The Process of Divorce

THE PROCESS OF DIVORCE

How Professionals and Couples Negotiate Settlements

KENNETH KRESSEL

Basic Books, Inc., Publishers New York

Portions of this book are adapted, with permission, from the following sources: Chapters 3 and 4 are from Kenneth Kressel and Morton Deutsch, "Divorce Therapy: An In-Depth Survey of Therapists' Views," *Family Process* 16(1977):413–43. Chapter 6 and parts of chapter 8 are from Kenneth Kressel, Allan Hochberg, and Theodore Sager Meth, "A Provisional Typology of Lawyer Attitudes Towards Divorce Practice: Gladiators, Advocates, Counselors, and Journeymen," *Law and Human Behavior* 7(1983):31–49. Chapter 11 is from Kenneth Kressel, Nancy Jaffee, Bruce Tuchman, Carol Watson, and Morton Deutsch, "A Typology of Divorcing Couples: Implications for Mediation and the Divorce Process," *Family Process* 19(1980): 101–16. Chapter 5 and part of chapter 7 are from Kenneth Kressel, Martin Lopez-Morillas, Janet Weinglass, and Morton Deutsch, "Professional Intervention in Divorce: A Summary of the Views of Lawyers, Psychotherapists, and Clergy," *Journal of Divorce* 2(1978):119–55.

Library of Congress Cataloging-in-Publication Data

Kressel, Kenneth.
The process of divorce.

Bibliography: p. 330
Includes index.
1. Divorce settlements—United States. 2. Divorce mediation—United States. I. Title. [DNLM: 1. counseling—popular works. 2. Divorce—popular works. 3. Marital therapy—popular works. WM 55 K92p]
KF535.K63 1985 346.7301'66 84–45346
ISBN 0–465–06389–6 347.306166

Printed in the United States of America
Designed by Vincent Torre
85 86 87 88 HC 9 8 7 6 5 4 3 2 1

To Roberta

Contents

Preface

This is a book about "uncoupling"—the manner in which divorcing husbands and wives take leave of each other. Its particular focus is the role of therapists, lawyers, and the newly emergent divorce mediators in the settlement negotiations over money, property, and children. Its intended audience is these professionals, the divorcing husbands and wives who employ them, and my fellow students of social conflict.

Settlement negotiations are only a part—often the shortest part—of the process of uncoupling. Typically they have been preceded by months or, more often, years of marital turmoil and unhappiness. Settlement negotiations may often appear to be the least psychologically interesting part of divorce—a cut-and-dried affair, more the product of legalisms and economic finagling than of the real concerns of human beings. In this view the psychologically interesting issues have either preceded the settlement process or are about to unfold as the parties enter the postdivorce period. This attitude may explain why so little systematic social research has been conducted on the divorce negotiation process.

This book takes a very different view. I have been drawn to the study of divorce negotiations because the issues dealt with in the settlement process and the manner in which they are resolved are no trivial matters in either material or human terms. Materially we are talking about the transfer of property and assets totaling billions of dollars annually; humanly, about the fundamental bond between parents and their children. It is during the settlement negotiations that the postdivorce family is given its psychological as well as its economic shape.

The uncoupling process, including both the informal negotiations by which couples arrive at the decision to end their marriage and the formal ones mandated by the legal system, represents a very sizeable industry in this country. If we consider that the "average" middle-class divorcing couple with a relatively uncomplicated settlement negotiation may spend about $2,000 in legal fees ($1,000 for him; $1,000 for her), and we allow for one million divorces per year, of which perhaps 40 percent represent our average case, the annual expenditure for legal services among only one class of persons works out to about $800 million per year. If one adds to this calculation the more litigious, complex, and conflicted cases, and the attendant additional costs for judges, courtrooms, court personnel, accountants, and therapists, it is by no means far-fetched to talk of a divorce negotiations industry with gross receipts of two or more billion dollars a year.

There is also good reason to believe that this costly industry is an inefficient one and, in some cases, is even destructive of important human values and relationships. It is clear that rates of compliance with the terms of divorce settlements are exceedingly low, that child support is often unpaid, and that children are not visited, or are infrequently and erratically visited, by the noncustodial parent. A large percentage of couples and their children end up in court time and time again, long after the divorce has been legally granted—with financial and emotional costs which need no belaboring.

This is not a muckraking book or one that seeks to attribute blame. On the contrary, one of its major themes is the multiplicity of forces that conspire to trip everybody up, including expert and well-intentioned lawyers, therapists, and mediators. But if we can gain a better understanding of the divorce negotiation process, then perhaps it can become a more constructive process.

My interest in divorce negotiations dates back to my final year as a graduate student in social psychology at Teachers College, Columbia University. I had recently completed a study of experienced labor mediators and their views on the management of industrial conflict, and was nearing the end of my doctoral dissertation on methods of resolving marital disagreements over money. As these topics illustrate, from the beginning my bent as a social psychologist tended toward the concrete and the practical. At that point, my then mentor, and now friend and colleague, Morton Deutsch, a leading figure in the social psychology of conflict resolution, suggested that we collaborate on a study to evaluate the application of professional mediators' techniques to intimate conflicts, such as those between spouses. Given my interests this was an extremely appealing proposal. And, with the explosive divorce rate of the mid-1970s, it was only one step further to think of exploring mediation in the context of divorce.

To establish a solid footing for implementing our divorce mediation idea, we set in motion a number of "preliminary" studies on the psychological and legal aspects of divorce. As is often the case, those preliminary studies began to take on a life of their own, raising new, unanticipated questions and leading to new investigations. Along the way we discovered, to our chagrin, that our plan to mediate divorce negotiations had been scooped by O. J. Coogler, a lawyer and marriage counselor. Chagrin turned to excitement, however, when I traveled to Atlanta to meet with Coogler, and learned that he had been systematically tape recording his divorce mediations and that he was enthusiastic about sharing his material with us.

In the meantime, my research and clinical interests had begun to complement each other. By the time our research program was about half completed I had begun working as a clinician, with a practice that included marital and family therapy as well as individual therapy with adults, many of whom were recently divorced or in the process of becoming divorced. It is the twists and turns in the research road, supplemented by clinical experience, that have provided the core of material from which this book is constructed.

In writing this book I have had three primary purposes: first, to set forth a profile of the main actors in the settlement drama—therapists, lawyers, mediators, and divorcing spouses—with specific reference to the manner in which the characteristics and experiences of each help shape the settlement process. Given the early stages of social research on this topic these are not presented as definitive profiles, but I trust that they will be useful in comprehending the forces at work at the divorce bargaining table. This is a modest objective but an important one; it is intended as an antidote to the frequent tendency among social commentators as well as the principal actors in the divorcing process themselves to put forward simplistic and scapegoating explanations for the admittedly dreary facts of destructive divorce conflict.

My second purpose has been to provide guidance for both professionals and lay persons with regard to the constructive handling of divorce conflict. The ideas presented here are by no means intended as definitive or exhaustive rules of conduct. I have attempted simply to draw from the research whatever implications of a practical kind it seemed reasonable to draw. The wise reader will approach these cautiously but will, I hope, benefit from them.

My final objective has been to stimulate others to study the settlement process. I have attempted this by offering speculations and hypotheses about why the process often goes wrong and what can be done to make it right. These ideas need to be tested, and I hope that others will join in that task.

The initial two chapters of the book set the stage for an appreciation of the complexities and hazards of the professional role. In chapter 1 I examine the evidence that suggests that divorce settlement negotiations frequently have disappointing results. The cumulative impression is of a process that often creates as many problems as it resolves.

It is common for the sorry record of divorce negotiations to be attributed either to the destructive influence of lawyers and the "adversary" legal system or to the emotional instability and irrationality of divorcing individuals. I believe that these are unfortunate oversimplifications. The bulk of chapter 2 is therefore devoted to a detailed examination of the full range of obstacles, headaches, and stresses that complicate the negotiation process for all concerned, few of which can be easily controlled. At various points later in the book I return to these complicating forces in describing why professional assistance in divorce has unpredictable and often unsatisfying results.

In chapters 3 through 12 the roles, activities, and problems of professionals involved in the divorce process are examined. The discussions are based on our own intensive interviews, case studies, and questionnaire surveys, as well as on an integrative reading of the relevant clinical and empirical literature in psychology and the law.

Chapters 3 and 4 are devoted to divorce therapists and their activities in the informal but crucial "negotiations" over the decision to divorce. These chapters should be of considerable interest to mental health professionals and lawyers, as well as to prospective consumers of therapeutic services in divorce. They are based on a series of in-depth interviews with twenty-one prominent marital and family therapists with extensive experience in the area of divorce therapy.

Despite the soaring divorce rate and the attendant increase in divorce therapy, systematic examinations of the therapeutic process in divorce are still relatively scarce. I have attempted to spell out the relevance of divorce therapy to settlement negotiations, since divorce therapists may exert powerful, if largely unheralded, effects on those negotiations, both in their capacity as experts on the needs of children and, perhaps more crucially, because of their impact on the process of divorce decision making. The testimony of clinical experience, described in chapter 4 and reiterated later in the case studies of divorce mediation, suggests that few couples understand what is going on between them during the divorce decision-making period or are aware that their ignorance contributes to their frustrating experiences with lawyers and each other during and after the divorce. This material should also be of interest to attorneys, since our research with lawyers suggests that even those who are well disposed toward psychological assistance have only a vague understanding of how the therapist's work may abet their own.

Chapters 5 through 8 are devoted to the divorce lawyer, clearly the central professional actor in the settlement process. While practicing attorneys and legal scholars have been relatively prolific on the subject of divorce, for the most part they have provided either firsthand accounts, of the war-in-the-trenches variety, or technical treatises on legal and economic issues. Systematic research on the interpersonal dynamics of the lawyer-client relationship is virtually nonexistent. Also lacking are systematic accounts of how divorce lawyers view their work and the complex pressures to which they are exposed.

One of our central discoveries, presented in chapters 5 and 6, is that there are a limited number of highly distinctive and contrasting attitudes that practicing attorneys take toward their clients and the objectives of legal representation in divorce. The identification of distinctive lawyer stances is based on an initial exploratory study of seventeen practitioners in and around New York City and a subsequent refinement of the typology based on interviews and questionnaires involving more than eighty members of the Family Law Section of the New Jersey State Bar Association. This typology of lawyers runs the gamut from attorneys with a narrowly competitive and technical approach to the divorce process, to those with a highly cooperative and psychological orientation. I refer to the former as *advocates* and the latter as *counselors.* These types have appeared in the "shop talk" of practicing attorneys for some time, but, to the best of my knowledge, this is the most extensive and detailed empirical evidence for their existence.

In chapters 7 and 8 I have attempted to go beyond the descriptive level to a consideration of how the distinctive lawyer types may be related to the stressful conditions of legal work in divorce and to the quality of legal service provided to the client.

Chapter 7 is an examination of the numerous problematic and ambiguous conditions with which the practicing attorney must typically cope. These include serious, hidden conflicts between attorney and client, unclear and contradictory norms for managing the relationship with opposite counsel, vague substantive criteria as to what constitutes a reasonable or "good" divorce settlement agreement—especially where the interests of children are concerned—and the lawyer's lack of training in psychological matters. The upshot of all this is that while divorce attorneys may often be well compensated they nonetheless experience a high degree of professional misery. I argue in chapter 7 that it may be useful to understand the advocate and counselor stances as mechanisms for coping with this distress.

The analysis of the lawyer's professional headaches also provides an opportunity for challenging two widely held beliefs about the lawyer's role in divorce: namely that the lawyer, more than the couple, typically does most of the direct negotiating; and that the typical effect of the lawyer's involvement is to escalate, rather than dampen, conflict. There is no good evidence for either of these assumptions. On the contrary, the little we do know suggests that, in the aggregate, lawyers play a more benign, less intensive role in the settlement process than is commonly thought.

The implications of the advocate/counselor typology for the quality of legal services in divorce is addressed in chapter 8. On the whole, a reasonably good case can be made that, all things being equal, the divorce client is better off in the hands of a counselor than an advocate. Direct evidence for this proposition is quite limited, but the hypothesis is consistent with several decades of research in social psychology. I have discussed the proposition cautiously, however, because all things are rarely equal in the divorce process. I have closed the chapter with several cautionary words against coming to any simple conclusions about the impact of lawyers on the settlement process, and I have attempted to sketch out the other, numerous aspects of the negotiating system in divorce that may well have a greater influence over what transpires.

The last major section of the book deals with divorce mediation. In mediation a trained third party, frequently a mental health professional, but sometimes a lawyer, assists the divorcing couple in negotiating directly with one another, rather than exclusively through their attorneys. Although a relatively small percentage of divorce agreements are currently negotiated through mediation, it has been widely touted as a more constructive and humane alternative to the presumed defects of the adversarial legal approach, and its popularity has grown rapidly in the last five years.

Chapter 9 reviews the rise of the divorce mediation movement, the general nature of the mediation process, and the differences between divorce mediation provided by the courts or court-related agencies and mediation paid for by the divorcing spouses. I have also reviewed in detail the small but growing literature on the effectiveness of divorce mediation. The evidence thus far is promising but far from conclusive, especially in regard to the important and often heated issue of mediation's usefulness compared to the traditional role of lawyers. It is partly to depolemicize this rather oversimplified debate that I have critically examined the literature and made several broad suggestions for its future development.

The lawyer vs. mediator debate also has ironic overtones because both roles share many of the same headaches. Indeed, for all its promise, and for all the plausible arguments that may be made on its behalf, the problems and stresses of the mediation role are in some ways even worse than those of the strictly legal one. Although it is still too early in the game to write definitively on the subject, in chapter 10 I have drawn upon both clinical research and theoretical literature to detail some of the more apparent role stresses to which divorce mediators appear to be exposed.

Chapters 11 and 12 report our research on the method of Structured Mediation pioneered by O. J. Coogler. Here the reader gets an overview of the mediation process as it is revealed in a small but intensive selection of case studies. The material in these chapters addresses three major issues: the very striking differences among divorcing couples in the manner in which the decision to divorce is arrived at; the implications of these differences for whether or not mediation will be successful; and the hazardous psychological and interpersonal currents with which the divorce mediator must struggle.

In Chapter 11 these matters are raised in the presentation of a typology of divorcing couples and the consequences for mediated negotiations. In chapter 12 one of these cases is examined in detail, providing an opportunity to further flesh out the complexities and quandaries of the divorce mediator's role and to make suggestions for the management of the highly dysfunctional couple during the mediation process. In this latter regard I have suggested that the line between therapy and mediation is not always usefully drawn, and that combining the two approaches *within* mediation may, under certain conditions, be necessary for a truly constructive, lasting resolution. All cases discussed in chapters 11 and 12 have been disguised with regard to biographical and other personal details in order to protect the anonymity of the divorcing couples involved.

In the concluding chapter I summarize the practical implications of our work for the selection and use of a divorce therapist, lawyer, or mediator. I have also treated the implications for students of conflict and conflict resolution.

Acknowledgments

Portions of the research for this book were supported by National Science Foundation grant number BN74–02477 A02 (principal investigator, Morton Deutsch), a grant from the Marshall Fund, and a Rutgers University Research Council faculty fellowship.

Many individuals gave generously of their time, energy, and intellectual resources to the making of this book. Foremost among them is Morton Deutsch, whose personal and professional support through the years of our association has meant so much. The work reported here began in collaboration with him. Although his involvement with the project eventually ended, and although he is not accountable for any errors or omissions of which I may be guilty, anyone familiar with his seminal work on the psychology of social and interpersonal conflict will have little difficulty detecting his influence on this volume.

I am also grateful to the other colleagues with whom I have worked in conducting the studies on which this book is based. They include: Cindy Elgart, Allan Hochberg, Nancy Jaffee, Martin Lopez-Morillas, Bruce Tuchman, Carol Watson, and Janet Weinglass. Theodore Sager Meth was not only a co-investigator, but a model of the caring and insightful divorce attorney. My understanding of the legal role in divorce has also been deepened by my association with James Boskey of the Seton Hall Law Faculty. Dick Ashmore, George Levinger, Dean Pruitt, and Jeff Rubin all provided useful comments and perspectives on various aspects of the manuscript.

The chapters on divorce therapy and the role of the divorce lawyer could not have been written without the professional experts in each of these fields who graciously took time from crowded schedules to be interviewed, frequently at considerable length. The therapists included Gerald Berenson, Ph.D., Edwin Church, M.D., Fredrick Duhl, M.D., Nina Fieldsteel, Ph.D., Esther Fisher, Ed.D., Helene Flapan, M.A., James

Framo, Ph.D., Abraham Franzblau, M.D., Richard Gardner, M.D., J. B. Hayes, M.D., Leah Horowitz, M.S.W., Arnold Lazarus, Ph.D., Vera Paster, Ph.D., Wardell Pomeroy, Ph.D., Robert Ravich, M.D., Ildaura Rhode, Ph.D., Olga Silverstein, M.S.W., Laura Singer, Ed.D., Jessie Turberg, Ph.D., Paul Vahanian, Ed.D., and Tilla Vahanian, Ed.D. The lawyers included Michael Atkins, Ira Bennett, Joseph D'Addario, Diana Dubroff, Irving Erdheim, Raoul Felder, Marjory Fields, Mitchell Fisher, Mildred Lesser, Thomas O'Hara, Harriet Pilpel, Miriam Robinson, Beatrice Rothaus, Steve Rubin, Diane Schulder, Shirley Schwartz, and Henry Wimpfheimer. Several judges with considerable experience in the legal aspects of divorce also spoke with us in the planning stages of the research, and we benefited greatly from their guidance. They included Justices Louis Heller, Lester Holtzman, and Sybil Kooper. I would also like to thank Dalton W. Menhall, Executive Director of the New Jersey State Bar Association, for his cooperation and assistance in helping us obtain a suitable sample of New Jersey attorneys. I am deeply appreciative also to the more than eighty members of the Family Law Section of the New Jersey Bar Association who answered our interview questions and completed our questionnaires. The interpretations and conclusions drawn from the comments of our respondents are, of course, my own and that of my co-workers. No inference should be made that the respondents necessarily agree.

In regard to the portions of this book that deal with divorce mediation I owe a very considerable intellectual and personal debt to O. J. Coogler. Jim enthusiastically shared his considerable knowledge of the mediation process and made available invaluable material on his pioneering experiments with his method of Structured Divorce Mediation. Although our ideas may have diverged in certain respects, this book would be very different and in no way improved had our paths not so richly crossed. His untimely death has deprived all of us in the field of conflict resolution of a great ally. To his early collaborators, Will Neville and Judi Wood, I also extend my thanks for permitting my colleagues and me to eavesdrop on their early mediation cases. I am also very grateful to the anonymous couples who permitted us to study their divorce and mediation experiences in the hope that we might learn things that would benefit others. I trust that their faith has been in some measure justified.

I would also like to thank my editors at Basic Books—Jane Isay, for her initial confidence and enthusiasm for this project, and Jo Ann Miller, for her congenial guidance and patience in the editorial process. To Abraham

Grinoch I owe a special note of thanks for his assiduous help in the preparation of the final manuscript.

My deepest gratitude goes to my wife, Roberta, whose steadfastness, warm support, and quiet wisdom have been the most enduring source of inspiration.

KENNETH KRESSEL
Highland Park, New Jersey

The Process of Divorce

1

The Terrain of Divorce Conflict

Vignettes from the Battlefield

The lawyers got involved and we had that situation where we were told not to talk to each other and there was a lot of mistrust. And it just got to be impossible. Like I was afraid anything I said would be used against me. Our communication just stopped completely.

I said, God, I just can't believe that it has come to this, where we have known each other for ten years and we can't say anything at all to each other. It was just a battle. He would say, "You're ripping me off. You got the house and the kids and now you are trying to get more money out of me." There was so much bitterness and so much anger and so much mistrust. (Weiss 1975, 265–66)

A woman has her door lock changed because her separated husband has been letting himself in whenever he pleases, ostensibly to look for mail or pick up a book. When he can't open the door, he kicks it in, breaking the lock and splintering the frame. His wife rushes to the kitchen and seizes a carving knife; they glare at each other speechless and unmoving for minutes, until at last he turns and stalks out, sweeping two porcelain lamps to the floor as he goes. (Hunt and Hunt 1977, 192)

When asked what happens if he wants to see his father between visiting weekends, Eric tried to be casual: "Oh, it's okay, it's usually not important." Painfully, quietly, Eric then talked of their unlisted phone number, obtained by his angry mother to prevent the father from calling his children. The absence of free communication greatly increased the possibilities of mishaps in visiting plans.

> Eric told of an incident when his father and sister failed to hear Eric calling at the apartment gate, whereupon he had to return home to call his dad. Once home, facing mother's anger, Eric decided not to call his father. The mother then called the father herself, venting her rage. After Eric's father arranged to pick him up a block from home, a scene ensued between Eric and his mother, Eric crying and refusing to visit his father, the mother angrily insisting that he must. As the therapist reviewed the event, Eric's sadness and hurt feelings began to emerge, as did his feelings of rejection by his father. (Kelly and Wallerstein 1976, 27)

War stories such as these are easy to come by. Any divorce lawyer, marital therapist, or family court counselor can give variations on the same theme. Divorce, like war, can be hell. However, a serious study of divorce conflict cannot be built on war stories alone. This book examines the role of lawyers and mental health professionals as they try to contain destructive conflict in divorce and, where possible, replace it with cooperation and mutual problem solving. In particular, the focus is on the divorce settlement negotiations, during which the parties attempt to satisfy the demands of practical necessity and of the state by reaching agreements on matters such as custody, visitation, child support, and the division of marital assets.

The settlement process commands our attention because, although it is certainly not the only source of conflict between divorcing spouses, the legal mandate that there be a formal document of agreement forces the parties to negotiate over concrete and far-reaching matters, thereby providing an opportunity for the management and resolution of conflicts, as well as an occasion for their exacerbation. Lawyers have a direct role in settlement negotiations while psychiatrists, psychologists, and social workers often affect them indirectly, but powerfully, through their treatment of the parties' emotional problems and the practical suggestions they may give. More recently, mental health workers are becoming centrally involved in the settlement negotiations through the newly and rapidly emerging field of divorce mediation.

It is no secret that many within and outside the legal profession are convinced that all too often the adversary bent of the law and the psychologically unsophisticated perspective of many lawyers, in combination with the emotional turmoil of the clients, produces a negotiating process of which nobody can be proud. We shall return to this hypothesis at various points throughout the book. For the moment it may simply be said that the orchestration of a constructive process of divorce negotiations must be considered one of the more demanding tasks that rational beings are expected to perform. To judge fairly the difficulties represented by the settlement process and the complex challenges it poses for divorcing persons and the professionals whom they consult, more is needed than clinical vignettes of the worst that divorce has to offer. In this chapter and the next, therefore, the frequency and sources of conflict in the settlement process are placed in empirical perspective. While research on divorce settlement negotiations is far from exhaustive or beyond scientific reproach, the evidence suggests that while the war story analogy may be exaggerated, a significant number of casualties are incurred nonetheless. (The cause of these injuries is a less self-evident matter.) Before reviewing this evidence, however, let us sketch something of the battle terrain.

The Structure of Divorce Settlement Negotiations

There are two principal arenas of conflict in divorce—one highly unstructured, the other much more rule-bound and societally prescribed. The unstructured arena concerns the decision to divorce itself; the more structured arena involves the negotiations over the terms of the divorce settlement. While the negotiating arena is the primary focus of the research to be reported in this book, especially in the chapters devoted to lawyers and mediators, the divorce decision-making process is an important prelude to those negotiations and often shapes dramatically how the parties will conduct themselves at the bargaining table.

The divorce decision-making process is generally more extended than are the formal settlement negotiations. For months, often years, the spouses may have been struggling to decide whether to end the marriage. Much of this will have occurred without the benefit of outside assistance, although in perhaps as many as 50 to 60 percent of middle-class divorces the help of a psychotherapist or marriage counselor is sought.[1] What transpires between the spouses regarding the decision to end the marriage is largely a private event; no records are kept and no accounting is required. In the chapters on divorce therapy and those on divorce mediation, I shall report on the nature of divorce decision making and its impact on the formal divorce settlement negotiations, as these matters were recounted by divorcing couples and specialists in divorce counseling.

But it is the nature and results of the divorce settlement negotiations themselves that principally concern us in this chapter. Divorce settlement negotiations revolve around five principal issues; custody of minor children; visitation; child support; alimony (or what is now often referred to as spousal maintenance); and division of marital property (most commonly the marital home but also including other material assets accrued during the marriage). Before a court will legally dissolve a marriage it expects an accounting from the parties of the manner in which these matters have been decided. This accounting is embodied in the divorce settlement agreement that sets forth in legal language the results of the parties' negotiations. Typically, these negotiations will have begun some time after a physical separation, in which one spouse, usually the husband, has moved out of the marital residence, and after a firm but usually one-sided decision to divorce has been made.

The principal actors in the settlement negotiations are the divorcing husband and wife and, often, the attorneys who represent them. The attorney's role is broad and highly variable, but, at a minimum, includes advising the client on how the state's laws governing divorce may affect the client's case and preparing and filing the necessary legal documents, including the divorce settlement agreement. Lawyers are frequently also the principal agents by which the divorcing spouses negotiate the terms of the settlement, although evidence suggests that a negotiating role for the attorney may be less common than is often supposed (Cavanagh and Rhode 1976).[2]

The role of the court in the settlement process is also a variable one. In the majority of cases the court serves essentially as a rubber stamp. These are the so-called uncontested divorces in which the parties have been able to reach agreement on all relevant issues concerning property, money, and children. Technically, the state reserves for itself final authority in all matters regarding children and equity. In practice, however, the courts have neither the time nor the inclination to cast more than a cursory glance at the arrangements which the parties present as their own. In uncontested divorces where no children or assets are involved, the average length of the court hearing to end a marriage is about three-and-one-half minutes; if there are children or assets, the hearing drags out to a full five minutes.[3] Only the most flagrant inequities or violations of law, it appears, will slow the rapid pace with which justice does its work.

In essence, then, the fairness and durability of the uncontested settlement agreement rests entirely on the parties' abilities as negotiators or on the ability of any agents they may employ. As we shall also see, in a large number of cases the term "uncontested" refers to the perspective of the court, not to what actually transpired among members of the divorcing family and their representatives, all of whom may have been embroiled in heated and nerve-racking exchanges. The fighting may stop only on the courthouse steps—and recommence at the exit.

Of course, there are cases in which the court is willing and able to play a greater role than it does in uncontested divorces. These are the contested divorces in which the parties have not been able to reach all the necessary agreements. Contested cases are in the minority—the traditional estimate is 10 percent of all divorces granted, although there is reason to believe that this figure may err on the low side.

In contested divorces the court serves as full-scale arbitrator, listening, sometimes at great length, to each side's version of what is fair and equitable. Although it is difficult to get precise figures, two-thirds of contested cases appear to be concerned primarily with disputes over child custody or visitation, while one-third concern some aspect of property or finances (Caron and Doyle 1979). If children are involved, the court may conduct psychiatric and psychological investigations of the parents and children, often as a supplement to the evidence on those matters that each side has marshaled through its privately-paid-for experts. Accountants, realtors, appraisers, and other relevant experts may also be appointed by the court when material issues are in dispute.

In most states there is no longer the possibility of a contest over the question of "fault" for the marital breakdown itself. Under the fault concept of divorce, before a divorce is granted, one party has to prove that the cause of the divorce is the noxious, immoral, or criminal behavior of the other spouse. These assertions are often contested by the spouse, either to protect his or her position in negotiations over money or children or out of moral or psychological outrage. Increasingly, fault statutes have been replaced in whole or in part by no-fault legislation in which all that must be proved is that at least one spouse wants the divorce and that the couple has not lived together for a specified period of time, usually a year to eighteen months. Opponents of no-fault divorce laws argued that such legislation would open the flood gates of divorce and seriously weaken the moral fabric of the institution of marriage, while its proponents argued that it would significantly reduce conflict during and after divorce settlement negotiations. There is no compelling evidence that any of these possibilities have occurred. What is clear is that there is still ample opportunity for divorce negotiations to break down and for divorcing spouses and their children to remain entangled in conflict long after the legal dust has settled. It is to evidence on this matter that we now turn.

The Outcomes of Divorce Settlement Negotiations

Precise evidence on the nature and extent of destructive conflict during and after divorce settlement negotiations does not exist. Given the soaring rates of divorce in the last decade and a half and the huge personal and social stakes involved, the absence of reliable information of this sort is dismaying. The data that are available are remarkably fragmentary, frequently come from small and unrepresentative samples, and are almost exclusively based on the subjective reports of divorced individuals or their lawyers. Moreover, almost all the data concern the end product of negotiations—how often the parties reach agreement, how they feel about the agreements they reach, and whether they live up to them after the divorce. On the process of negotiating itself there is virtually nothing. This is unfortunate because, by any reasonable definition, the destructiveness of a conflict is also measured by the manner in which the parties interact in resolving their differences as well as by the results of the settlement process. A diligent search, however, enables a rough portrait of the extent of destructive divorce conflict to be drawn. In general, it is a gloomy one.

Indices of Conflict at the Time of Settlement Negotiations

The data are most sparse on the state of relations between divorcing spouses during their initial efforts to negotiate a settlement agreement. This is a striking void since there are more than a million such negotiations every year and since each of the fifty state court systems routinely files a dossier on most of these cases. For the most part, however, this potentially rich source of information lies dormant and unanalyzed in all but the most superficial way.

The traditional, if crude, index of the frequency of destructive conflict at the divorce bargaining table is the percentage of divorces involving a court contest at the time the divorce is granted. There is little argument with the notion that couples who require the assistance of a court to decide the terms of their settlement have had a significant problem with each other during the settlement process. The often cited claim is that in 10 percent of all divorces such a court contest occurs. However, there is little reliable evidence to support this figure other than it seems to be what most judges and attorneys reply when asked to give an estimate (Woolley 1979). A random sample of 500 cases drawn from California court records confirms the 10 percent estimate (Weitzman and Dixon 1979), but more detailed data from Minneapolis (Caron and Doyle 1979) suggest that court battles may be much more common among divorcing couples with children, who represent approximately 60 percent of the entire divorce population. Thus, in Minneapolis from 1975 to 1978, custody battles occurred in an average of 11 percent of the cases involving children. For couples who did not have a custody fight, approximately 31 percent had a settlement dispute over visitation serious enough to require court intervention. We must also include among our litigants those couples who did not fight over their children but about money or property. The study is mute on this matter, but as a conservative estimate we may assume that an additional 10 percent of divorcing parents are in this category. (This estimate is conservative because while the 10 percent rate is for property and money disputes between childless couples, clinical experience strongly suggests that the presence of children greatly heightens the probability of conflict over all issues.) Overall, then, the Minneapolis data suggest that 50 percent or more of divorcing couples with children cannot resolve their differences without the help of the court.

Of course, the percentage of contested cases is a poor guide to the frequency of serious conflict in divorce settlement negotiations. Many couples who have had a truly miserable time negotiating their settlement agreement have neither the money nor the stomach for a court battle. An indication of how little the settlement process has been studied is that, at the time of this writing, there was but one empirical investigation that shed even tangential light on the levels of conflict during settlement in these "uncontested" cases. In that investigation, 331 uncontested divorces granted in 1975 were drawn at random from divorce records in New Haven and Bridgeport, Connecticut. From an examination of the court dossiers and interviews with a subset of the clients involved, the researchers concluded that in approximately 30 percent of these nominally uncontested cases there were disputes heated enough to warrant the active intervention and negotiating assistance of lawyers on both sides (Cavanagh and Rhode 1976). The researchers did not break down this figure by family composition but we may assume that in a good deal more than half of these cases —let us say two-thirds—the heated disputes were between divorcing parents. (Again, this estimate is based on clinical experience that the presence of children increases the likelihood of conflict.) Combining the estimates for contested cases and high-conflict uncontested cases, we may tentatively conclude that in perhaps 70 percent of all divorces involving children there may be levels of turmoil serious enough to require active intervention by courts or lawyers.

For childless couples the estimate of "high" conflict is on the order of 20 to 30 percent contested cases and 10 percent uncontested but acrimonious. The overall estimate of destructive conflict for all divorcing couples, with and without children, averages out to between 40 and 50 percent. Given the absence of research, these calculations represent no more than educated guesses, but they are bolstered by a study by Kitson (1982). In her survey of 172 recently divorced persons, Kitson found that 32 percent described the process of reaching a settlement agreement as "somewhat" or "very" difficult. However, because a sizeable portion of the original sample did not supply data, this figure may be conservative. Nonresponders included those who, despite repeated efforts, could not be reached (10 percent of the original sample), those who had moved without leaving a forwarding address (6 percent), and those who simply refused to participate in the survey (20 percent). It is easy to imagine that a large portion of the individuals in these categories represent the higher levels of the divorce conflict spectrum—moving without leaving a forwarding address or being unwilling to talk about one's divorce, for example, are often associated with a bitter divorce experience—thus, the true proportion of those who had significant difficulties in the initial settlement process may be closer to 50 percent.

What happens when the settlement documents are finally signed and the parties begin living with the agreements they have reached? On this matter there is more to report. The data on postdivorce conflict may be summarized under two headings: conflicts concerning the divorce settlement agreement per se, and more general conflicts in the co-parental relationship.

Conflict Over the Terms of Settlement

Postdivorce litigation rates are the crudest but most direct evidence of conflict over the divorce settlement agreement. There are a handful of published studies that provide estimates of postdivorce court fights ranging from 14 to 52 percent. This wide variance may be attributed to differences in the types of samples studied, none of which can be considered representative of the divorcing population at large, or to differences in the time since the divorce at which the data were collected.

The 14 percent figure is from Goldsmith (1980), who studied forty-four couples drawn from Chicago court records. However, Goldsmith's respondents had been divorced for only one year, and, since the primary purpose was to investigate the co-parental relationship among "typical" divorced parents, the study excluded couples in which the father had not visited his children for the preceding two months or where the parents lived more than two-and-one-half hours apart by car. These latter criteria undoubtedly screened out many couples at the higher end of the conflict spectrum. In addition, like many studies which draw their samples from court files, nearly half of the eligible respondents either refused to participate or could not be located. For these reasons the 14 percent estimate must be regarded as conservative.

Wallerstein and Kelly (1980), in their widely cited study on children and divorce, report that 20 percent of the divorced mothers and somewhat fewer of the divorced fathers in their sample of sixty families had initiated litigation within five years after the divorce. Almost all of these were disputes over alimony and child support. Since Wallerstein and Kelly report data only for individuals, the rate of postdivorce litigation per divorced *family* falls somewhere between 20 and 40 percent of their sample. It is not possible to say whether this is a conservative or liberal estimate of conflict among divorced parents. The figures may overestimate postdivorce litigation rates because the project had been advertised as a combination of research and clinical service, and thereby probably attracted a disproportionate number of high-conflict couples. On the other hand, the figure may be an underestimate because, unlike many divorced parents, participants received six weeks of counseling aimed at helping to resolve problems with children. Presumably, the clinical services they were given provided sufficient motivation to remain with the study over its five-year course. Wallerstein and Kelly do note that postdivorce litigants had three important characteristics: they could afford to litigate; they were sufficiently angry to do so; and they all felt they had a good chance of winning.

Higher rates of postdivorce litigation have also been reported from studies in which the litigants had experienced high levels of conflict at the time of the initial settlement negotiations. Milne (1978), for example, reports that in Dane County, Wisconsin, 34 percent of the cases in which the court undertook an initial custody study returned to court for further custody litigation within two years. Cline and Westman (1971) report even higher rates of litigation for a somewhat earlier period in Dane County. In reviewing 105 consecutive divorces passing through the family court (presumably representing couples who were already having significant disagreements with each other), 52 percent had hostile interactions requiring at least one court intervention in the years after the divorce and 31 percent were back in court anywhere from two to ten times in that period. Wheeler (1980) indicates that there are several small-scale studies that are consistent with a 52-percent rate of postdivorce litigation.

Pearson (1981) gives similar figures concerning custody and visitation battles for a Denver sample that consisted of subjects whose initial settlement negotiations over the children were troubled enough to have them referred to the project designed to evaluate mediation as a method of curtailing parental fights in the divorce process. Approximately two years after the divorce, 35 percent of the parties who had been randomly assigned to a control condition which involved no special assistance were already engaged in a court fight; an additional 20 percent of the control group had taken the first steps toward a court battle by filing a motion to modify the existing agreement.

The data from these studies of divorced parents whose initial settlement experience was embittered and difficult lead to a tentative conclusion: if high levels of conflict characterized the initial settlement negotiations, there is an approximately 50 percent chance of a court contest in the postdivorce period. Presumably this rate would be lower for couples whose initial negotiations went relatively smoothly. There is no good evidence on the subject, but an investigation by Ahrons (1981) is not reassuring: in a study that shared many of the same sampling criteria as those of Goldsmith, and therefore underrepresented high-conflict couples, 48 percent of the cases had at least one ex-partner who was planning to contest a settlement provision in court within one year after the divorce.

The available studies do not separate out those who just complain from those who actually litigate, but the findings on expressed dissatisfaction or noncompliance with the settlement terms are entirely consistent with the rates of postdivorce litigation. The evidence suggests that from one-third to more than one-half of divorced individuals are seriously unhappy about the settlement provisions.

In his classic, if dated, study of over 400 divorced women, Goode (1956) found that 32 percent of the respondents who split the marital property with their ex-husbands regarded the division as unfair. More recent investigations report comparable levels of dissatisfaction with the property settlement (Albrecht 1980).

Custody and visitation arrangements appear to be a particularly intense source of displeasure. Estimates of dissatisfaction range from one-quarter to two-thirds of all respondents. Jones (1977), in a random sample drawn from divorce petitions in Oregon, reports that among the fifty-two couples, more than one-quarter of the respondents were dissatisfied with the parenting arrangement and more than one-fifth of the fathers were unhappy being the noncustodial parent. Fulton (1979), who studied 560 individuals divorced in three urban Minnesota counties in 1970, reports that one-third of the fathers claimed that they would contest custody if they had it to do over again. In about one-third of the sample one or more of the children had, in fact, moved back and forth between the parents or had changed legal custodians since the divorce.[4] Pearson's respondents, who, like Fulton's, were in conflict over the children during the initial settlement negotiations, experienced a similar level of dissatisfaction: 40 percent acknowledged "serious problems" with the custody and/or visitation agreement and 32 percent said they would "surely want to modify" the agreement in the future (Pearson 1981).

For divorced couples with children one of the most important terms of the settlement agreement is that governing child support payments—how much the noncustodial parent, almost always the father, shall pay to the custodial mother, usually on a monthly basis, to fulfill the legal obligation to contribute to the support of minor children. The evidence on this subject is the most complete of all those bearing on the durability of the divorce agreement and it is consistent with the data on postdivorce litigation and dissatisfaction: Men do not like to pay and in a very high proportion of cases they do not pay. Widespread noncompliance has been documented in at least five studies in the last decade and a half.

The general pattern may be summarized succinctly: The first year after divorce is the worst and sets the tone for what will follow. Within that first year approximately 50 percent of noncustodial fathers pay little or nothing of the child support to which they are legally obligated as a result of the arrangements set forth as part of the divorce decree. This rate of noncompliance increases slowly but steadily with time; by the third year the rate of noncompliance is approximately 60 percent; by the fifth year it is up around 70 percent to 80 percent. In the rare jurisdictions in which men are routinely jailed for failure to pay, compliance is better. The effects of coercion have been documented by Chambers, who summarizes his results thusly: "In one important sense, jailing seems to work. At the end of our study the evidence is strong that, in the context of child support, the use of jailing, when coupled with a well-organized system of enforcement, produces substantial amounts of money both from men who are jailed and from men who are not" (Chambers 1979, p. 9). Even at that, rates of noncompliance in the most punitive county studied still hovered around 40 percent.[5]

As would be expected, court fights to compel payment appear to occur far less frequently than does noncompliance. Weitzman and Dixon (1979) report that within the first year postdivorce, orders to show cause why the provider husband should not be held in contempt of court for noncompliance occurred in between 8 and 26 percent of the sampled cases, depending on year and venue. (In the years since the enactment of no fault statutes the rates appear to have fallen to the 8 to 16 percent range.) In other words, it is in a good deal less than half of the cases of significant noncompliance that the custodial mother has the will or the financial resources to legally pursue a defaulting ex-spouse.

In cases where child support is paid it appears to amount to less than one-half, on the average, of what is owed. For example, in a Michigan sample, divorced men earning over $7,000 a year were paying about 12 percent to 16 percent of their income in child support, but the average support stipulation in Michigan at the time of divorce is pegged at around 35 percent of one's income. There are even data which suggest that as a payer's income increases, the amount of support paid as a percentage of earnings often decreases.[6]

Cassetty (1978) reports that men earning between $3,000 and $5,000 a year paid an average of 14 percent of their income in support. Men earning $15,000 and over averaged 11 percent of income in support payments. She cautions, however, that while these figures suggest that conflict and hostility, rather than resources, are the major issue in nonpayment, the data may inflate the impression of noncompliance among more affluent men who may have been married to women with greater earning power or who may have made a large property settlement in lieu of high support payments.

The most graphic evidence of the extent of noncompliance with child support stipulations was the passage by Congress in 1975 of an amendment to the Social Security Act aimed at improving support payment rates (Public Law 93–647, H.R. 17045). In essence, this legislation declared war on defaulting fathers. It required the states to utilize more vigorous enforcement procedures in order to qualify for matching federal funds to support children from single parent homes living at or below the poverty level. It also established a controversial Parent Locator Service to track down divorced fathers who have fled to escape their support obligations, opening previously sacrosanct IRS files to locate defaulting individuals.

The results of this legislation for the period 1975 through 1978 are revealing. While the costs to government of location and collection were $457 million, the search netted $1 billion in child support that otherwise might have gone unpaid! Slightly more than half of this billion dollars was collected from men whose families were not on the welfare rolls, and were therefore presumably able to make a significant voluntary support contribution. The Parent Locator Service found 453,000 of an estimated five million men who had kept their whereabouts hidden from the custodial parent. As Wheeler (1980) notes, the need for this legislation has been widely viewed as an indication of individual and social failure.

Conflict in the Postdivorce Family

The relationships that develop among parents and children after divorce are a less direct measure of the success of the settlement negotiations than are postdivorce litigation and noncompliance data. Nonetheless, in theory, a constructive negotiating process should help dampen tension, foster more benevolent attitudes, and improve parental cooperation. Conversely, a destructive negotiating process should leave the parties with a greater inclination to fight, less good will, and fewer of the skills of conflict resolution than they had at the start. The evidence suggests that the less sanguine of these two possibilities is also the more probable.

The failure of the settlement process to help foster a cooperative climate in the postdivorce family is nowhere better illustrated than in the state of the co-parental relationship. Research suggests that the relationship between divorced parents may be distrustful and conflicted in anywhere from 75 to more than 90 percent of the cases during the first year after divorce. The longitudinal evidence is scanty, but even five years postdivorce a significant minority of parents appear to be having conflicts.

The first postdivorce year is clearly terrible for nearly all couples. Even in the benign samples of Goldsmith (1980) and Ahrons (1981), substantial levels of co-parental conflict are reported. The co-parental relationship is described as conflictual, highly stressful, and involving basic differences of opinion about child rearing in approximately three-quarters of the cases in both investigations. Dissatisfaction with the quality of the co-parental relationship was expressed by 25 to 51 percent of the fathers and 19 to 30 percent of the mothers (Goldsmith reports the higher rates of dissatisfaction for the fathers, Ahrons for the mothers). Forty-one percent of the fathers and 20 percent of the mothers were dissatisfied with the amount of co-parental communication, and 16 percent of the couples did not communicate at all regarding their children (Goldsmith 1980). Distrustful perception, one of the hallmarks of any destructive conflict, was also evident. Each spouse tended to see himself or herself as more helpful, cooperative, and supportive than they were felt to be by the other. The discrepancy was especially evident regarding the level of the ex-husband's involvement with the children, with fathers perceiving themselves as much more involved than they were felt to be by their ex-wives.[7]

The same phenomenon is evident in Fulton's (1979) study. The couples in her investigation were not doing much better two to three years following divorce than they had been at the time of the initial settlement. Fewer than 20 percent of the custodial mothers said they worked jointly with their ex-spouse to solve problems concerning the children, and most admitted they had excluded the father intentionally. At the same time, however, two-thirds of these women complained that the father "takes too little interest" in the children.

These high levels of conflict between divorced parents are confirmed in two recent and influential longitudinal studies, those of Hetherington, Cox, and Cox (1976, 1979a, 1979b) and Wallerstein and Kelly (1980). Hetherington and her co-workers studied forty-eight families undergoing marital dissolution, at two months, one year, and two years after divorce. Divorced families were obtained from court records and referrals from lawyers. This is one of the rare studies on divorce which, for comparative purposes, included an equal number of intact and divorced families that were matched on various demographic characteristics. At each time period data were collected by observing parent-child interaction in home and laboratory as well as through interviews with each parent concerning the relationship of the noncustodial parent with the children.

Hetherington et al. report that in the two months following divorce, 66 percent of the exchanges between ex-spouses involved conflicts, primarily over child support, visitation, and intimate relations with others. In only 8 percent of the couples was acrimony and painful conflict absent. By the two-year point much of the hostility had attenuated, but anger and resentment was sustained longer in the women than in the men.

Wallerstein and Kelly (1980) studied sixty divorcing parents and their children at the point of physical separation and again at eighteen months and five years after separation. In return for their cooperation with the research aims of the study, parents received six weeks of counseling designed to help them manage their children during the divorce process. Although the investigation did not include a comparison group of intact marriages or employ standardized measurements of interaction or adjustment, it is rich in clinical detail gleaned from over thirty hours of in-depth interviews with each family. Regarding the co-parental relationship, Wallerstein and Kelly report a pattern similar to that observed by Hetherington and her colleagues. For the vast majority of their sample, "bitter and explosive" is their characterization of parental interaction immediately after separation. Money was an especially intense focus of parental hostility, particularly over matters that had not been spelled out and agreed upon explicitly in the separation agreement, and visitation "provided a rich arena for struggles around the issue of who should be in control" (Wallerstein and Kelly 1980, 27). During this initial period fully 80 percent of the fathers and an even higher proportion of the mothers expressed anger and bitterness toward the other partner. The most common expression of this ill feeling was denigration of the other parent in front of the children, an activity in which the children were frequently invited to participate.

> More than half of the mothers, and almost as many fathers, were extremely critical and abusive about the other parent. For the most part, children heard their parents describe each other in new terms. Men were "liars, bastards, terrible parents, unreliable, sleeping around with cheap women, disgusting and crazy." Women were "whores, unfit mothers, drunken bitches, greedy and grasping, sexually inadequate, and crazy." Children were invited to participate in these hostilities. Some did, with alacrity; others felt anxious, some were disgusted. (Wallerstein and Kelly 1980, 28)

At eighteen months after separation the researchers note a distinct reduction in hostilities. Nonetheless, 50 percent of the mothers and 20 percent of the fathers continued to make bitter, disparaging remarks about their former mate in front of the children. At the five-year mark, 29 percent of the children were still witness to "intense bitterness" between their parents, and an even larger group continued to be aware of limited anger or friction. At this relatively late date only one-third of the children were completely freed from the burdens of continuing hostility between their divorced parents. Like Hetherington et al., Wallerstein and Kelly also note that mothers were angrier and less friendly toward their former partners than were the fathers.

As with child support perhaps the most dramatic indication of destructive conflict in the co-parental relationship derives not from an empirical study but from a piece of legislation. In 1980 Congress passed the Parental Kidnapping Act, which authorized the use of the Federal Parent Locator Service to search for parents who flee with their children. The law was a response to estimates that each year between 25,000 and 100,000 children are kidnapped by a parent who has lost custody or contact with his or her children. The kidnappings are thought to be a means of redress and revenge (*New York Times,* 23 July 1981, sec. B, p. 4).

Conflicts in the co-parental relationship appear to contribute significantly to the troubled course of the parent-child relationship after divorce. In this sense, the failure of the settlement process to attenuate conflict are amplified well beyond the divorcing couple, as the children interact with their parents as well as with schoolmates and teachers.

Perhaps the most poignant issue in postdivorce parent-child relations is the frequency and quality of the contact between the divorced father and his children. In 90 percent of the cases the children will continue to reside with the mother, and the father will be granted "visitation"—the legal right (and, in the eyes of many, the moral obligation) to see his children on a regular basis. The terms of visitation are set forth in the settlement agreement. Among the various aspects of postdivorce family life, the course of visitation is thus the most accurate measure of the success of the settlement negotiations. By that criteria the settlement process must be judged unsatisfactory for a considerable number of divorced families.

Several studies suggest that serious problems with visitation occur in anywhere from 15 percent to more than one-third of all divorces. (The size of the estimate appears to vary with the nature of the sample.) Ahrons (1981), in a generally optimistic report, found that in 15 percent of the cases parental rapport was so badly deteriorated that the parents avoided all personal contact with each other in managing visitation, preferring either to let the child make arrangements with the noncustodial parent or sticking rigidly to the terms of the visitation agreement. As has been noted, Ahrons's sample excluded couples at the higher levels of conflict and therefore probably underestimates the rate of conflict over visitation.

Samples chosen in a more representative manner indicate that conflict over visitation may be more common. In their random sample of uncontested divorces in California, Weitzman and Dixon (1979) report that in roughly 20 percent of the cases the court detected sufficient parental disharmony to set additional conditions to the exercise of visitation (for example, required the husband to notify his ex-wife prior to seeing the children; required visitation to take place only in the children's primary residence). For problems of this kind to come to the attention of the court at least one of the parents must have been sufficiently angry and financially robust to take legal action. Therefore, the 20 percent figure must also be regarded as a conservative estimate of visitation discord.

In Jones's (1977) random sample of Oregon divorce filings visitation was unsatisfactory to 21 percent of the fathers and 34 percent of the mothers. The study by Fulton (1979), which included all available cases in which there had been either an initial court contest or much "uncontested" fighting, reports the highest rate of visitation conflict. In that study, 34 percent of the parents reported that visitation had either ceased entirely or occurred only once or twice a year. Forty percent of the custodial mothers said that they had refused visitation at least once to punish the father and 25 percent of the noncustodial fathers reported that they had tried legally or informally to change the visitation schedule but had been unable to do so because of their ex-wives' lack of cooperation.

The most detailed evidence on visitation comes from the Hetherington et al. and Wallerstein and Kelly studies. The unsatisfactory course of father-child contact after divorce is confirmed in both.

Hetherington and her co-workers report that, in spite of an initial increase in father-child contact in the first two months after the divorce, over the two-year period of the study there was a distinct decline in the frequency with which fathers saw their children. By the second year after divorce nearly one-third of the fathers saw their children once every three weeks or less. Laboratory and home observations indicated that compared to fathers in intact marriages, divorced fathers were ignoring their children more and showing them less affection (Hetherington, Cox, and Cox 1976).

The investigators summarize their findings on visitation by observing that although the divorced fathers in their study were probably more motivated and concerned about their children than is the average divorced father (as evidenced by their two years of cooperation with the project), there was nonetheless a notable decline in the father's influence on and intimacy with his child: ". . . two years after the divorce, divorced fathers clearly are influencing their children less and divorced mothers more" (Hetherington, Cox, and Cox 1976, 426).

The researchers later noted that visitation was a source of continuing conflict in the postdivorce family. "As time went on, fathers more often were late for visits, cancelled visits at the last minute, or failed to appear when the child expected him"—a pattern which infuriated the custodial mother (Hetherington, Cox, and Cox 1979c, 113).

Wallerstein and Kelly report that in the first year following separation, visitation was an area of conflict and alienation for a sizeable minority of families. In at least 20 percent of the cases the mothers saw no value in visitation and actively tried to sabotage it. In 75 percent of the families overnight and weekend visits between father and child did not occur. Most visitations lasted only a few hours at a time. One-quarter of the parents were in active competition for the affection and loyalty of the children and one-third of the children were exposed to "intense anger" between the parents at the time of visiting. Two-thirds of the mothers and about 80 percent of the fathers found the visits in the first year following separation moderately or severely stressful.

Five years postseparation, fathers and children had maintained contact with each other to a greater degree than the researchers had expected. Nonetheless, one-quarter of the children continued to be visited erratically or not at all, and 20 percent did not enjoy the time spent with father. In a vein similar to that of Hetherington et al., Wallerstein and Kelly report that even in cases where visitation occurred on a regular basis the influence of the father on the child decreased notably.

Problems with visitation tell only part of the story regarding disturbances in the parent-child relationship after divorce. Generalized conflict and alienation between parents and children appear to be common and frequently represent a significant deterioration from conditions prior to the divorce.

Again, the principal data on the fate of the parent-child relationship come from the two longitudinal studies. Parent-child conflict after divorce appears to have three principal sources: the children's modeling of the fighting they observe between their separated parents; the acting-out by the child of anxieties and resentments aroused by the parental separation and aggravated by continuing parental conflict; and the deterioration in the parents' ability to control their children which results from the problems that the parents are experiencing in their relationship with each other. The mother-son relationship appears especially vulnerable in all of these regards.

Hetherington and her co-workers found that, relative to parents in intact marriages, divorced parents communicated less with their children, were less affectionate toward them, showed marked inconsistency in discipline, and were less able to exercise parental control.

By the second year postdivorce the situation had improved but the divorced family continued to exhibit significant problems (Hetherington, Cox, and Cox 1979b). The mother-son relationship, which had been bad at the outset, remained troubled. Divorced mothers were significantly more coercive toward their sons than were divorced fathers or parents in intact marriages. The researchers describe a "coercive cycle," in which the divorced mother's antagonistic and ineffectual behavior elicited a corresponding oppositional and aggressive stance toward her by the son. Divorced mothers of boys were less able than other parents to control or terminate this type of behavior in a child once it had begun.[8]

When the divorced couple had a good co-parental relationship the negative cycle of interaction between mother and child and the overall adjustment of the child were greatly improved and stabilization of the relationships in the postdivorce family occurred more rapidly. The impact of visitation was also correlated with the quality of the co-parental relationship. When cooperation between the parents prevailed, frequent contact with the noncustodial father had a beneficial impact on the child's overall adjustment and improved the relationship between mother and child.

When parental cooperation was absent or interaction was hostile, the adjustment of the child suffered and tension rose in the relationship between mother and child.

Themes of family conflict and disharmony were echoed in the child's behavior and relationships beyond the home. This was especially true for sons, whose struggles with the outside world continued into the second postdivorce year. There were two poles to the boys' difficulties. On the one hand, they were considerably more antagonistic, oppositional, and uncooperative than were girls from divorced homes or children of intact marriages. These hostile tendencies were evident in interactions with peers and adults, especially female adults. On the other hand, children of divorce, especially boys, were more dependent, more passive, and more in need of support and nurturance. The net effect of these opposing tendencies was increased social isolation. Children from divorced homes, especially boys, wanted to interact with others, but did so in such a nagging, demanding, and offputting way that they elicited counter-hostility and, ultimately, rejection. (Ironically, at the two-year point, boys were still rated by their peers as aggressive, although observational data indicated that this was no longer the case.)

The Wallerstein and Kelly study tells a very similar tale. At the time of parental separation three-quarters of the children were strongly opposed to the divorce, and fears of abandonment, especially by their fathers, were common. The greatest anxiety was found in those children whose families were involved in a custodial battle. Children of all ages experienced an increase in aggression, and over one-quarter exhibited "explosive anger" towards one or both parents. At this early point in the divorce process the mother-child relationship was in serious disarray and had deteriorated in two-thirds of the cases from what it had been prior to the separation. Decreased cooperation and trust and increased fighting were characteristic. The net result in many cases was a coercive cycle reminiscent in spirit, if not in detail, to the one described by Hetherington and her co-workers (Wallerstein and Kelly 1980, 112).

At eighteen months postseparation one-quarter of the children continued to be intensely angry at one or both parents and, for close to one-fifth of the children, mainly boys, this anger was expressed in frequent, explosive outbursts. The anger of children was directly linked to the occurrence of mayhem in the relationship between mother and father. Another visible consequence of the child's anger was a deterioration in the quality and quantity of visitation: the angrier the child was, the less the father visited; the less the father visited, the angrier the child became (Hetherington, Cox, and Cox 1979c).

Wallerstein and Kelly report that five years after the separation over one-third of the children were consciously and intensely unhappy with family life; 39 percent felt rejected by their fathers and for 40 percent the relationship with their mother either deteriorated or remained poor. The quality of the parent-child relationship prior to the divorce was an uncertain guide to the child's postdivorce adjustment. The strongest predictor of child adjustment was the individual adjustment of each parent and the quality of the co-parental relationship in the postdivorce period: "When one or both parents continued to be distressed, or when the divorced parents continued to fight with each other as bitterly as they had during the marriage, or when the bitterness following the divorce even exceeded the bitterness of the marital conflict, children felt unable to master the resulting stress and psychic pain" (Wallerstein and Kelly 1980, 224).

A study by Hess and Camara (1979) suggests that the strongest predictor of child adjustment is the individual relationship between the child and each parent, with the state of the co-parental relationship playing a significant, but distinctly secondary role. However, the psychological adjustment of each parent—and hence their ability to be effective parents—is undoubtedly conditioned by the state of the co-parental relationship. Indeed, individual adjustment, co-parental adjustment, and child adjustment are all so complexly intertwined and reciprocally influential that it is no easy task to establish the direction and magnitude of causation. At least it may be said that continued parental battling is no asset to child adjustment.

Summary

The conflicts that so often occur in divorced families—the broken promises, unpaid support, missed visits, and angry scenes—cannot be attributed exclusively, or even primarily, to unsatisfactory settlement negotiations. In the first place, the evidence regarding settlement negotiations is far from complete. The major defects include too few studies, especially studies concerning the quality and nature of the negotiating process itself; the uncertain representativeness of samples used; and too much reliance on self-reports, with a corresponding dearth of observational data. In nearly all of the investigations reviewed here, the absence of information on intact families is also a shortcoming, suggesting by implication that the situation that prevails in the postdivorce family departs radically from the erstwhile tranquility and cooperation of the "average" American home. This assumption is seriously in need of testing. In the Hess and Camara study (1979), for example, the quality of parental communication and parental time spent with the child varied more *within* the divorced and intact family groups than between them. More crucially, the child's adjustment was predicted better by the prevailing dynamics within the family than by whether or not the family happened to be divorced. The study involved only sixteen families per group, but the results underline the need for including intact families wherever possible in research designs.

Second, some of the conflicts that occur during the divorce process must surely be considered unavoidable—they are products of predivorce problems in getting along, which the parties bring to the divorce; the emotional stress produced by the separation; and the introduction, with time, of new life-styles and personal attachments that weaken the commitment to the old, now inconvenient agreements. In order to assess the contribution of these factors to postdivorce conflict, longitudinal studies are needed that begin not with divorce, but with marriage, tracing a representative group of families from their inception. In the scheme of things some of these families will break apart and an understanding of their subsequent fate can be sought with more complete data than are presently available.

We must also consider that a portion of the conflicts that result from divorce is probably desirable, representing cathartic outbursts that help break the old bonds of attachment and help pave the way to a better future. For this reason, among others, researchers in the area of divorce conflict need to become more sophisticated in defining and distinguishing constructive from destructive forms of interaction.

Depending on one's subjective beliefs, it is also possible to stand the evidence on its head and remark on the surprising number of divorced spouses who, in spite of the difficult circumstances surrounding most divorces, do *not* end up in court disputes or badgering each other eternally about the children. Indeed, this is the perspective taken by some of the researchers whose studies have been reviewed. Five years from now, perhaps, when research on the settlement process and the sources of postdivorce conflict is further along, we will be in a better position to identify which of these various perspectives should be assigned the greater weight.

All of this notwithstanding, a basic fact is clear from the high degree of general agreement among the reported studies, which are otherwise so heterogeneous in their samples, methods, and points of focus: for a great number of divorced persons the process of separation and the settlement negotiations which accompany it fail to produce enduring, mutually acceptable agreements. They also fail to create a more positive climate of cooperation and trust, especially concerning co-parenting.

But is it reasonable to expect the separation/negotiation process to do so? The answer, I believe, is "yes," at least for a proportion of divorcing couples now listed among the casualties. This belief is based on a sizeable body of research in other areas of interpersonal conflict which has shown that where there are incentives for cooperation, however obscured they may be, there exists a powerful potential for deescalating the fighting and for channeling interaction along more benevolent paths (Deutsch 1973). The incentives for cooperation between spouses are certainly present in divorce, especially when children are involved. For divorcing parents the settlement negotiations do (or can) establish the basic terms of interaction over a deeply shared concern that may last a lifetime. In addition, the settlement negotiations occur at perhaps the one moment in adult life when the help of others is most likely to be sought. Divorced persons are more likely than any other group in the population to seek psychotherapy (Veroff, Kulka, and Douvan 1981), and are among the largest group of consumers of legal services (Curran 1977). The potential for containing and re-directing conflict in this group must be considered correspondingly large.

Any improvement in the prevailing modes of "uncoupling," however, depends on a clear understanding of the obstacles to be overcome. In the following chapter the psychological, interpersonal, economic, and social circumstances that condition the settlement negotiations are examined in detail. These conditions may well be among the worst surrounding any personal negotiations. They are worth elaborating for a variety of reasons, not the least of which is to gain a fairer appreciation of the hazards and frustrations faced by divorcing couples as well as by the lawyers and therapists to whom they often turn for assistance.

2

The Context of Professional Intervention

In the previous chapter we traced the frequently unsatisfactory results of divorce settlement negotiations. Broken agreements, mutual recrimination, coercion through litigation or threats of litigation, and an absence of cooperation between the spouses are common. It is also common for therapists and the lay public to attribute many of these difficulties to the psychologically unsophisticated, combatative orientation of lawyers. Lawyers, on the other hand, are prone to blame the "irrational" client and, occasionally, the ineptness or legal naivety of the client's therapist. In this chapter, I suggest that the poor outcomes in settlement negotiations can be attributed to no single cause, but are the product of many unfavorable circumstances that conspire to make the divorce bargaining table extremely problematic.

It is useful to begin with a consideration of the objectives to which a truly constructive divorce negotiation might aspire. We may then proceed to an examination of the hurdles that typically stand in the way of attaining such objectives. On both of these topics theory and research is sparse if we restrict our attention exclusively to the legal and psychological literature on divorce. However, researchers and practitioners in other arenas of human conflict have much to say that is germane to the divorce context. A comparative perspective is also useful for defusing the argument over who is "to blame" for the spotty record of divorce negotiators, since the problems faced in divorce negotiations appear remarkably similar to the kinds of difficulties that beset negotiators in other forms of conflict.

Criteria of a Constructive Divorce Settlement Negotiation

A constructive settlement negotiation can refer to the manner in which the parties conduct themselves during negotiations or to the outcome of the negotiations. The distinction is important, since there is considerable evidence that certain modes of interaction during negotiations are more conducive to constructive conflict resolution than are others. Let us begin, however, with the more obvious and tangible matter of outcomes. A constructive outcome in divorce settlement negotiations may be defined by the following criteria:

1. *Resolution of all relevant issues.* The imposition of a settlement by an outside authority, such as a court, is a less desirable occurrence because of the additional financial and emotional costs involved and because, psychologically, the parties are unlikely to experience an imposed settlement as their own. To be sure, there are instances where a court verdict may be extremely useful as a means of terminating hostilities—at least legal ones. Court orders may also allow the parties to save face; all responsibility and blame can be placed on the judge, although secretly the parties may welcome the arrangements imposed. But these instances may be best regarded as cases of judicial faute de mieux.
2. *Tolerable financial and emotional costs.* Neither spouse should be emotionally or financially depleted in an effort to reach a negotiated agreement, nor should the emotional costs to the children be excessive.
3. *Technically correct agreements.* The final agreement should be expressed in clear, unambiguous language; it should cover all matters required by law and by the circumstances of the parties, and violate no legal statute.
4. *Agreements that are fair and equitable—relative to broadly prevailing norms and community expectations for comparable cases—and are perceived as such by the parties.* One can argue whether the fact of fairness and equity is more or less important than the perceptions of the parties, but the two are clearly interrelated; e.g., it is likely that an agreement that is grossly out of line with prevailing standards will ultimately be viewed as such by the parties.
5. *Agreements that protect the rights, interests, and welfare of affected third parties, especially children.* For divorcing parents this is a crucial matter whose importance is perhaps matched only by the difficulty of determining precisely what arrangements are, in fact, best for their children.
6. *Creative agreements.* This type of agreement is inherently difficult to define.

Innovative, imaginative, and flexible are the adjectives that come immediately to mind. In the case of divorce a creative agreement might refer to one in which: resources are conserved or maximized for the entire postdivorce family (as opposed to being diluted in unnecessarily paid taxes or poorly coordinated child care arrangements); new opportunities for growth and independence are established (as in an innovative plan for the continuing education of the wife-homemaker); foreseeable or probable changes in circumstances are taken into account (such as those caused by inflation or remarriage); and provisions are included for handling future disputes or dissatisfactions arising out of the settlement (as in a clause to seek mediation or arbitration for postdivorce disputes).

7. *Satisfaction with the overall results.* Given the difficult and unhappy nature of the task we would perhaps expect this satisfaction to be of a tempered, sober kind. Certainly neither side should emerge from negotiations feeling either triumphant or humiliated. Such extremes of feeling bode ill for future compliance with the agreement.
8. *The couple experiences a sense of "ownership" of the agreement.* Both spouses should conclude with the feeling that, for better or worse, the final product represents their own best efforts and values, as opposed to the efforts and values of outside parties such as lawyers or judges.
9. *Parties comply with the terms of the agreement.* The feelings of tempered satisfaction with and psychological ownership of the agreement should be translated into compliance with its terms. Expensive and emotionally draining postsettlement litigation and/or chronic postdivorce conflict over the agreement should not occur.
10. *Spouses are better able (and certainly not less able) to cooperate.* A constructive negotiation should leave the relationship between the parties improved in areas where future coordination of activities is necessary and desirable. In the case of divorced parents this refers particularly to co-parenting.

What needs to happen in the negotiating exchanges between the parties and their representatives to produce such lofty outcomes? It is in response to this question that disagreement and uncertainty are most likely to arise among professionals and researchers. Partly this is because judgments concerning desirable negotiating strategies and tactics are invariably subjective. More crucially, I believe, it is because legal training and the legal system itself have established as normative an adversarial style of bargaining which stresses the use of pressure tactics, concealment, and competitive legal strategems aimed at "winning." While there are many in the legal community who believe that an adversarial stance is inappropriate in divorce, the legal norms in its favor are still quite strong.

In contrast to the legal debate (which, incidentally, is largely devoid of appeals to objective evidence), stands the empirical record from several decades of research in the social psychology of conflict resolution. Criteria of a successful settlement process may be drawn from diverse but rich sources within social psychology, including field studies of interpersonal and intergroup conflict (Bach and Wyden 1968; Blake and Mouton 1964; Deutsch 1973; Sherif 1966); research on bargaining and negotiation (Pruitt 1981; Rubin and Brown 1975); investigations of productivity and achievement (Johnson et al. 1981); and conflict theory (Deutsch 1973). It is this research tradition from which I have drawn for the criteria of a constructive process of settlement negotiations.

1. *Cooperative orientation to the negotiating encounter.* Perhaps the principal criteria of a constructive negotiating process is that, *at some point,* the parties define the task as a cooperative effort to achieve mutual or compatible goals. Research in other areas of conflict has repeatedly demonstrated that a cooperative orientation produces greater satisfaction, better feelings toward and more accurate perceptions, of the other, higher joint profits, and an increased willingness to compromise, than does a competitive or individualistic orientation in which the parties are motivated either to "beat" the other or attend solely to their own gain (Deutsch 1973; Rubin and Brown 1975). A cooperative orientation in divorce settlement negotiations is not unrealistic if the many potential shared objectives, such as keeping down legal costs and protecting the welfare of the children, are borne in mind. There are also potential compatible goals that may form the basis for cooperation. For example, the husband's desire to pay less alimony and the wife's wish to achieve a greater degree of self-sufficiency can produce an agreement wherein the husband underwrites career training for the wife in return for a schedule of alimony payments that gradually reduces as her earnings increase.
2. *"Open" communication.* Deutsch (1973) and others have shown that when a cooperative orientation prevails, exchanges over the bargaining table are likely to assume certain other desirable characteristics, such as an open style of communication. Cooperatively motivated negotiators communicate to each other all information that might facilitate their search for an acceptable agreement. Concealment or distortion of information in the interest of outwitting the other does not typically occur under such conditions.

   Full and honest disclosure is not, however, equivalent to naivety or passivity. On the contrary, open communication implies active, mutual participation in the give-and-take of negotiating. The failure of one or both sides to take such a stance suggests nonacceptance of or guilt about the decision to divorce. The consequence of such passivity is that the final settlement, arranged by lawyers or the courts, will not convey a sense of psychological ownership and may not adequately reflect the realistic needs or wishes of both parties.

   An open style of communication also encompasses the direct expression of anger. Anger may take various forms and serve different functions at each stage of the negotiating process, a matter I will discuss in more detail later. For the moment, we may simply note that when negotiators are cooperatively motivated, anger tends to be expressed for the purpose of communicating feelings or priorities relevant to reaching a sound agreement, rather than for the sake of inflicting punishment. Thus, disagreements are based on realistic, current issues rather than on past hurts, real or imagined, or on pseudo-issues (such as a husband's threats to contest custody which are merely a bargaining ploy to gain leverage over his wife).

3. *Respectful task-orientation.* When negotiators are cooperatively oriented, their approach to the work of bargaining emphasizes the enhancement of mutual power and resources. The legitimacy of each other's interests is acknowledged, attempts to influence the other rely more on persuasion than on threats or coercion, and the issues in conflict tend to become increasingly well-focused and specific rather than expanding into matters of "general principle" (notoriously hard to resolve because nobody likes to compromise on "principles"). The motivational significance of the issues also remains within reasonable bounds, instead of intensifying the parties' emotional involvement to the point where mutual disaster (spelled C-U-S-T-O-D-Y B-A-T-T-L-E) is preferred to limited achievement of goals.
4. *Benevolent perceptions and attitudes.* A cooperative orientation heightens sensitivity to common interests and similarities, while downplaying the complete opposition of interests and values. Neutral or conciliatory actions by the other are correctly perceived, rather than being misattributed to malevolent or deceptive purposes. A tendency to attribute positive, or at least legitimate, motives to the other predominates. Within the broad confines of pursuing legitimate self-interest, attitudes remain trusting, if not friendly. There is a willingness to respond helpfully rather than exploitatively or antagonistically, to the other's needs and requests.
5. *A gradual pace, involving a shift from a competitive to a cooperative orientation.* This is perhaps the most speculative of our criteria because there has been little systematic research on the time element in formal negotiations. What has been reported (see Pruitt [1981] for a review) and what is known about the effects of time on the psychological adjustment of divorced persons leads to a tentative conclusion, however: that a successful divorce settlement process is likely to be *gradual,* involving a shift from an initial *competitive stage,* in which hostility, coercion, and other flamboyant manifestations of destructive interaction are at their peak, to a *cooperative stage,* in which the more benevolent characteristics of joint problem solving are present.

   That constructive settlement negotiations should be gradual is a reflection of the well-recognized emotional turmoil inevitable in the early stages of adjusting to divorce. During this early period neither spouse is likely to be in full control of his or her capacity for rational, informed decision making. As one divorce therapist put it, the best rule for the recently separated is, "Don't just do something; stand there." In addition, the parties need time to familiarize themselves with the new, complex realities of finances, work, social life, and family responsibility to which their negotiations must ultimately be addressed. For these reasons, rushing into detailed and demanding settlement negotiations in the early stages of psychological adjustment to divorce is likely to end either in frustration or in an unrealistic and unworkable agreement. In a successful negotiating process the parties' serious, formal negotiations (as opposed to informal, temporary agreements on matters of necessity) should not begin until both sides are at least moderately in command of themselves and the principal issues to be resolved.

The need for a shift from an initial hostile stage to a more cooperative one is supported by research findings in the area of industrial and international negotiations. Several researchers have proposed that such a shift is characteristic of successful negotiating encounters in those areas (Douglas 1962; Morley and Stephenson 1977). In the early stages of negotiations, angry exchanges may help the parties see more clearly and quickly which issues are the most significant to whom, thereby preparing the ground for compromises and trade-offs in the later cooperative stage. In the case of divorce settlement negotiations, an early period of hostility may also serve important psychological functions, helping the parties accept the need for a divorce by allowing them to work through their anger. Given the characteristic human resistance to ending intimate ties, the initial stages of fighting may also help to break the marital ties by imposing such significant costs to continued warfare that ambivalence about the divorce is overcome.[1]

DIVORCE NEGOTIATION: THE IDEAL VS. THE REALITY

The foregoing criteria of an ideal settlement negotiation are not unassailable or necessarily exhaustive. Moreover, in some instances they are general, when what is wanted are specifics. I have said, for example, that a successful outcome is one that is "fair and equitable" or involves a "gradual" shift from competition to cooperation, but how are such terms to be defined? Whatever their shortcomings, however, these criteria provide a useful metric, based on wisdom accumulated by researchers and practitioners in other domains of human conflict, beside which may be set the psychological and practical circumstances in which divorce negotiations are typically conducted. The ideal negotiation that we have been describing may be summarized as a gradually evolving, cooperative search for mutually acceptable, equitable, and creative terms toward which the parties feel a sense of psychological ownership. In this search several elements must be held in delicate balance: self-interest vs. mutuality; impetuosity vs. patience; and explosive anger vs. controlled debate. Under the best of circumstances, attaining all of these objectives is no small order. In the typical divorce negotiation circumstances are very far from the best.

Obstacles to a Successful Divorce Negotiation

What factors frustrate the search for a constructive settlement negotiation? This was one of the central questions we put to the expert practitioners who we interviewed in the first phase of our research. They responded in the language of law and psychology familiar to their respective professions. These views are presented in more detail and in the terms in which they were originally stated in the following chapters. Here I would like to summarize in more general language what our respondents told us and what our own subsequent analyses confirmed. In so doing it is apparent that the obstacles that complicate the negotiating task of the divorce lawyer, the divorce mediator, and the divorcing couple themselves include many of the same factors which negotiators, mediators, and combatants in other settings have identified as problematic. That is, in a sense the problems posed for constructive dispute resolution in divorce are the same obstacles encountered elsewhere; the concrete guise in which each obstacle presents itself may differ from one type of conflict to another but the underlying difficulties appear to be much alike. This is heartening to the general theorist of conflict resolution, whose pleasure it is to find similarities beneath surface disparity, but it holds an important message for divorce practitioners and their clients as well: namely, that no single person and no single thing is likely to be to blame if settlement negotiations are frustrating and difficult; all of the parties, including highly experienced and competent professionals, are contending with many forces not of their making and by no means under their control.

If we restate the views of our expert divorce practitioners in language applicable to other domains of conflict, nine shared obstacles to a constructive negotiating experience can be identified:

1. High levels of intraparty conflict
2. Well-established and rigid patterns of destructive interaction
3. Inexperience in the art of negotiating
4. Scarcity of divisable resources
5. Complex issues which threaten loss of face or self-esteem
6. Elevated levels of stress and tension
7. Social norms and institutions for conflict management that are weak or that unintentionally provoke destructive interaction
8. Disparities in the parties' relative power
9. Disparities in the parties' degree of interpersonal sensitivity

The last two of these obstacles are closely associated with the male-female context in which divorce negotiations occur.

The presence of any one of these nine factors heightens the prospect for difficulty in the negotiation process. This is so because in varying ways and to varying degrees each tends to impair communication, inhibit rational decision making, reduce the prospects for informed compromise, and, perhaps most significant, discourage the parties from defining the negotiations as a cooperative effort to strive for mutual or compatible objectives. When all of these obstacles are present, as they may well be in the case of negotiations between divorcing spouses, the negotiating experience is likely to give everybody fits.

HIGH LEVELS OF INTRAPARTY CONFLICT

In labor-management disputes, international negotiations, and other forms of institutionalized bargaining, factional conflicts frequently impede progress in the external negotiations. For example, union leadership facing a strong dissident group within the rank and file may experience considerable pressure to appear tough and unyielding at the bargaining table, lest they lose credibility with and power over their internal rivals. Internal rivals may also conceal important information from the negotiating leaders, in the hopes of either frustrating the search for a settlement or arriving at one more favorable to their own interests.

In divorce negotiations internal conflict is principally of the intrapsychic variety. The precise nature of the emotional turmoil in divorce is discussed in chapter 3, but it may be summarized in a word—*ambivalence.* The principal sources of ambivalence are threefold: ambivalence produced by concrete events surrounding the marital dissolution, ambivalence connected with separation distress, and ambivalence resulting from the nonmutual nature of the decision to divorce.

Of the three, the ambivalence arising from events that occur during dissolution is the simplest to comprehend and the most emotionally straightforward. A husband who feels humiliated about losing his wife to another, a woman made to feel anxious by her husband's threats of nonsupport, a mother who is guilt-ridden about her children's distress when their father leaves the home—all of these individuals are experiencing feelings that are sources of ambivalence toward settlement negotiations. These feelings introduce motives of revenge or capitulation (depending on the circumstances) which are directly at variance with the need to negotiate an end to the marriage. The parties, that is, may wish to "settle" with each other in more ways than one. Such contradictory tactical objectives may have very adverse effects on negotiations.

> Mrs. K. initiated the divorce. Dr. K. claimed repeatedly during mediation that he loved his wife and children very much and did not want the divorce. On the other hand, he was often openly angry and bitter at having been "deserted" by his wife. Mrs. K. was consumed by guilt at ending the marriage. The effect of these conflicting emotions was apparent in the negotiations over division of

> marital assets, during which Mrs. K. said nothing in her own behalf, and simply acquiesced to her husband's offer to take 25 percent of their $83,000 in assets, although at the time she had no job and the custody of three young children. (Kressel et al. 1979, 270)

Nonmutuality of the decision to divorce and distress caused by separation add more profound elements of ambivalence because they are likely to engender not merely divided tactical objectives, but a divided attitude about the fundamental premise on which the settlement negotiations are built: the necessity or desirability of ending the marital relationship.

The decision to divorce is a complex event which cannot be done justice by a simple summary. One aspect of the process, however, is the nonmutual nature with which the majority of couples arrive at such a decision. Empirical and clinical evidence suggest that in 75 to 90 percent of all divorces one spouse wants the marriage to end more than does the other (Ahrons 1981; Goldsmith 1980; Wallerstein and Kelly 1980; Zeiss, Zeiss, and Johnson 1980).[2] A situation is thus created in which one party is likely to have strong inclinations to obstruct or sabotage the movement toward a final agreement in the hopes that the unwanted dissolution can be avoided. It does not make matters easier that this wish, which is so intimately tied to feelings of self-esteem and self-worth, is often unconscious. When pressed into consciousness (by a well-meaning attorney or divorce mediator, for example) the effect may be to escalate the conflict even more.

> The M's were divorcing because Mrs. M. had fallen in love with a co-worker whom she wished to marry. In the mediated settlement negotiations which followed, Mr. M. insisted on sole custody and refused to consider his wife's proposal for joint residential custody on the grounds that her relationship with the new man made her an unfit model for the children. He also interpreted the boyfriend's efforts toward the children as proof of his lack of moral standards.
>
> The mediator tried to break the impasse over custody by suggesting to the husband that his inflexible bargaining position might be the product of his understandable, but misplaced hurt and anger at being rejected, rather than from any realistic consideration of his wife's abilities as a parent or the efforts of her boyfriend to form a relationship with the children. Mr. M. rejected these ideas vehemently, and accused the mediator of favoritism and lack of understanding.

Nonmutuality in the decision to divorce may also produce ambivalence in the initiator, whose flexibility in the settlement negotiations may be compromised by self-doubt and guilt. In the case of the M's the problem revolved around the wife's concerns about her image as a parent, the chord upon which her husband played so insistently.

> Mrs. M. could have reached a negotiated settlement with her husband if she had agreed to give up her stubborn refusal to consider anything less than a legalistic "50–50" arrangement for sharing time with the children. She acknowledged that, because of her husband's career objectives and his past inclinations to share parenting responsibilities, there was an excellent chance that whatever the final legal stipulations, in practice she would have as much time with the children as she wished. Her rigid insistence on a "50–50" arrangement was unswayed by such realistic considerations, however, since it stemmed from her need to "prove" to the children, her husband, and perhaps most importantly, to herself, that she was a good and caring mother and not the harlot her husband insisted she was. The rigidities on both sides led to a stalemated mediation and ultimately, a court battle over custody.

The most profound source of ambivalence at the divorce bargaining table is what Weiss (1975) has aptly labeled "separation distress": that painful constellation of emotions, including anxiety, irritability, anger, and depression, experienced by the "leaver" as well as the "left," touched off by the prospect of severing the marital bond. The hallmark of separation distress is psychological attachment—the persistent, wistful dwelling on the former mate and marriage, even in the face of a conscious desire to give up such thoughts. As yet there is little reliable data on the frequency with which separation distress and continued psychological attachment occur in the divorced population at large or of their relationship to the behavior and adjustment of divorced persons. Several such studies have been reported, however.

Spanier and Casto (1979), using a questionnaire which asked respondents how frequently they thought about or wished to be with their ex-spouse, reported that 36 percent of the sample showed strong attachment, 36 percent mild attachment, and 28 percent no attachment feelings at all. However, there was only a slight and statistically nonsignificant tendency for those showing higher degrees of attachment to be more poorly adjusted psychologically to the divorce.

Kitson (1982) employed a four-item, factor-analyzed self-report measure of psychological attachment in a random sample of 172 recent divorce petitioners drawn from court records. Her study revealed that 25 percent reported high continuing psychological attachment to the spouse, 18 percent moderate attachment, 42 percent low attachment, and 16 percent no discernible attachment feelings. There was a significant correlation between attachment and independent measures of psychological distress.

Brown et al. (1980), using a five-item questionnaire to measure attachment within a clinic population, found that there was a significant relationship between attachment and distress but that while attachment accounted for most of the variance in distress (22 percent), other economic and social factors were also related to dysphoria.

Another line of evidence suggestive of high levels of postdivorce psychological attachment is that regarding continuing doubts about the dissolution. Feelings that the divorce might have been a mistake appear to occur in a large majority of respondents during the first year after the divorce and persist in at least a quarter of those sampled as many as two years or more after the dissolution (Goode 1956; Hetherington, Cox, and Cox 1976; Hunt and Hunt 1977; Wallerstein and Kelly 1980). The remarriage of the ex-partner has been reported to resurrect intense feelings of psychological distress in as many as 25 percent of sampled individuals (Hunt and Hunt 1977) and to be a common source of renewed hostility between the former spouses (Hetherington, Cox, and Cox 1976).

Both Goldsmith (1980) and Ahrons (1981) downplay the significance of continuing contact between divorced spouses as a sign of psychological ambivalence and unhealthy attachment. Goldsmith argues, for example, that "caring feelings and friendly interaction appear to be normative and should not be 'automatically' considered indicative of an unhealthy entanglement or an inability to separate" (Goldsmith 1980, 17). There may be merit in this perspective, but data in both investigations suggest that for a sizeable minority of the respondents continued dwelling on the marriage was common. Thus, Goldsmith reports that one year after the divorce 48 percent of the sample reported talking with each other about the marriage and 36 percent talked about why they had divorced. An equally high proportion appeared to use the former spouse as a continuing source of emotional and psychological support; 64 percent talked with the ex-partner about "new experiences," 44 percent about personal problems. Slightly more than half of the sample reported that on occasion they spend time together with the children "as a family." With all of this contact occuring, the majority of Goldsmith's respondents were dissatisfied with the nonparental aspects of their relationship. Some were unhappy because they wanted more contact and more intense involvement; others because they desired less. Neither the Goldsmith nor the Ahrons study report the relationship between level of nonparental contact and either degree of postdivorce conflict or psychological adjustment.

It is logical to suppose that psychological attachment and the distress it may cause is highest during settlement negotiations, and it is, of course, this source of ambivalence which is most germane to our argument regarding the inherent difficulties of the settlement process. Unfortunately, there is little direct evidence on the subject. Theoretically, the challenge that attachment poses to the negotiating process is obvious enough: to create still further motivation for procrastination, obstruction, and continued destructive fighting in the interest of maintaining the marriage. As one therapist indicated, "hate is a relationship."

Kitson (1982) is the only investigator who, to my knowledge, reports directly on the negative impact of psychological attachment on settlement negotiations. In her investigation, great difficulty in negotiating a settlement was reported by 33 percent of those who scored high in attachment, 3.3 percent of those with moderate attachment scores, and 25 percent of those with low attachment. The relatively high figure for negotiating difficulty among persons scoring low in attachment hints at the possibility that too little emotional investment in the marriage may be as problematic as too much attachment, perhaps because low attachment reflects a generalized impairment in the ability to respond to the needs of another.

There is one important additional form of intraparty conflict that may occur in settlement negotiations. It is of the interpersonal, rather than intrapsychic variety. I refer to the tensions that sometimes arise between each of the divorcing spouses and their respective attorneys. In chapters 5 through 8 I shall consider the legal role and its tensions in detail. Here let us simply note that there is every reason to believe that serious, if unarticulated, conflicts may and do occur between the divorce attorney and his or her client. The rise in malpractice claims against divorce attorneys is one concrete expression of lawyer-client conflicts. One experienced observer has noted that "the practice of family law has been recognized as such a significant area of liability claims that many insurers are rating the family lawyer for a higher professional liability premium" (Mallen 1978, 10).

There are several sources of potential tension between lawyers and their divorce clients. For one, while duty-bound to pursue the client's wishes, the attorney cannot help but form his or her own views about what is fair, desirable, or legally feasible. The stereotypic version of the conflict that may develop from these differing perspectives is that of the decent but "naive" client seeking compromise and fair play and the legal shark determined to "win" for the client at any cost. In fact, because of the ambivalence and emotionality that characterizes many divorce clients, there is an equally good probability that the client's wishes will be more extreme or unrealistic, at least in their initial form, than those held by the lawyer.

There is also a potential for conflict between lawyer and client when determining what kind of negotiating process will be theoretically good for the client and best suited to the practicalities of the law office. Once again, the stereotypic version of this dilemma is that of the unscrupulous attorney who generates conflict for the sake of an inflated fee. The other, equally plausible scenario is the lawyer who wants to orchestrate a gradual negotiating process that would permit passions to cool and realities to become clearer, when the client is unable or unwilling to afford the fees or expend the patience that such a course of action would require.

To further complicate the picture, the attorney's negotiating preferences are shaped not only by pressures to observe the needs and wishes of the client, but by a set of professional norms and expectations governing the attorney's relationship with the opposing counsel. At times these two sources of allegiance may be in distinct opposition. The husband, for example, may make it plain to his lawyer that he wishes the most devoted of legal warriors, but the attorney for the wife may indicate equally plainly to the husband's counsel that moderation and compromise are appropriate. The fact that the attorney will, in all probability, serve his client but once, while he will have numerous occasions to deal with the opposing counsel, may add an additional incentive to follow a more cooperative path than that preferred by the client.

Choosing between allegiance to the client and allegiance to professional expectations can become even more complicated because there appear to be several distinctive postures that govern attorneys' behavior in divorce cases. These range from a belief in the most tenacious and uncompromising pursuit of the client's wishes (especially regarding money), to quasi-therapeutic notions of inducing compromise and restraint. There may be as many as six such distinctive lawyer stances, as will be discussed in detail in chapter 5. That this mix of professional styles can produce headaches in the negotiating process is suggested by the finding that, next to the emotionality of the client, differences of philosophy and approach with the opposing counsel are the obstacles to successful negotiation most frequently cited by divorce attorneys.

How attorneys and clients handle their not necessarily compatible interests and what effects these conflicts of interest have on the quality of legal representation in divorce are matters much in need of investigation. There is evidence in personal injury cases that such conflicts can produce awards that are unfavorable to the client if the client does not participate vigorously in the handling of the case (Rosenthal 1974). At least one investigation in the area of divorce (Hochberg 1984) found that the most stable and satisfactory settlements occurred when the client took an active role in the negotiating process. Clients who allowed the attorney to do most of the negotiating reported worse outcomes. This finding was statistically significant even when other factors (such as the quality of the divorcing spouses' relationship with each other) were controlled for.

In summary, the negotiating parties in divorce are likely to be beset by internal problems and conflicts as intense and problematic to the negotiating process as any faced by the most beleaguered union leader or international statesman. Only the sources of the internal divisions—and, perhaps, the parties' experience and sophistication in managing them—are different.

WELL-ESTABLISHED, DYSFUNCTIONAL PATTERNS OF INTERACTION

In some types of negotiations the parties meet over the bargaining table for the first, and perhaps last, time. Negotiations between a salesman and a customer or the buyer and seller of a house are examples of such ahistorical transactions. In many forms of negotiations, however, the parties have had long experience with one another and that experience may profoundly shape their negotiations in both form and substance. One needs only to think of the conflicts between Catholics and Protestants in Ireland or between Israelies and their Arab neighbors to appreciate the extent to which the mutual past of some parties will cast an ominous shadow over the bargaining table.

In divorce, a troubled pattern of interaction is more likely to be the rule than the exception. Indeed, we may surmise that in the majority of cases difficulties in communication, decision making, and conflict resolution have already contributed significantly to the marital breakdown. The precise nature of these handicaps must remain a matter of conjecture, since systematic research on the interactions of divorcing couples is virtually nonexistent. However, behavioral studies comparing the interactions of happily and unhappily married couples hint at the kind of impairments in conflict management that characterize the parties at the divorce bargaining table.

Gottman (1979) has provided a useful summary of the accumulating evidence. Compared to nondistressed couples, couples who seek help with a marital problem or who are otherwise seriously unhappy with their marriage are far more likely to attempt to influence each other by criticism, by insults, and by responding to one complaint with another. In the event of a disagreement they are more likely to get locked into long chains of reciprocating negative behavior, both verbal and nonverbal. Overall, they have fewer pleasurable exchanges and are less supportive of one another, especially in problem-solving situations. Emotionally, the husband is likely to be less responsive to the wife than she is to him. Needless to say, this profile, or anything close to it, will not prove an asset should the parties decide to negotiate an end to their connubial misery.[3]

Our case studies of divorcing couples (reported in detail in chapter 11) suggest that a more specific historical inheritance may frustrate the process of divorce negotiations: the manner in which the couple has arrived at the decision to divorce. My colleagues and I have identified four such decision-making patterns—*enmeshed, autistic, disengaged,* and *direct.* The enmeshed and autistic patterns have particularly unfavorable implications for settlement negotiations. In different ways both patterns represent fundamental difficulties in conflict resolution.

In the enmeshed pattern the couple's relationship during the process of reaching an agreement to divorce is marked by high degrees of ambivalence, extremely high levels of destructive conflict (including violence and threats of violence), and endless but inconclusive arguments about the pros and cons of getting a divorce. One or both parties derive psychological gratification in continued fighting and display anxiety at the prospect of giving up the marital tie. The settlement negotiations that follow the ostensible agreement to divorce recapitulate these unfortunate characteristics of the divorce decision-making period, leaving a shambles of the bargaining table, not to mention placing more stress on the mediators or lawyers.

In the autistic pattern the divorce decision period is marked by a phobic-like avoidance of conflict and virtually no discussion of the possibility of divorce. The parties avoid each other physically and emotionally until one of them unilaterally announces that the marriage is over, to the shock and dismay of the other. In the autistic case discussed in chapter 12, the settlement negotiations reflected this inheritance. During most of the settlement process overt conflict or even mild disagreement was avoided, but it was at the cost of an informed and realistic give-and-take. Toward the end of negotiations there was an explosive and unanticipated outburst on the part of one of the parties, which subsided as mysteriously as it had come without producing any more realistic movement toward a viable agreement.

INEXPERIENCED NEGOTIATORS

According to expert labor mediators, the single greatest obstacle to effective mediation is parties who are new to collective bargaining. Said one such mediator:

> The sophisticated parties know that a mediator will be looking for alternatives. They will assist him in indicating what might be acceptable. They are more open to suggestion. The non-sophisticated party has a single-track mind. They win or they lose completely without salvaging what they can of the situation. This "all or nothing" approach doesn't lend itself to proper mediation. (Kressel 1972)

In divorce negotiations the inexperience and negotiating naivety of the parties is virtually guaranteed by the "first time around" characteristic of the divorce itself and the fact that, by and large, ours is not a culture in which people are well-schooled in adopting a negotiating posture. In the case analyses of divorce mediation the inexperience and ignorance of the parties was a major problem for mediators. In nearly all of the cases studied the level of ignorance about basic details of family finances was high. Annual net income, outstanding indebtedness, monthly cash flow, and a host of other important details were unknown or highly uncertain in the minds of one and frequently both spouses.

For the mediator there were at least two major consequences of this ignorance. In the first instance, the absence of sound information on the financial state of affairs made the search for viable compromises more difficult. Second, the mediator spent much time trying to educate the parties about certain fundamental principles of money management while in the midst of negotiations, a time when ambivalence and emotional turmoil created strong obstacles to comprehension.

One of the arguments against divorce mediation and in favor of adversary representation by attorneys is that the presence of an attorney is an antidote to the havoc that might otherwise be wreacked by the parties' inexperience. This is a complicated issue because significant liabilities may be introduced along with the attorneys. In any case, interviews with divorce lawyers indicate that they too are often troubled by the inexperience and ignorance of many of their clients regarding the nature of the negotiating process (Kressel et al. 1979).

The obstacles to a successful negotiation which we have considered thus far refer primarily to the psychological and related characteristics of the divorcing spouses. There are additional obstacles to constructive negotiating which derive from the objective circumstances in and around the dispute.

SCARCITY OF DIVISIBLE RESOURCES

In many ways the heart of negotiation is the ability to arrange compromises and trade-offs. A scarcity of resources is likely to represent a serious impediment to such efforts. When each side is worried that even its marginal needs may not be met, intransigence and a competitive win/lose orientation have a high probability of occurrence. Deadlocks arising out of such an orientation may yield only to the injection of large amounts of material incentives by interested and powerful third parties. (Note, for example, the role the United States played in smoothing the path to an agreement between Israel and Egypt by proffering both parties economic and military assistance on a grand scale, as discussed by Kressel [1981].)

Without belaboring the sorry economic plight of the typical middle-class divorcing couple we may simply note that there is usually limited potential for expanding the financial pie in the interest of making agreements more palatable. The principal source of difficulty is the necessity of supporting two households with the same resources that had previously supported—or perhaps barely supported—one household. The situation is typically more acute for divorced mothers, whose economic circumstances after divorce show a precipitous decline. Nor is it an optimum situation for the divorced father, since, especially during the negotiations themselves, it is usually from his pockets that much of the cash will necessarily be extracted.

Financial and material insufficiency as a source of protracted conflict in divorce negotiations deserves emphasis because marriage counselors and psychotherapists may easily overlook such seemingly mundane factors in seeking to understand their clients' inability to reach a settlement. For example, one experienced therapist whom we interviewed remarked:

> I think where people have had no conflicts around money prior to the divorce, they don't have them in the divorce process. The kinds of quarrels that go on around money have nothing to do with the realities of money and how much there is to be shared. It has to do with the feelings people have about money. (Kressel and Deutsch 1977, 424)

Compare this with the perspective of one of the lawyers whom we interviewed:

> There are typical cases where the man makes $15,000 a year and there are three or four children and a nonworking wife. There you have complete chaos, and anybody who tried to introduce so-called "equity" would be much better off introducing money, because it's the only thing that's going to solve this insoluble problem. (Kressel et al. 1979, 251)

COMPLEX ISSUES THAT THREATEN LOSS OF FACE OR SELF-ESTEEM

It is clear from both descriptive and experimental accounts of the bargaining process that the nature of the issues in dispute and the manner in which these issues are formulated by the parties can have a profound influence on the course and outcome of negotiations (Iklé 1964; Pruitt 1981; Rubin and Brown 1975; Walton and McKersie 1965). Perhaps the single greatest problem is posed by disputes in which the issues directly threaten the negotiators' self-image or public reputation for competence, strength, or decency. When one or both parties feel that concession making or compromise pose such a threat, significant increases in inflexibility, distrust, and belligerence are to be expected at the bargaining table.

In negotiations between divorcing parents there is a very high probability that a preoccupation with self-esteem and pride will occur. One source of difficulty is the child-related nature of many of the issues to be negotiated.

Divorcing parents frequently worry about their competence as parents and the long-term effects on their children of their decision to separate. These fears are likely to be highest during settlement negotiations because behavioral and emotional problems in children are especially prominent during and shortly after the stressful period of separation (Hetherington, Cox, and Cox 1976; Wallerstein and Kelly 1980), during which negotiations take place. At the moment when worries and self-doubts about parental competence are highest, divorcing spouses must simultaneously contend with self-doubts about their worth as lovable and successful marriage partners. For the noninitiator such concerns are especially predictable but even the initiator of the divorce is not immune to worries of this type. Under such conditions negotiations can easily be bogged down as each spouse attempts to "prove" that he or she is a competent person and a fit and caring parent. The problem is compounded by the deep personal knowledge that divorcing spouses have of each other. Such knowledge arms each spouse with an exquisite ability to penetrate the other's already vulnerable ego and thereby decreases the willingness to compromise even further.

Issues touching upon the negotiator's fragile self-esteem or concerns about saving face may be more successfully managed if such issues are formulated in concrete, rather than abstract terms, if they are broken down into smaller subunits ("fractionated"), and if they are considered simultaneously, rather than one at a time, so that trade-offs may be seen and arranged (Pruitt 1981; Rubin and Brown 1975). Negotiations between divorcing parents may pose obstacles in each of these regards.

Casting the issues in concrete terms may be a problem because emotionally vulnerable spouses are low in self-esteem and often prefer to couch their negotiating positions along lines of lofty but abstract principles. For example, it was common in the sessions of divorce mediation we analyzed for the rejected wife to speak insistently of her husband's "obligations as a father" and "his responsibilities as a parent," all the while disclaiming that her unrealistic financial demands had any source other than her deep maternal concerns. Such a tactic may have provided the wife with a degree of catharsis and protected her from ego-damaging admissions of hurt, but it did little to inspire a more forthcoming attitude in her husband.

Simultaneous consideration of the issues may be difficult due to the sheer number of items on the bargaining table. In addition to the five principal issues of custody, visitation, child support, alimony, and division of marital property—each of which may have a number of subcomponents—there may be additional matters of insurance, education, and health care to resolve. As a matter of simple cognitive organization and coordination, simultaneous consideration is likely to prove challenging and stressful, particularly to inexperienced and emotionally labile negotiators. As Pruitt (1981) has noted, a viable alternative to simultaneous consideration is *mutual responsiveness,* an explicit or tacit agreement between the negotiators that, although issues will be considered one at a time, on any given issue the greater concessions will be made by the party for whom that issue is of lower priority. When there is a reasonable mix of priorities across the range of issues, as there usually is in divorce negotiations, mutual responsiveness may work well. Alas, the foundation of mutual responsiveness is mutual *trust,* a commodity likely to be in short supply in divorce proceedings.

The chance for a negotiating deadlock is increased by the uncertainty and lack of clear standards surrounding many of the most deeply felt issues, especially those concerning children. In arriving at agreements over visitation, child support, or education, for example, the parents must grapple with unforeseeable contingencies covering periods of ten to twenty years or more. In matters of custody and visitation there is no professional consensus about which arrangements are best or even which factors should be given priority in formulating a plan (e.g., under what circumstances, if any, is joint custody to be preferred to sole custody?).

ELEVATED LEVELS OF STRESS AND TENSION

The direct evidence that high levels of stress result in increased rigidity and belligerence during negotiations is admittedly limited. There are few such investigations relative to the other sorts of negotiating variables that have been studied. For example, Rubin and Brown's (1975) compendium of experimental research on bargaining and negotiation has no headings for "stress" or "tension." However, the indirect evidence is substantial. In the last decade an extensive research literature has accumulated which documents the deleterious effects of stress on human performance and social behavior (see Cohen [1980] for a comprehensive review). Individuals recently exposed to high levels of stress from such diverse sources as noise, crowding, sex discrimination, and task overload have consistently been found impaired on a host of characteristics relative to nonstressed persons. These include impairments in cognitive flexibility, problem-solving skills, and tolerance for frustration and ambiguity. Highly stressed individuals have also shown a generalized decline in sensitivity toward others, including reduced willingness to help and an increased tendency toward aggression. The decrements are greatest when the stressors are both unpredictable and beyond the control of the exposed person. Performance and social impairments of these kinds would constitute significant handicaps for negotiators attempting to master the complex intellectual and interpersonal challenges of the bargaining situation. There is evidence from the field of international negotiations that this is indeed the case (Walcott, Hopman, and King 1977).[4]

In divorce settlement negotiations both spouses generally experience high levels of stress, much of which is attributable to the psychological forces set in motion by the dissolution process. However, additional sources of stress of an altogether more practical and concrete kind are likely to be at or near their peak during the negotiating period.

For the husband, divorce typically involves disruptive changes in residence, in daily routine, and in work. In one study, for example, within two years of the divorce only 15 percent of divorced fathers were living where they had resided during the marriage; in many instances they had moved repeatedly over that time period (Fulton 1979). Compared to married men, divorced fathers have been found to lead more erratic and chaotic home lives—sleeping less and reporting more difficulty and frustration with shopping, cooking, and cleaning (Hetherington, Cox, and Cox 1976; Kitson and Sussman 1977). Perhaps out of loneliness or because of the new economic pressures they face, divorced men also have been found to spend more time at work than do married men, but with diminished feelings of job competence (Hetherington, Cox, and Cox 1976). Social isolation can also be a problem. Hetherington and her co-workers report that 75 percent of their sample of divorced fathers felt that they were functioning less well socially and in their relationships with women and 19 percent reported an increase in sexual difficulties. Perhaps most important, as the noncustodial parent the divorced father must adapt to seeing his children less frequently, often on a schedule not of his own choosing. His lessened involvement in his children's lives may occasion an extremely painful and continued emotional distress (Hetherington, Cox, and Cox 1976; Wallerstein and Kelly 1980).

For the divorced mother, the changes set in motion by the separation are usually even more radical than those experienced by her ex-husband. Residential instability may be nearly as common among women as it is among men (Fulton 1979), and as bad as divorce is financially for men, for women it may amount to an economic disaster. Because of these economic pressures most divorced women are obliged to work outside of the home, for which, because of economic discrimination, they can generally expect to be paid about half of what a man doing comparable work would earn.

While adjusting to the new and unremunerative responsibilities of employment, the divorced wife is simultaneously playing the role of both mother and father to her children. Mastering all of these challenges is not easy. Hetherington, Cox, and Cox (1979c) note that, compared to intact households, the homes of divorced mothers are generally more erratic regarding mealtimes, bedtimes for children, and relaxation time between parent and child. The internecine warfare between mothers and their offspring, particularly their sons and especially during the early period of separation, has been described in chapter 1. Divorced mothers also report having significantly less contact with adults than do other parents, and often comment on a sense of being locked into a child's world. Divorced mothers have been found to have fewer friends, belong to fewer organizations, and participate in fewer recreational activities than do married women. There is evidence that the divorced mother's relative social isolation may be more debilitating emotionally than the stresses attendant to dealing with her children or relating to her ex-spouse (Berman and Turk 1981; Hetherington, Cox, and Cox 1979a).

Establishing a satisfying dating and sex life may be retarded by inexperience, uncertainty about prevailing norms, and fear of being an inappropriate model of social behavior for her children. Compared to her ex-husband, the ex-wife with custody often has a more narrow range of possibilities for remarriage. Surveys of marital happiness have found that remarried women are less satisfied with married life than are once-married women or remarried men (Glenn and Weaver 1977; Renee 1971; White 1979). Remarried divorcées have also been found to have lower educational status and to be in lower paying jobs than are divorced women who have not remarried (Renee 1971). Evidence of this kind has been cited in support of the view that when a divorced woman does remarry she may well do so as much out of felt economic necessity as from desire.

The entire situation for both divorced parents is complicated by the absence of clear social norms.

> Parents who are uncertain about what to do have no reliable place to turn. Most cannot draw on their own personal histories for models in the new situation; there is little accumulated wisdom and the many new roles of the visiting parent,

> joint custody, father custody, and stepparent are in the process of evolving—and the rules are not clearly defined. As a result, people are thrown back even more on the passions or anxieties of the moment in making decisions with long-range consequences for themselves and their children. (Wallerstein and Kelly 1980, 317)

The psychological vulnerability which may result from the ambiguous or absent social norms governing divorce is suggested by the finding that, relative to widows, divorced women are much more likely to report feeling "like a fifth wheel;" being taken advantage of; and of having lost social status (Kitson et al. 1980).

Finally, impairments in psychological and physical health are more common among the separated and divorced than among persons of any other marital status. Whether these health-related difficulties are regarded as predating the divorce, as a reflection of the stresses to which divorced persons are exposed, or as some combination of the pre- and postdivorce conditions, they nonetheless constitute an additional source of stress in their own right.

With regard to physical health, data from both the 1960 and 1970 censuses, as well as from health surveys conducted by the National Center for Health Statistics in the 1960s and 1970s, disclose that on a wide variety of age-adjusted indices of ill health and disability the rates are nearly always higher for the separated and divorced than for individuals of any other marital status. With very few exceptions these differentials persist when income and race are controlled for. These indices include: incidence of acute physical illness, average number of physician visits per year, days of restricted activity due to illness, and the percentage of persons limited in activity due to a chronic condition. The separated and divorced have the most partial work disability and rank second (to single people) for complete work disability. When ill or injured the separated and divorced take the most disability days per condition. They have the highest hospitalization rates and the longest hospital stays (Verbrugge 1979).

Regarding psychological adjustment, at least three national surveys on representative samples covering a nearly twenty year span indicate consistently more subjective distress among the separated and divorced than among persons of any other marital status. In these surveys separated and divorced persons are generally more likely than others to describe themselves as stressed, dissatisfied, and anxious; to report fears of an impending nervous breakdown; to feel inadequate as parents; and to have sought psychotherapy or felt they could have benefited from it (Campbell, Converse, and Rodgers 1976; Gurin, Veroff, and Feld 1960; Veroff, Kulka, and

Douvan 1981). Psychiatric hospitalizations have been found to be anywhere from three to eight times more likely for separated and divorced women than for married women and from seven to twenty-two times more likely for separated and divorced men than for married men. Suicide and alcoholism are also more common among those who have experienced marital dissolution (Bloom, White, and Asher 1979).

The two principal longitudinal studies of divorce adjustment (Hetherington, Cox, and Cox 1976; Wallerstein and Kelly 1980), as well as various survey and epidemiological studies (Goode 1948; Kitson and Sussman 1977), generally agree that the psychological impairments are greatest in the earlier stages of dissolution, the period when the settlement negotiations are most likely to be occurring. In one investigation divorced persons were found to be at particularly high risk for automobile accidents in the period from six months before to six months after divorce, with the accident rate for the group doubling during that time (Bloom, White, and Asher 1979).

Perhaps the most extensive and commonly cited evidence that marital disruption is related to impaired functioning is the research relating changes in life events to onset of psychological and physical illness. In such research marital disruption contributes most heavily to a high life change score which, in turn, has invariably been found to be significantly related to the onset of disability. In an incisive critique of this literature, however, Rabkin and Streuning (1976) note that most of the studies fail to report the degree of association; those that do so indicate that no more than 1 to 2 percent of the variance in illness rates can be explained by the association with life change scores. In their critique they conclude that, "in practical terms, . . . life event scores have not been shown to be predictors of the probability of future illness" (Rabkin and Streuning 1976, 1015). They also wisely note that "most people do not become disabled even when terrible things happen to them" (p. 1018).

On the other hand, physical and emotional ill health are relatively gross indices of the effects of stress. Our concern is with the considerably more subtle behaviors and attitudes involved in settlement negotiations. The basic point is that during these negotiations both husband and wife are likely to be experiencing transient but relatively high levels of stress arising from *numerous* quarters, of which the health-related is only one. If research in other areas of human behavior is any guide, the net effect should be distinct impairments in their intellectual and emotional resourcefulness as negotiators. The testimonies of experienced divorce lawyers, who regularly list client unpredictability and "irrationality" as one of their greatest problems, suggest that this is indeed the case.

DEFECTS IN THE NORMS AND SOCIAL MECHANISM FOR REGULATING THE CONFLICT

The importance of social norms and institutions for regulating and containing conflict needs no belaboring. The legal system is perhaps the most obvious manifestation of the value which society places on institutionalized mechanisms for conflict resolution, but many other examples can be cited. The regulation of labor-management disputes, for example, is virtually unthinkable without the network of federal, state, and local agencies for mediation and arbitration. But institutions of conflict resolution may not only help resolve or contain conflict, however inadvertently, they may exacerbate or provoke antagonisms as well.

The institutional framework in divorce is the legal system and the laws governing marital dissolution. The impact of this system on the process and outcome of divorce negotiations is a topic of heroic proportions on which, as has been noted, remarkably little systematic research has been done and about which, therefore, no firm conclusions may be drawn. Experienced observers have, however, noted several ways in which the legal environment may instigate or exacerbate destructive conflicts during divorce negotiations.

Perhaps the most serious and frequently made charge is that the lawyer-regulated adversary system of divorce is an extremely poor vehicle for constructive conflict resolution. In chapters 5 through 8, in reporting our research on lawyers' differing conceptions of their role in divorce negotiations, we shall examine this viewpoint and its ramifications in more detail. A brief summarization of the arguments against the lawyer-controlled adversary process can be given here, however.

1. The adversary system may escalate conflict through the use of legal threats and counter-threats in an atmosphere already made volatile by strong feelings of anger, guilt, failure, and humiliation.
2. The lawyers' ability to form an accurate picture of the marital situation is frequently handicapped by the ethical injunction under which they operate —namely, that they represent and therefore see only one of the marital partners.
3. The necessity of negotiating with the other attorney, while it may enhance matters if both attorneys share similar attitudes about the goals to be achieved in a divorce, is just as likely to worsen things. The reasons for this derive from the widely divergent conceptions that lawyers are likely to have of their role in divorce. Our own investigations of divorce lawyers have identified a range of lawyers' attitudes, ranging from "winning" at any cost to protecting the psychological welfare of children, even against client demands. In addition, the lawyer's role in divorce is essentially that of a repre-

sentative. There is a fairly substantial body of literature that suggests that because of the pressures on the representative to champion his or her own constituent's position, to make a show of competence and strength, and to take an extreme position, the representative's ability to reduce interpersonal conflict may be drastically curtailed (Blake, Shepard, and Mouton 1964; Benton and Druckman 1974). There is also evidence that attorney litigiousness may differ from one jurisdiction to another, even within the same state. Los Angeles divorce attorneys, for example, appear roughly twice as likely as those in San Francisco to become involved in protracted legal battles with one another (Dixon and Weitzman 1980). (No explanation for this disparity is reported, however.)

4. The issues to be resolved are as much matters of psychological judgment and expertise, or of personal values, as they are of law and economics (e.g., what custody and visitation arrangements would best meet the emotional and social needs of children and parents?). There is no reason to believe that, as a group, lawyers are uniquely well qualified to provide guidance on such extralegal matters.
5. The psychological costs of divorce are high. While there are numerous sources for the psychological problems involved in the divorce and post-divorce periods, lawyers, who are untrained in psychology and counseling, may play an unwitting role in exacerbating this distress. Or, more probably, they simply fail to be of much psychological assistance.

Aside from the direct influence of attorneys there are other ways in which the legal infrastructure has been hypothesized to impede constructive negotiations in divorce.

The legal preference for awarding custody to one parent, for example, has been frequently mentioned as creating an undesirable situation in which one parent "wins" the children while the other is doomed to "lose" them (Folberg and Graham 1979; Fulton 1979). Such a climate, it is argued, promotes tactics of deception and coercion at the bargaining table and may contribute significantly to the high levels of noncompliance with child support by fathers who feel cheated and deprived of a truly equal parental role. The movement toward a legal presumption in favor of joint custody has gained strength from such arguments, the merits of which, however, are ultimately in need of empirical verification.

Destructive conflict at the divorce bargaining table may also be promoted by the uncertain and idiosyncratic basis on which matters such as child support, alimony, and division of property appear to be decided. Conflict resolution can be facilitated when outside standards for fashioning agreements are widely known and clearly understood by the disputants or their advisors. Such standards provide a common frame of reference which may have the tonic effect of narrowing the range of possible solutions, thus simplifying the negotiating task facing the parties. Clear judicial standards may also motivate the parties to accept otherwise unpalatable compromises which, for all their distastefulness, can still be seen to be either superior on material or psychological grounds to what a judge would order, or preferable to a costly legal battle which would only produce a highly similar result.

Unfortunately, clear judicial standards appear to be largely absent in divorce negotiations. A study of 1,300 judicial opinions regarding alimony and child support concluded that while individual judges appear to have their own models for determining an award of child support there was no consistency among judges in the use of a model, or even uniformity in the choice of which factors to take into account in fashioning an award (White and Stone 1976). The researchers concluded that "consistency as to what constitutes equity is absent from divorce cases" (p. 83).

Mnookin and Kornhauser (1979, 166) have suggested that one reason why the vast majority of divorcing spouses settle out of court is to avoid the uncertainties typical of judicial involvement. In this sense, the absence of judicial norms is an incentive to negotiated agreements. On the other hand, while the absence of standards may promote out-of-court settlements, it may do so in the interests of expediency, not quality. The frequency with which postdivorce litigation occurs in initially uncontested divorces suggests that the settlement deliberations may have left much to be desired.

Vagueness also appears to be characteristic of the standards for drafting the terms of the settlement agreement. It has been argued, for example, that a well-drafted visitation agreement is one which specifies times, dates, and the manner in which children are to be picked up and returned. The value of such specificity from the point of view of conflict management is that it provides the parties with a clear-cut standard upon which to fall back in the (likely) event that disagreements arise in the postdivorce period. Two recent studies suggest that specificity is typically not attained by the parties or their attorneys; nor is it insisted upon by the courts (Cavanagh and Rhode 1976;Weitzman and Dixon 1979). In the words of one of these reports, "Visitation rights of the non-custodial spouse were detailed in a small minority of cases. For the rest, the phrases 'reasonable rights of visitation,' and occasionally, 'liberal rights of visitation' constituted the sole contribution made by the decree to laying the foundation for future parent-child interaction" (Cavanagh and Rhode 1976, 133). Indeed, vagueness or the complete omission of relevant issues such as life insurance, medical insurance, and educational provisions was typical in cases involving minor children (Cavanagh and Rhode 1976).

It may be argued that vagueness in settlement language is a virtue in many divorce cases and represents a constructive form of conflict management in the sense that obscuring the differences permits a settlement—because any agreement is better than a court fight. This is undoubtedly a valid argument in some cases and specious in others. The point is that there appears to be no professionally well-established criteria for a sound settlement agreement under varying circumstances—and very little debate on the matter to boot.

Disparities in Power and Interpersonal Sensitivity: The Male-Female Context of Divorce Negotiations

We have been reviewing obstacles to a constructive negotiating process that appear to be as problematic in divorce settlement negotiations as they are in other forms of bargaining. There is one characteristic of divorce negotiations, however, which is unique: at the divorce bargaining table, one negotiator is always a man, the other always a woman. What, if anything, does this imply for the smoothness or difficulty of the negotiating process?

There is no simple answer to this complex question. As Bloch (1980) notes, the study of sex differences is so beset with inconsistent, emphemeral, and unreproduceable findings, and the entire subject has such obvious implications for social policy, that it is easy for people to honestly differ about the appropriate conclusions to draw. Sex differences in negotiating behavior have been studied in the experimental laboratory with inconclusive results—some studies have found that men bargain more cooperatively than do women; others have found that women bargain more cooperatively than do men; and still others report no differences based on sex (Pruitt 1981; Rubin and Brown 1975). Most of these studies have involved pairs of strangers, mainly college students, bargaining for little or no real stakes in experimental tasks that typically restricted the kinds of communication and ability to terminate interaction that normally exist in "real world" negotiations. The relevance of this type of research for husband-wife bargaining, including divorce negotiations, is unknown.

With these cautions duly noted, I believe there is, nonetheless, sufficient evidence to suggest that the male-female context may be a liability for the divorce settlement process. The research in support of this proposition comes from studies on the psychological differences between the sexes, the behaviors of husbands and wives in distressed and nondistressed marriages, and male-female differences in coping with divorce. The argument boils down to this: divorce settlement negotiations are likely to bring together over the bargaining table a husband who has a high degree of power vis à vis his wife, but who is relatively insensitive to the interpersonal and emotional dynamics that operate during negotiations, and a wife who is highly attuned to the interpersonal cues in the situation but who possesses a relatively low degree of power. Research and theory in the general area of bargaining and negotiation suggests that when parties are mismatched in this way the prognosis for a constructive negotiation is unfavorable.

DISPARITIES IN RELATIVE POWER

When the parties involved in negotiation differ markedly in their access to information and material resources, or in their ability to withstand prolonged, unresolved conflict, the prospects for a constructive, negotiated settlement are not good. The stronger party is likely to be less motivated to compromise and more likely to use tactics of coercion and intransigence. The less powerful party may react with either passive concession making or reactive defiance, neither of which provides a sound basis for arriving at a durable settlement (Deutsch 1973; Rubin and Brown 1975). Mediators dislike conflicts in which the parties are ill-matched in this way because, among other things, they must direct a good deal of their efforts to redressing the balance of power, at least psychologically, with the attendant risk that they will become suspect to the stronger side and thus lose their acceptability (Kressel 1972, 1980).

In divorce negotiations an acute imbalance of power is likely to exist because of the general economic dependence and disadvantages of wives relative to their husbands. The financial plight of the divorced mother relative to that of the divorced father has been documented by numerous investigators (Albrecht 1980; Bane 1976; Chambers 1979; Espenshade 1979; Glick 1979).

The relative financial dependency of divorced wives on their husbands not only influences the settlement negotiations, but continues into the postdivorce period, since many women cannot adequately support themselves after divorce even if they find employment, as most of them are obliged to do. In one investigation, 42 percent of divorced mothers living on their own wages alone had incomes below the poverty level. In cases where the husband continued to pay support, only 15 percent of divorced mothers were in such dire economic straits (Chambers 1979). The subjective reports of divorced men and women mirror the objective discrepancy in resources: much more frequently than their former husbands, divorced wives report anxiety regarding their limited finances, resentment for the economic discrimination they face, and distress and worry about their own ignorance in understanding and managing the finances (Campbell, Converse, and Rodgers 1976; Hetherington, Cox, and Cox 1979c; Kitson and Sussman 1977; Spanier and Casto 1979).

In our analysis of the tapes of divorce mediation cases the imbalance of power issue was prominent and generally stemmed from the disadvantaged position of the wife, who often had given up college or a career in order to assume the role of homemaker. Moreover, although husbands were frequently uninformed about financial matters, they were paragons of financial expertise in comparison to their wives. Husbands had almost exclusive control of important financial documents and were aware of financial arrangements of which their wives were ignorant. The ignorance of the wives, combined with their heightened anxiety at their poor post-divorce prospects, created strong pressures on the mediator to shore up the wives' side of negotiations.

> Mrs. W. had dropped out of college to send her husband through medical school. She was to have custody of their three children and was clearly anxious about how she would manage after the divorce. She was highly suspicious of her husband's reporting of his financial assets during mediation, but also found it difficult to ask informed questions or to follow explanations involving tax and business terminology. She relied increasingly on the mediator to explain matters to her ("What's depreciation?"). Dr. W. acquiesced verbally to repeated requests from the mediator to provide documentation of his assertions as to what he could and could not afford in child support and alimony, but continually failed to provide such information. An adversarial stance gradually developed between Dr. W. and the mediator. (Kressel et al. 1979, 271)

The power disadvantage of wives at the bargaining table may also have been increased, paradoxically enough, by changes in the law and the prevailing social climate favoring greater equality between the sexes. For example, based on their analysis of patterns of divorce filings and settlements in California before and after the change to no fault divorce, Dixon and Weitzman (1982) conclude that the change in the legal statute may have shifted the balance of negotiating power toward the husband. Prior to the no fault provision, they argue, the tendency was for the wife to initiate divorce proceedings, probably due to "chivalrous" norms that called for the husband to play the "defendant" role (rather than bring unseemly charges against his wife); to the greater ease with which certain grounds, such as cruelty, had been applied against the husband; and to the greater likelihood that the courts would grant a divorce if the wife had filed. Under no fault divorce none of these legal implications applies, and since the statute went into effect there has been a corresponding increase in the likelihood that husbands will initiate legal proceedings.

> The shift to a higher percentage of husband-petitioners suggests that the change in the law reduced the normative (both legal and moral) restraints that had previously prevented a number of husbands from taking the active role. Men could now proceed without fear that their wives would contest the divorce or file damaging countercharges leading to protracted court battles. A husband no longer had to negotiate an agreement with his wife in exchange for her acquiescence to the divorce, and no longer had to allow her to file (even if he most wanted the divorce), in exchange, perhaps, for some financial or child-related considerations. (Dixon and Weitzman 1982, 114)

Most important, the no fault law also requires judges to order an equal distribution of marital assets in the event of a court contest. Although the parties are free to negotiate whatever private arrangements suit them, the effect on settlements in or out of court has been a dramatic reduction of the wife's share of the marital pie. For example, a random sample of San Diego court records before and after the change to no fault divorce reveals that in 1968, under the old law, 65.8 percent of divorced wives either successfully negotiated for or were awarded the marital home. In 1976 this figure had dropped to 42 percent. Similar proportionate decreases in the assets going to the wife occurred for home furnishings, automobiles, and other marital possessions. Wives were also more likely in 1976 to end up assuming a share of the responsibility for paying off the marital debt (58 percent, as opposed to 30 percent in 1968) as well as a portion of the legal fees (44 percent, compared to only 12 percent in 1968). Alimony and child support awards had also decreased (Seal 1979). (See also Dixon and Weitzman [1982], who report similar data for Los Angeles and San Francisco.) In other words, a strategy of obstinancy at the bargaining table, a power tactic if ever there was one, may no longer be the weapon it once was for the negotiating wife. If she and her husband cannot reach their own agreement the court may well impose one, and on terms far less likely to favor her than was once the case.[5]

No discussion of disparities in negotiating power between the sexes would be complete without mention of the possible contribution of sex-linked differences in personality. In their influential review of the literature on sex differences, Maccoby and Jacklin (1974) could find relatively little evidence that males and females differed substantially on personality characteristics that would affect social interaction. More recent studies and reviews have called this conclusion into question (Bloch 1980; Cooper 1979; Eagly and Carli 1981; Hall 1978). A reading of this debate, along with evidence from a much smaller number of studies on husband-wife differences in troubled and untroubled marriages, leads to the conclusion that in settlement negotiations, especially those involving unassisted, face-to-face bargaining (as opposed to the use of lawyers or mediators), husbands may hold the upper hand. The findings are as follows:

Relative to males, females have consistently been found to be less aggressive and more susceptible to anxiety; to have less confidence in their abilities, especially in problem-solving situations, including those explicitly labeled "negotiations" (Pruitt [1981, 46] calls this "perhaps the most consistent sex difference in the experimental bargaining literature"); to be more conforming and susceptible to persuasion, especially in situations of uncertainty; and to describe themselves as being less powerful, energetic, and ambitious and less in control of external events. Although after the age of ten or eleven females show greater verbal ability, men have been reported to be more likely to initiate topics, more likely to interrupt another speaker, and more likely to get back the conversational "ball" after being interrupted themselves. Males also have greater mathematical interest and ability than do females. All of these findings suggest that in a competitive social encounter with a partner of the opposite sex, the man will be more "powerful" than the woman.

Surprisingly, studies of marital interaction have devoted relatively little attention to husband-wife differences based on gender; certainly no unequivocal support for the greater power of men is discernible. However, certain lines of evidence are suggestive of this possibility. For example, in his review of the marital adjustment literature, Barry (1970) reports that the personality characteristics of the husband, but rarely those of the wife, have routinely correlated with measures of marital adjustment. Barry interprets this to mean that marriage is more stressful for the wife and more central to her feelings of self-esteem than it is for the husband, for whom career plays a more salient role. These circumstances make the wife's marital adjustment highly contingent on her husband's emotional responsiveness and personal flexibility. This argument receives a measure of support from a study of conflict management among newly-wed couples (Rausch et al. 1974). Overall, the husbands in this study were found to be more conciliatory and positive, while the wives made greater use of tactics of coercion, guilt induction, and appeals involving moral persuasion. As the researchers note, the wives' influence strategies are consistent with a position of relative low power and dependence.

(Clearly, there are sources of power and power discrepancies at the divorce bargaining table other than those tied to gender. The relative strength of the parties' wishes to end the marriage is one example. The noninitiator is likely to feel psychologically less "powerful" than the initiator at the time of settlement negotiations in terms of self-confidence or feelings of well-being. On the other hand, the ability to induce guilt may also be regarded as a source of power—here the noninitiator may be more "powerful."[6])

DISPARITIES IN INTERPERSONAL ORIENTATION

The degree to which we are interested in and reactive to the emotional and psychological cues coming from persons with whom we interact is referred to as our interpersonal orientation. Some people are closely attuned to such cues; others are relatively indifferent to them. While interpersonal orientation has been cited by several investigators as a dimension that has a potentially important impact on the negotiating process (Hermann and Kogan 1977; Rubin and Brown 1975), the effect of disparities in the negotiators' degree of interpersonal orientation is more a matter of conjecture than is the effect of disparities in their relative power (Rubin and Brown 1975). I have included a discussion of the topic for two reasons. First, there is indirect evidence from experimental laboratory studies that a high level of interpersonal sensitivity creates problems when there are already forces at work pushing negotiations toward mutual distrust and competitive conflict (Rubin and Brown 1975). These are precisely the conditions which are likely to prevail in divorce negotiations. Second, research on the psychology of sex differences, including studies of bargaining behavior, and on the coping styles of divorcing husbands and wives is highly supportive of the idea that a mismatch in degree of interpersonal orientation is likely to exist at the divorce bargaining table. The research suggests that the wife is highly reactive to the interpersonal messages emanating from her husband, while the husband is focused instead on the tangible and concrete demands and objectives of the bargaining situation.

Research on sex differences in social behavior routinely shows that, relative to males, females are more interested in and reactive to the interpersonal dimension (Bloch 1980; Deaux 1976). Thus, females have been found to be more self-revealing and to like other women who behave in a similar manner. Men, on the other hand, tend to dislike other men with a propensity for self-disclosure. In conversation women prefer eye contact and engage in more eye contact than do men, and they are less comfortable than men are in situations that do not permit eye contact. Females have been shown to be substantially more accurate in decoding nonverbal cues concerning emotional states, as well as to be more accurate in sending such cues about themselves (Eagly and Carli 1981; Hall 1978). Women also prefer less physical distance between themselves and other people. Under situations of environmental stress (e.g., crowding) women have been reported to share their distress with each other while men tend to hide their discomfort (Epstein and Karlin 1975). The absence of social support has also been correlated with dysfunctional coping styles (including drug addiction) in women, but not in men, suggesting again the greater affiliative needs and interpersonal orientation of women (Binion 1982; Tucker 1982).

Two independent reviews of the experimental bargaining literature (Deaux 1976; Rubin and Brown 1975) reach the identical conclusion regarding sex differences: females alter their bargaining behavior much more than do males in response to all manner of changes in the interpersonal context of the bargaining situation, including sex of the other, attractiveness of the other, sex of the experimenter, availability of communication channels, and cooperativeness of the other. In negotiations in which alliances are possible women are more interested in forming coalitions with a second player even when they are strong enough to succeed without such support. Men show no such affiliative tendencies when they are powerful enough to succeed on their own. Deaux (1976), in her summarization of the extensive literature on male-female differences in experimental studies of negotiations—using one particular research format, the so-called Prisoner's Dilemma game—reaches a conclusion which may well stand for the differences in the motivation and orientation of the sexes in more complex bargaining situations:

> Men seem to be more oriented toward the game itself, attempting to develop tactics that will guarantee them the largest financial payoff. In part this may be a function of the task itself. Men's greater interest in mathematical tasks predispose them to take the game more seriously. Women, on the other hand, seem less concerned with the game itself and more concerned with the interpersonal setting. (Deaux 1976, 99)

Rubin and Brown, summarizing a broader body of experimental literature on negotiating, make an almost identical point (Rubin and Brown 1975, 173). These findings from the experimental laboratory are echoed in recent research on the motives of men and women for accepting or rejecting divorce mediation as the method for negotiating their settlement agreements. Pearson, Thoennes, and Vanderkooi (1982), for example, found that "women . . . seem predisposed to mediate because it appears to be less remote and impersonal than the court system and more like their satisfying counseling experiences. For men, on the other hand, the decision is largely a function of their perceived chances of winning in the adversarial process" (p. 31).

Unfortunately, there are few studies of marital interaction in which the focus has been differences in interpersonal orientation between husbands and wives. Several investigators have failed to find any evidence in support of the thesis, initially proposed by Parsons and Bales (1955), that husbands are the task leaders and wives the socio-emotional specialists in family life. However, these are studies of normal families observed in relatively low conflict situations (O'Rourke 1963; Leik 1963) or are reports of their remembered modes of behavior (Levinger 1964). There is evidence from a number of more recent observational investigations that, under conditions of tension or conflict, wives are more emotionally responsive to their husbands than vice-versa (Gottman 1979; Margolin and Wampold 1981). These findings are very much in line with the notion of the expressive female and the inexpressive male.

Against the relatively few studies of differences in interpersonal orientation in the research on marital interaction may be stacked a much greater body of evidence on husband-wife differences in coping with the stress of divorce. This evidence comes from epidemiological studies, surveys of divorced men and women, and the clinical impressions of seasoned investigators. The overall pattern that emerges is that women react to the stresses of divorce in a highly interpersonal manner whereas men react with much more nonpersonal, instrumental, and nonemotional ways of coping.

Compared to divorced men, or persons of any other marital status, for that matter, divorced women express much higher levels of subjective distress. Although there are occasional reports to the contrary, generally speaking, divorced women admit to being more depressed, more anxious, and generally more miserable than do divorced men. For example, divorced women typically score higher on measures of depression, whether depression is measured by a formal psychological scale or by a single question about mood (Chiriboga, Roberts, and Stein 1978; Radloff 1975). Similarly, on measures of tension and perceived life stress, divorced women also report higher distress than any other group in the population. In three surveys on nationally representative samples over the last twenty years, divorced or separated women were more likely than persons of any other marital status to admit to having had fears of a nervous breakdown (Campbell, Converse, and Rodgers 1976; Gurin, Veroff, and Feld 1960;

Veroff, Kulka, and Douvan 1981). This is not to say that divorced men express satisfaction with their lives. In most studies they are second to divorced and separated women on measures of felt distress, and are the second most frequent to seek psychotherapy. The distress of divorced men is only less striking when compared to that of divorced women.[7]

Divorced women also seek help with their problems with greater frequency than do persons of all other marital statuses, including divorced men. Thus, in the 1960 study by Gurin et al., 40 percent of divorced women had been in psychotherapy, the single highest percentage of any marital status group. Sixty-two percent of the divorced or separated women either went for help or felt that they could have used therapy at some point in their lives; only 37 percent of divorced or separated men responded in a like fashion. The study was replicated twenty years later (Veroff, Kulka, and Douvan 1981) with the same pattern of results, although the differential between divorced men and women had narrowed. Divorced women were still the most frequent users of psychotherapy of all marital status groups (54 percent), with divorced men in second place (46 percent).

While these survey results do not demonstrate that women sought therapy as a means of coping with the stresses of divorce, this implication is supported by other studies that deal specifically with divorce: when figures are reported on percentages of individuals seeking counseling during the divorce process, the figures are always greater for women than for men. Differentials in seeking counseling by divorcing men and women have been reported by Kitson and Sussman (1977) (60 percent of women vs. 40 percent of men), and by Hetherington, Cox, and Cox (1979c) (15 percent of women vs. 8 percent of men). Wallerstein and Kelly (1980), who studied help seeking both before and after marital separation, found that more than 50 percent of the women and more than one-third of the men sought counseling prior to separation. Within eighteen months postseparation, 44 percent of the women and 20 percent of the men had sought counseling.[8]

This pattern of greater help seeking among divorced women also occurs in regard to visits to physicians' offices. According to census data, across all marital statuses women are more likely to go to a doctor than are men, but the differential is greatest for the divorced, where 71 percent of the women compared to 51 percent of men report visiting a physician in a one-year period. The high differential between divorced men and women reflects both the relatively high rate of visits to a physician by divorced women and the relatively low rate of such visits for divorced men, who rank next to last of all men in frequency of physician usage (Carter and Glick 1976). The preponderance of women over men in unsuccessful suicide attempts—by more than two to one in one large-scale study—has also suggested to some researchers a greater proclivity among women to signal their distress to potential sources of help (Bloom, White, and Asher 1979).

It can be argued, of course, that differentials in subjective distress and help seeking between divorced men and women reflect either the greater problems that divorce creates for women or the greater coping skills and resiliency of men. There may be truth to these perspectives but there are some striking data to the contrary. Divorced and separated men, for example, are much more likely than divorced or separated women to end up in a psychiatric hospital. The admission ratio into psychiatric hospitals of divorced men to married men is anywhere from 7:1 to 22:1, depending on the study; for women the ratios of divorced to married are much smaller (3:1 to 8:1 across various investigations). In an analysis of psychiatric hospitalizations for the city of Pueblo, Colorado between 1969 and 1971, divorced and separated men constituted 46 percent of the ever-married male patients, whereas divorced and separated women represented only 32 percent of ever-married female patients (Bloom, White, and Asher 1979).

The death from suicide ratios of the divorced to the married has also been found to be greater for men than for women, in spite of the fact that women are much more likely than men to attempt suicide. In a study by Shneidman and Faberow (1961) of suicidal behavior in Los Angeles, 70 percent of 768 completed suicides were by men, whereas 69 percent of 2,652 attempted suicides were by women.

Finally, although separated and divorced women have higher illness rates, especially during the initial separation, more divorced men than divorced women die from nearly all causes, especially those with an "elective" or life-style component—e.g., suicide, homocide, auto fatality, and cirrhosis of the liver (largely a function of alcoholism).[9]

Findings such as these suggest that men suffer fully as much as women in divorce but are more likely to either deny their distress or seek nonpersonal ways of coping—ways that may ultimately create more problems than they solve. Several investigators who have studied the divorcing process at close range, including my colleagues and I, have noted that, relative to women, divorced men seem less able to articulate plausible psychological explanations for the breakup and generally seem more bewildered by the entire experience, whether or not they initiated the divorce (Chiriboga and Cutler; Kressel 1980). "I'm not sure what happened" appears to be a much more popular response of men than of women to inquiries about the cause of divorce (Kitson and Sussman 1982). Hetherington, Cox, and Cox (1976) note a phenomenon which may be related to the distance that men appear to put between themselves and the emotional and interpersonal aspects of separation and divorce: the "Hip, Honda, and Hirsute" syndrome—the statistically significant increase among recently divorced men, relative to men in intact marriages, of beards, mustaches, sports cars, hairy-chested dress, and modish clothing—all of which represent instrumental, nonpersonal ways of coping.

As we have seen, research in a variety of contexts suggests that there is likely to be a discrepancy between the divorcing wife and her husband regarding sensitivity to interpersonal dimensions of the relationship and the emotional and psychological cues by which interpersonal issues are communicated. What is the relevance of this to the prospects for successful divorce settlement negotiations?

The simplest answer is that a disparity in the spouses' degree of interpersonal sensitivity may create problems in communication and coordination, because the parties are attentive to different aspects of the bargaining task and are therefore more easily mistaken or befuddled in their efforts to understand each other. A simple, if exaggerated, example may make the general point. It has been shown that females not only smile more frequently in conversation than do males, they also tend to smile even though they may not be in agreement with what has just been said. For males, smiling does not have these kinds of compliant overtones (Deaux 1976)—a difference which may be regarded as another illustration of the greater interpersonal, affiliative concerns of women. Now, if, in the course of settlement negotiations, the wife smiles benignly in response to her husband's proposal that he wants the house, the children, and 80 percent of the marital assets—and he takes her smile as an indication of assent—the only thing that may be difficult to predict is how much money the attorneys will make and which judge will end up hearing the case.

A more poignant illustration of the difficulties created when the parties are attending to different elements of their relationship may be taken from the negotiations of one of the divorcing couples whose mediation experience is discussed in more detail in chapter 11. The thirty-five-year-old wife in this case had been unable to bear a child throughout the seven years of their marriage. Two months prior to the beginning of mediation she had experienced yet another in a series of spontaneous abortions. This disappointment, with all its intense emotional ramifications, was clearly reverberating when negotiations began. She at first resisted her husband's push for mediation (after the abortion he felt there was no longer any reason to delay a divorce); then agreed to it, and then reneged again before finally consenting. In the first session her emotional distress was evident and was most certainly intensified by the highly business-like manner of her husband and the mediator (also a man), who were intent on discussing and clarifying the administrative and technical aspects of the mediation process, little of which the wife was able to comprehend. Her husband was visibly irritated at her slowness in grasping the details but the problem was clearly not her lack of intelligence, but her emotional distress, to which he was, or wished to appear, impervious.[10]

A CAUTIONARY NOTE ON SEX DIFFERENCES

In this discussion of the obstacles to a constructive divorce negotiation I have included disparities in power and interpersonal orientation because there is evidence from other domains of conflict that this is indeed what such disparities represent. The evidence is particularly strong for differences in power; it is clear that in divorce negotiations a discrepancy in the spouses' relative power, particularly on economic grounds, is likely. The evidence for the negative consequences of disparities in interpersonal orientation is plausible, but much weaker because it derives primarily from laboratory research in which levels of interpersonal orientation have not been directly measured. In addition, to the best of my knowledge, the effect of disparities in the bargainers' degree of interpersonal orientation has been inferred only from studying dyads in which both sides were either high or low on this dimension (see Rubin and Brown [1975] for a review).

In linking the discussion of differences in power and interpersonal orientation to the male-female context of divorce negotiations, I have succumbed to a temptation about which I have mixed feelings. On one hand, I believe that without unreasonable intellectual straining much of the research on the psychology of sex differences may be legitimately summarized under the twin headings of "male superiority" in an attribute that may be variously defined as social power or potency and "female superiority" in emotional and interpersonal sensitivity. These differences are made more believable by research that demonstrates that there are systematic differences in the ways in which males and females are brought up in our culture. These child-rearing differences are consistent with the observed differences between males and females in later social behavior (Bloch 1980).

On the other hand, there are a variety of good reasons for reserving judgment about the extent to which psychological differences between men and women have an influence on the course of divorce negotiations. First, in the general literature on sex differences, the focus is on the statistical significance of average scores. While such differences are reliable (i.e., have a high probability of being obtained in study after study), they are frequently small and show a considerable overlap in the scores of men and women. Second, the extent of sex differences often goes unreported, and this is by no means a trivial omission. In their intensive examination of the research documenting women's greater capacity for being influenced, for example, Eagly and Carli (1981) conclude that only about 1 percent of the variance in this capacity is accounted for by sex differences, and that "a sex difference as small as this may have few implications for social interaction." (This is not the case, however, for gender differences in interpersonal orientation, where Eagly and Carli [1981] estimate that the advantage of women over men in accurately judging nonverbal emotional cues is substantial.) Third, much of the research on sex differences is of uncertain relevance to divorce negotiations since the bulk of it has been done on children and involves same-sex dyads. The relevance of such research to divorce negotiations must be regarded as intriguing but uncertain.

The research on husband-wife differences in handling conflict is more germane to our purposes, but there are relatively few such studies. And, while husband-wife differences have been reported, the findings have not been consistent across studies and the differences are usually far less powerful in their effects than the differences in behavior produced by external aspects of the situation such as the type of issue being discussed, the degree of conflict that the issue represents, or the couple's characteristic style of interaction (Raush et al. 1974). Sex differences in coping with divorce appear to exist, but no studies have attempted to measure the impact of such differences on the settlement negotiations. Indeed, what transpires during settlement negotiations from almost any angle is shrouded in mystery.

Finally, in divorce negotiations the spouses are regularly assisted by third parties, especially attorneys but also therapists, judges, mediators, friends, and relatives. The intervention of a third party may substantially alter or altogether eliminate the putative effects introduced by sex differences. There is some evidence that suggests that women may benefit considerably by third party assistance, especially in a negotiating task, in which their insecurity and dependence may be alleviated by information and guidance (Caplan 1979; Crandall 1967; Lockheed 1976; Stake and Stake 1979). The evidence, however, is still too scanty and of too uncertain relevance to divorce for reliable conclusions to be drawn.

Perhaps the best conclusion that can be reached at present is that sex differences are an intriguing, plausible, but as yet unproven source of difficulty at the divorce bargaining table. The variables with which sex differences are associated however, especially those firmly rooted in objective disparities in material power and resources, seem important negotiating hurdles indeed.

Summary

The foregoing account of the obstacles to a constructive divorce negotiation leaves many important questions unanswered. We do not know, for example, how each of the factors I have identified is distributed in the divorcing population at large. Nor can we say much, based on the available research, about their relative impact on the settlement process; some are undoubtedly more crucial than others to the establishment of destructive patterns of negotiating behavior, but *which* are more crucial? We also have no reliable information on the possible interactions that may occur among these variables. Does, for example, the inexperience of the negotiators have different effects when there is a scarcity of divisible resources than when assets are abundant? Does intraparty conflict in the form of ambivalence become crucial only when the power discrepancy is great and the attorneys combative, but play a more modest role when the power discrepancy is small and the lawyers more cooperatively oriented? Finally, we cannot be certain that all the key variables have been identified. Perhaps because of the idiosyncratic nature of the available evidence and the clinical perspective of our respondents, important factors have been overlooked.

What can, I think, be said with certainty is that the terrain of divorce negotiations is replete with pitfalls and obstacles. The failure to traverse that terrain successfully is unlikely to be the result of any single factor or cause. I have introduced the comparative perspective with other forms of negotiations to try to bring home this point more clearly. What is true of labor or international conflict seems just as true of negotiations between divorcing spouses and their lawyers: none of the participants holds all the cards and none is likely to be totally responsible when matters go wrong. It is against this complex backdrop that we now turn to an examination of the role of therapists, lawyers, and mediators in the divorce and settlement process.

3

Divorce Therapy: The Context and Goals of Treatment

The three principal professional groups to whom divorcing couples turn for help are psychotherapists, lawyers, and the newly emergent divorce mediators. The remainder of this book is devoted to the research that my colleagues and I have conducted on the role of each of these groups in the management of divorce conflict.[1]

The overall focus of our research program was divorce settlement negotiations. Of what relevance to this matter is a report on the role of psychological counselors who are untrained in the legal issues of divorce and without formal legal standing in the preparation and finalizing of settlement agreements? The next two chapters answer this question more completely but certain key themes are worth enumerating at the outset.

By virtue of their training and because they are frequently the first professionals from whom help is sought when a marriage turns sour, divorce therapists seemed to us uniquely positioned to answer our questions regarding the psychological and interpersonal dynamics that often disrupt the formal settlement process orchestrated by lawyers and the courts. Furthermore, although it was not as clear to us when we began our research, in a variety of ways divorce therapists may exert a powerful, if unheralded effect on the settlement negotiations.

In the first place, divorce therapists are often consulted by couples in the throes of making a decision about whether or not to divorce. Clinical experience and the investigation we subsequently conducted with couples seeking divorce mediation strongly indicate that the manner in which a decision to divorce is arrived at can have profound consequences for the ease or difficulty with which the formal settlement negotiations proceed. As the frequent "mediators" of this decision, therefore, divorce therapists play an indirect, but often crucial role in helping determine the subsequent fate of the settlement process.

Second, divorce therapists often play a direct and active role regarding the child-related issues with which the settlement negotiations are concerned, particularly custody and visitation. This is one realm in which lawyers, who are often suspicious of mental health professionals, willingly admit the potential value of psychotherapeutic intervention.

Finally, divorce therapy is often sought by persons soon to be or currently involved in settlement negotiations. In so far as therapeutic assistance reduces emotional turmoil and unhappy modes of interaction it may provide an important impetus to the evolution of a cooperative negotiating climate.

At the time we began our research on professional intervention in divorce, little of a systematic nature had been published on divorce therapy and considering the magnitude of the divorce phenomenon not much has appeared since. We therefore undertook an intensive series of interviews with a highly expert group of therapists regarding their conceptions of the divorcing process and the nature of therapeutic assistance in divorce. These interviews were conducted in the spring and fall of 1975 and the results were first presented to professional audiences in 1977.

We began that investigation with a straightforward query: Given that two people have agreed to end their marriage (even if only one of them really wants to), what can be done to insure that they will do so in a constructive and cooperative manner, rather than destructively and with lingering hostility? That is to say, our focus was on the process set in motion when a marriage is being terminated, rather than on the causes of the divorce or efforts to prevent its occurrence. We wished, in particular, to answer three questions:

1. What are the criteria that distinguish a "constructive" divorce from a "destructive" one?
2. What obstacles in the marriage, in the milieu surrounding the marriage, or in the spouses themselves, stand in the way of achieving a constructive

divorce, and make difficult the task of a therapist wishing to help produce such an outcome?

3. What strategies and tactics of therapeutic intervention are most useful and how can they be classified?

The answers our expert practitioners gave to these questions are presented in this chapter and the next, supplemented by my reading of the research and clinical literature which has appeared since we conducted our interviews and by my own increased experience as a therapist. None of these developments has appreciably changed my understanding of divorce therapy as it was described to us by our panel. I attribute this to the complex challenges of the work itself and to our fortunate choice of respondents: they represented the state of the art then and they pretty much represent it now. However, an attentive review of my own experience and the published views of others suggests that certain aspects of therapeutic practice in divorce deserve additional comment. I have inserted these where appropriate. I have also reflected on the relevance of divorce therapy to the central concern of this book—the formal settlement negotiations. The idea that lawyers and therapists should collaborate during the divorce process has been around for a long time but the collaboration continues to be sporadic and uneasy. Although the problem undoubtedly reflects the very different perspective and training of the two professions it may be attributable as well to an insufficient appreciation of how therapy may favorably alter the special obstacles with which attorneys and their clients typically struggle.

After a few preliminary words about the method of our survey this chapter describes the practical and psychological climate in which divorce therapy typically occurs, along with our expert panel's views concerning the appropriate objectives of treatment. The following chapter is devoted to the clinical work itself.

Method of the Study[2]

Our investigation took the form of a series of in-depth, semistructured interviews. An effort to locate highly expert practitioners was made through professional organizations, personal contacts, and the referral of one respondent by another. The sample thus assembled consisted of twenty-one respondents. (Their names will be found in the Acknowledgments.) By any standard they are a highly experienced, influential group. Each interview lasted nearly two hours and was tape-recorded for later transcription.

The interview was in two parts. The first involved a general discussion of the topics just enumerated. In the second, respondents were asked to discuss in detail (but without revealing information which would permit identification of the clients) a case in which they felt that they had been particularly successful.

The average age of the respondents was fifty-three; they practiced mainly in and around New York and Boston. Most characterized themselves as specialists in marital and/or family therapy and all had more than five years of experience in which divorce work was at least part of their practice. On the average, approximately 20 percent of their professional time is spent specifically on divorce cases. They serve a predominantly middle-class, college-educated clientele with a median income of $30,000 and an average length of marriage of twelve to fifteen years. Approximately 50 percent of the divorcing couples with whom they work are Jewish, 30 percent Protestant, and 20 percent Catholic. Fifty percent of the couples have dependent children.

The respondents' views are presented under two major headings: criteria of a constructive divorce and obstacles to obtaining that objective. It may be useful to begin, however, with a discussion of the practical and psychological context in which divorce therapy typically occurs.

The Context of Intervention

PRACTICAL ASPECTS

Several important practical characteristics of divorce therapy may be noted. First, well-defined training programs for specializing in divorce work do not exist. Recruitment to the field can occur by numerous routes, of which training in individual or marital therapy, child psychiatry, and counseling are among the more common. One does not as yet, however, set out to be a divorce counselor.

Second, there are two distinct sources of therapeutic or quasitherapeutic help in divorce. At the time our interviews were conducted in the mid-1970s almost all such assistance was largely privately arranged. Apart from the opportunities for litigation there were no highly visible, well-structured public agencies or procedures for the resolution of conflicts arising out of the termination of the marriage contract. Family or conciliation courts established by various states came the closest to playing such a role. However, they generally sought to reconcile marriages rather than to provide assistance for those wishing to end them (Brown 1976). In the intervening several years this situation has begun to change radically. Largely in response to the burgeoning divorce rate and the concommitant increase in pre- and postdivorce litigation, the court systems in many states and municipalities have begun to institute formal counseling procedures for the resolution of divorce conflict. This movement is still in its early stages but informal observation suggests that the nature and quality of these programs is highly variable, and rarely do they attempt the kinds of intensive interventions with the kinds of fundamental objectives as those recounted by our private practitioners. Much of what they do attempt may be subsumed under the narrower heading of divorce mediation aimed at resolving focal substantive conflicts around issues such as child custody and visitation. I shall consider this mediation approach in detail in the final section of this book. Divorce therapy as described in this chapter remains in the private sphere.

Reflecting perhaps the absence of institutionalized support, as well as the idiosyncratic nature of divorce itself, the external details of therapist involvement in the private realm described here are likely to be extremely varied. Table 3.1 summarizes the respondents' characterization of the specific case discussed during the interview. While these cases are not necessarily representative, they do convey something of the flavor of private therapeutic practice.

The modal case was relatively long (median of two years), involved sessions of approximately one hour per week, included both spouses, and, at one time or another, some form of contact with a variety of other individuals (most often children and lawyers or other therapists). There were, however, numerous variations on this modal theme. Thus, therapist contact with a case varied from three months to nine years; sessions occurred less than once a week or more than twice a week; in half the cases only one spouse was involved for at least part of the therapy (and this was equally likely to precede as to follow the use of joint sessions); virtually any permutation or combination of joint or separate meetings, couples' groups, and sessions with extended family was possible; therapist involvement began at any point from marital stress through postdivorce readjustment and ended at any time along this continuum.

Finally, there was no commonly used term to describe what it is that our respondents do for the divorcing couple. Although several respondents used the term divorce therapy (or divorce counseling), this rubric was not

Table 3.1

Respondents' Characterization of the Divorce Case Discussed During Interview

Item	*Number of Respondents*
Initiator of First Contact	
Husband or wife equally likely to initiate	3
Wife more likely to initiate	10
Husband more likely to initiate	0
Duration of Contact	
3 months to 1 year	5
1½ to 2½ years	6
4 to 9 years	5
Hours of Contact Per Month	
3 or less	3
Approximately 4	5
More than 6	6
Identity of Client(s)	
Both spouses from start to finish	8
Both initially, then only one	3
One initially, then both	4
Only one and children	1
Types of Contacts During Case[a]	
Client(s) only	1
Clients and:	
Children	10
Relatives	7
Friends (or other nonrelatives)	6
Other professionals (lawyers, therapists, etc.)	9

NOTE: Completed or nearly completed questionnaires were available for 16 of the 21 respondents.
[a]Totals more than 16, since most respondents had contact with more than one collateral person.

always accepted. On several occasions it was criticized as too narrow to describe what was considered to be either a general practice in marital therapy or a concern with individual growth through any therapeutic channels that seem indicated. (Here, too, a change, albeit a relatively minor one, has occurred. The term "divorce therapy" now appears to be accepted professional nomenclature.)

PSYCHOLOGICAL ASPECTS: THE PROCESS OF PSYCHIC DIVORCE

> Talking about divorce, I think, really misses the point. Because you're not talking about divorce, we're talking about needs—needs not to be alone and needs to be related; needs to be attached and needs to avoid anxiety.[3]

The work of the divorce therapist occurs in an often treacherous psychological climate, a climate which owes many of its most distinctive characteristics to the phenomenon of psychic divorce.

Numerous terms were used to allude to psychic divorce: "decourting," "individuation," "differentiation of self," "emotional divorce." Whatever nuances of meaning may differentiate these phrases, all rest on a distinction between what may be called "parallel" vs. "passionate" marriages. Parallel marriages are those in which the partners have not had any intense psychological involvement with each other. Most often these are relatively brief marriages involving young people who have no children. They may have been marriages of "convenience" (e.g., a means of escaping the parental home) or may reflect an underlying problem in both mates in forming intimate attachments. In any case, as divorces they produce relatively few fireworks and are accomplished with relative ease.

Passionate marriages are another matter entirely. The vast majority of couples seeking divorce therapy have had marriages of the passionate type. Generally, these are marriages of relatively long duration out of which children have been born, and in which there has been an intense, deeply felt emotional attachment between the partners.

As divorces, perhaps the most problematic of the passionate marriages are those which owe their intensity to a deeply neurotic component in the original marital attraction, specifically to an unrecognized expectation of one or both partners that the marriage would heal a deep childhood wound. One of the therapists commented:

> Where a person has looked to marriage to supply and make up for early infantile deprivations—where they really see the spouse as a substitute parent, I think those are very often unrealistic and unsuccessful marriages. Unless people grow in the process of ending the marriage, it leads to very acrimonious divorces with feelings of once again being done in by an ungiving parent.

The rupturing of deep emotional bonds, however tattered, is difficult and painful. As one respondent noted, "In our culture most people marry for romantic-passion reasons, and the divorces are passionate affairs as well." Psychic divorce is the term that describes the more or less predictable course which this "passion" takes. The concept of psychic divorce, while fundamental, was rarely articulated in all its complexity by any one respondent. We therefore constructed a composite account of the process. While it is unlikely that this composite would be assented to in every detail by each of the respondents, it will serve to convey the dimensions of the phenomenon and the challenge it poses to the work of the divorce therapist, the divorce attorney, or the mediator.

There are certain general characteristics of psychic divorce. Within broad limits the process is unavoidable and unmodifiable (although self-awareness and/or professional intervention can mitigate its more extreme manifestations). Throughout, decision making and rational planning are impaired, at certain points markedly so. The process occurs in distinct stages that embody powerful swings in mood and in quality of marital interaction. On balance, the more painful moods and types of relating predominate.

The painful emotions associated with psychic divorce are not easily distinguished from such feelings as loneliness or jealously whose roots are easier to trace in the concrete events surrounding the divorce. However, in the view of the clinicians the pain of psychic divorce is a distinctive element, more or less independent of such other feelings. From the emotional perspective the process of psychic divorce adds insult to emotional injury.

The experience of the partner who has initiated the breakup, while basically similar to that of the noninitiator, is less difficult. The distinctiveness of the initiator's experience is related to the relatively earlier occurrence of some of the psychological stages and the relatively shorter time span of the entire process. Much of the difficulty in adjustment attributed to the noninitiator can be viewed as a consequence of a lack of psychological preparedness and intense feelings of diminished self-regard. Some respondents noted that the noninitiator could not be expected to recover for as long as three years or more.

Although the phenomenon of psychic divorce is inevitable, the successful completion of the process is not. Thus, legal divorce may, and frequently does, occur in the absence of psychic divorce. The worst examples of postdivorce legal battles, bitterness, and general mayhem may be most often ascribed to a failure of psychic divorce.

The Stages of Psychic Divorce The stages of psychic divorce include the predivorce decision period; the decision period proper; the period of mourning; and the period of re-equilibration.

THE PREDIVORCE DECISION PERIOD. Strictly speaking, this is not a part of the process of psychic divorce. It is, however, the preliminary skirmish, from which the parties may emerge already badly shaken onto the field of divorce.

1. The first stage is one of increasing marital dissatisfaction and tension on the part of both spouses, but often felt more acutely by one spouse.
2. The couple attempts reconciliation. These attempts may include frantic efforts to recapture a sense of mutual caring and the seeking of advice from

friends or relatives. Psychotherapeutic help may be sought here or at any subsequent stage.

3. A clear decline in marital intimacy. One or both spouses may take a lover as psychological "insurance" for the impending separation.
4. A break in the facade of marital solidarity. It is now public knowledge that the marriage is in serious trouble; there is open fighting, and lawyers may be contacted. Physical separation may occur at this or any subsequent stage, or it may never occur. In extreme cases the spouses do not separate even after the divorce!

Stages 1 through 4 may last for weeks, months, or even years. In some cases the process neither moves to the next stage nor attains resolution in the form of a return to marital harmony.

THE DECISION PERIOD.

1. The decision to divorce is firmly made by at least one partner; there is a sense of relief, perhaps exhilaration: a difficult, but liberating, step has been taken.
2. Anxiety and panic at the prospect of separation: "Can I survive alone?"
3. A stage of renewed marital intimacy. In reality, it is a mutually dependent clinging and unwillingness to face the underlying rupture because of separation anxiety.
4. Renewed outbreaks of marital fighting, revealing the true nature of the immediately preceding stages. Stages 3 and 4 may be repeated several times. In fact, the entire decision-to-divorce period may be marked by what one respondent labeled the "marital flip-flop," as the partners take turns alternately pushing for and opposing the divorce, until the inevitability of the divorce is accepted.
5. Final acceptance of the inevitability of divorce involves renewed anger, now expressed in conflict over the terms of settlement: "I promised you that I was going to give you half the money in the bank; well, I changed my mind."

Two additional points may be noted about the divorce decision period. First, the composite account that we have constructed omits important differences between couples. Our later research (described in detail in chapter 11) suggests that there may be at least four different patterns by which the decision to divorce can be reached. A similar observation, stated from a somewhat different perspective, has been made by Federico (1979). Based on extensive clinical experience with divorce adjustment groups, Federico has identified two distinctive styles of couple interaction during the decision-making process. In one such pattern, which he labels "provocation," the spouse who has consciously or unconsciously given up on the marriage engages in increasingly hostile or distancing acts to which the noninitiator responds by denial and efforts at keeping the marital peace in however unsatisfactory a form. To each such accommodation, however, the other responds with more serious provocations. There thus ensues an escalating series of increasingly problematic provocations-accommodations, until at last, the noninitiator "gets the message" and finally sues for divorce.

The second pattern Federico refers to as "sabotage." In this style of divorce decision making the noninitiator does not march under the banner of denial and peace at any price, but responds to the partner's provocative behavior with acts of hostility of his or her own. The result is that the initiator's hidden wish for a divorce is flushed out ("sabotaged") and the initiator is obliged to accept the unwanted role of marriage breaker.

A second and related point about the divorce decision-making period is that it appears to be highly prognostic of whether the settlement negotiations will take a productive or destructive path. This may be because reaching a decision to divorce is itself a type of "negotiation" and therefore reveals the communication and decision-making strengths and weaknesses endemic to the couple throughout their relationship. This is what clinical theory and experience would lead us to expect. The prognostic value of the divorce decision period may also be attributable to its length (several months to several years) and to its close temporal proximity to the settlement negotiations: when destructive modes of relating have long been at work in a marriage, deterioration in each partner's self-esteem and the decline in mutual trust may present formidable obstacles to a constructive settlement negotiation particularly one begun hot on the reactive heels of the divorce decision.

THE PERIOD OF MOURNING. This is a complex and critical period. It is during this period that the terms of settlement may be agreed upon.

1. Feelings of guilt and self-reproach for having caused the breakup; an acute sense of failure and diminished self-worth; loneliness and depression are typical during this stage. Several respondents noted that mourning a spouse lost through divorce is in some respects more difficult than mourning a dead spouse, since the partner in divorce is alive and there may be a strong temptation to re-establish ties.
2. Anger toward the spouse. This signals a return to psychological equilibrium and an upswing in self-regard.
3. Acceptance of the positive as well as the negative side of the marriage. Realistic sadness.

THE PERIOD OF RE-EQUILIBRATION. This is a period of heightened self-growth and diminished dwelling on the marriage. If the mourning process has been successfully completed, this stage will increasingly take on the characteristics discussed later in this chapter under Criteria of a Constructive Divorce.

In short, through much of the process of psychic divorce, both partners are viewed as being buffeted by strong emotional forces over which they have little control; their behavior, whether loving or hostile, may belie their actual feelings and is, in any case, an uncertain guide to their deepest intentions. The partners are unpredictable and their ability to plan constructively for their own needs and those of their children is reduced.

It is perhaps because of the vagaries of psychic divorce that every once in a while there surfaced in the respondents' remarks a certain bemusement about their chosen work.

> They came to me for what seemed to be a marital problem, and about the third or fourth session I learned that they were divorced. As a matter of fact, they didn't go on a honeymoon when they got married; they went on a sort of honeymoon when they got divorced. They celebrated by going away together. See, people do strange things—and how the therapist is supposed to follow and understand all those strange things, I don't know.

The primary implication of the psychic divorce process for the nonpsychological counselor—lawyers, mediators, accountants, real estate agents —whom divorcing individuals are likely to consult, is that normal assumptions about what can be expected from a client are likely to be disappointed. It is more realistic to assume that divorcing clients will be slow to act, unable to comprehend or retain information, and changeable in their decisions. As far as the divorce settlement negotiations are concerned, the potential for displaced and particularly intense conflict is high, and the prospects for enlightened and realistic negotiations (even in the absence of overt conflict) are low.

Criteria of a Constructive Divorce

What distinguishes a successful divorce from an unsuccessful one? If therapeutic assistance in terminating a marriage is sought, what should it accomplish? From the perspective of our clinicians, and speaking in the broadest sense, a constructive divorce is one in which the process of psychic divorce has been successfully completed. There was consensus that psychic divorce has occurred when certain conditions prevail with regard to the attitudes and behavior of the former spouses toward one another, the welfare of children, and the level of functioning of each of the ex-mates as a newly single person.

THE ATTITUDES AND BEHAVIOR OF THE FORMER SPOUSES TOWARD ONE ANOTHER

A good divorce, like a good marriage, is a mutual enterprise. Both partners must wish to end their relationship just as they once wished to start it.

> One member may be sadder than the other about the disruption of the marriage, or feel more distressed, but I think a constructive divorce is when both people realize it is the best solution for the two of them—not necessarily the most wanted solution, but the best solution—the only possible solution.

> Where one member of the divorcing couple still feels that it could have worked — or that, "if only,"some other kind of magic could have kept it going—I think there's bound to be bitterness.

Mutual acceptance of the need to divorce should find concrete expression in mutually active negotiating over the terms of settlement, particularly in cases involving dependent children and the division of accrued material assets. Such negotiations should be undertaken by the parties with a healthy sense of their respective needs and in a spirit of equity and fair play. When a mutual readiness to end the marriage does not exist, these negotiating conditions are unlikely to occur.

It is important and interesting to note, however, that the respondents as a group were relatively indifferent to assisting in negotiations over practical matters. (Only two, for example, mentioned an equitable financial settlement as an important criterion of a constructive divorce.) The paucity of interest about the practical side of divorce reflects, in part, the belief of many of the respondents that difficulties in arranging practical issues are only symptoms of more profound—and "real"—conflicts.

> I think that the issues are emotional and that they get played out in terms of money; they get played out in terms of visitation; they get played out in terms of a lot of things. I think the basic issues are emotional. In a good divorce, those things just don't come up as issues.

We shall return to this important matter in the next chapter when we focus on the process of therapy.

The successful divorce should also leave each partner with a balanced view of the other and of the marriage, and with a sense of psychological closure.

> The good outcome to me is where the individual without either self-blame or blaming the other, has been able to look at the marriage and retrospectively say, "Here were the good things, which were nice, and they are part of me; here are the things that went wrong, for these and these reasons . . ."

> A critical element is where they can look on their ex-mate with a certain degree of objectivity. You know, there are some people who go to their graves still hating that mate that they divorced twenty-five years ago. It's a vendetta for the rest of their lives.

> I suppose if I could ask the people three years later, "Are you glad you did it?" "Do you have regrets?" I would say that a good outcome is if people can feel that they really have no more than some minor misgivings about having chosen that path—if there's a minimum of looking back. You know, people sometimes have a way of continuing to relive a marriage—which suggests to me that the marriage isn't finished.

In the postdivorce period it is desirable that the former partners be able to work together cooperatively when the situation requires it—whatever their feelings toward each other may be. The need for such cooperation is greatest for couples with minor children.

> It's worked out in such a way that he will not welch on payments, and they conduct themselves very civilly; she doesn't like him; she says he's a real bastard, but they do meet occasionally to discuss business matters and things regarding the children, and they're very civil about it.

While postdivorce civility is an asset, few respondents were in favor of continued postdivorce involvement between ex-spouses beyond those necessitated by co-parenting. Seemingly pleasurable postdivorce interactions were seen as suggesting an unconscious wish to "hang on" to the marriage. A minority viewpoint, expressed by two therapists, was that friendship between ex-mates was desirable when it could be achieved.

> There are many couples who are divorced and still maintain all kinds of contacts —even without children—of telephone calls, or of problems with alimony, or whatever, or in terms of friends, of sharing friends, keeping them involved in the process. So that there are divorces which are not divorces; and I think those are the most destructive.

> Sometimes they can become friends for the first time in their lives. It's a strange thing, I mean, I've heard people say, "You know, we have never been so open with each other . . ." because, what more is there to lose; and they can sometimes

> say truths to each other which they haven't said before. It may simply be that there is a kind of recognition: "We really aren't going to make it with each other. You're going one way and I'm going another. But that doesn't mean I have to hate you for it or you have to hate me for it. We can hold each other's hands."

One unambiguous sign that psychological divorce has not occurred is continued court battles.

> They get divorced legally, but the fight continues. I think that's really where I came into divorce counseling—where after the legal divorce the emotional divorce doesn't truly occur; and the anger is so great that they proceed to use each other. They fornicate in court instead of fornicating in bed. . . . So often they get the satisfaction of battle—they get their orgasms by going to court.

Indeed, so violent may the conflicts be which erupt in the process of severing the marital bond that facilitating a legal divorce may represent a considerable therapeutic achievement. One respondent cited the case of a man who threatened to kill his wife at her mere mention of the word "divorce." The respondent congratulated himself on helping the couple achieve a divorce without anybody—including the therapist—getting hurt.

THE CHILDREN

> Kids are always hurt when their parents break up; there's no such thing as, "better have a divorce for the sake of the children." No, the kids are always hurt. We try to hurt them as little as possible.

Whether or not each of our respondents would agree that children are *always* hurt in a divorce, this comment captures the prevailing view of the sample: that children of divorce, particularly very young children, are at considerable psychic risk. The idea of children's vulnerability rests on two major notions: that for optimal psychological growth, children need two parents, one of each sex; and that, because they are cognitively and emotionally immature, children are poorly equipped to handle any significant estrangements in their relations with parents. For the child under the age of six or seven such an event signals, in fact, a major life trauma.

The risks to children are heightened by the temporary, but often considerable impairment in the care-taking ability of the parents, who are undergoing one of the great stressful periods of their own lives.

> Even people who are absolutely determined that they're not going to use their kids will do so in some form. For example, the father picks them up on Sunday.

> He's run out of places to take the kids. You know, after a while he does. And then the kids are crying, if they're little: they don't have their toys with them and they don't have their playmates. And he's kind of uncomfortable with them at times. And then he takes the kids home and the mother says to the kids: "What'd your father give you today? Another hamburger? Another hotdog? He didn't give you a full course meal? Who's he dating now?" Even people who are determined not to do it are going to do it in some form. Then the kids become message carriers. Even if the parents don't use the words, the kids can pick up the feelings.

More devastating to children can be the emotional and legal guerrilla warfare between the parents in which the children become primary weapons. It is psychologically easier and publicly more acceptable to give vent to feelings of anger, humiliation, and diminished self-worth by attacking the spouse in one's parental role, than in the unflattering capacity of rejected husband or wife.

> The fighting goes on for years, after the real part is over with; the wife brings the husband to court again for additional alimony, for additional child support, and eventually he starts some sort of counter-action . . . and the kids pay a terrible price for that. And that is the main criterion for a bad outcome. The adults get bruised in the process. I think they can usually handle it. But the kids are pretty helpless and if they get destroyed, I think that's really the worst sort of outcome that can happen.

The constructive divorce then, is one in which psychic injury to children is minimized, principally through the maintenance of a good co-parenting relationship between the former spouses. In particular, children should be free of the apprehension that loving either parent will jeopardize their place in the affections of the other.

> Those kids should feel that they can love one without having to feel antagonism to the other; that it's not an act of disloyalty to love both; and those kids should feel that in an emergency that they've still got a mother and father and they can count on them.

The children's relationship with the noncustodial parent was mentioned by several respondents as having special importance. One therapist, for example, felt that the success of her assistance consisted, in part, in the working out of postdivorce living arrangements which took into account the children's need for both parents.

> One issue was who was going to move; that was a major issue. The other one was what was going to happen to the kids and how that was going to happen.

> It was dealt with by deciding that the kids went with her, to her apartment, but they would be close enough so that they could walk over and visit their father whenever they chose to. And they spent a lot of time with him. And she feels free to let them do that and not interfere with the relationship. I mean, that's a very big thing with me. I work very hard at working this through for the children, exacting that they should be allowed to have a separate relationship with each parent.

A constructive divorce is also one in which children have mastered the painful experience they have been through, and, if possible, grown in the process. Absence of the fantasy that they were the cause of the divorce was seen as evidence that the worst of the children's difficulties have been resolved.

> I believe that every person who had divorced parents has the secret fantasy that he's going to bring them together again. Even when they're grown up. Analysts, of older adults frequently hear the fantasy, "I can bring my mother and father together, who were divorced thirty years ago." I even knew one person who made sure that his divorced parents were buried together.

THE SELF

The minimal criterion for a constructive divorce is the absence of strong, unrelenting feelings of failure and self disparagement. The truly successful divorce, in addition, entails increased self-understanding, the ability to form satisfying new intimate relationships, and a heightened sense of personal competence. In a word, "growth." This was the single most reiterated theme in the interview.

Most often, an increase in self-knowledge referred to what one respondent termed a "victory over a neurotic choice of a mate." The primary purpose of such a victory was to avoid a subsequent identical marital choice—the "same mistake twice" (or thrice) syndrome. (Although the ability to form new intimate relationships was considered important, few respondents went so far as to suggest that the *sine qua non* of healthy postdivorce adjustment was remarriage.)

> You can't really tell whether the divorce, or the therapy associated with it, was successful, until you've seen what kind of relationship the divorced person forms. If they get themselves into the exact kind of neurotic binds, then the divorce hasn't solved anything. But if they are able to form healthy relationships, it has.

The specific components of self-understanding that innoculate against the same mistake twice syndrome are insight into one's unconscious conflicts and distortions, and an appreciation of one's contribution to the dysfunctional behavior in the old marriage. It is an important therapeutic strategy to elucidate these matters over the course of treatment. A one-sided view of the marital breakdown was taken as prima facie evidence that something far short of an optimal divorce had been achieved.

> Another kind of destructive divorce is when there is so much animosity between two people that both of them cling to the view of the other as the evil one; and there really is no recognition that each has played a part in—has made a contribution to the situation.

Increased feelings of personal competence may be a direct result of terminating a psychologically abusive marriage.

> The man was very dependent on his wife—she had an income from stocks and bonds—and unquestionally this was one of her attractions for him. But she had very little respect for him and tended to side with his children against him, and was mildly paranoid. He was really selling his soul to the devil for money, and his extracting himself was a healthy sign.

In other cases, the growth in self-mastery comes from an active process of coping with the demands of the divorcing process or the postdivorce period.

> He was one of the people with whom I've worked who found lawyers at the university who were concerned with the rights of children. He became knowledgeable in finding these people for himself. This was a man who in many other areas of his life was a very competent man, but in terms of his personal life there'd been a lot of dependence and helplessness. So that being able to do some of this was part of his growth—to fight for the custody of his children, to face that.

Obstacles to a Constructive Divorce

The major obstacle to a constructive divorce in the eyes of the clinician is, as we have noted, the turmoil of psychic divorce. That is not the only obstacle which may exist, however. Additional complications may arise because of certain characteristics of the marital relationship and from the involvement of third parties, particularly the involvement of lawyers.

CHARACTERISTICS OF THE MARRIAGE

The single most frequently cited predictor of a difficult divorce was one spouse's eagerness to end the marriage coupled with reluctance to do so on the part of the other. The interviews leave the impression that in the clinical practice of the respondents such cases are very common.

Typically, unequal motivation to divorce was linked not only to a changing balance of affection but to a realistic imbalance in postdivorce prospects. A divorced man of thirty-eight or forty, for example, may be just reaching the peak of his professional and financial attainments. Such a man may have reason to believe that, in the event of divorce, his social and sexual horizons can, with some minor time out for readjustments, be easily and gratifyingly extended. Not so for his homemaker wife with custody of their two minor children. She may have cause to suspect that her postdivorce social and financial situation will be far less easy to arrange and far less satisfying. When, in addition to differing levels in postdivorce "marketability," the less marketable spouse has been rejected for a new lover, the barriers to a constructive divorce can be formidable.

Most often the husband was pictured as the spouse wishing to end the marriage because of a new lover, although the rising rate of women who have found new partners was noted by several therapists. A wife's desire to end a marriage, however, was more often linked not to a new man, but to a new consciousness—the wish for a career and/or a greater degree of autonomy and fulfillment than that provided by a traditional marriage. Reluctance to divorce on the part of husbands was viewed more as a function of psychological overdependence on their wives and the painful prospect of diminished contact with their children, than of a poor post-divorce social or financial outlook.

The precise effects of an unequal desire to divorce may be difficult to predict, but certain reoccurring patterns were noted.

Frequently, the partner who wishes to end the marriage feels guilt about abandoning the spouse. A frank discussion of the desire for divorce is therefore made more difficult, and a series of escalating but misplaced marital conflicts may then occur. Several respondents also noted that much of what is ostensibly joint therapy designed to save a marriage is actually a covert form of divorce therapy, resulting from the deserting spouse's desire to assuage his or her guilt ("I tried my best to save it") and, perhaps unconsciously, to provide the mate with a "lover" in the person of the therapist.

Once the initiator finally broaches the topic of divorce, continued guilt combined with the equally strong desire to leave, may produce a virulent form of the "settlement at any cost" mentality. At the same time, the settlement terms demanded by the spouse who wishes to keep the marriage may escalate. Such escalating, and often unreasonable, demands may be motivated by feelings of humiliation combined with anxiety at the prospects of a bleak and unchosen future. They may also be a means to prolong the marriage and ultimately prevent the marital breakup.

An opposite pattern was also noted: Guilt in one spouse at leaving the marriage may be expressed as anger directed at the other. In the reluctant partner, diminished feelings of self-worth may inhibit the ability to bargain constructively and effectively, or worse, produce an abject acceptance of almost any terms dictated by the other. Under such circumstances, a settlement may be quickly arrived at. Its inequitable and ultimately unworkable nature, however, may not become apparent until several years and several court fights later.

Chances for a constructive divorce are also much reduced for couples in which one or both partners have a heavy investment in casting blame or in bringing up past grievances; for "Virginia Woolf" couples who experience gratification in wounding one another and are thus committed to a pathological fighting process; and for couples in which one partner plays a dominating, aggressive role in marital disputes, while the other adopts a passive, submissive stance.

There was also wide consensus that for divorcing couples with minor children the potential for a destructive divorce is greatly increased. First, there must be planning for the children's welfare—their immediate needs as well as those ten or fifteen years in the future. Such planning is complex and difficult even under the best of circumstances. For many parents there are also extensive feelings of guilt at the damage that they feel the divorce will do to the children's emotional development. Guilt may result in defensive anger at the mate, or uncritical acceptance of any child care proposals, however ill-conceived. As has been noted, children also provide a psychologically inviting opportunity for both spouses to embellish their feelings of anger and bitterness towards one another in a socially acceptable manner. It may be difficult to de-escalate a conflict of this kind since its true roots are unacknowledged.

The effect of wealth or its absence on the divorcing process was one aspect of the marriage on which there was no consensus. Two positions were articulated: One view was that either poverty or wealth can produce complications. If there is very little money the partners may have great difficulty in negotiating a settlement because the small economic pie makes it difficult to arrange trade offs, and the clear reduction in circumstances that looms ahead produces anxiety and a corresponding increase in self-protectiveness. If there is much money the high financial stakes may ruin the climate in which negotiations take place.

> In one couple I treated, the guy was a millionaire; he was following his wife while they were separated, and having infrared pictures taken of her with men, so the flash wouldn't be seen. This was the kind of thing I was trying to avoid; but he said to me, "Look, Buster, there's a half a million dollars at stake, if I don't protect myself with this information."

Large sums of money may also provide increased opportunities for the expression of revenge seeking and the desire to punish.[4]

The second view was that in and of itself money has no predictable effect on the divorcing process. When money does become an issue it is because "something deeper" is involved. We have noted this perspective earlier but it is worth repeating because it is so much at variance with the perspective of attorneys and others who have studied the economic consequences of divorce.

> I think money is very often used in our society and in marriages as a way of expressing needs, controls, expectations, wishes—and it continues in the divorce process. And it sometimes is used as a way of punishing or exacting payment for pain. I think where people have had no conflicts around money prior to the divorce, they don't have them in the divorce process. The kinds of quarrels that go on around money have nothing to do with the realities of money and how much there is to be shared or distributed. It has to do with the feelings people have about money.

THIRD-PARTY INVOLVEMENT

The ability of relatives and friends to hinder the divorcing process was a minor theme in the interviews. Several respondents discussed situations in which outside parties made things worse—the boyfriend who eggs on the unhappy wife, the mother who fuels her daughter's resentment against a husband—and there were some who felt that relatives or friends, however well meaning, could rarely be objective. There was also agreement that of all outside parties, the client's own parents loomed largest as complicating factors in the divorce. However, it was not the actual meddlesomeness of parents which was the cause of difficulty but the internalized anticipations of how the parents would react to the divorce.

The place of preeminence as enemy of a constructive divorce was reserved, in the respondents' views, for the divorce lawyer. Although the respondents' attitudes toward the lawyer's role in divorce can best be described as ambivalent—positive relationships between therapists and lawyers do develop—the great majority of the therapists expressed a wary, critical view of the legal profession.

Three major criticisms of lawyers reappeared continually. Under the present legal system lawyers are part of an adversary process and thus under a professional obligation to defend the client's interests and attack those of the spouse. From the therapists' perspective as agents of a constructive divorce, this is the least desirable posture imaginable. Lawyers are untrained in psychology, and in family and marital dynamics in particular. Consequently, they may easily become unwitting pawns in the escalation of marital conflict. The lawyer's objectivity may be compromised by financial considerations, since his fee is contingent on the amount of time and energy required to produce a final settlement.

Two of the respondents also mentioned cases in which they had been subpoenaed by one spouse's lawyer to testify against the other spouse. Such legal action not only violates in a direct manner the therapist's jealously guarded impartiality, but also raises the unresolved and highly problematic issue of confidentiality between therapist and client in divorce counseling.

> I once got caught in my early years in a custody case. That was, first of all, a lousy position to be in; and secondly, it seems to me that, really, nobody knows very clearly what the role of the therapist should be in relation to two people as opposed to one person. There's confidentiality, and that's pretty clear when you're talking with one person; but when you're talking with two people, what is the confidentiality? And particularly if you're in a situation where people are separating and so on, you begin to get mixed up. What was said when you were alone with them, and together with them?

To what degree are the obstacles to a constructive divorce which our clinicians identified characteristic of the over one million divorces which have occurred every year in the United States since the mid-1970s? No precise answer can be given to this question but it is logical to assume that those who seek help represent an especially distressed—and relatively well heeled—segment of the population. If data on representative samples were available, the incidence of nonmutuality, destructive psychological enmeshment, lawyer-instigated mutual torment and so on, would undoubtedly be less common than they are in the cases which appear at the clinician's door. For example, the data on the persistence of psychological attachment between divorcing spouses—the phenomenon which is the prime mover in the great engine of psychic divorce and the attendant havoc which it wreaks—appears to lie somewhere in the 25 to 70 percent range (Kitson 1982; Spanier and Casto 1979). This is a considerable figure when translated into sheer numbers of cases, and even an appalling one when considered in terms of human misery, but by no means suggestive of a universal phenomenon.

By the same token, we cannot say with any assurance how frequently our panel's criteria of a psychologically constructive divorce are met by the divorcing population at large. It is in this realm that the greatest amount of research has accumulated since the time of our interviews, but reliable answers are not yet available. Research certainly confirms the clinical impression that divorcing persons and their children are high-risk groups for psychological problems and continuing interpersonal conflict with one another. I have reviewed earlier much of the evidence on the frequency of the postdivorce suffering of adults. Generally speaking these estimates are in the 25 to 50 percent range, depending on the criteria of adjustment and on the study; relative to other adult groups in the population, separated and divorced persons are invariably found to have the worst psychological adjustment. Research on the psychological impact of divorce on children is equally sobering. Relative to children from intact homes or children who have lost a parent through death, children of divorce appear worse off on a variety of indices of adjustment, including depression, delinquency, and cognitive ability. The problems appear more common in boys than in girls, a finding echoed in research on the adult adjustment of children of divorce.

The evidence both in adults and children must be regarded cautiously, however. In the first place, on some of the criteria of a constructive divorce mentioned by our panel little or no systematic data are available. For example, virtually nothing is known about the degree to which divorcing spouses take an active role in the settlement negotiations, nor on the extent to which insight into self, and a balanced, objective view of the former mate and marriage are achieved.

There is some survey evidence that suggests that the "same mistake twice" syndrome may be an empirical reality, but this data refers principally to statistics on divorce rates in second marriages (they are higher than for first marriages) and the tendency for divorced women to make what the sociologists refer to as heterogamous marriages (marriages between persons with different racial or religious backgrounds) the second time as well as the first. More detailed evidence regarding the degree to which divorce is or is not a "learning experience" is largely anecdotal.

Second, research on the impact of divorce is marred by serious methodological weaknesses. The most important of these include unrepresentative samples, a preponderance of female over male respondents, a failure to evaluate adjustment in relation to multiple factors besides the global "divorced" vs. "not divorced" dichotomy (e.g., in terms of socioeconomic status before and after the breakup; type of custody arrangement; availability of support networks of family and friends, etc.), an absence of control groups, and the lack of sound longitudinal studies. The absence of longitudinal research is a particularly grievous defect since there is good reason to believe that for both adults and children the psychological impact of divorce attenuates markedly with the passage of time. The absence of longitudinal studies on representative samples also leaves unanswered the degree to which poor postdivorce adjustment can be attributed to the divorce experience, how much to pre-existing problems, and how much to a mix of these factors. There is evidence that those who divorce do have a greater frequency of prior emotional illness than those in stable marriages (Kitson and Raschke 1981).

Third, as noted in chapter 1, it is easy to overstate the degree to which divorce is associated with emotional debilitation. The sheer number of studies demonstrating the effect is impressive, but the magnitude of the difference in adjustment between separated and divorced persons and the rest of the adult population may be relatively small in practical terms (Rabkin and Streuning 1976).

Finally, whatever the psychic costs of divorce they must be weighed against the costs associated with staying in a bad marriage. Here too, the evidence, while far from complete, suggests that continuing marital distress is more emotionally and physically injurious than ending the relationship (Renee 1971).[5]

Whatever the limitations of the empirical record, however, our respondents' criteria of a psychologically constructive divorce and the obstacles which they perceive to attaining such a result shape their conceptions of their therapeutic role. It is this central issue that concerns us next: What does the clinician do to mitigate the suffering in divorce?

4

Divorce Therapy: The Nature of Treatment

Divorce therapy may focus on helping clients with the often difficult struggle of deciding whether or not to end their marriage or in assisting them in negotiating practical matters such as custody, visitation, and division of marital assets in the event a decision to divorce has been made. In this chapter I describe therapist activity in both these spheres. The emphasis, however, is on therapeutic assistance with the decision to divorce since this was the primary concern of our respondents.

Some readers may be dissatisfied with this uneven distribution of emphasis in a book on the psychology of settlement negotiations on the grounds that the treatment that precedes those negotiations is only marginally relevant, at best, to the vicissitudes of the settlement process. I believe such a view to be seriously mistaken. Although I shall devote considerable attention in later chapters to divorce mediation over substantive matters—an activity in which mental health professionals are coming to play a major role—most clients who appear at the lawyer's doorstep after having tried psychological counseling will have experienced not divorce mediation, but help in evaluating their marriage, since this is what most therapists are trained to do in cases of impending divorce. Experience suggests, however, that even attorneys well disposed toward psychological assistance in divorce are only dimly aware of what actually transpires in the therapist's office. This ignorance may be one of the factors impeding greater cooperation between lawyers and therapists—a professional obstacle widely believed to operate against the client's interests (Fisher and Fisher 1982; Perlman 1982; Steinberg 1980).

Even more to the point, if successfully executed, the decision-making phase of divorce therapy is likely to extend far beyond the circumscribed task of helping the parties choose between divorce or continued marriage but lead instead to fundamental changes in the psychological forces at play in their relationship. These changes may very substantially improve the climate in which the eventual settlement negotiations occur and the parties' ability to make constructive use of legal counsel.

For both these reasons a detailed account of the decision-making phase of divorce therapy may well repay our attention.

The Decision-making Phase of Treatment: Exploratory Divorce Therapy

Because the scope of therapy for couples seeking help with the divorce decision is so broad I shall refer to this phase of treatment as exploratory divorce therapy. The interventions of the therapist in both the exploratory and settlement phases are extremely numerous and, in theory, limited only by the ingenuity and zeal of practitioners. However, the therapeutic behaviors which our respondents described can be classified into three more or less distinctive categories: *reflexive* tactics, by which therapists seek to improve their usefulness by increasing their understanding of the underlying conflicts or by gaining the trust and confidence of the parties; *contextual* tactics, by which therapists endeavor to improve the ability of the couple to settle matters on their own, with minimal substantive advice on the therapist's part; and *substantive* tactics, intended to produce movement toward a solution on terms which the therapist has come to believe are inevitable or desirable. I first used this classificatory schema in a study of the behaviors of labor mediators (Kressel 1972). Its usefulness for describing the work of divorce therapists is more than simply fortuitous. Whether focusing on the divorce decision or the settlement terms, the divorce therapist is very much the "mediator."

While the classification of therapist activity into reflexive, contextual, and substantive interventions is highly useful for expository and analytic purposes, the intervention of a therapist in a complex marital situation is a fluid, multi-faceted activity in which many things are occurring simultaneously. Breaking down such a process into discrete "units" of intervention is an obvious oversimplification. With this important caveat in mind, however, our three classificatory terms can usefully organize an otherwise bewildering array of therapist behaviors.

REFLEXIVE INTERVENTIONS

Building Trust and Confidence A pervasive theme in the therapists' conceptualization of their role was the importance of developing in the clients a sense of trust and confidence. (Since divorce therapy typically involves both spouses, either in conjoint or concurrent sessions, I have employed the plural, "clients," throughout. It is clear, however, that many interventions are employed when only one spouse is in treatment.) A concern with rapport continues throughout therapy, but is likely to be central to the therapist's behavior in the initial stages when therapist and clients are new to each other. In a sense, this is the most subtle of therapist strategies, conveyed as much by the therapist's tone and general bearing as by his or her concrete actions. Among the specific tactics by which a sense of trust and confidence may be fostered are explicit statements of reassurance and support, the judicious use of self-disclosure, and the maintenance of confidentiality. While there was a general distaste for becoming the repository of marital secrets, respondents accept and even encourage confidences, but at the same time attempt to provide constraints and rules for "secret"-telling. (Except where otherwise noted, the quotations that accompany the account of therapist behavior are taken from the interviews with the therapists in our sample.)

> I tend to see them alone for two sessions and then bring them back together. When I'm seeing them alone I make it very explicit that they are free to tell me things that they want kept confidential, and I will respect that. The advantage is to get them to open up and begin to look at themselves, because if they're constantly worried that their spouse is going to learn this, then they aren't going to open up. I make two exceptions. First, I want the freedom to tell the partner things he is telling me that could be discussed right now by all three of us sitting here together, and I make it very plain that I'm clued in to what is sensitive and what is free. Second, if there is some sensitive material that I think the other person needs to know, I might urge him to tell the partner. I won't do it myself, but I might urge him to.

Diagnosing the Marital Situation Before they can intervene effectively or, indeed, know what interventions are needed, therapists must educate themselves about the nature of the situation confronting them. The key issue on which information is needed is whether or not the marriage is headed for divorce. Three aspects of divorce and divorce therapy make the task of accurate diagnosis particularly difficult.

THE PREVALENCE OF CLIENT MISDIAGNOSIS. In a large number of cases the client's initial self-diagnosis is incorrect or grossly misleading. Perhaps most common is the request to "save" a marriage, which is actually an implicit request (at least on one spouse's part) to help end it. Less frequently, the initial request is for help in divorcing. Here too the probability of client misdiagnosis is high.

> What we have to tune in to in working with people is: What do they mean at this time when they hurl the word "divorce" at each other? Is it done like a threat? Is it done as some straw to hold onto and get an escape route? Or is it really a calmly thought through decision, so that this is really the logical route to follow?

The high degree of ambivalence that is typically associated with the divorce decision-making process is perhaps the most formidable barrier to accurate client self-assessment. The sources of this ambivalence may include the social stigma attached to divorce; a sense of personal failure at a prescribed cultural task; guilt about possible damage to children or to the spouse who still wants the marriage; fear of living alone and functioning autonomously; reluctance to offend or disappoint one's parents; and the inevitable emotional turmoil of the divorce process. Because of this high degree of ambivalence and the pain associated with it, a decision to divorce may occur but be warded off from conscious awareness as a form of emotional self-protection. Only in retrospect may the initiator be able to recognize that long before the protestations of love had ceased, the point of marital no return had secretly and unconsciously been passed (Federico 1979).

Partly because the clients are such unreliable guides, and because the diagnostic issue is such a complex one, when respondents were asked at what stage of a potential divorce case they prefer to become involved, the overwhelming response was, "as early as possible"—generally meaning before the issue of divorce has been seriously raised, but in any event, well before lawyers have been called in.

THE MULTIPLE POSSIBLE LOCI OF THE IMPETUS TO DIVORCE. Although our expert clinicians generally preferred the view that an unhappy marriage is usually the result of the highly mutual contributions of each partner, it is also clear that there are other cases in which a divorce is precipitated by a conflict or crisis whose locus is only in one of the partners. In addition, the movement toward divorce, whatever its locus, may represent a reactive flight from a basically sound relationship or a more or less healthy response to an inappropriate or no longer viable marital situation (Beal 1980; Federico 1979; Martin 1976). These multiple possibilities greatly complicate the diagnostic problem facing the practitioner, particularly since the notion of "good" and "bad" divorce decisions is at once clinically useful as well as highly subjective and at variance with the view that the therapist should remain strictly impartial regarding the decision to divorce. The result is that professional motivation to explicitly formulate and defend criteria for deciding whether or not a marriage is (or should be) headed for divorce is relatively low and laced with its own peculiar form of ambivalence. I believe that this state of affairs contributes to diagnostic uncertainty within the field.

THE NASCENT STATUS OF DIVORCE THERAPY. Another explanation for the significant diagnostic problems in divorce therapy has to do with the professional status of the treatment itself. A review of the literature conducted in conjunction with our interviews found only a handful of publications on strategies of intervention in divorce. The situation has changed since then, but not by very much. Moreover, although all our respondents were highly expert, on the average only 20 percent of their time was spent on divorce work. We were unable to locate any practitioner for whom divorce therapy was the preponderant or exclusive area of practice. With the exception of the small cadre of divorce mediators this too continues to be the norm in the private practice of divorce counseling. These, I believe, are continuing signs that we are dealing with a specialty which has not yet achieved full and independent status. To some degree, then, the diagnostic issue looms large because couples who have made a firm decision to divorce, and who, therefore, represent no diagnostic problem, do not present themselves for help in dealing with the practical and psychological problems of separating. Quite simply, they are unaware that such help is available.

At the time we interviewed our expert panel my colleagues and I did not appreciate that determining the status of the case is one of the central conundrums of divorce therapy. Consequently, it is in the realm of diagnostic criteria and diagnostic tactics that we asked the fewest questions and learned the least. I would like to rectify that oversight to some degree by drawing upon my own clinical experience, which has grown considerably in the intervening years, and on several recent useful papers which treat the diagnostic issue (Beal 1980; Bloch 1980; Federico 1979; Lazarus 1981). I hasten to add that what follows is far from the definitive statement on the subject. Much remains to be learned about the divorce decision-making process and the clinician's role therein.

As has been suggested in the foregoing discussion there are three principal diagnostic issues in the decision-making phase of divorce therapy:

1. Is the marital distress primarily a result of problems in the marital relationship or in the personal conflicts of one of the marital partners?
2. Regardless of its locus, is the movement toward divorce a positive or negative development?
3. Regardless of whether the movement toward divorce is positive or negative (from the clinician's perspective), from a practical point of view, is it too late to do anything about it?

Of the tactics for answering the first two questions the preferred one may be to simply observe the marital interaction at first hand. In the early stages of treatment the therapist may be content to do so passively.

> In the beginning, I listen to the story. As a matter of fact, I never make any interventions the first couple of sessions. I don't want to affect the process—let it come out spontaneously. I listen to him and then I ask her, how does she react to what he is saying. And then I listen to her.

In other cases the therapist may structure the interaction so as to maximize information.

> Where I think that the people are not sure about divorce I will try and test out their ability to be together by moving them together, kind of forcing them together. There are people sometimes whom you see that, every time they come close together it's like they have an allergic attack. And you really want to examine that. They can talk about it, but now you want to see it in operation. And I will sometimes do that by actually physically moving the people closer together in the room, to see if they can do it. I'll pay a lot of attention to what they pile up between them here, and talking about it. But it's the things that they do in front of me that are more important.

Friends, parents, and other relatives may also be consulted to expand the therapist's understanding.

> Often I've had people come in with their best friends. The friends have been very helpful to me. I'll get information that it would be very difficult to pick up in the confines of the four walls in which I see the person. "How are they socially? What do they do, and how do they interact? What have you noticed with the couple, and how do you and your husband socialize with them? And how does she really treat him? She tells me that she's a model mother, but what do you see?" And I get a lot of factual information that only a home visit on

> a lucky day could elicit. Of course, you set it up in such a way that they don't feel that they are betraying: I say, "You know, you could really paint a picture which will mislead me; you could really screw them up. As a loyal friend, you must understand that I really need to know the facts; then I can be helpful." I've found that I often do get information that doesn't color the person all beautiful. And it's helpful as all hell in certain cases.[1]

Beal (1980) has provided several useful criteria which should alert the clinician to the likelihood that a reactive divorce, based principally on individual conflicts within one of the partners, is in progress and to the probability that, without further therapeutic assistance a destructive divorce process will ensue. These signs all refer to the initiator's attitude toward the divorce decision. They include the belief that the problem is exclusively in the current relationship; high levels of denial about the possibility of feelings of loss, either in oneself or other members of the family; and a compulsion to "get away" or to do "what feels right," unaccompanied by any insight into self or the nature of the marriage. Beal notes that the appropriate therapeutic strategy in a case of this kind is to head off the impulse to divorce by establishing a supportive therapeutic calm and then to proceed to direct the patient's attention to the historical roots of the problem in his or her growing-up years. The goal of self-understanding is in the service of a more informed basis for divorce decision making.

To these few diagnostic hints little can be added except to say that a spirit of inquiry, patience, and a strong therapeutic alliance are imprecise but valuable components to the diagnostic endeavor. Several procedural elements may also help clarify matters. For example, it is useful to clearly describe to the client the nature of the diagnostic task, as enumerated earlier, and why an accurate answer to these questions is so crucial. The sooner this is done the better. A didactic approach also imposes a meaningful structure on the initial phase of treatment, which itself may allay anxiety and produce confidence that the clinician, at least, knows what he or she is doing—a feeling that clients often do not have about themselves and which is often a central part of their distress. The initial presentation of the diagnostic task should also reinforce the theme that the locus of divorce decision making is the client's and that the therapist's role is that of guide. Presenting the purpose of therapy to the client in this manner clearly models an important element of the guide's role—that of identifying issues that need to be addressed.

Second, individual sessions early on are usually an essential part of a thorough diagnostic assessment. It is true, of course, that joint sessions can be used to assess the extent to which a personal crisis is fueling the marital problems and it is often useful to have the other spouse hear and understand such material. However, in the initial stages of treatment, when clients and therapist are still strangers, and anxiety and defensiveness are correspondingly high, individual meetings may be more effective. Thus, an initial joint "get acquainted" meeting, followed by an individual session with each party is often the most useful way to proceed.

On occasion, the partner making the initial contact will indicate a preference for an individual session. This may be a sign that personal conflicts are the primary issue and it is usually best to accede to the client's wishes. Rarely is acceptability to the other partner compromised by such a course, assuming that the therapist makes clear the strictly diagnostic purpose of the meeting and the rationale for possible future joint sessions. In any case, insistence on joint meetings in the face of the client's continued preference for an individual meeting is very likely to undermine rapport, without which no productive intervention is possible.

Third, the diagnostic endeavor should, in my opinion, be avowedly weighted on the conservative side. This does not mean, of course, that it is the therapist's job to coerce people into staying married. It is a valid therapeutic task, however, to apprise clients of the concept of a reactive divorce; to persistently raise the possibility that the client has contributed significantly to the misery which he or she is seeking to escape; to examine with the client the likely psychic, economic, parental, and practical consequences of a divorce decision; and to keep the marital relationship in focus by combining individual sessions with joint ones. All of this may sound like simple therapeutic wisdom, but with mental health professionals writing books with such titles as *Creative Divorce* and *The Courage to Divorce,* one can no longer be sure. I hasten to add that there is most certainly a point beyond which the conservative approach is both unproductive and unethical. Most people soberly approach the task of deciding whether or not to divorce and they appreciate a sober approach on the part of the therapist. When a conservative emphasis by the therapist is not appreciated by one or both spouses, it is most likely a sign that the marriage is no longer salvageable.

It is to the last of the three diagnostic questions enumerated earlier that the most precise, although far from exhaustive answer can be given: When in doubt as to whether an irrevocable decision to divorce has been reached by one of the marital partners, look for patterns of *behavior* aimed at destroying the marital bond, regardless of whether or not such behavior is accompanied by protestations of love. To this theoretically simple but practically arduous injunction several clarifications can be given.

The patterns in question may be relatively straightforward embodiments of the decision to divorce. Thus, if one partner has begun a serious love affair; admitted the affair openly to the other; taken up residence with the paramour; consulted an attorney; and closed bank accounts as part of a legal strategm of divorce, it does not take the clinical sophistication of a Freud to surmise that the marriage is irretrievable. The significant clinical problem in such cases may be overcoming the massive denial in the noninitiator that divorce is imminent. In such instances the most useful therapeutic service may lie in reviewing in detail with this partner the last two or so years of the marriage for the inevitable signs that the relationship was far from ideal (Federico 1979).

Conversely, the inability of one or both partners to complete the legal and practical arrangements for a divorce in the absence of convincing objective obstacles suggests that the proper therapeutic role is to redirect attention to psychological and interpersonal issues within the marriage on the assumption that the point of no return has not been truly passed. Cases of this type include those in which the parties cannot conclude a separation agreement or make extremely complex and unworkable plans for custody and visitation which require constant contact with one another (Bloch 1980).

The diagnostic problem is frequently more complicated. Often only one or two steps toward divorce have been taken and the possibility is distinct that these are genuine cries for assistance in saving the marriage. In other instances there is an absence of divorce-related actions of any kind. Indeed, the mere mention of divorce may be studiously avoided by both partners. These are the kinds of cases which were most puzzling for our expert panel and they remain so. The best approach in these instances is to accept the protestations of caring at face value and begin therapeutic work on the marriage, while simultaneously paying close and unrelenting attention to the behavior of the couple, rather than to their words. In the face of repeated sabotaging of the efforts at reconciliation and the persistence of ever-increasing (or, at least, non-decreasing) hostilities, the case that the point of no return has been passed becomes more compelling and should be examined closely with the parties. As Federico (1979) notes, imperviousness to intervention is the single best indicator that at least one of the partners has consciously or unconsciously given up on the marriage.

Maintaining Impartiality Of all the strategies of intervention, maintaining impartiality was the one on which there was the greatest agreement. A therapist who has lost his or her impartiality was viewed as having made the most serious of professional blunders. The therapist must maintain impartiality both toward the spouses as individuals and toward the prospects of their divorce or continued marriage.

> You've got to remain totally open, objective, and unbiased; as soon as you start taking sides and get into an adversary situation with one party against the other, you're gone. Forget about any constructive work at that point—unless you can recognize what's happening and go back and correct it.

> If someone comes in and says, "Listen, I'm finished and I don't want to work on it; I want a divorce," then, if they want my help at that point, I will help them to make some kind of a resolution. But I don't say, "Listen, I think this marriage stinks, and you really better get out." That's a value judgment I don't bring into a session.

Impartiality is not synonymous, however, with an absence of a point of view. The therapist's commitment is to his or her conception of reality and the best interests of all concerned. In defense of this commitment the therapist may be obliged at times to differ very sharply with one or the other spouse.

> You know what I have written here of my four o'clock patient? "Document the wife's errors. She doesn't know where she went wrong." When I met with her I said: "Tell me, did you make any errors?" She couldn't see any—not one error that she made. "He's a bastard. I have been the model wife. You name an error for me."
>
> And I said, "I'm going to do better than that; I'm going to ask your husband when I see him on Friday to tell me the errors he sees, and when I meet with you we will discuss what he sees as your errors." They're in the stage of her being bitter, bewildered, angry, blaming; and that's why I'm trying to show her: "Look, you're not a saint, and he's not a bastard."

The stress on impartiality is clearly related to strategic considerations because the task of producing meaningful alterations in a relationship cannot be accomplished if either party perceives the therapist as biased. There are other characteristics of divorce work, however, that appear to accentuate the respondents' concern with impartiality—even to the extent, at times, of leading them to deny that they have goals of what should be done when, in fact, they may have them.

The emotional strain and upheaval of couples in the process of getting a divorce is one such factor. In the view of the respondents, such couples are particularly likely to want a decision as to who is "right" and who is "wrong," and cues as to whether to end the marriage.

> I think that the original goal of every couple who is on the verge of divorce and comes to a therapist is to lay blame on each other. So they come originally for you to act as a judge and tell the other guy that he was wrong and all the terrible things she's doing to me. That's their original goal—to be proven right.

The emphasis on therapist impartiality may also be a function of the respondents' highly developed awareness that they operate in an area of interpersonal conflict that, by its very nature, is apt to touch uncomfortably upon their own unresolved childhood and family conflicts.

> One of the major pitfalls in working with a couple or family is that you begin to form such strong counter-transferences that you become identified with one member of the family, or one partner of the couple. Therefore, part of my function, part of the job I do on myself, is to think very carefully about what I am doing and what kind of contract has been set up—about my own unconscious role; it becomes very important to deal with it and to think about it and to be aware of how I'm responding.

Finally, the prominence of the theme of therapist impartiality also appears related to the highly active role to which nearly every respondent subscribed.

> I am a very active therapist; I don't sit passively; I can't imagine doing family therapy passively—nondirectively.

Therapists with a highly activist stance are more likely to be impressed with the importance of "impartiality" for the simple reason that their role conception puts them at a higher risk of losing or appearing to lose it.

The therapists' tactics for guarding their impartiality toward the mates as individuals may involve explicit statements of therapeutic even-handedness.

> I've often had husbands come around and say, "Would you sign an affidavit to the effect that my wife is really unstable and I deserve to have the children?" And I point out that's not where I come in. "I'm the family agent; I'm not going to do something that's going to screw her up. You have to convince me that this is to everybody's advantage. Go to your lawyer. He'll sign affidavits. I'm not a lawyer, I'm a psychologist. I'm an agent of the family." That's the kind of thing you stress again and again.

Therapists may also safeguard their impartiality by inviting clients to openly criticize or question them. One respondent's amplification of his reasons for inviting the parties to evaluate his behavior illustrates well the close relationship between an intense concern with impartiality as well as a concern that the therapist play a very active role.

> There is an occupational disease that we all suffer from—it's called omniscience. And another occupational disease is called omnipotence. And in a case like this,

> where you're manipulating, where you're dealing with realities and angry people, and all kinds of things like that, there is the danger that you may feel you know all the answers. And that what you say ought to be done is the thing that *must* be done. And if they won't do it, then you whack them, spank them, and kick them out. I think these are very great dangers. The one is handled by careful analysis of one's own counter-transference to both parties. The second can be handled, I believe, by a great flexibility in letting the parties respond to your proposals. In other words, I could say, "It seems to me the only thing to do is thus-and-so. And I think that's what you ought to do." I rarely say that. I usually say, "Well putting A and B and C together, it seems to me as though the path to be followed is thus-and-so. What do you think?" And I state at the outset that the people sitting before me always have the right to challenge any statement that I make and ask me why I make it. And I have to present what thought process led me to that conclusion. If it's in error, as it sometimes is, they can correct it, if I allow this kind of openness. That is a counterploy to the omnipotence fantasy which we're apt to have.

The therapist's impartiality may be protected not only behaviorally—that is, by what he or she says during therapy—but also structurally—by therapist decisions about who should participate in counseling sessions. The strong preference for seeing both spouses, and the common use of co-therapy and marital groups are all, at least in part, justified on the grounds that doing so helps keep the therapist "honest."

> I try at the beginning to see people together. And while I'm doing that, I don't engage in individual sessions—unless it's by agreement by all of us. And usually, if that occurs, I will balance it off with the other one, too. I will also not get drawn into telephone communication with one person, which I think is an alliance-seeking tactic that is often used.

A respondent who works frequently in co-therapy with her husband explained her rationale:

> Working together as therapists allows each of us to make sure that somebody gets supported. It's very important. My husband reacts very badly to hostile, aggressive women, and he's going to find himself giving it to her. I, on the other hand, can soften that; I can say: "Hey, wait a minute, Fred," because I don't react that way to that kind of woman. So I say, "Mary was just attempting to get across to John the strength of her feeling on this; it really is very important to her."

The therapist's impartiality toward the issue of the couple's divorce or continued marriage is protected by making two things clear: the decision-making responsibility is the client's, not the therapist's, and the aim of treatment is the growth and well-being of each spouse as an individual.

> I can't take your burdens on my shoulders. These are your problems, not mine. I can give you a new way of looking at things, new ideas, or new suggestions about how you interact with each other, but you have to do it.

> I do not allow people to say, "We feel," and "we think," because the "we" hides differences. And I insist that each person is responsible for himself. His first obligation is to himself; then to the mate; then to the children; then to the family of origin; and lastly of all, to society, and the world.

CONTEXTUAL INTERVENTIONS

Several respondents took exception to our use of terms like "constructive," "amicable," or "civilized" divorce. To these respondents, such phrases suggest that the breaking of once deep emotional ties can be a relatively simple matter, a proposition that, as the concept of psychic divorce illustrates, contradicts clinical experience.

> A husband and wife who've had sexual intercourse and children together and smelled each other and had a lot of shared experiences—they can only separate violently and savagely. I think, in a sense, anger is a necessary part of the process. It's unrealistic when it's not. I think a friendly divorce is a little bit phony.

The therapeutic task is not to deny or circumvent anger, but to reduce the level of hostility to more manageable levels.

> The first task of a therapist is to lessen the emotional intensity, because unless you do that, you're not going to get anywhere. And I consider divorce therapy to be an extremely difficult, very tenuous kind of therapy that is always on the edge of termination. The couple, for example, can have an argument right before a session, and if one thinks that the other wants the therapy, may say, "I'm not going back to that doctor." The need to get back at the partner is more important than working things out in therapy. It is very tricky. I can never tell from one session to the next whether it's going to be the last one.

Respondents' tactics for attempting to reduce the emotional pitch were of two kinds: tactics involving direct interventions during sessions—what we have referred to previously as *behavioral* tactics—and activities involving the manipulation of the context and environment in which the couple interacts—what we have called *structural tactics.*

Reducing the Level of Emotional Tension: Behavioral Tactics A major source of tension and escalating hostility is the tendency of one or both partners to feel victimized by the other. A variety of tactics may help defuse the situation when this occurs.

CLARIFYING THE REAL SOURCE OF ANGER. The educative function of the divorce therapist is an important one. A certain amount of the anger which the spouses direct at each other is either a mask for more painful feelings (such as lowered self-esteem, grief, or anxiety), or an over-reaction to the spouse based on an unconscious distortion of the present situation. If the therapist can help clarify these matters, the heat of the marital battle may be significantly reduced.

SHIFTING THE FOCUS FROM OTHER TO SELF. If the parties continue to attack each other and make no serious efforts at self-examination, hostilities are likely to escalate. The therapist will often attempt to raise the salience of self-examination.

> The average spouse will be talking about the other: "what he did to me"—"what she did to me." And you've got to try as much as possible to refocus the individual's attitudes and feelings. "What am I doing? What am I contributing to this relationship? How am I acting? When this happens, what do I do?"—we know what they do—what do *I* do in the situation?

RELABELING BEHAVIOR. The therapeutic climate may improve if the parties modify, even slightly, their evaluations of each other's behavior.

> I try to delabel the behavior as much as possible. For instance, a guy tells me that his wife never leaves him alone, that she's constantly ready to go, and she's driving him out of his mind. I'll say something like, "What did you do to deserve such a lively lady?" I delabel the sting of the epithet—the sense that this is a terrible way to be, that she's demanding.

> When one partner reaches out, let's say, in a kindly, concerned way toward the other, and then the other sees that as an attack, I'm in there trying to clarify the way I saw it. What was there that made the other person see it in his way, when it's clear that if you look at it in terms of what was happening at the time, it was really an attempt to do something in a very positive kind of way. So I try to emphasize the healthy and respond very positively to that kind of thing happening—sort of watch for that.

FOCUSING ON SUBSTANTIVE ISSUES. The resolution of practical matters seemingly remote from the "real issue" may have an immediate calming impact on the marital dialogue. Thus, one respondent on the question of the dinner menu:

> The husband's home for dinner, and the wife has fixed spaghetti and meatballs. And if there's one thing he detests, it's spaghetti and meatballs. So he gets

triggered off and they begin to fight, and the next thing you know, there's a big conflagration. "Why has she made spaghetti and meatballs two or three nights running?" "Well, the bastard won't give me any money. I can't afford to give him steak."

When you eliminate many of the practical problems, it defuses a lot of the emotional response. I always try to eliminate the obstacles in the practical area before we get into any of the deeper dynamic aspects, because those can only be handled when you don't get interference and static from the practical problems.

REDUCING ANXIETY THROUGH BEHAVIORAL TECHNIQUES. One respondent described the use of cognitive desensitization with a man whose virulent opposition to his wife's request for a divorce was based on his jealousy of her new lover.

The idea of the other guy produced very high anxiety; so I used a simple desensitization process: Just sitting with him and getting him to picture very vividly the wife and some other guy in various acts of intimacy; having him simply relax and at the same time cognitively say, "this takes nothing away from me," until he was able to picture this with equanimity. And then he proceeded apace; he was then quite keen to go through with the divorce.

Reducing the Level of Emotional Tension: Structural Tactics Among the contextual modifications the therapist may introduce to reduce the destructive levels of hostility are modifications in the format of therapy sessions, physical separation of the parties, and regulation of the client's contact with lawyers.

MODIFYING THE FORMAT OF THERAPY: COUPLES' GROUPS. Approximately half the respondents discussed employing this procedure during some part of their work with a couple. A couples' group may inhibit destructive fighting by "embarrassing" the partners into more socially restrained behavior and make them less accusatory of one another by giving them perspective on the common stresses of marriage.

MODIFYING THE FORMAT OF THERAPY: CO-THERAPY. The value of co-therapy for protecting therapist impartiality has been noted. Impartiality is, of course, itself a means of lowering the emotional temperature. Co-therapy may also contribute to a hospitable emotional climate by making treatment less "psychiatric," thereby reducing the defensive tendency to seek judgments against the spouse. It may also provide a useful model of constructive methods for resolving differences.

For us, the whole business of modeling is very important—that my husband and I can disagree with each other; that one of us can back down gracefully. If we disagree with each other, we don't have to get into a great big fight. We don't

> have to because we allow each other to have different opinions on matters. And couples will sometimes pick this up. Also, we listen to each other.

ENFORCING PHYSICAL SEPARATION. In cases of physical assault or where verbal hostility has become so extreme that constructive problem solving is blocked, a physical separation, either in terms of the therapy sessions, the living arrangements, or both, may be suggested or even required. Respondents spoke of ordering violent husbands out of the home as a condition for continued therapy, and suggesting that a couple heavily invested in blaming each other begin by negotiating a "structured separation"—Will dating others be permitted? How often will they see each other? Will extramarital sex be permitted?—so that "they no longer can play the game 'if it weren't for you'."

REGULATING CONTACT WITH LAWYERS. Although the respondents generally viewed lawyers as a major source of destructive conflict in divorce, the implications for therapeutic intervention drawn from this belief differed widely. One conclusion was that no constructive therapeutic work can occur if lawyers are involved. The task of the therapist is to prevent such involvement.

> I try to help them see that their lawyers are doing them a terrible disservice. On the one hand, they use their lawyers as weapons; on the other hand, the lawyers foment more conflict and hostility. I might say that I do not counsel people who have already gone to the point of getting lawyers. You can't do meaningful counseling at that point because they are no longer interested in resolving problems. The lawyers say, "Listen, don't mention this, because it'll compromise your case" and once you have that kind of contamination you don't have treatment. And it's a farce to think that you can conduct any meanful counseling when you have that kind of external contamination.

Ruling lawyers out, however, was a decidedly minority preference. Several respondents prompt clients to have an initial legal consultation as an aid to decision making about the fate of the marriage. Legal consultation may also serve to reduce the level of tension and conflict by removing anxieties due to ignorance; by introducing a lawyer who is committed to a constructive, equitable divorce; and by serving as a corrective to fantasies of revenge and destruction.

> Occasionally people come in to the treatment situation with fantastic ideas about what they're going to get if the opposing spouse doesn't give in and do what they say. I don't give legal advice—so sometimes it's necessary for them to get an individual lawyer in order to determine realistically what can be done

> in the specific situation. This frequently will help the total situation, because when the individual is brought back to reality and confronted with the facts—"No, you're not going to be able to do this, and no, you're not going to get that, and you just can't hit him over the head for fifteen years because he didn't do what you wanted him to"—this sometimes makes it easier to work.

GETTING PAYMENT IN ADVANCE. One respondent noted that a very effective aid for producing a workable emotional climate was to insist on payment in advance.

> In many cases I sense right away that I'm going to have trouble with one or the other of the partners. You know what I do? The second they come in and want my services—they put a check on the table buying a certain amount of time—and my time is expensive. This guarantees continuity of their participation in the work we do.

Clarifying the Sources of Marital Dysfunction

> A couple comes in and they say: "We've been thinking about divorce but we don't know . . ." So I say, "Look, let's have a period of exploration before either of you decides to leave. When you understand yourself better and the situation better, then you're in a better position to make a decision about the fate of your marriage."

The educative function is focused on two areas: promoting understanding about current patterns of marital interaction and, particularly, each spouse's own role in destructive marital interchanges, and explicating the historical roots of the marital difficulties in terms of each spouse's own psychological development.

PROMOTING UNDERSTANDING OF CURRENT PATTERNS OF MARITAL INTERACTION. Understanding current dysfunctional patterns is facilitated by structural arrangements, such as joint sessions, marital groups, and the use of audio or video playback. The goal is to keep the couples' interactions "on display" as much as possible to encourage the development of "observing egos." For example, in a couples' group the therapist may focus attention on one couple for half an hour and then invite the others to comment on what they have seen. Video and audio playback may be used to point out particularly dysfunctional marital interactions. The couple may even be given the tape for at-home training in self-observation. Another respondent discussed arranging sessions between one spouse and the new lover in order to help the client see, in a concrete and compelling fashion, that identical patterns of interaction are occurring in the supposedly idyllic and "totally different" relationship with the new partner.

EXPLICATING THE HISTORICAL ROOTS OF THE MARITAL CONFLICT.

It's important to find out just exactly who they're getting divorced from. Often, it has to do with things still being worked out in the family of origin. For example, if a woman has a brutal, tyrannical father, she's absolutely determined that no man is ever going to push her around again. So she marries a nice, sweet, passive guy; but then when they come in for therapy later on, she can't stand his weakness and passivity. Unless she does something about her relationship with her father, she's not going to be able to make a rational choice either about this divorce or about selecting another mate.

He's the kind of guy who came in saying, "Oh, I never had any problems with my parents; I loved them all the time; they're the greatest people who ever lived." When gradually we began to scratch underneath this very hard facade, we found the fear of his parents not loving him, anger toward them, or their inability to give him what he wanted. Since he was a little boy, he has been asking for the same things that his wife was asking from him. If he never got it from his parents, he wouldn't have much of a capacity to give it.

The historical roots of marital dysfunction may be clarified by client-therapist discussions and the "lesson" taught directly via therapist interpretations:

It's rather common for me to say something like this during the course of the divorce counseling session: "Look, the problem with you"—turning to one or the other spouse— "is that you've been raised with this desire to be treated like a prince or princess, as the case may be. And you've had this incredible need to be served; and your whole trip really seems to be that of being served. And you equate that with love; you haven't quite sorted out the difference between being loved and being served. This carries over into the relationship; you feel terribly hurt whenever you are treated as an adult, because then the child in you is not being properly fulfilled." And these things may be said with a view either to saying, "So, we've got to do something about this, so that you don't screw up another marriage," or "if you do get married again, you're going to need somebody who's really going to want to pander to that and love doing so."

A minority of the respondents discussed therapy sessions with the client's family of origin as a more ambitious method for disentangling the past from the present. One respondent, in particular, placed heavy emphasis on this approach.

First of all, the mate is not present. And I don't allow talk about the marriage to go on. You know, the patient's mother and father will come in and say, "Well, I know what's wrong with our daughter; it's that son-of-a-bitch she's married to . . ." That diverts from the main purpose. The purpose is to review with the family what happened in that family while the patient was growing up. What were the nodal events? What were the alliances? Its like the traditional kind of family interview. I must tell you that, of all the things I ask clients to do, this is where there is the greatest resistance.

I do it toward the end of the therapy when I feel that people have changed and they're ready to start dealing with their family. And I do a great deal of rehearsal before they bring their family in. "What do you want to take up with your family?" And some people say, "Well, I don't have any issues with my family; that was too many years ago; I get along okay with them." "Alright let's go over the history again." And then, of course, people have thousands of issues with their family. And then they're prepared, and I turn the session over to them; they essentially run the session. I'm sort of traffic manager. They may start out: "You know, Dad, I never really felt close to you"—that kind of thing. I've had scenes right out of Arthur Miller in my office.

I find it especially important to do this in divorce therapy, but remember I said that a lot of people terminate prematurely. The family-of-origin work, I think, is the most important aspect of the work that I do.

SUBSTANTIVE INTERVENTIONS: ORCHESTRATING THE MOTIVATION TO DIVORCE

The more successful divorce—I mean, the least painful divorce—is one in which the two people are at equal points of readiness to split. I think for both partners, when one is more ready than the other, it is much more difficult. For the one there's going to be guilt for deserting the one who doesn't want to be left; for the other one there's the pain of being left. Arriving at equal readiness is one of our tasks as marital therapists; to help people time a separation in such a way that they both move to a more or less balanced point of readiness and acceptance of where they're going. So that neither one of them feels too awfully abandoned.

Orchestrating the motivation to divorce emerged in our interviews as the most distinguishing characteristic of therapeutic work with divorcing couples—and one of the most professionally delicate as well. The importance of the strategy rests on three assumptions: first, for most couples, and certainly for those seen in clinical practice, the motivation to divorce is highly ambivalent; second, in spite of mutual ambivalence, one partner typically wants out of the marriage more than the other; and third, a constructive divorce and a stable and cooperative postdivorce co-parenting relationship are highly improbable if the motivation to end the marriage is not approximately the same in both partners. Consequently, once the likelihood of divorce becomes apparent, a central task of the therapist becomes that of shoring up the motivation to divorce wherever it is weakest and strengthening it whenever it begins to flag too markedly under the stress of separating.

Orchestrating the motivation to divorce appears, at first, to be a delicate and even contradictory intervention because it conflicts directly with the professional norm of zealously guarding the clients' right to independently decide the fate of their marriage. Moreover, precise and unassailable diagnostic criteria for identifying hopeless marriages do not exist, depriving the therapist of a clear mandate to press for a divorce.

In practice, however, the professional conflicts in divorce therapy are less problematic than they appear. In the first place, the professional injunction to prevent harm to children is at least as strong as the one to encourage marital stability. To the extent that equalizing parental recognition that a divorce is inevitable (if not mutually desired) can replace marital deception and destructiveness with a modicum of parental cooperation, therapists may well justify "pushing" for divorce. Second, orchestrating the motivation to divorce does not occur in a therapeutic vacuum. It is quite clear from the interviews that the strategy occurs within the supportive confines of a trusting and collaborative therapeutic relationship. Only within this context, and after repeated and determined efforts to save the marriage, do therapists become concerned with pressing the issue of divorce. Even here, the style is empathic and respectful of the clients' right and obligation to decide their own destinies.

Finally, in my experience, the forces at work within a couple's relationship are generally far stronger than those that a therapist can marshall to redirect things. The principal value of therapeutic intervention, in my view, is not of "saving" or "ending" marriages, but of altering the forces at work just enough so that the path the couple's own dynamics and history prompts them to take is followed in as constructive and mutually beneficial a manner as possible. Thus, in my experience, if one party is determined to end a marriage there is little that either the other spouse or the therapist can do to head off dissolution; the intent becomes clear soon enough. Conversely, in the context of a sound therapeutic alliance, if a therapist tries to "orchestrate" the motivation to divorce and both partners are not truly ready or desirous of pursuing such a course, the effort will collapse of its own weight and, lo and behold, the therapist will discover that "orchestrating the motivation to divorce" was really "catalyzing recommitment to the marriage."

With these caveats in mind, six major tactics for orchestrating the motivation to divorce can be identified from our interviews: weakening attitudinal impediments to divorce; arguing in favor of divorce; disputing negative assertions about self; enforcing physical separation of the spouses; increasing marketability; and enlisting the support of family and friends.

Weakening Attitudinal Impediments to Divorce Various fears, realistic and unrealistic, may keep a couple from broaching the issue of divorce or from pursuing it steadily once it has been raised. Therapists may smooth the divorcing process by addressing these fears directly.

> There's often a lot of shame related to mothers and fathers and relatives and friends. And, dependent upon what we know about the parental situation we help them see that there are ways of getting support from their parents. If they can't get it because of the hangups of that other person, then that's the way it has to be. That doesn't change anything—"you don't die from it," is a favorite statement that I'll make. "It hurts, but you don't die from it."

One respondent discussed a sequence of steps by which he gradually shifted marital therapy to divorce therapy by attacking the underlying fears about divorce that, for different reasons, had been aroused in each partner. The following schematic account may make matters appear simpler than is the actual case. I wish primarily to focus attention on the "orchestrating" quality of the therapist's role in producing a mutual readiness to divorce:

1. Repeated efforts were made during joint sessions to solve marital problems and enhance the marriage. All such efforts were sabotaged by one or the other spouse.
2. A separate meeting with the wife was held, during which the therapist asked directly whether she had considered divorce. The therapist found that, "yes, in fact she had, and he had threatened to kill her and had actually come after her with a gun, and she was just terrified. Therefore, she put divorce out of her mind, and she felt imprisoned."
3. The therapist raised the possibility that he might be able to reduce the husband's rage at the idea of divorce and aim the therapy in that direction in a constructive, protected manner, and asked whether the wife was interested. Her response: "Definitely."
4. Separate sessions were held with the husband to uncover the source of his deep-seated rage.

> Why is he sticking around? Why is he putting up with it? And all this kind of thing. Not saying she wanted a divorce, but saying, how come *he's* never thought of divorce. Never. And it was becoming very clear to me that he would see himself deprived of the children. That was the main thing.

5. Attempts were made to reassure the husband about his parental role.

> The intervention that was really concrete and specific was my saying to him, "Look, even though the two of you may get divorced, I want you to remember one thing: you will always be the biological father of those children. No other man can possibly take your place as the father"—giving him some kind of

identity, some separation, because his feeling clearly was that the divorce spelled the end of everything.

6. Joint sessions were resumed, during which the possibility of divorce was discussed and the prospect of a continuing postdivorce alliance was used to control the husband's anxiety.

"I see the divorce is over, and you people have been able to do what few people can do, which is to have an amicable relationship as friends. And you go over to her place; you know she's married or has another guy, and it doesn't bother you. Of course that man is not the father of those children; and you're really going over there primarily to be with your kids, to pick them up, and to see her as a friend. And whatever she has going with that guy is immaterial."

7. Continued strengthening of the parental alliance by emphasizing to the husband the wife's importance as mother to their children.

Then he got into another of these death fantasies—that she would die, and he would have the children, and his mother would look after the children, and she'd raise them properly. And then we got into, "What would that really be like?" And he began to see very clearly that his mother didn't do a very good job with him and wouldn't do a very good job with his own kids—and that his wife was doing a pretty good job. That was a very important breakthrough there. And not just saying, you know, "Take my word for it," but getting him to see that this was true. I was drawing him a picture, with his wife present, of her death and what would happen to the children. And I painted this picture, which I really believed to be true, of the children crying for their mother and not being able to find a true biological substitute who had the caring that she had. The wife started crying, and so did he. It was an amazing thing. Finally he was so glad that she was alive, that it produced a great feeling in her that he wasn't going to kill her.

8. A return to separate sessions with the husband to dissipate another emotional road block to divorce—his intense jealousy of the idea of his wife with another man. This was accomplished through the desensitization procedure described earlier.

Arguing in Favor of Divorce While attacking the fears that are holding up the divorce process, the therapist may also become a subtle or not-so-subtle advocate of divorce. The most commonly described tactic for advocating divorce was an appeal to self-interest combined with an articulation of the drawbacks of the marriage.

The task was to help her get angry enough—instead of pleading—"I need you"—to recognize: "I deserve something better. Why shouldn't I be genuinely loved by a man, instead of having you, who's really wanting to be with somebody else. . . ." The task so often in marital therapy is helping people to build sufficient self-esteem so that when they're making the decision or the choice, they make it really with a greater sense of what's in their own best interests—and not out of fear. The therapist's goal was for her to recognize that, even though she at first cried bitterly and understandably about feeling so abandoned, she could come around to the view that there was plenty wrong with him; she had idealized this man to a point that he was quite unreal. Because he was not giving her all that many good things. And so her view changed from the feeling that "I'm being betrayed and abandoned" to "I don't really need you any more than you need me."

In another instance, a respondent referred to a more fanciful method for illustrating to both partners the dubious value of staying married to each other.

I used a paradoxical technique there: "Why don't the two of you decide to stick together—and make a really good job of being unhappy. I mean, up to this point the level of unhappiness has been only at the sixtieth or seventieth percentile; you could bring it up the ninetieth percentile with a little bit of effort. The two of you are so talented and so almost compatible for unhappiness that, you know, you may be able to make the *Guinness Book of World Records* as the Unhappiest Couple." I find very often that this kind of approach—when the people know I'm not being sarcastic and mean, but am clinically in tune and caring—highlights some of the ridiculous ideas that the people don't want to acknowledge.

Disputing Negative Assertions about Self

I, as a professional, know this is what is going to get in your way: You're going to say, "I failed." What can we do to combat it?

Although many respondents spoke of the importance of being supportive and caring of clients in the throes of a divorce, the nature of this therapeutic assistance was most often reflected in comments about the importance of contradicting negative self-assertions rather than in direct praise or encouragement. Depending on the source of self-doubt, the therapist may directly challenge the notion that the failure of the marriage was due exclusively to one spouse's shortcomings (the other spouse also played an important role); that one spouse's decision to leave the marriage is a reflection of the other's undesirability (both spouses had their own problems, distortions, or needs); or that ending a marriage is an admission of failure (it may be a sign of, and an opportunity for, growth).

Enforcing Physical Separation Physically separating the parties may be used as a tool for assisting in the decision to dissolve the marriage.

> Maybe the people are hanging on to each other, and yet they are obviously on the way toward divorce—or I believe that they're going toward divorce. I will suggest some movement apart that will allow them to draw back from each other—figuring that drawing back will allow them to decide either that they want to come back together, or that they really want out—instead of talking about one person leaving the house, maybe he or she *should* leave. I'm suggesting a change in the space between them. Sometimes what happens is, instead of doing that, they'll move into different rooms, for example.

Several respondents felt that once a decision to divorce has been made, joint sessions are no longer indicated since such sessions may foster unrealistic fantasies of reconciliation. Given the notion of psychic divorce as an inherently ambivalent and unstable process, such a concrete representation of the new reality was viewed as particularly desirable. (The disinclination to see the couple jointly after the divorce decision was correlated with the view that the therapist has no role to play in the mediation of the terms of divorce settlement agreements. For respondents who do see such a role for themselves, joint sessions in the postdecision phase are viewed as desirable and even necessary.)

Increasing "Marketability" A client cannot be expected to work constructively on divorce if divorce might impose a condition of poverty and social isolation. An important therapeutic task, therefore, is to assist in the development of needed work or social skills. In addition, development of such skills can facilitate withdrawal from psychological dependency on the spouse. One therapeutic technique is to make very specific suggestions:

> "Who are your friends? Do they have friends who give parties? How about a political club? How about going to church?" I'm very specific about pushing them out into the world, because if they don't get out into the world they're going to continue to feel the loss and abandonment and resentment of their spouse. When they bump against their own real world outside, the separation and loss of the spouse ceases.

Couples' groups can also provide useful positive social feedback for a client with an unrealistically low sense of his or her appeal to the opposite sex.

It may be necessary for the therapist, supportively but firmly, to put the client in touch with the apprehensions that have motivated avoidance of constructive problem solving:

> A technique that's been quite useful is a future-projection technique in which I get the person imagining that they are divorced—time is passing—and what they anticipate. And very often if they get into it, they get in touch with the loneliness, the aloneness, and so on. And then it's a matter of my saying, "What could you do to offset that? What kinds of reinforcements could you

look for—and how do you go about doing it?" And then you get a kind of a modus operandi: "Well—would I advertise in a 'Singles' newspaper? Would I go to a singles bar?" And then we begin to explore the various options.

Role-playing techniques may also be used:

I'm a great believer in all kinds of therapy, of having fire drills. . . . We do a lot of rehearsals; we'll role play party scenes and small-talk.

In some instances, however, a more blunt approach may be needed:

At one point I said to her, when she was talking about whether she should get a job, [that] she'd always delay. I said, "You've been agreeing to get a job, talking about it, doing nothing; don't come back until you get a job." She said that she was indignant. She said, "I've never heard anything like that; that's terrible." It was that sort of high-pressure tactic I was using.

Enlisting the Support of Family and Friends Ambivalence about the decision to divorce may also be lessened if the client's closest associates can be enlisted as allies.

Where a husband has left a rather dependent wife, partially as a means of controlling her, partially as a threat—if she doesn't do as he says, he's going to stay away—sometimes I utilize friends to help provide support. Immediate emergency support [is needed] for the wife, in order not to give in to the husband's threats—in order for the wife to maintain some kind of stability . . . the husband is not able, then, to come back, find the wife shattered psychologically and then take over and be twice as bad as he was before.

The Settlement Phase of Treatment: Mediating Terms

While the distinction between the decision-making, exploratory phase of divorce therapy and the settlement phase of treatment is useful for descriptive purposes, it raises a critical issue on which there was sharp disagreement: Should the therapist, in fact, play any significant role in helping arrange the terms of settlement?

Five of our respondents ruled out such a function as inconsistent with their training and the primary goal of divorce therapy—to help clients make the difficult decision to end or maintain the marriage. These respondents become involved with negotiating issues of settlement only to the extent that unacknowledged emotional conflicts in the client are viewed as blocking effective problem solving. In these instances, therapeutic efforts are needed to explore and resolve the emotional problem. In the absence of such emotional conflicts, substantive differences between the spouses were viewed as solvable without third-party assistance, except for the technical advice of lawyers. The flavor of opinion in this group may be best conveyed by some typical comments:

> People who can already decide to differentiate and separate really need very little help; I'm not a lawyer, and I can't help to decide how to separate an estate or make legal commitments for the children.

> I absolutely don't want to get involved in the financial settlements; that really doesn't concern me, unless it gets into the dynamics of the case.

Eleven of the remaining respondents, while stressing the psychodynamic aspect of their role, acknowledged that there was a place in their activities for helping couples negotiate terms of settlement. In the interviews, however, they did not detail the nature of this assistance to any great degree. Three respondents stand apart in their explicit, detailed concern with working to arrange the terms of divorce. The strategies and tactics discussed under the settlement phase rely heavily on their comments.

The reflexive strategies of establishing trust and confidence, maintaining impartiality, and accurately diagnosing the issues and forces at work, are as important in the settlement phase of divorce therapy as they are in the decision-making phase, although the specific referrents change with the changed nature of the therapeutic focus. Little, however, was said by the respondents about reflexive strategies in the settlement phase of treatment. The discussion therefore revolves around contextual and substantive interventions.

CONTEXTUAL INTERVENTIONS

Establishing a Favorable Climate for Negotiations Reducing the level of emotional tension is a fundamental strategy that underlies therapeutic intervention from beginning to end. Once direct negotiations have begun, the level of tension may rise again, stimulated by the complexities of working out an agreement as well as by the anxieties produced at the intensified prospects of psychological separation which the agreement so concretely represents. Hence, controlling the emotional climate may take on renewed salience as a therapeutic task. Many of the earlier tactics for so doing may be repeated, but this time with an eye to facilitating negotiations. Two tactics with particular relevance to the negotiating phase of therapy may be noted:

STATING NORMS OF EQUITY, REASONABLENESS, AND COOPERATION. At the commencement of serious settlement negotiations there are strong pressures on the parties to adopt a competitive strategy of trying to outsmart or outmaneuver the other. The therapist will often attempt to rechannel things along more cooperative lines.

> When they decide to get a divorce, then they get involved with lawyers for whom it is an out and out battle to do the best for their clients under a set of rules that have nothing to do with the couple's rules. That can become very bitter and nasty. I think I can help the couple to maintain a perspective on their continued relationship in the future and that there are reasons to cooperate as well as compete. I take a position: "Look, this doesn't have to be the kind of fight that ends in bitterness. It can end fairly and equitably and more or less to everybody's satisfaction."

DISCOURAGING VENGEANCE AND REVENGE SEEKING. The angry emotions re-aroused during the settlement phase may seek expression in vindictive behaviors. Here, too, the therapist may try to act as a brake by putting matters into perspective.

> I try to help people appreciate the futility of vengeance, of "I won't let him get away with this." It's often more prudent to let the other person get away with it—to see that the price you're going to pay for fighting back will be greater than any price of victory; that the victories of vengeance and retribution are often empty. So, for instance, a wife will say, "I'm not going to let him get away with paying so little. I'll fight him in court and everywhere else." "But the years of tension and litigation," I try to point out, "aren't worth what you're ultimately going to get. And even if it's granted, there's still no assurance that your husband's going to continue to pay, and they generally don't put people in jail for not paying. So know a lost cause when you see it. And stop batting your brains up against a stone wall. Just admit defeat in certain situations. It's the healthiest thing to do."

Structuring Negotiations The therapist may increase the flow and ease of negotiations by giving the couple a framework in which to conduct joint bargaining sessions. One respondent has evolved a highly structured format for this purpose. He was unique among his colleagues in this regard. The couple is provided with a detailed memorandum entitled "Factors to be Considered in Working Out Separation Agreements," which serves as a checklist of issues to be settled. The respondent described his approach in the following way:

> The procedure that I outline here is a way that I use to get them to go down the line on all the things that might be sources of contention—like considerations of property, and of support, and of maintenance; all the things that in my years of experience have come to be problems: one list for the spouse who is to be left, and the other list for the children that are going to be left with this spouse. Another consideration has to do with visitation—which often is a big hurdle, a big problem. I try to suggest different topics for them to discuss and to reach an agreement on. And then a last group of considerations concerns relinquishment of the premises—who does the leaving and when does he or she go? Also the costs: the legal fees, psychiatric fees, traveling, living expenses. These are things which cause trouble later on, after the divorce has been accomplished. I try to discuss all those things and reach agreements.
>
> I see both spouses, and they sit here and battle everything out, so that when it's all finished, when they have reached agreement on all of these points—the topics alone covering two pages of my outline—when it's all finished, I sit down at my little typewriter and I draw up a memorandum of separation, embodying all the points of agreement. And I leave room at the bottom for the husband to sign, and for the wife to sign. Now I sign it as a witness.

Mediating Between Lawyer and Client Several respondents discussed their role in helping clients choose a lawyer once the decision to get a divorce has been made. Three kinds of lawyers may be recommended, depending on the circumstances: (1) *experts,* lawyers who specialize in matrimonial law; (2) *conciliators,* lawyers who will try to arrange a settlement in the best interest of all parties and will do their best to avoid pressure tactics and protracted litigation; and (3) *tigers,* lawyers who are able and willing to protect their clients' interests if efforts at constructive, equitable negotiations break down. Such lawyers may also be required when, for reasons of guilt or low self-esteem, the client has ceased to protect his or her own interests.

> It sometimes happens that a wife is terribly, terribly hurt and she gets a lawyer who pats her cheek and says, "Look, you got enough trouble; you don't want more trouble, so let's work it out quickly and smoothly." The result is that she gets knocked on the head by the lawyer. And my job with a woman like that is to get her real angry, and to get her to want to defend her rights, and to know what her rights are in the law. And her first right is to have a lawyer who's a tiger.

Once the client has established a relationship with a lawyer, the therapist may act as a useful go-between. The therapist may help the lawyer by building up the self-esteem and psychological resources of a client so that the client is better able to participate in and withstand the rigors of divorce negotiations, or by giving the client some understanding of the lawyer's role.

The therapist may also interpret the client to the lawyer:

> Frequently I'm able to give a lawyer an insight into what's happening with a couple—where they're at, how he could perhaps support the process—because frequently they're tremendously unsophisticated and do not know what goes on between people. We're also able to help in the process of settlement; to help the lawyers see, for example, that the father would be a much better person to have the child.

> To make up an example: say I get into the whole question of money with a woman who has gone to a lawyer and wants a divorce, and it turns out that her whole family background is one of her being frightened and abandoned; they were poor and the father walked out on them and this is evoking the abandonment fears she had before. So when she tries to grab onto the husband's money, the more the lawyer knows about where this comes from the better he can help work it through with her.

Overall, however, collaboration between lawyer and therapist was mentioned infrequently, although several of the respondents indicated that they would enjoy having information about attorneys whose views were compatible with their own. Since the time of our interviews, calls for collaboration between lawyers and therapists in divorce have increased, but there is evidence that the alliance continues to be sporadic and uneasy (Sabalis and Ayers 1977; Steinberg 1980). The major difficulty appears to be the fundamental differences in training and style of the two professions.

In general, lawyers are taught to be objective, eschew emotions, and to attend to the facts, the law, and above all, to the rights and interests of their clients. Therapists operate in the realm of the emotions, of subjectivity, and of the complex interrelationships within the family. The therapeutic aim is not to "win," but to clarify. The relationship between lawyer and client is likely to be hierarchical, with the lawyer the active and controlling expert, and the client the passive consumer of advice; the therapeutic relationship is more likely to develop into a partnership of activity and control. As Hancock (1982) observes, ". . . attorneys are trained talkers and therapists are trained listeners." Differences such as these represent significant barriers to interdisciplinary cooperation, although as we shall see in chapter 5 there are interesting and important differences among attorneys of which the lay public and many mental health professionals often appear ignorant.

SUBSTANTIVE INTERVENTIONS

Making the Parties Face "Reality" Because they are undergoing an emotionally trying experience and because there are many complex matters to decide, a divorcing couple may need help in planning the terms of their divorce in a realistic manner. While permitting the husband to visit the children whenever he likes may have the appearance of a generous concession on the part of the wife, wouldn't a clearly defined visitation schedule allow her the necessary freedom to begin dating again? A man may wish to contest the financial demands of his wife, but how do the anticipated gains compare with the predictable costs?

Fights over money, in particular, may lend themselves to the forceful presentation of reality:

> I had one couple come in here, and they were going to divorce, there's no question about it. And the wife said, "Look, I need twelve hundred dollars a month and he won't give it to me." And the husband said, "But the most I can give her is six hundred dollars; that's all I can afford." Why twelve hundred? Why six hundred? And I pulled out paper, and I said, "Do you think that what you're going to offer and what you're going to get bears no relationship to reality? What is your rent? Let's put it down. What is your telephone bill? Let's put it down. How much do you use for groceries and for the butcher and the baker and so forth?"

Introducing a needed time perspective is another function the therapist may perform:

> Very often people fight like hell with lawyers about the agreement when it deals with visitation. They fight over that so hard, when actually the needs of the children at this age level will not be so important five years from now. They will have their own lives; they are going to say "no" to you on occasion. I point this out—that this is for now, that she needed this structure, but that life would change; other things would happen. She would get married. There are certain things that seem important now—and they are important, but they will change; it is temporary.

The therapist may also make the partners see the psychological facts of life with regard to their spouse:

> Well, he's a very funny fellow, and he was willing to be very generous if she would agree not to have a lawyer make the terms. He's willing to be a very generous man if he is in control. He's afraid of loss of control. So it was quite possible to help her to see that she could leave him that sense of control without being too scared that he was not going to take care of her properly; he'd take care of it for her. And he is more generous and loyal than I have been able to get him to be any time.

However important making the parties face reality may be, the ambiguous quality of therapeutic claims of impartiality is nowhere better indicated than in a consideration of the reality-orienting function. This function, it would appear, is a fairly common method—and perhaps the principal method—by which therapists may encourage substantive agreements which seem desirable to them and, at the same time, avoid the appearance of partiality. Not bias, but an accurate perception of matters as they are is the ostensible motive behind such interventions. Pointing to the "reality" involved in a complex divorce settlement, however, is not the same kind of gesture as pointing to the reality of a chair sitting in the middle of the room. It is apparent that at times, the definition of "reality" that the therapist chooses may represent an implicit but nonetheless firm value position. That therapists stress the impartial role and gloss over their more substantive interventions is ascribable, I believe, not to any generalized tendency towards deviousness or Machiavellianism, but to the considerable tactical and subjective pressures to appear impartial, as sketched earlier in this chapter.

Making Suggestions for Compromise Although this is an obvious third-party function, and one that was alluded to, there is little in the interviews detailing the role of the therapist in this regard. A more common strategy for arranging compromises was trying to work through the emotional barriers to accepting reasonable proposals, or dealing with self-critical feelings that are blocking the pursuit of a viable solution.

Protecting the Welfare of the Children The one area in which respondents were not reluctant to acknowledge having goals for settlement other than those chosen by the marital partners had to do with the interests of the children. One explanation for their lack of reticence may be that the risks of appearing biased are much lower here than in other areas where therapists might take a substantive position. Presumably, both parents love their children and want to do the best for them. A therapist can scarcely be accused of partiality by either partner if the therapist shares this concern with the parents, even if the therapist does not share their concept of what should be done.

The therapists' interventions on behalf of minor children fall into four categories: preventing the worst; mediating terms of custody and visitation; handling emotions; and promoting constructive postdivorce arrangements.

PREVENTING THE WORST. Several respondents took a very firm stance with regard to preventing children from becoming pawns in a parental battle. The list of abuses that can occur in such a case is extensive, but may include violent fighting in front of the children; demeaning of the other spouse to the children; angry and sullen handling of visitation arrangements; and the use of custody fights purely as a bargaining ploy—"I'll give up the custody battle if she'll ask for less money." "Laying down the law" was the preferred tactic for handling such excesses.

> There's a lot of talk now about child abuse, but there are a lot of other ways of abusing children without beating them—and these kids were taking a beating, in a real, psychological sense. So I laid down the law as far as I saw it—that they didn't have a right to do this to their children; that we should get on with a discussion of how to do it so that the kids aren't caught in between.

MEDIATING TERMS. Preventing the worst represents minimal standards for protecting child welfare. Most respondents who discussed their role vis à vis children attempt to do more. Fostering cooperative negotiation of custody was one. One therapist advises that this important decision be deferred until the emotional climate between the spouses has cooled down. Two respondents mentioned inviting children to therapy sessions so that their wishes with regard to custody and the frequency of visitation could be taken into account.

During negotiations the therapist may also assume the role of advocate of the present and future financial needs of the children. The therapist may suggest close postdivorce physical proximity of the parents to make it easier for children to see the noncustodial parent, and may give advice on how the moment of the physical separation of the parents can best be handled to involve minimal emotional turmoil for the children.

Our respondents did not directly address the issue of sole vs. joint custody, in part because the debate on this topic had not yet begun at the time of our interviews. A complete discussion of joint custody is beyond the scope of this chapter but it is evident that many mental health professionals have come to favor the idea as an antidote to the "I win the children/you lose them" climate associated with the traditional sole custody arrangement and as a means of promoting maximum contact between children and both of their parents (Eider 1978; Grote and Weinstein 1977; Roman and Haddad 1978). Joint custody has its detractors, however, including those who argue that it fosters loyalty conflicts in children, is unworkable except when parents are already highly cooperative with each other, exposes children to too many simultaneous adjustments in living arrangements, and fosters continuing psychological attachment between divorced parents. Unfortunately, at the present writing the arguments for and against joint custody rely more on plausability and ideology than on well-conducted research (Clingempeel and Reppucci 1982).

HANDLING EMOTIONS. Three respondents discussed conducting therapy sessions with parents and children together for purposes of dispelling in children notions of guilt about the parental break and the fantasy that the parents can be reunited through some behavior of the child. Joint sessions of this kind may also serve to de-escalate the parental battle by making vivid the turmoil and pain being inflicted on the children.

PROMOTING CONSTRUCTIVE POSTDIVORCE ARRANGEMENTS. Tactics designed to foster the postdivorce welfare of the children include such things as encouraging regular visitation, advising against the simultaneous presence of both parents during visits (to prevent fantasies of reconciliation in the child), and suggesting dating patterns that will do the least damage to the child's sensibilities.[2]

THE SETTLEMENT PHASE OF DIVORCE THERAPY AND DIVORCE MEDIATION: SOME DIFFERENCES

Many of the activities described by our respondents in the settlement phase of treatment constitute a form of divorce mediation. However, the "mediation" which they outlined has a distinctly different flavor than the mediation which has begun to mushroom since the time of our interviews and which shall occupy our attention in later chapters. The differences can be captured in the form of two related questions.

The first concerns the matter of timing: When is it best for a mediator to become involved with the disputing parties? This is an issue which has long been of concern to mediators in other forms of social conflict (Kerr 1954; Kressel 1972). The involvement of our respondents with their clients typically begins early in the divorce process, frequently even before any clear decision about divorce has been made. The "new" divorce mediation typically occurs without any antecedent involvement with the couple on the part of the mediator and focuses primarily on the negotiation of settlement issues. Both mediation with and mediation without prior involvement of the mediator have their justifications and problems, but the distinction is worth keeping in mind. The argument can certainly be made that in the absence of a thorough exploration of the manner in which the decision to divorce has been made, a keen appreciation of the couple's characteristic style of interaction, and a modification of that style where needed, the mediation of durable and creative settlements, as opposed to merely expedient ones, becomes an improbable achievement.

The second, related question concerns the degree of sophistication about marital, family, and individual dynamics which a divorce mediator should possess to be effective. As with the issue of the timing of entry, this too is a question which only empirical study can begin to answer. Let me simply record here my impression that the lack of enthusiasm that the majority of our highly experienced therapists had for mediation seems to reflect less on their inability to see a need for it than on the basic lack of appeal that divorce mediation, narrowly construed, has for well-established marital and family practitioners. For example, in the recent writings of influential clinicians there is both explicit endorsement of the value of divorce mediation, combined with very little evidence that its practical and substantive focus has much more appeal now for this type of therapist then it did at the time of our interviews. Thus, Bloch (1980), one of the leaders in the field of family therapy and, until recently, the editor of its most prestigious journal, *Family Process,* notes the value of the therapist taking an active role in discussing financial arrangements with divorcing couples for both "substantive" and "symbolic" reasons. The case illustration he gives, however, is entirely devoted to the symbolic issues—in this instance, how the couple's negotiating posture over money recapitulated the highly dysfunctional pattern of "a whiny, dependent woman, alternatively indulged and restricted by a powerful male figure" (Block 1980, 98–99). Similarly, Lazarus (1981), one of the most informative respondents in our study, has recently expanded on his views, explicitly endorsing therapist involvement in negotiations over custody, visitation, and the division of property. As with Bloch, however, the case details are entirely concerned with marital evaluation and the subsequent orchestration of the couple's motivation to divorce. A perusal of a recently published national directory of divorce mediators (Association of Family Conciliation Courts 1982) also conveys the impression that it is primarily the less well-established practitioners who list themselves among the ranks of divorce mediators.

That divorce mediation may draw most of its recruits from the less experienced in the mental health community is logical. Younger therapists are more likely than their senior colleagues to possess the economic and professional motivation to acquire the distinctive skills and wrestle with the distinctive headaches which mediation involves. Whether this trend will continue and, if it does, how serious a matter it will be for the future of divorce mediation remains to be seen. In part the answer may depend on yet another unanswered question: whether the problems posed by the mediation of divorce settlement agreements are principally in the realm of psychological and family dynamics unique to divorce or lie more in the area of acquiring problem-solving and negotiating skills of a kind similar to those needed in any form of bargaining. If the obstacles facing the divorce mediator are found to be uniquely psychological, the absence of an active and influential core of mediators with a solid grounding in traditional approaches to therapy may represent a genuine handicap for the new subspeciality.

Divorce Therapy and Divorce Settlement Negotiations

At the outset of this chapter I noted that exploratory divorce therapy, which is primarily concerned with helping couples examine the basis for divorce or continued marriage, may contribute significantly to easing the task of the parties and their attorneys in the formal settlement negotiations should a decision to divorce be reached. By way of summarizing this chapter I should like to briefly consider that proposition in more detail. My comments are necessarily speculative since empirical evidence regarding the value of divorce therapy of any kind does not exist. The few relevant studies do little more than ask persons who have received some undefined or ill-defined form of counseling during marital dissolution how they would evaluate that assistance. These assessments suggest either that therapy during divorce is likely to be perceived as helpful by most persons (Brown and Manela 1977), unhelpful by most (Albrecht and Kunz 1980), or to have but a modest probability of being experienced as helpful relative to therapy for other types of difficulties (Veroff, Kulka, and Douvan 1981). Of all the aspects of divorce in which an absence of sound data exists none is more striking than the lack of evidence on therapeutic effectiveness, since separated and divorced persons are among the most frequent consumers of mental health services (Veroff, Kulka, and Douvan 1981).

Given the robust tradition of research in other areas of marital and family therapy I am confident, however, that we shall gradually begin to have more reliable estimates of the value of divorce therapy, particularly with regard to the impact of treatment on the psychological adjustment of the parties and the relationships among them and their children after divorce. I am less certain that attention will be paid to assessing the value of exploratory divorce therapy for the negotiations over money, property, and the legal status of children. To the casual eye (especially the casual legal eye) these are matters to which the decision-making phase of treatment is only vaguely related. Theoretically, however, exploratory divorce therapy has as much to offer settlement negotiations as any other form of professional assistance, including divorce mediation. In pursuing this perspective I wish to do more than merely reiterate the view commonly held by clinicians that once the psychological problems are resolved the practical and legal ones will pretty much fall into place. I believe that there is truth in that view, but the potential of exploratory divorce therapy can be stated in terms that are more directly relevant to the very real obstacles that settlement negotiations present to the divorcing spouses and their lawyers.

Let us briefly consider the promise of exploratory divorce therapy in terms of some of the major obstacles to settlement negotiations described in chapter 2.

Reducing Levels of Ambivalence In chapter 2 I observed that ambivalence regarding the decision to divorce may well be the most serious obstacle to a constructive settlement negotiation. Perhaps the most consistent goal of exploratory divorce therapy is the reduction of such ambivalence. This is the central theme in the strategic efforts summarized under the heading "Orchestrating the Motivation to Divorce." The reduction of ambivalence about the divorce decision is also a logical effect of the therapist's efforts to instigate a thorough-going diagnostic process in which the parties are encouraged to understand the basis for their marital difficulties. Presumably, a decision to divorce based on such understanding is less likely to be charged with ambivalence than one not so informed—and the prospects for a constructive negotiation that much improved.

Attenuating Destructive Patterns of Interaction A major liability for the negotiating process are the destructive patterns of relating that divorcing couples bring to the bargaining table, either as a reflection of their longstanding difficulties with each other and/or as a result of the forces set in motion by the divorce decision-making process itself. Many of the contextual interventions of the decision-making phase of treatment are directly addressed to improving the climate of interaction and fostering in the partners a better understanding of their marital dynamics. The result for the settlement negotiations may be the difference between a hard won but durable settlement agreement or years of postdivorce strife and litigation.

Imagine, for example, a not atypical clinical picture: The couple arrives at the therapist's door with the wife having already made an unequivocal decision to divorce. The husband is opposed, but has reluctantly come to accept the inevitable. More striking to the therapist is the obvious and longstanding pattern of conflict avoidance. The wife has believed from the inception of the marriage that a woman who complains to her husband is nothing but a "bitch" and a "crab." Further, she believes that if a husband truly loved his wife he would not need to be told of her dissatisfactions but would "know" what she needs to be happy and act accordingly. The husband, on the other hand, appears a man of such brittle self-esteem that the occasional marital crises which have occurred during the marriage he has always defined exclusively in terms of his wife's problems, to which he has made no contribution and in which he can play no role—except perhaps in the passive sense of paying her psychiatric bills. She has never dreamed of correcting this belief of his directly, although her seething resentment has expressed itself covertly for years. This exquisitely dysfunctional match of marital philosophies has not only sunk the marriage, it will most certainly do the same to any divorce settlement negotiations, whether orchestrated by lawyers or mediators. For couples of this type the need for exploratory divorce therapy prior to settlement negotiations is crucial in order to introduce into the relationship a modicum of flexibility and tolerance for conflict. The paradox, of course, is that their phobic attitude toward conflict makes such couples tenuous candidates for therapy itself. If they can be persuaded to remain, however, the gain may be enormous.

Of equally profound value to the settlement negotiations may be the therapist's efforts to bring the manifest process of divorce decision making in line with the latent one. As we have seen, one prominent characteristic of the decision-making process is the frequent refusal of one or both partners to acknowledge the reality that a covert decision to divorce has been reached. The result of such denial is likely to be a series of escalating conflicts which cannot be resolved since their true source is the wish to end the marriage, not improve it. The problem with such a state of affairs is that by the time attorneys are called in the parties may have tormented each other into such a state of belligerence and despair that all prospects for a constructive negotiation are gone forever. By enabling the parties to face the reality of the divorce more quickly and with more insight, exploratory divorce therapy may do much to forstall the development of such a climate and leave the parties' trust of each other sufficiently intact to permit compromise and cooperation in the settlement negotiations.

Raising Levels of Self-esteem If the complex and personally sensitive issues involved in the settlement negotiations are to be handled with tact and flexibility neither party should feel too diminished in self-worth. A major thrust of the decision-making phase of divorce therapy is to replace self-blame with self-acceptance and the feelings of control and mastery associated with it.

Reducing Stress and Tension Negotiators experiencing high levels of stress are likely to be poor negotiators. No form of treatment can eliminate stress during the divorce process but a number of therapeutic activities may help reduce stress to more manageable levels. Since much of the stress of divorce derives from the psychological and interpersonal conflicts associated with "letting go," therapeutic success in reducing ambivalence, interrupting destructive interactions, and raising self-esteem are also modes of stress reduction. On a more concrete level, the therapist may help reduce stress by emotional supportiveness, guidance in handling practical issues, and counsel to proceed cautiously and gradually. The therapist may also help marshall external resources and support from family and friends and increase the parties' ability to reach out for such assistance.

Increasing Relative Power Typically the divorcing wife is in a less powerful economic and social position than her husband. An inbalance of this kind can be fatal to a constructive settlement negotiation. Lawyers who come to the aid of such women, for example, may find themselves engaging in acts of obstinancy or belligerence at the bargaining table which may only make things worse—and in the long run it is the client-wife, not her lawyer who will have to live with with the result. Divorce therapy cannot eliminate discrepancies in power between divorcing spouses but it can improve the balance of power by bolstering social and occupational coping wherever they are weak. Power also has psychological referents. One important aim of exploratory divorce therapy is to foster conditions in which neither spouse feels overwhelmed by the other, but in which each emerges with a sense of competence to hold his or her own.

Heightening Interpersonal Sensitivity In the previous chapter I argued that disparities in interpersonal sensitivity are likely to characterize negotiations between divorcing couples, with the husband typically less interpersonally oriented than his wife, and that such disparities may cause problems at the bargaining table. In theory, an effective course of exploratory divorce therapy should help redress this imbalance since a primary focus of treatment is to educate the parties to the psychological and interpersonal sources of their difficulties, training them, in effect, to become mutually sophisticated about interpersonal issues and cues.

Reducing ambivalence, attenuating destructive patterns of interaction, improving self-esteem, moderating stress, and equalizing the parties' power and sensitivity to one another are explicit and interrelated objectives of exploratory divorce therapy. To the extent that these objectives are met, the effects on the parties' ability to participate in the rigors of the settlement negotiations should be greatly improved, even without any specific coaching on the substance of those negotiations. The indirect benefits of treatment may also be substantial. It can be argued, for example, that the potential problems introduced by the adversary legal system and the opportunities it provides for particularly destructive forms of conflict are far less likely to occur in cases where the parties enter the legal arena with their lines of communication opened, their mutual understanding of the need for a divorce strengthened, and their ability to manage their differences with each other in a constructive manner already demonstrated. Likewise, raising self-esteem and self-confidence in the social and economic marketplace may bode well for the parties' ability to overcome the negotiating problems posed by an insufficiency of divisible resources.

Obviously, arguing that exploratory divorce therapy has as much to offer settlement negotiation as the use of skillful lawyers or mediators is not the same thing as proving it. I have argued the point partially in the hope of increasing the likelihood that the proposition will be put to an empirical test and to encourage divorcing couples and lawyers to understand more clearly the potential value of this mode of treatment.

Let us now turn to a topic whose relevance to the settlement negotiations has never been in any doubt—the role of the divorce attorney.

5

The Divorce Lawyer Elite

If divorcing persons avail themselves of any professional help it is almost certain to be provided by an attorney. Hence, lawyers are the central professional actors on the divorce stage. In spite of their central role, however, surprisingly little is known about the attitudes of attorneys toward divorce work and next to nothing is known about their actual behavior with and on behalf of the divorce client. At the time my colleagues and I began our research on professional assistance in divorce in the fall of 1975, there was but one empirical study on the subject (O'Gorman 1963) and only a few more by the time we completed our work in spring 1982 (Cavanagh and Rhode 1976; McKenny et al. 1978).

Given the skimpy empirical record a definitive statement about the lawyer's role in divorce cannot presently be written. However, it is possible to shed light on the key ways in which lawyers think about their work and the divorce client.

Our central discovery is that, unlike the divorce therapists and clergymen whom we have studied, who expressed some unanimity about their function, there are strong differences among attorneys regarding the appropriate professional role in divorce. These differences are not idiosyncratic, however. On the contrary, in two separate investigations, involving nearly one hundred attorneys, it has been possible to classify them into a small number of highly distinctive types.

The first of these investigations is described in this chapter; the second in chapter 6. Although I shall discuss methodological and other cautions regarding the types of attorneys we have identified, the data are firm enough to justify speculation as to why the lawyers differed among themselves and what these differences may mean for settlement negotiations and the quality of legal services in divorce. These matters will be considered in chapters 7 and 8.

The Study of the Elite Practitioner: The Typology Emerges

Our research began with a series of in-depth interviews with a highly elite group of divorce specialists practicing in and around New York City. The investigation paralleled that of the divorce therapists (reported in chapters 3 and 4) and was conducted during the same period, in the spring and fall of 1975. As with the therapists, we sought out expert practitioners on the assumption that in the early stages of our research they would be the most useful type of respondent to provide insight into the central issues that concerned us. These were the same general issues on which we queried the therapists: (1) What are the criteria that distinguish a "constructive" divorce from a "destructive" one? (2) What are the major obstacles to effective professional assistance? (3) What are the most important strategies and tactics of professional intervention?

We located our respondents through professional associations, personal contacts, and the referral of one respondent by another. The final sample consisted of seventeen lawyers, eight men and nine women (their names can be found in the Acknowledgments). By any standard they constitute an elite group. Their average age was fifty and all of them had many years of legal experience. Divorce constituted 90 percent or more of their practice. Nearly all of them belonged to professional associations of matrimonial lawyers and several have occupied positions of leadership in such groups. Their typical clients were middle- to upper-middle-class, married ten or more years, parents of young children, and with enough material assets and/or disagreements to require the level of expertise which the respondents represent. In sum, they were as highly experienced and influential within their fields as the divorce therapists with whom we spoke were in theirs.

With appropriate modifications to accommodate the specialized nature of legal work the interview was the same one we used with our informants in the therapeutic community. The first half of the interview involved a general inquiry concerning the topics enumerated above. The second half asked respondents to discuss in detail a case in which they felt they had been particularly successful. The interviews lasted two hours on the average and were tape-recorded for later transcription.

THE TYPOLOGY DESCRIBED

Formally, at least, the legal role in divorce is far better structured than that of either therapist or clergy. Allowing for individual differences in style and personality, we might therefore expect that the views of lawyers would show a far higher degree of consensus than would be true for the other two groups. In fact, just the opposite pattern was reflected in the interviews. While therapists and clergy occasionally differed from their colleagues on important issues, differences among the lawyers were far more common. There were three key areas in which systematic differences of opinion among the lawyers were evident: attitudes toward the client, the objectives of legal intervention, and the nature and value of collaboration with mental health professionals. A lawyer's views in one of these areas tended to be highly correlated with the views that he or she held in the other two. On the basis of these differences it proved possible to outline a set of six distinctive stances with which different groups of lawyers viewed their work.

I shall present these in ascending order from those that involve a more narrow, legalistic rationale for intervention to those which are broader and marked more by social or psychological, rather than legal concerns. (While the concept of stance is best thought of as a continuum, rather than as representing sharply defined categories, respondents fell rather clearly into one or two adjacent classifications.)

The Undertaker The analogy (supplied, incidentally, by one of our respondents) rests on two assumptions: that the job involved is essentially a thankless, messy business, and that clients are in a state of emotional "derangement." It is also characterized by a general cynicism about human nature and the pessimistic view that a good or constructive outcome is never possible in divorce, as evidenced in the following statements.

> The lawyer is the agent of the people's misery. In other words, it's very rare that you could ever get anybody what they want in divorce. You can't do it.

> There's never a good outcome. You're not solving their problem, you're just giving them relief for a very brief period of time.

It is also the only stance in which, in its more extreme manifestations, a clear derogation of the client occurs.

> I'm not interested in my client's personality; that's not my function. I knowingly represent psychotic people. All of my clients are neurotic, some of them actually psychotic. If mine aren't, the other side is.
>
> The ideal client would not be in a lawyer's office. In other words, the ideal client is somebody who is well-adjusted, able to cope with reality and with their problems, and one who can enter a relationship with a lawyer where they could be helpful. They're not the kind of people who get involved in divorces.
>
> The only time it ever works out is if a woman comes in and has a boyfriend; she wants a divorce so she can marry him and she doesn't want money from her husband and so forth. But even *that* is not a happy client because, chances are, whatever made her miserable in the first marriage will make her miserable in the second—she will marry the same guy again. Maybe a little more hair maybe a little thinner, maybe richer—but the same guy.

This last comment reflects a viewpoint that is very much in line with the beliefs of mental health professionals: that human beings tend to repeat patterns of attachment. However, whereas divorce therapists agree that the tendency to repeat past mistakes is one of the strongest arguments for marital or divorce therapy, the undertakers are dour, to put it mildly, about the value of psychological counseling. They may refer clients to psychotherapists, but the purpose is narrowly utilitarian and the expectation of benefit to the client nil.

> I put them [emotionally disturbed clients] into the hands of people who are equipped to help them—"equipped" in quotes. I mean psychiatrists, psychologists, certified social workers, all that garbage. What I try to do is shuffle them off to psychiatrists and psychologists, secure in the internal knowledge that it relieves me of a burden and, most important, a responsibility.

The undertaker's scepticism about psychotherapy appears to derive, in part, from a commitment to help the client "win" and from the practical exigencies of orchestrating a legal finale to the marriage.

> I have had clients come to see me who have admitted extramarital affairs as a result of counseling by a psychiatrist. It may be good therapy but I think the psychiatrist was totally unaware of what the ultimate impact might be.

The context in which this remark was made indicates that "the ultimate impact" to which the attorney was referring concerned the negotiations over dividing the marital assets. The husband's admission of an extramarital affair represents a handicap to securing for him the lion's share of those assets. Thus, both the adversarial objective and the pace of the legal process may be fouled by the client's involvement in therapy:

> A psychiatrist will often say to a client, "Don't take a definite step at this time. Let's wait and see." I can't wait. The case is coming up for trial, an answer is due, an offer made. I cannot go to court and say, "Supreme Court, Mrs. so-and-so is in therapy and needs time."

The Mechanic This is a pragmatic, technically-oriented stance that assumes that clients are basically capable of knowing what they want. The lawyer's task primarily involves ascertaining the legal feasibility of doing what the client wants.

> If a husband says he wants to give $25,000 a year to his wife, I don't think it's the duty of the lawyer to say to him, "you're out of your mind." I think that if a lawyer is asked, "What risk do I run in the courts?" then he has a professional responsibility to give his opinion as to what the risk is.

Like the undertaker, the mechanic tends not to call the existing legal system into question. Unlike the former, however, he is not actively disparaging of the client, but accepts the notion that "good" outcomes are possible. A good outcome lies in producing "results" for the client.

> When all is said and done one of the most important things you do is what you do as a lawyer—not as a comforter, not as a surrogate father—it's what you do professionally to get the best results.

Comments about other professionals centered around their usefulness in buttressing a case or corroborating evidence. Thus, if there are allegations that the client is alcoholic, the mechanic might seek the testimony of a doctor or psychiatrist to disprove it.

The Mediator This stance is oriented toward negotiated compromise and rational problem solving, with an emphasis on cooperation with the other side and, in particular, the other attorney. Generally, there is an appeal to the client's "better nature" or a view that what the client wants should be tempered with a sense of "what's fair." There may also be a posture of emotional neutrality or noninvolvement in response to emotional or conflicted clients:

> I may raise my voice, if yelling and screaming avoids me getting an ulcer. But I don't get emotionally involved. It's their life, not mine.

Unlike the undertaker and the mechanic, but like the three stances that follow, the mediator tends to downplay (but not deny) the adversarial aspect of his role. Only when provoked by the other side does the mediator accept the responsibility to fight:

> I think that my most important role initially is to try to keep waters calm and work out, if at all possible, a settlement with which everyone can live. Nobody's going to be happy with it, but as long as they can live and function properly I've done my job. When there is no such situation then the greatest contribution I can make is to prepare the case so that my client is in the best position in an adversary situation.

> If the man [the client's spouse] cuts off the telephone, if he changes the lock on the door, I don't talk; I get into court and get that remedied immediately. That doesn't preclude negotiations at a future date, provided it is understood that we're not going to enter into an agreement because of economic pressure.

On the other hand, mediators' commitment to negotiated compromise will occasionally result in a refusal to carry out the aggressive, conflict-oriented demands of their own clients:

> If there was a situation where I felt that the client was acting so detrimentally to his or her own best interest that I did not have the heart to continue, I would withdraw from the case. And on occasion—actually very few occasions, because I find most people in the long run turn out to be reasonable—I have said to a client, "In my opinion you're making a terrible mistake, because this is a better thing you're getting by agreement than you're ever going to get in a court fight —not to mention the anguish and expense of a court fight; and I think that under the circumstances you should probably get someone else whose heart would be more into arguing for what you're insisting on."

For the mediator a good outcome is a "fair" negotiated settlement that both parties can "live with" (a frequently quoted phrase). A primary motive in maintaining contact with other professionals is in using them as resources for de-escalating conflict:

> You can talk to the therapist and try to have the client understand that it's not necessary to proceed with the divorce on the grounds of adultery.

The Social Worker This stance centers around a concern for the client's postdivorce adjustment and overall social welfare. In the case of women clients in particular, there may be an emphasis on the "marketability" of the client:

> The main thing is to fully explore her ability to contribute to her own support. I had agreements where I have been able to get money for college or a business course. Or a course in one case in cooking.
>
> If the client is a woman, is she employable? Is she going to remarry? How is she going to live? How will this breakup of the marriage affect her future?

There may also be a tendency to keep the entire family in mind, even though the attorney represents only one of the parties:

> I think the family unit should be treated as a unit that is having an illness or problem that can be solved by the separation of the spouses; and a whole solution be worked out that would be best for each of the family members, in a cooperative venture.

The social worker may also attend to long-range plans for the children (summer camp, higher education, and the like). The social worker stance is also frequently associated with the view that, contrary to the expectations of many clients, divorce is not usually an easy solution to marital unhappiness. This perspective is shared with the undertaker, but is without rancor toward the client.

> I think most people come into the office with a storybook idea of divorce—that somehow divorce is going to solve all of their problems. It is a panacea that will suddenly make them happy. Most of them fail to take into account any of the problems involved in the divorce process.

Of the stances described thus far, the social worker is the first involving more than a perfunctory attention to the possibility of reconciliation. For undertakers, mechanics, and mediators such an inquiry is viewed as largely a waste of time, although one which the lawyer is legally and practically obliged to make. Not so for the attorneys whom we begin to describe here. For the social worker pursuing reconciliation is a muted but genuinely accepted obligation.

> I don't think divorce is a panacea. That's my own view. Sometimes I try to inculcate people with this view. I tell them what the story is and tell them to think about it a bit more and not run into it—unless of course they're in love with somebody else, which is very common.

It is in the social worker stance, too, that we encounter for the first time some enthusiasm for psychotherapy. The involvement of therapists is welcomed either before entry of the lawyer (with a view to providing a troubled family with assistance) or after the divorce as an aid to post-divorce recovery. As might be expected, a "good" outcome is perceived to be one in which the client achieves social re-integration.

The social worker stance is perhaps the most accepting of all the lawyer postures of the notion that social institutions and services for families of divorce need to be expanded:

> I don't think the State should only be involved in divorcing people. I really think the State should take an interest in trying to work out the problems facing the family unit after divorce.

The Therapist This stance involves active acceptance of the fact that the client is in a state of emotional strain and turmoil. There is a concomitant assumption that the legal aspects of a divorce situation can be adequately dealt with only if the emotional aspects are engaged by the lawyer. Correspondingly, there is an orientation toward trying to understand the client's motivation:

> I don't see that there's any difference in my work and the work of the psychiatrist or psychologist. I have to understand the individual. When the individual comes in for an interview, I think the most important part of the case is right there in the first interview. If I know how to ferret out the motivations. If I know how to ferret out the interpersonal things that are happening.

For lawyers with a therapist stance, involvement in reconciliation seems to be an aspect of the general orientation toward understanding the client's motivation:

> You may get a person who says they want a divorce and many times they really don't—they still love their husband or wife. Then it becomes a question of going back to the rapport. If you have the rapport, ultimately you'll get from them what's really on their minds.

A good outcome is conceptualized more or less as it would be in a therapeutically-oriented crisis intervention situation: personal re-integration of the client after a trying, stressful period. Predictably, this is also a stance that welcomes involvement of and collaboration with psychotherapists.

> I'm representing a young lady now who's in the care of a psychiatrist. She's got a lot of hang-ups. It's useful for me to find out what her breaking point is. I delayed for over a year before I even brought the action, because I thought it might affect her so adversely. And the psychiatrist said, "It's OK now, she's strong enough to handle it."

> A family is in therapy as the result of the rupture. There are hostilities, the children are being torn, there is difficulty on visitation. There are problems arranging for the various experiences that the children shall have, be it camp or school or something else. Now, the lawyer is meeting with the therapist who is seeing the children to ascertain the effect of all these stresses. Shall we send the kids to another camp at this time? Shall we pull them out of school and send them to visit their grandmother in Israel? Shall we have them where they are not able to communicate with either parent? You may have a situation where a husband has been having a love affair with another man and wants to get out of the marriage; there you may have a wife who is shattered by the fact. You can talk to the therapist and try to have the husband relate to this woman again, at least in so far as she and he do share the children.

The therapist stance tends to be accompanied by a strong feeling that the legal system is not adequately meeting people's psychological needs, combined with a commitment to de-escalating conflict wherever possible:

> The matrimonial laws today do not work. They are not serving the needs of people. They are hurting people.

> If I get a client with a "get even" mentality *at this point* in my practice I'm very independent about it. I tell them to leave.

I have underlined the temporal qualifier in this last remark because it hints at the tensions that may be generated in the lawyer-client relationship and the professional security that may be required to resolve those tensions for the lawyer. That the attorney may feel the need for financial independence from the client in order to work effectively is part of a much larger dilemma facing divorce lawyers which I shall explore more fully in chapter 7.

Another element in that dilemma is the tunnel vision which may be induced in the lawyer by the one-sided view of the case provided by the client. For attorneys who are committed to a cooperative, problem-solving orientation to settlement negotiations such a distorted perspective poses a serious hazard. The therapist stance is perhaps the most notable in its emphasis on strategies designed to expand the lawyer's field of vision without violating the ethical and legal obligation to avoid direct contact with the client's spouse. "Listening with the third ear" is one of those strategies:

> I'm not so interested in what you tell me. I'm interested in what you don't tell me.

There are more active approaches:

> I listen to the wife present her story. I say, "Oh, that's terrible, terrible." Then I will say: "You know, I wonder Mrs. X, if your husband had come through that door instead of you—I know from what you tell me that he's a pathological liar, a horrible person, and so on—but I'm a little interested: What are these lies he would say about you?"

The Moral Agent In this final stance there is an explicit rejection of neutrality; it is assumed that the lawyer should not hesitate to use his or her sense of "right" and "wrong":

> Oh, that's my trouble. The criticism I get from judges is that I get emotionally involved. I don't get that emotionally involved as far as the litigation is concerned; I get emotionally involved as far as what's right or wrong.

Perhaps the most striking aspect of the moral agent stance is the degree to which opposition to the client's wishes is viewed as not only legitimate, but positively mandated by the lawyer's role. The latitude that moral agents permit themselves in this respect is impressive:

> You can often talk people out of divorces or separations. While it doesn't work in every case, I think that at least the lawyer will feel he or she has done everything humanly possible to save the marriage—particularly where there are children involved.
>
> A man will often walk in feeling that his marriage is over. He took good care of her while she was with him; now his attitude is: "What's the least I can give her?" Well you've got to change his thinking; you've got to let him know that a woman has a right to be sheltered, clothed, fed, and maintained and that this continues whether he shares life with her or not.

It is in regard to the protection of children that the moral agent stance is most clearly evoked:

> Where there are children I have a duty and an obligation as an attorney to represent not only my client but to represent the child, because that child at this stage of the game does not have a representative.
>
> I try, very desperately, to get the parents to put the children into professional hands, because I am thoroughly convinced that the average parent, because of the emotional reaction to the situation, doesn't even realize that they are using the children.
>
> I think I'm successful if, in the normal run of things, after the divorce, if the child needs help he comes to me and he says he'd like his father to pay for a psychiatrist; and his mother says that maybe if I speak to his father's lawyer I can get it for him.

Whether the moral agents' level of involvement in their clients' lives is based on a sound appreciation of individual psychology and family dynamics is open to question. The interviews leave little doubt, however, that the stance includes an optimistic faith that constructive outcomes are indeed possible in divorce and that such outcomes are best defined as those which satisfy the lawyer's own sense of fair play and parental duties.

Summary

Our initial foray into the realm of the divorce lawyer turned up an unanticipated finding: the specialized divorce practitioner did not appear to be a single beast but any one of a number of distinctive types, some of whom were decidedly more psychologically minded, nonbelligerent, and "tender-hearted" than their more ferocious relatives of stereotypic fame. When the study was completed we learned that O'Gorman (1963) had made a similar discovery more than a decade earlier.

Given the small size and elite composition of our sample and the badly outdated nature of O'Gorman's pioneering work, the concept of distinctive types of divorce lawyers was an intriguing notion, but one in need of further corroboration. An invitation from an experienced lawyer colleague, Theodore Sager Meth, to work together in an advanced seminar in psychology and law at the Seton Hall Law School in the fall of 1980 provided an opportunity to subject the notion of a typology of lawyers in divorce to further study. That investigation is the subject of chapter 6.

6

Counselors vs. Advocates

Our interviews with the elite of the matrimonial bar produced the serendipitous finding that divorce lawyers are not of one piece. Lawyers of the undertaker and the therapist stances are each legally empowered to represent clients in divorce, but their respective attitudes toward the job could scarcely be more different.

The notion of distinctive styles of lawyering raised important questions in our minds about the quality of legal services and the course and outcome of settlement negotiations. We wondered if certain types of clients are more likely to choose and/or be better served by one type of lawyer than another or if there are different consequences for settlement negotiations of the pairing of lawyers with similar or contrasting styles. Before such questions could be taken seriously, however, it was necessary to verify our findings on a larger and more representative group of attorneys. To this end, members of the Family Law Section of the New Jersey State Bar Association were contacted and asked to participate in a study of the lawyer's views on divorce practice. Membership in the family law section suggests a special interest in divorce practice, but not necessarily the degree of specialization and experience that was characteristic of the elite practitioners in our first study.

We asked participating lawyers to complete a sixty-one-item questionnaire, dubbed henceforth The Lawyer Role Questionnaire (LRQ), and to submit to an interview of roughly one and a half hours. The project was conducted as part of an advanced seminar in Law and Social Science given at the Seton Hall Law School. Graduate students in psychology or third-year law students served as the interviewers.

Fewer than 5 percent of the lawyers whom we contacted refused to participate. In all, eighty-one respondents were interviewed and, of these, and additional 58 percent (n=46) returned usable questionnaires. As far as we can judge our respondents were representative of the Family Law Section membership. The vast majority were men in their thirties and forties with ten or more years legal experience and with a case load that is approximately 50 percent divorce related. Thus they were clearly practitioners with much experience in divorce work, but younger and less highly specialized, on average, than the lawyers in our first study. (Details on the selection of respondents and the sample characteristics may be found in appendix 2.)

The LRQ (reproduced in appendix 1) is a standardized effort to gather information in the several broad areas which had emerged as most salient in classifying the elite practitioners. It taps respondent attitudes on settlement objectives and obstacles; sources of satisfaction in doing divorce work; the value of collaboration with mental health professionals; and general feelings about divorce and the divorce client. Respondents were also presented with a brief description of each of the six role stances which had emerged in our earlier study (without the labels "undertaker," "mechanic," and so forth) and were asked to rate the degree to which each was similar to his or her own style of practice.

The interview surveyed the same broad areas as the LRQ but in an open-ended format. The respondents were asked what major goals or objectives they strive for in divorce cases; what the major obstacles are to achieving those objectives; and what are their major sources of gratification in doing divorce work. Finally, respondents were queried on the major ways in which the present system of divorce in New Jersey might be improved and for what kinds of couples, if any, a nonadversarial form of mediation might be useful in settlement negotiations.

Because the focus in this chapter is on the classification of lawyers into differing types I will primarily discuss the responses to the LRQ because these data permit systematic and uniform comparisons across respondents. The interviews will be used to provide information not touched on by the questionnaire and to flesh out our efforts at a descriptive typology.

General Attitudes of the Sample

Table 6.1 sets forth the most and least popular views of the sample on the major areas tapped by the LRQ. The most salient concern of the respondents was to protect children; furthering the welfare of children was both the goal of settlement endorsed more strongly and the greatest source of satisfaction in divorce work. On the whole, the respondents disassociated themselves from the view that the lawyer should be a hired legal gun out to do the client's bidding. Equity, not winning through intimidation, was the preferred objective.

The most significant problem in divorce practice was seen to be the unrealistic and divergent goals of the parties, and the highly charged

Table 6.1

Most and Least Important Attitudes of Lawyers (N=46) Toward Divorce Practice

Most Important Attitudes	*Least Important Attitudes*
Goals of Settlement (7 Items)[a]	
Protecting children (91.5, 13.7)[b]	Satisfying client's wishes, no matter what (56.6, 33.4)
Settlement both parties can live with (79.9, 21.8)	Achieving emotional adjustment for client (63.4, 33.07)
Obstacles to Settlement (14 Items)[c]	
Unrealistic client expectations about legal feasibility (4.8, 1.5)	Client's ambivalence about divorce (1.9, 1.1)
Highly charged emotional atmosphere between partners (4.8, 1.7)	Emotional strain on the lawyer (2.2, 1.8)
Differences of parties' settlement goals (4.5, 1.7)	Inadequacy of New Jersey divorce laws (2.3, 1.9)
Sources of Satisfaction (10 Items)	
Protecting children (5.8, 1.4)	Legal combat (2.9, 1.6)
Producing equitable settlements (5.5, 1.7)	Gaining insight into reasons for divorce (3.0, 1.8)
Helping in time of need (5.2, 1.8)	Learning about human psychology (3.2, 2.1)
Role of Mental Health Professionals (9 Items)	
Protecting children (5.3, 1.7)	Helping parties resolve substantive differences (3.1, 1.9)
Helping with custody disputes (5.1, 1.8)	Relieving lawyer of burden of listening to emotional problems (3.2, 2.2)

[a]The scale ran from 100, "a goal I usually strive for," to 1, "a goal I usually do *not* strive for."
[b]Numbers in parentheses represent the mean and the standard deviation, respectively.
[c]The scale ran from 1 to 7, the higher the number the greater the perceived obstacle, source of satisfaction, or usefulness.

atmosphere between them. Client ambivalence about the divorce was not seen as an obstacle, however, nor was the strain of working with distressed individuals. Although helping a person in time of need was an important source of satisfaction, on the whole, the respondents disavowed any gratification in the "softer" aspects of their work—learning about human psychology or gaining insight into the reasons for divorce.

Their attitude toward mental health professionals was fundamentally positive, but only in terms of traditional mental health roles. The least popular item among those dealing with mental health workers was the one which referred to mediation in all but name; i.e., that therapists might help the parties resolve substantive differences.

Allowing for the limitations of the fixed-alternative questionnaire format, the respondents overall portrait of themselves was of fair, but tough-minded professionals, who are oriented principally toward the protection of the innocent, the avoidance of legal warfare, and the mandates of equity. The air of firm, but sweet reasonableness gave way to something a good deal more interesting and more recognizable, however, when we turned from an analysis of average responses to a focus on individual variation.

Dimensions of Lawyer Attitudes

In order to explore variations among lawyers in the way they perceive their role in divorce the questionnaire data was subjected to a two-stage analysis. First, the responses were factor analyzed to identify the principal attitudinal dimensions being tapped by the LRQ. A cluster analysis was then performed to determine whether the attorneys could be classified into distinctive types based on their attitudinal differences.

FACTOR ANALYSIS

Four principal factors, accounting for 35 percent of the total variance on the LRQ were identified. The items that contributed most heavily to each of these factors are presented in table 6.2.[1] Generally, these four factors are highly similar to the attitudinal dimensions that were identified more impressionistically in our study of elite practitioners.

The first factor, accounting for 13 percent of the variance, we have called

Table 6.2

Illustrative Item Factor Weights on Lawyer Role Questionnaire

Items	*Factors*			
	Psychological	*Advocacy*	*Social Work*	*Client as Problem*
Goals of Settlement				
Creating cooperative postdivorce climate	.62*	.09	.19	−.22
Emotional health of client	.67*	.12	.28	−.07
Best possible financial settlement	−.39	.53*	.25	.01
Settlement both parties can live with	−.10	−.31	.47*	.30
Obstacles to Settlement				
Inherent neurotic personality of client	.08	.27	.09	.62*
Unrealistic client expectation	.23	.17	.28	.60*
Lawyers' lack of training in psychology and family dynamics	.49*	−.08	−.12	.04
Sources of Lawyer Satisfaction				
Learning about human psychology	.61*	.13	.02	.09
Challenge of legal combat	−.01	.69*	−.01	.31
Winning for client	−.09	.59*	.26	.23
Protecting welfare of children	.19	−.26	.48*	.15
Usefulness of Therapists				
Helping parties resolve substantive differences	.64*	−.18	.13	.16
Relieve lawyer of burden of listening to client's emotional problems	.12	.49*	.07	.08
Protecting welfare of family	.24	.06	.63*	−.05
Protecting welfare of children	−.01	.08	.66*	.15
Helping client achieve social integration	.16	.25	.56*	.02
Strategies and Tactics				
Giving great attention to reconciliation	.56*	−.12	.28	−.09
Adversarial relationship with opposing counsel	−.01	.48*	−.06	−.01
Telling clients when they are unfair to spouse	−.06	−.10	.44*	−.03
Carry out wishes of client, don't give own view of fairness	−.03	.03	−.47*	−.02
Attitude Toward Client				
Divorcing people least mature, unstable members of society	−.02	−.03	.04	.64*
Personal selfishness major cause of divorce	−.07	−.01	−.07	.52*

*Scores from these items were summed to obtain factor scores on the respective factors.

a *psychological factor.* It includes items which picture the lawyer in a quasi-therapeutic stance—emotionally supportive, concerned with understanding the client's psychological makeup, and focused on promoting reconciliation, the client's emotional health, and a cooperative postdivorce climate between the parties. The satisfactions of divorce work are those involving learning about human motivation as well as gratification in helping the client as a person in need. The major obstacles to settlement are also those which stress psychological issues: the lawyer's lack of training in psychology and marital dynamics and the client's emotional ambivalence about the divorce. Items favorable to formal psychological counseling do not contribute heavily to this factor, with the exception of the one item advocating a role for mental health professionals as mediators over substantive matters.

The second factor, accounting for 9 percent of the variance, we have labeled an *advocacy factor.* The items that contribute most to this factor picture the lawyer as a devoted warrior in the client's (largely financial) cause. The goal of legal assistance is to produce the best possible financial settlement, and the satisfactions of divorce work are the challenge of legal combat, winning for the client, and gaining professional recognition. An adversarial stance with the opposing attorney is thought necessary and taking a stand against the client who is being unfair to his or her children is rejected. The only heavily weighted item on this factor that concerns mental health professionals is the one that views them as useful in relieving the lawyer of the burden of listening to emotional problems.

A third factor, accounting for approximately 7 percent of the variance, we have labeled the *social work factor.* The lawyer is portrayed in this factor as an enthusiast of formal psychological counseling for a variety of purposes (with the exception of mediation) and as someone committed to equitable settlements and the protection of children, even at the cost of opposing the client's wishes when these objectives are threatened.

Finally, a *client as problem factor* accounted for 6 percent of the variance. The items in this factor attribute difficulties in divorce cases to undesirable qualities in the client, including neurotic behavior, emotional instability, unrealistic expectations, and an inability to make sound decisions. Two items that represent divorcing individuals as selfish and more emotionally unstable than most people also contribute heavily to this factor. ("Client as nuisance" might be an equally apt label for this entire set of items.)

Typology of Lawyers

In a broad sense the factor analysis confirmed that the distinctive attitudes toward the client and the lawyer's role which were salient to the divorce specialists of our first investigation were also important to the general practitioner. It was still not clear, however, whether the typology of elite attorneys was also applicable to the generalist. To address that question a statistical technique called cluster analysis was employed, using each lawyer's score on each of the four dimensions of the factor analysis as data.[2]

The cluster analysis indicated that a meaningful typology of the sample was indeed possible. The respondents could most adequately be divided into two major clusters: a group of twenty-two attorneys whom we called *advocates*, and another group of twenty-four respondents whom we called *counselors*. The differences between the two types make it apparent that the typology of our first study was no fluke. The term counselor appears to be but a broader rubric for the therapist, moral agent, and social worker stances, while the term advocate captures well the underlying spirit of the undertaker, the mechanic, and the mediator.[3]

THE COUNSELORS AND THE ADVOCATES

The counselors and advocates had contrasting views on the four principal dimensions tapped by the LRQ. The counselors were more positive in their endorsement of items describing a psychological orientation to divorce work. They were also above the sample mean on the social work/moral agent dimension. The advocates were below the sample mean on both factors. On the remaining two factors the pattern was reversed. The advocates were more enthusiastic about items portraying the lawyer as a legal combatant and the client as a source of irritation and difficulty. The counselors were below the sample mean in their endorsement of either type of item.[4]

There were statistically significant differences ($p < .05$) between counselors and advocates on fifteen of the questionnaire items. These are presented in table 6.3.[5]

Although there was considerable overlap between the two types of lawyers on all of the items, the table indicates that relative to the advocates, counselors were more concerned with producing a cooperative post-divorce climate and protecting the welfare of children; derived greater satisfaction from the opportunity which divorce work provided them to learn about human psychology; were more inclined to the view that law-

Table 6.3

Attitudinal Differences Between Counselor and Advocate Lawyers on Lawyer Role Questionnaire

	Mean Scores		
Items	*Advocates* (N=22)	*Counselors* (N=24)	*F Value*
Goals			
Best financial settlement	89.5	70.8	9.29**
Cooperative postdivorce climate	63.9	78.5	5.52*
Welfare of children	87.9	96.5	5.26*
Obstacles			
Neurotic personality of client	3.7	2.6	5.51*
Lawyers' lack of training in psychology and family dynamics	2.3	3.6	4.62*
Sources of Satisfaction			
Technical/legal challenges	5.1	3.4	8.86**
Winning for client	5.5	4.0	10.69**
Challenge of legal combat	3.8	2.3	10.55**
Learning about human psychology	2.6	3.8	4.35*
Strategies and Tactics			
Not lawyer's job to provide emotional support	3.5	2.2	8.50**
Lawyer's job to tell clients they are being unfair to children	6.1	6.8	11.68**
Strong adversary relationship with opposing lawyer necessary	2.4	1.6	5.09*
Where children involved, lawyer's job to give great attention to reconciliation	2.8	4.6	8.77**
Role of Mental Health Professionals			
Relieve lawyer of burden	4.0	2.7	4.90*
Helping parties resolve differences on substantive issues	2.1	3.8	11.23**

NOTE: The higher the number, the more important the goal, the greater the obstacle, satisfaction, endorsement of strategy, and positiveness towards an activity of mental health professionals. All scales ran from 1 to 7, with the exception of goals, for which respondents were asked to assign a number from 1 to 100.

*$p < .05$ $F(1,45) = 4.06$.

**$p < .01$ $F(1,45) = 7.23$.

yers' lack of training in psychology is an obstacle in the settlement process; and were more favorably disposed toward the idea of divorce mediation by mental health professionals. By contrast, advocates gave greater weight to achieving a superior financial settlement; enjoyed divorce work for the challenge it poses for the exercise of legal skills in the pursuit of victory for the client; felt that a principal obstacle to settlement was clients' neurotic behavior; were readier to endorse the value of an adversarial relationship with the opposing attorney; and were stronger in their rejection of responsibility for providing the client with emotional support. They were, however, enthusiastic about being relieved of this "burden" by psychotherapists.

The respondents' pattern of identification with the six lawyering styles of the elite study reinforces the impression that the counselor-advocate typology is basically a replication of those earlier results (see table 6.4). The trend on all of the items is in the predicted direction: counselors are more inclined toward the three people-oriented descriptions; advocates toward the more legal or technical ones.

The interviews conducted by our student interviewers proved to be a more difficult basis for classifying lawyers than did the LRQ. However, seventeen attorneys were identically classified by the two sources of information. Ten of these respondents were advocates, seven were counselors. They may be thought of as the purest representatives of the two types in our sample. Their remarks pungently convey the stylistic differences between the two stances.[6]

The counselors' interviews confirm an orientation toward the psychological and interpersonal side of divorce practice which contrasted sharply with the hardnosed, occasionally dyspeptic views of the advocates. All seven of the counselors referred in various ways to their interest in and acceptance of the client's emotional turmoil; the need to combine financial and practical advice with emotional support; and an interest in helping the client toward greater maturity and personal insight. To be sure, these remarks were not always couched in language of the greatest psychological

Table 6.4

Preference of Counselors and Advocates for Hypothetical Lawyer Stances

	Mean Scores		
Stance	*Advocates (N=22)*	*Counselors (N=24)*	*F Value*
Undertaker	5.8	6.1	0.38
Mechanic	3.5	5.2	14.25**
Mediator	3.6	4.2	1.28
Social Worker	4.2	3.3	3.12
Therapist	5.5	4.3	5.44*
Moral Agent	3.6	2.6	3.22

NOTE: The scale ran from 1 to 7; the lower the score, the stronger the endorsement of the description.
*$p < .05$ $F(1,45) = 4.06$.
**$p < .01$ $F(1,45) = 7.23$.

subtlety, and the tone was occasionally paternalistic, but the acceptance of a quasi-therapeutic role for the lawyer was clear.

> I'm a shrink. When people come to me with problems that are deeply rooted in emotions, such as divorce, I must bring a lifetime of understanding to be of assistance.

> Many times you feel as though you helped them directly because of your role as a mother confessor. You must listen and console them like little lost children.

> People are usually "tender" and upset when they seek a divorce attorney, so I see my role, to some extent, as that of a counselor. . . . The legal method is not necessarily the best and I try to add some counseling into my work. Lord knows they need it.

Five of the seven counselors also spoke favorably of psychotherapy and refer at least some of their divorce clients to therapists with the expectation of positive results.

The ten advocates' views contrasted sharply with those of the counselors. Of the five who touched upon the possible value of a quasi-therapeutic stance in divorce practice, two were mildly positive, although they had little to say on the subject. The other three respondents rejected any role which had even a hint of therapeutic coloring.

> I will not treat the emotional aspects at all as a matrimonial lawyer because I'm not qualified or trained to be minister, priest, rabbi, analyst, or psychiatrist. I'm trained as a matrimonial lawyer to handle the financial aspects of divorce.

Psychotherapy and psychotherapists were also unpopular. Of the four advocates who mentioned therapy, one gave it a lukewarm endorsement, while the other three were outspokenly against it.

> It is neither my responsibility nor my prerogative to attempt reconciliation or emotional counseling. Psychological counseling, whether done by myself or professionally, is of little or no value during the divorce process.

> I think psychiatrists are crazy doctors. You get ten on one side, ten on the other. What do they do for us other than charge us $500 a sheet for all this testing?

One respondent referred to the psychologists whom he has used for "testimonial" purposes as "nothing more than whores" who "can't agree on anything."

In at least two instances, advocates expressed a degree of cynicism and negativism that was absent in the interviews with counselors. One respondent, for example, gave the following response when asked to describe his greatest source of professional satisfaction:

> First, it's an interesting view of human nature, as well as what you'd call the institution of marriage and the family. It's an interesting view of the social fabric of American life, which is all bound up with one thing—M-O-N-E-Y. I'll tell you the truth, if I ever write a book on divorce I'll call it *Money.*

Another advocate expressed a constellation of opinions, including the view that divorce clients are inherently neurotic, childish, and selfish; that there are never any satisfactory outcomes or emotional rewards in divorce work; that such work is inevitably frustrating and depressing; and that to protect themselves emotionally lawyers must learn that their role is a limited one at best, for which the only outcome worth caring about is the fee.

The stereotypic view of the divorce lawyer as a hired gun was no more popular when the respondents expressed themselves freely during the interview than it was in their responses to the fixed-choice items of the questionnaire. There was, however, a clear difference in emphasis between the counselors and the advocates.

Among the five counselors who addressed themselves to the issue, efforts to "beat" the other side were viewed as having little or no place. The preferred image was of the lawyer as an agent of compromise. Of the seven advocates who commented on the merits of an adversarial stance, three expressed views more or less consonant with those of the counselors. The remaining four, however, admitted in varying degrees to a desire to "win," tempered with the recognition that nothing like total victory was possible or appropriate.

> I always consider the other person's interest, but, very frankly, from an adversary point of view, for the benefit of my client. And sometimes I selfishly look after the interests of the person I represent; not to take advantage of the other party, but to selfishly preserve my client's interest—guard it jealously. Generally my attitude is that of a strong advocate.

One advocate commented that, although he won't "go too far" because he is a "professional," he sees nothing wrong with trying to get more than is reasonable for his client if at all possible, since he is a strong believer in the adversary system.

The contrasting opinions of the two types about needed legal reforms are a further illustration of the underlying philosophical differences which separate them. Advocates complained more about the absence of consistency and predictability among judges, particularly with regard to financial matters, presumably because these judicial shortcomings complicate the lawyer's efforts to gauge the prospects for "victory" and the scope for hard bargaining. The counselors on the other hand, complained less about the bench and more about the need for ancillary psychological services. When they did complain about the judiciary it was in terms of psychological insensitivity, particularly where the interests of children were concerned.

Advocates also complained about judges' intemperance in the treatment of counsel, an issue mentioned by none of the counselors. This hints at the negative impact which the competitive orientation of the advocate may have on other parties to the settlement process. Interestingly, counselors and advocates complained with equal frequency about problems caused by undue competitiveness in the opposing counsel.

Counselors and advocates also differed in their views on the potential value of divorce mediation. The mediation model presented to them was that of a mental health professional assisting parties who also retained legal counsel. All but one of the counselors felt that mediation of some type could be worthwhile for properly motivated couples. The advocates were against the idea to a man, vociferously so in a few instances:

> [Mediation] would be an outrage as far as I'm concerned and ruin our practice. Arbitration and mediation are a blot on the escutcheon. They'll put us all out of business. As far as I'm concerned they ought to destroy all arbitrators and mediators tomorrow.

Finally one counselor saw a problem mentioned by nobody else: "Very often you yourself are an obstacle. Let's face it—there are a million ways to screw up."

Review of the Research on a Descriptive Typology of Lawyers

Our research on the counselor-advocate distinction is not without its imperfections. Perhaps the most obvious are those inherent in asking people about their work instead of watching them go about it: we cannot be sure that what we have been told corresponds to what actually occurs. There are significant obstacles to conducting observational research on lawyer-client interaction, however. These include concerns about lawyer-client privilege; the reluctance of lawyers to impose on their clients; the lack of motivation among attorneys to subject themselves to an enterprise with a high, if uncertain probability for embarrassing them and no clear likelihood of doing them much good; and the enormous gulf in style and purpose separating the social scientist from the practicing attorney.[7] I believe, however, that such problems can be intelligently and sensitively resolved, as they have been in medical and psychotherapeutic settings. Certainly, studies of lawyers at work are very badly needed. Among other things, such research would go a long way in clarifying the degree to which counselors and advocates differ in deed as they appear to do in word.

There are several additional reasons for a restrained attitude toward the findings. The total number of lawyers who participated in our two investigations is large compared with the numbers in the few previous studies; but it is still relatively small, especially since the statistical methods which we have employed yield more stable results with much larger samples.[8] It is also clear that no claims can be made that our respondents are necessarily representative of the thousands of attorneys who handle the nation's divorces each year. The LRQ is a pioneering instrument which served us reasonably well, but the relatively modest percentage of the variance in responses accounted for in the factor analysis suggests that it also is not as complete an inventory of how lawyers think about their work as one might wish.[9]

Finally, cluster analysis, which provided some of the most important evidence regarding the two lawyering styles, is still an inexact technique, with few sure guidelines to either the selection of the appropriate clustering procedure or the appropriate place at which to stop partitioning the sample (Blashfield 1980; Everitt 1974). It would strengthen support for the typology to replicate the results using an alternate clustering approach (Everitt 1974). With a larger sample this additional effort would have been justified.

These caveats notwithstanding, there are reasons for believing that our research has succeeded in identifying in a crude, but basically accurate fashion, two relatively stable and sharply contrasting approaches to legal work in divorce.

First, despite differences in method and type of practitioner, both of our investigations yielded comparable evidence in favor of the counselor-advocate typology and the attitudes underlying it. Second, the typology will come as no surprise to many practicing attorneys who have long talked of some such division in their ranks (Areen 1976; Bass and Rein 1976; Mnookin and Kornhauser 1979). This anecdotal evidence is supported by a small but gradually increasing number of research reports other than our own.

The earliest of these is by O'Gorman (1963) to whom we are indebted for the terms counselor and advocate. In the late 1950s O'Gorman classified seventy-nine New York City attorneys into these two categories based on their responses to several general questions regarding the satisfactions and frustrations of divorce work. Perhaps because of the wider range of questions which we asked, our counselors and advocates emerge more clearly on a number of issues not touched upon directly by O'Gorman, including attitudes toward mental health professionals, the client, and judicial reform. However, in major respects O'Gorman's results parallel ours. O'Gorman's counselors, like ours, were highly oriented to the interpersonal side of divorce practice and had a noncompetitive, problem-solving orientation. His advocates share with ours a desire to "win" for the client and a strong inclination to see this victory in largely financial terms.

Several more recent investigations lend further corroboration to the counselor-advocate dichotomy, at least in so far as it rests on differing preferences for cooperation or competition during the settlement process.

In the study of Connecticut divorces by Cavanagh and Rhode (1976) the researchers asked attorneys to identify "the lawyer's most important functions in an *uncontested* divorce action" (italics mine). Twenty-three percent of the ninety-nine lawyers who answered and 33 percent of the fifty-two attorneys handling more than ten divorces per year gave responses that stressed competitive advocacy as opposed to an equitable and cooperative adjustment between the parties.

These findings are echoed in a recently completed doctoral dissertation by one of my students, Allan Hochberg. Hochberg extensively queried nearly one hundred recently divorced persons, selected at random from New Jersey court records, on their settlement negotiations and their experience with lawyers (I shall return to other aspects of this study subsequently). Among their tasks, respondents were presented with several hypothetical lawyer profiles and asked to indicate how closely each fit the lawyer whom they had retained. Approximately 38 percent of the sample identified the advocate description as a highly accurate portrait of their attorney. The counselor description was rated a best fit by 53 percent of the sample.

In the only other effort to study lawyer attitudes toward legal negotiations with which I am familiar, Williams (1983) has reported data on 351 Phoenix, Arizona lawyers who were asked to consider their most recently completed case and describe the attorney on the other side using an extensive battery of rating scales. The study was not focused on divorce negotiations (although divorces were among the cases in question), but its results are highly relevant to our discussion. The data indicated that 24 percent of the attorneys being appraised by their colleagues could best be described as having a competitive approach to negotiations, while 65 percent could be clearly classified as cooperatively oriented. Eleven percent of the attorneys fell into neither pattern and shared no discernible pattern with each other.

Williams's generalized characterizations of the most highly rated attorneys of each type are strongly reminisicent of what we have been describing in the arena of divorce negotiations. Of his cooperatively oriented lawyers Williams has this to say:

> Cooperative effectives seek to facilitate agreement, they avoid use of threats, they accurately estimate the value of cases they are working on, they are sensitive to the needs of their clients, and they are willing to share information with their opponent . . . their strategy is to approach negotiation in an objective, fair, trustworthy way and to seek agreement by the open exchange of information. They are apparently as concerned with getting a settlement that is fair to both sides as they are with maximizing the outcome for their own client. (Williams 1983, 22)

He also describes the competitively oriented attorneys:

> In contrast to the friendly, trustworthy approach of cooperative effectives, effective/competitives are seen as dominating, competitive, forceful, tough, arrogant, and uncooperative. They make high opening demands, they use threats, they are willing to stretch the facts in favor of their clients' positions, they stick to their positions, and they are parsimonious with information about the case. They are concerned not only with maximizing the outcome for their client but they appear to take a gamesmanship approach to negotiation, having a principle objective of outdoing or outmaneuvering their opponent. Thus, rather than seeking an outcome that is "fair" to both sides, they want to outdo the other side; to score a clear victory. (Williams 1983, 24)[10]

The typology is lent further credibility by the wide currency which its underlying dimensions of interpersonal sensitivity vs. task orientation and cooperation vs. competition have long enjoyed in other domains of social psychological research. For example, the most prominent general theory of leadership in social psychology is built on a distinction between leaders with a high concern for good interpersonal relationships with their subordinates and those motivated more by getting the job done, whatever the costs in interpersonal terms (Fiedler 1967). In studies of bargaining, problem solving, and small group behavior a similar distinction has proven useful (Bales 1950; Blake and Mouton 1979). Over the last two decades the cooperative-competitive dimension has probably been the most central theoretical construct in research on bargaining and negotiation (Rubin and Brown 1975) and on interpersonal conflict generally (Deutsch 1973).[11]

There is one final consideration which strengthens my belief that counselors and advocates are not mere figments of the unreliable or arcane methods of social research: the typology can be systematically related to the highly problematic conditions under which divorce lawyering typically occurs. Indeed, I shall argue in the following chapter that the typology may be very plausibly understood as a mechanism of coping with just those difficulties.

7

The Conditions of Legal Work: Stress and Coping in Professional Practice

> I have often told my law students that if I were setting up a system designed to have the maximum potential to drive its practitioners bonkers I could hardly improve on the conflicting roles in divorce.
>
> —*Andrew Watson*
> *University of Michigan Law School*

I have reviewed in the preceding chapters the evidence that there are two widely held and contrasting views that attorneys have about the proper legal role in divorce. A sizeable group of lawyers ascribe to the counselor stance, the primary characteristics of which are a concern for psychological and interpersonal issues in the attorney-client relationship and a cooperative orientation to divorce settlement negotiations. Another large group of lawyers hold to the advocate philosophy. Relative to the counselors these attorneys eschew psychological and interpersonal issues, defining their role in a more exclusively technical-legal fashion. An important component of this task orientation is a competitive approach to settlement negotiations. The counselor-advocate labels do not perfectly describe everybody and lawyers of both types undoubtedly agree on a good many things. Overall, however, the categories capture a central stylistic division among practicing attorneys. To what is this division attributable?

As a social psychologist I am not completely satisfied with the most obvious answer: namely that counselors and advocates differ because they have different "personalities." In the first place, the personality explanation does not explain why these two particular lawyering styles are so prominent. Secondly, there is good evidence from psychological research that personality alone is not a particularly robust explanation for belief or behavior when it is invoked without regard to the circumstances in which people find themselves. The evidence in this regard is as clear in the area of bargaining and negotiation as anywhere else (Rubin and Brown 1975).[1]

By all accounts, the circumstances in which the divorce lawyer functions are extremely difficult. The lawyers whom we studied complained much more commonly than did the divorce therapists or clergy whom we have interviewed of the stresses inherent in their work and much more frequently expressed exasperation about the people with whom they must deal, including each other. Legal training and formal codes of legal conduct provide little guidance to the lawyer in handling the stresses of professional life. On the contrary, they appear to contribute to them in significant ways. Consequently each lawyer is obliged to solve the dilemmas of the professional role as best he or she can. I believe that the counselor-advocate typology should be understood as a response to these difficulties. The point will become clearer if we examine in detail the ambiguous and often conflict-ridden nature of the attorney's role in divorce. The principal sources of the lawyer's problems are the client and the nature of the legal system and legal training.

The Problematic Client

Surface bonhomie not withstanding, the lawyer-client relationship is likely to be rife with undercurrents of mutual wariness. Many of the tensions are directly attributable to the client's difficult psychological and financial circumstances.

The emotional instability of the typical divorce client has been detailed in chapter 2. I would simply note here that attorneys have at least a 50–50 chance of finding themselves with clients suffering from severe bouts of lowered self-esteem, impaired powers of concentration, and ambivalent feelings about reaching a settlement. In other words, from the attorney's perspective the divorce client is anything but a prize. This is pretty much what the lawyers in both our investigations told us when we asked them to rate the most significant obstacles to settlement. The emotionality of the parties or factors associated with it (such as unrealistic expectations) were most frequently cited. In our second study, "client as problem" emerged as one of the four principal dimensions of lawyer attitudes toward divorce work.

The economic plight of the average divorce client is also well known. A national survey indicates that of persons seeking the help of a lawyer, only those with criminal or employment problems earn less than the average divorce client (Curran 1977). Thus, the client will almost certainly be worried about the affordability of legal fees and the lawyer about their collectability. Between one-third and two-thirds of divorce clients appear to be seriously dissatisfied with the fees which they paid to their lawyer (Cavanagh and Rhode 1976; Curran 1977; Hochberg 1984) and there is good reason to suspect that attorneys are not too thrilled about the way in which clients uphold their end of the bargain either.[2] In reviewing the *Family Advocate*, a quarterly publication of the American Bar Association aimed primarily at divorce lawyers, I commented on the number of articles treating the matter of fees. One such piece, with the appealing title, "Setting the Tone for a Successful Relationship," was exclusively devoted to increasing the probability of client payment through a properly drafted letter of retainer (Kressel 1980). This emphasis may not be entirely misplaced. Hochberg (1984) reports that client satisfaction with lawyer services in divorce was significantly correlated with the degree to which the client felt that the lawyer had clearly set forth the basis for professional charges at the start of the relationship.

The strained financial circumstances of the client also impose real barriers to what can be accomplished on the client's behalf. Thus, attorneys may often find themselves in the unflattering position of being the bearer of bad news. We quoted one of our legal respondents to this effect in chapter 2. His comments bear repeating here:

> There are typical cases where the man makes $15,000 a year and there are three or four children and a nonworking wife. There you have complete chaos, and anybody who tried to introduce so-called "equity" would be much better off introducing money, because it's the only thing that's going to solve this insoluble problem. (Kressel et al. 1979, 251)

The position of either the therapist or clergyman is much more comfortable in this regard. Therapists can avoid the entire topic on the grounds that disputes over money are not a proper area of psychotherapeutic intervention (except insofar as unconscious, neurotic conflicts are concerned); a position which many of them take, as we have seen in chapter 4. Clergy are more often willing to address financial matters, but their role is the positive one of trying to augment resources through congregational funds over which they have control or by making a referral to a charitable agency (Weinglass, Kressel, and Deutsch 1977). It is only the lawyer, who, in the course of professional duties, is obligated to confront the client with unpleasant financial realities.

It is also worth noting that unlike the therapist or clergyman, much of the lawyer's time on a case consists of work done in the client's absence. Whatever dissatisfactions may exist on the client's part about the financial side of the settlement or the lawyer's fee may therefore be exacerbated by doubts as to the nature of the attorney's services.

Finally, divorce is basically an unhappy occasion, whose (hopefully) happy denouement is many months or years in the offing. This circumstance inevitably places rather modest limits on the degree of gratitude and fellow feeling which can be expected to develop in the lawyer-client relationship. The decrease in contact with children, for example, which is the common experience of the divorced father, is not in most cases attributable to deficiencies in the lawyer. Yet in one investigation significant dissatisfaction with the attorney was nearly universal among noncustodial fathers but rare among those awarded custody (Gersick 1979).

The Problematic Nature of the Legal System and Legal Training

The hazards posed to the attorney-client relationship by the client's difficult circumstances are significantly compounded by the nature of the legal system and the lawyer's own training. The adversarial bent of the law is the most well advertised of these problems. Although no fault statutes may have reduced the level of legal warfare (Dixon and Weitzman 1980) the parties may still contest each other over the financial terms of the settlement and the arrangements to be made for the children. Thus, the formal adversarial bias of the law, the availability of legal threats and counter threats, and the emotional agitation of the parties, may push even the most cooperatively oriented lawyer toward serious escalation of conflict.

The matter is more complicated than this, however, because the lawyer is simultaneously exposed to pressures which run counter to the official norms of zealously protecting the client's interests. For example, it is also part of the unwritten code that lawyers should play the role of mediators, resolving as much through compromise and cooperative problem solving as possible. This role description was among the more popular with our sample of New Jersey lawyers. Moreover, the lawyers' dependence on each other for the successful resolution of the case, their anticipation of future interaction once the case is completed, and their concern for their professional reputation, all represent significant collegial bonds which run counter to the adversary spirit. Indeed, the positive ties between the two lawyers may well be stronger than those between the lawyers and their respective clients.

The bonds of attachment between attorneys, as well as the attorneys' dependence on other actors in the legal system, such as judges and court personnel, have been identified by numerous writers as an important factor conditioning the lawyer-client relationship (Blumberg 1967; Carter 1983; Mnookin and Kornhauser 1979; Ross 1970). The point has been most often documented in studies of criminal justice, personal injury, or legal services to the poor. There is general agreement that these professional ties tend to work in the direction of compromise and settlement, but opinion is divided as to whether this is good or bad for the client. The negative view holds that the solo private practitioner, representing the "one shot," low-power client, tends to be co-opted—if not corrupted—by his dependence on the legal system and his own relatively low status, often at the expense of the client (Blumberg 1967; Carlin 1962; Galanter 1974). The more favorable perspective is that the lawyers' interdependence and objectivity, combined with their shared allegiance to legal standards, serve to moderate client belligerence and, in the final rendering, better serve the client's true interests.

To my knowledge there is only one study on this subject which is directly relevant to divorce. In that investigation of English lawyers, Cain (1979) observed lawyer-client interaction in seventy-seven cases. Of the four lawyers whose practice was followed, only one was prone to reject the client's objectives in favor of his own. Three of the six cases where this occurred involved divorce. Cain describes the attorney in question as more dependent on his colleagues than his clients. "He was not willing to fight matters if there was a risk of being viewed as 'unreasonable' by court officers or fellow lawyers" (p. 347). The implication is that in these instances the clients' interests were sacrificed but no direct evidence in that regard is provided.

There is also a relevant literature in social and organizational psychology which treats the dilemmas of the "boundary role" occupant, who, like the lawyer, is accountable both to those whom he represents and those with whom he must negotiate. Here, too, opinion is divided as to the effects of the chief negotiator's divided loyalties. In one view, the boundary role occupant, such as the negotiators for union and management, are described as more often than not serving as voices of moderation and informed compromise (Walton and McKersie 1965); in the other view they are portrayed as subjected to strong pressure to prove their loyalty by striking poses of belligerence and inflexibility, which may ultimately produce poor outcomes (Adams 1976).

It is clear from both the psychological literature as well as that devoted specifically to the work of lawyers, that there are many important variables which mediate the precise effects which will occur as a result of lawyer interdependence. At the moment, however, the research is insufficiently developed to allow for clear statements other than that the boundary role position is a significant component of professional stress.

This, at least, may be said of the professional dilemma of the divorce attorney: while the official code of conduct prescribes a zealous pursuit of the client's interests, the informal norms and the realities of professional life prompt compromise and cooperation. Unfortunately, clear guidelines for helping attorneys decide which path to take are nonexistent.

Two obvious determinants of the lawyer's choice are the client and the opposing attorney. Research suggests that in a good many cases the lawyer is not happy with the influence exerted by either.

In the prevailing stereotype it is the client who is likely to end up the unsuspecting victim of the lawyer's competitive zeal. Several recent investigations suggest that more often than not lawyers prefer to avoid conflict, but find themselves pressured into assuming a combative posture by their aggressive clients. The findings are as follows:

LAWYERS ARE MORE LIKELY TO BE DISCHARGED (OR TO REJECT THE CLIENT) WHEN HOSTILITY BETWEEN THE SPOUSES IS HIGH. Hochberg (1984) reports that 29 percent of his sample switched lawyers at least once during the settlement process. (Ten percent of the sample switched two or more times.) *The strongest predictor of multiple lawyer usage was high levels of reported conflict between the divorcing spouses at the beginning of settlement negotiations,* as indicated by measures of verbal aggression, physical violence, and hostility. These data suggest that when the client is in a state of war with the spouse, the lawyer may be in a state of incipient unemployment—either because the client may give the attorney the gate or because the lawyer may want to withdraw. (The data do not show how or why the lawyer-client relationship was terminated.) Conversely, clients who were most likely to report satisfaction with their lawyer and were willing to refer the lawyer to a friend, were those respondents reporting the greatest self-confidence and emotional stability during the settlement process.

LAWYERS EXPRESS CONCERN ABOUT CLIENT COMPETITIVENESS AND WELCOME CERTAIN KINDS OF HELP IN CONTROLLING IT. At heart, the generalized complaint that lawyers make about client "neurosis" may be a complaint about the inflexibility of their clients. In a study of 150 cases in Phoenix, Williams (1983) reports that lawyer-client misunderstandings were the single most important factor cited by attorneys for the breakdown of negotiations. "When the attorneys whose cases went to trial were asked why, over 50 percent said it was due to the unwillingness of one or the other of the clients to accept a settlement figure recommended by their own attorney" (p. 59).

Lawyers have also been reported notably more enthusiastic than judges about judicial pressuring of recalcitrant clients to settle in pretrial conferences (Wall, Schiller, and Ebert 1983). The list of judicial tactics about which lawyers were so enthusiastic is instructive. It included the judges' emphasizing to the client the risks of jury trial; pointing out to the client the strengths and weaknesses of the client's case; suggesting a settlement figure to the client; and speaking personally to the client to persuade the client to accept a compromise settlement. Judges may be uncomfortable about using such tactics because they may be taken as coercive and incompatible with notions of judicial restraint. Lawyers may welcome them, however, as an effective solution to their own dilemma of aggressively pursuing the client's wishes while simultaneously serving as agents of negotiated compromises.

WHEN LAWYERS PLAY AN ACTIVE ROLE IN NEGOTIATIONS IT IS OFTEN BECAUSE THE PARTIES' OWN NEGOTIATING RELATIONSHIP HAS BROKEN DOWN. It appears to be a myth that lawyers typically play the leading role in settlement negotiations. More often it is the clients who control things (see chapter 8). However, Hochberg reports that lawyer involvement was positively associated with highly problematic couple interaction. That is, couples who were most likely to rely on their attorneys in settlement negotiations were also more likely to report that during the settlement process they used coercive tactics of influence, were anxious at the thought of communicating directly with the spouse, and felt they had very significant differences with the spouse over settlement terms. There is no certain way to rule out the possibility that it was the lawyers' involvement which precipitated these problems, but the weight of the evidence suggests otherwise. It seems more likely that, in the majority of cases, the lawyers were drawn in by the spousal conflict rather than the instigators of it.[3]

CLIENTS REPORT GETTING MORE COOPERATIVE THAN COMPETITIVE TACTICAL ADVICE FROM THEIR LAWYERS. Hochberg presented his respondents, all of whom had retained a divorce lawyer, with a list of eighteen tactics a lawyer might suggest to the client during settlement negotiations. Half of these items represented competitive tactics (e.g., "protect yourself by misleading spouse as to your true position on custody or visitation, "hide as many financial assets as possible"); the other half cooperative ones (e.g., "avoid doing things that would unnecessarily irritate or provoke spouse," "try to see spouse's point of view on some issues"). The respondent was asked to indicate how frequently each tactic was suggested by the lawyer. Only 16 percent of the sample reported getting significant amounts of competitive advice from their attorney, whereas 53 percent reported moderate to high levels of cooperative advice. Spanier and Anderson (1979) report a comparably low level of attorney competitive zeal in their study of two hundred Pennsylvania divorces (a state, incidentally, still functioning under fault grounds).

CLIENT DISSATISFACTION WITH LAWYER SERVICES MAY REFLECT HIGH LEVELS OF CONFLICT IN THE SPOUSAL RELATIONSHIP. There are at least five studies that report levels of overall client satisfaction with the services of lawyers in divorce. Contrary to the prevailing stereotype, the reports indicate that the majority of divorce clients are satisfied with the assistance they have received. At least one-third, however, are strongly dissatisfied (Cavanagh and Rhode 1976; Hochberg 1984; Pearson 1983; Spanier and Anderson 1979; Spanier and Casto 1979). This percentage corresponds reasonably well to estimates of the proportion of divorce clients who enter the lawyer's office with a highly competitive orientation to the settlement process or in relationships with their spouse which are seriously deficient in problem-solving ability.[4] The correspondence between the two sets of findings suggests that, at least in regard to receiving a positive evaluation from the client, the lawyer may be more often the victim of spousal antipathies than their instigator.

I am not arguing from the preceding kinds of evidence that lawyers never or rarely play the role of self-conscious troublemakers in previously pacific spousal waters. My point is rather that the degree to which this occurs is probably seriously overestimated in the popular imagination. I also very strongly suspect that the negative reputation from which divorce lawyers suffer is well enough earned, but results from inadvertent mismanagement, rather than calculation. The roots of this mismanagement are deeply embedded in the mismatch between lawyers and clients and lawyers and their own colleagues. A good illustration of the point is provided by the case of the passive client. The lawyer's contribution to escalating hostility between the principals may lie in not challenging such passivity. The absence of a challenge may be due to lack of skill or interest, rather than to intent.

I have occasionally experienced this aspect of the unsuspecting lawyer's dilemma when listening to the accounts which my patients give of the legal advice they are getting. Thus, one woman patient very much wanted to return to part-time employment for psychological as well as financial reasons. She reported that she was advised against doing so by her attorney on the grounds that it might compromise her chances for a larger financial award should the case wind up before a judge (which, at the time, it had a very good prospect of doing). Of course, a more emotionally and financially secure wife might have made a more tractable client and eased the lawyer's task of arranging a negotiated settlement. However, like many persons in the midst of divorce, the patient's demoralized psychological state was making her a very passive contributor to the lawyer-client dialogue. I suggested to her a more vigorous exploration with her lawyer of the motives behind her desire to seek employment. She followed this suggestion and was surprised to find that her lawyer promptly withdrew his objections. I imagined him happy to do so, since her initiative relieved him of responsibility for practicing law so defensively—that is to say, competitively.

The lawyer's most valuable potential ally in managing the client is likely to be the opposing attorney. Working together the two lawyers may be able to inject enough reason and reality into the proceedings to produce a constructive negotiating climate. Alas, as the dichotomy of lawyers into counselors and advocates makes clear, in many instances such a collaboration is not possible. Stories of problems with opposing counsel were frequent in the interviews with the elite practitioners:

> If you are lucky enough to have an adversary with whom you have had experience to know that the person has the same philosophy you have, then you have very few problems; you can work out something beautifully. You're lucky if you find one who is really in complete consonance and communication with you and understands the way you want to handle the divorce. That is very rare, I want to tell you.

> Often it is the character of the lawyer you're working with which will set the stage for whether or not the issues can be resolved without bloodletting.

> I think those of us in the matrimonial field recognize that when there is a certain lawyer that you have as an adversary there will be no settlement. There just will be none. You know it; you prepare; and you recognize that this must be a Donnybrook.

When we asked New Jersey attorneys to identify the most significant problems with the legal system in regard to divorce nearly half (41 percent) complained of inappropriate behavior in opposing counsel. Of these complaints the great majority were of undue competitiveness.[5]

Another source of potential difficulty for the divorce lawyer is the lack of consensus within the profession regarding the substantive criteria for a sound settlement agreement. I have cited in chapter 2 the study of judicial opinions (White and Stone 1976) which documents the lack of agreement among experienced members of the bench on the criteria to use in fashioning judicial awards on alimony and child support. Lack of judicial predictability represents a problem for the attorney who is trying to fashion a negotiating strategy and calm the anxieties of the client. Next to excessive delays in the processing and granting of divorces, our New Jersey lawyers complained most about inadequate and unpredictable judges (67 percent of the respondents complained about court delays; 65 percent about the judiciary). The absence of consensus on the bench, however, may well mirror a similar problem among members of the bar. In one study (McKenry, Herman, and Weber 1978), when attorneys were asked if they believed that support should be continued for a child's higher education, 27 percent said "no," 36 percent said "yes, sometimes," and 32 percent said, "yes, definitely." A similar diversity of opinion was elicited regarding whether support awards should take into account the wife's earning power. Fourteen percent of the respondents felt that the wife's earning ability should not be a consideration. Informal conversations with attorneys also suggest that there is very little professional agreement regarding detailed, as opposed to broad and vague, visitation stipulations or the circumstances under which joint, as opposed to sole, custody is to be preferred. The lack of objective standards for settlement presumably opens a Pandora's box if the two attorneys and their clients should have widely differing notions of what is "fair and reasonable." One practical upshot may be vague, inadequately detailed settlement terms.[6] Another may be the professional unease of the attorneys who produce them. In the study by McKenry, Herman, and Weber, nearly half of the twenty-two lawyers interviewed felt that most clients are dissatisfied with the legal services they have received. This appears an overestimate of how badly clients actually feel, but it may say something about the lawyers' own discomfort about the services they have rendered.

The efforts of lawyers to produce viable negotiated settlements may also be impeded by the one-sided perspective forced on them by the professional rule that the lawyer deal directly with only one of the parties. This obligation is a concrete manifestation of the adversary legal philosophy which continues to surround the practice of divorce law. Our elite practitioners referred frequently to the difficulty of ascertaining the true state of affairs from the perspective provided by their client. Those attorneys with a therapist stance, as we have seen, try to do something about it within the ethical constraints imposed on them. However, even lawyers who do not care a whit for gaining a balanced perspective may be adversely affected by their lopsided vantage point when the case blows up in their face because of overzealous identification with the client's perspective.

The economics of the law office, in conjunction with the client's poor financial circumstances, may create yet another obstacle to a trusting lawyer-client relationship. The most talked about aspect of the problem is that the lawyer's fee is directly tied to the amount of "work" the case requires. This may tempt the less ethical, impecunious members of the bar to provoke conflict between the divorcing parties. In both our lawyer studies the problem was acknowledged as an infrequent, but troubling aspect of the work. (Of the twenty-two New Jersey lawyers who complained of problems with overly competitive colleagues, 38 percent attributed the difficulty primarily to attorney greed.)

Client suspicions about where the lawyer's real interests lie are not necessarily offset by the lawyer's actual handling of the case, much of which is hidden from the client anyway. In the Hochberg (1984) study, one respondent who had intentionally made very little use of his lawyer (with good results) echoed a theme commonly heard among consumers of legal services in divorce: "We were intelligent enough to work it out for ourselves. The lawyers want to make a fight so they can make more money. We felt the less we fought, the more there would be to divide."

Tensions between lawyer and client may also be engendered by the fact that the wife's legal fees are frequently paid in whole or in part by the husband. (In the Hochberg study this was true for more than one-third of the sample.) Unconscious pressures may thus be created for something less than totally effective representation of the wife's interests. The wife herself may have doubts about the degree of allegiance which she can expect from this type of arrangement.

There may be other, more subtle aspects of the "business" of running a law firm which promote covert misalliance in the lawyer-client relationship. In chapter 2, for example, I speculated that the inability of many clients to afford high legal fees may often constrain attorneys to do less than that which they feel the case optimally requires. (The data on the limited role which attorneys appear to play in settlement negotiations—

reviewed in chapter 8—are consistent with this thesis.) The tension between client need and client pocketbook can also occur for divorce therapists but there the problem may be eased considerably if the patient has insurance coverage. While such coverage is widespread for psychotherapy it is almost unheard of for legal services.

Extended, time-consuming involvement with the client may also run counter to cost-effectiveness notions, in which, for the average practitioner with a not so well-heeled clientele, greater profit may be associated with the expeditious processing of a higher volume of cases (much of which can be done by less expensive paralegal help) than by detailed attention to a few. I have seen nothing on this subject in the area of divorce law, and none of our respondents discussed the matter. However, at least two studies in the area of personal injury cases make it clear that the client's interests may be compromised because of economic and other institutional pressures on the attorney for expeditious case management (Rosenthal 1974; Ross 1970).

When all is said and done, perhaps the most grievous handicap with which lawyers must contend in the handling of divorce cases is the near total neglect of such areas as child development, family dynamics, and counseling skills in their training. Indeed, it is a common suspicion that sensitivity to psychology is positively trained out of aspiring lawyers, even those who have such an interest to start with. In divorce work this is doubly unfortunate. In the first place, as the preceding discussion has argued, the lawyer-client relationship is difficult for both parties. If the distrust and tension are to be managed, it is the lawyer who will have to set the tone and take the lead. Without rudimentary training in the skills of empathic listening and effective communication, many attorneys are ill prepared to do so.

Second, relatively few of the issues that arise in a divorce settlement negotiation are legal issues in the strict sense. Moreover, even many legal and financial issues are as likely to engage psychological expertise or personal values (e.g., custody or visitation arrangements that would best meet the emotional needs of children and parents), rather than established legal doctrine.

To put it simply, in major areas of their activity with and on behalf of the divorce client lawyers are operating outside the domain of law and legal training. There are indications that many lawyers are aware of this and discomfited by it.[7] One highly expert practitioner in our first study noted plaintively that although lawyers are described as Counselors at Law, their training is almost entirely in law and not at all in counseling.

Summary

The role of the divorce lawyer is unenviable in many ways: the unhappy emotional and financial circumstances of their clients introduce significant tensions in the lawyer-client relationship; the adversary nature of the legal system pushes lawyers toward tactics of competitive conflict, while the informal norms and ties to their colleagues introduce strong counter-pressures to adopt a more cooperative stance. Unfortunately, choosing between these starkly contrasting alternatives must be done in the absence of clear professional guidelines. The attempts of lawyers to predict how the dynamics of the marital relationship will affect the proceedings over which they are nominally in charge are hampered by the one-sided source of the information available to them and by their own psychological naivety. Finally, the ability of attorneys to orchestrate the settlement negotiations is hobbled by the lack of consensus within the profession on substantive criteria of settlement and by the probability that each lawyer will be matched with either a client or another attorney—or both—whose views are quite different than their own and with whom it may be difficult to work. Besides this quagmire of professional tension and uncertainty the frustrations and headaches of the divorce therapists and the ministering clergy appear humdrum indeed.

In the jargon of the social sciences the description is that of very high degrees of occupational role strain (Komarovsky 1976; Sell, Brief, and Schuler 1981). The potential for role strain to cause distress and alienation has been extensively documented in professional and managerial settings (Kahn 1980; Sell, Brief, and Schuler 1981). There is every reason to believe that the motivation to cope effectively with such tension is correspondingly high.

Although social scientists have conducted much research on the nature and extent of role strain, there are relatively few studies on mechanisms of coping with it. Those of which I am aware are stated in terms of discrete tactics of coping rather than in terms of encompassing styles of belief and behavior. Thus, in their study of union and management negotiators, Walton and McKersie (1965) articulate a variety of tactics by which the pressures emanating from the conflicting demands of constituents and the opposing negotiator are managed (e.g., persuading the constituents to revise their expectations, obscuring or misrepresenting the failure to achieve constituent objectives). Sell, Brief, and Schuler (1981) provide a useful summary of the general literature on the effects of role strain and the few studies which have investigated adaptive mechanisms.

The counselor-advocate continuum along which lawyers divide is most aptly viewed as one such adaptive mechanism. Although the adoption of one or the other stance is certainly the product of each lawyer's own experience, personality, and judgement, the principal dimensions along which the two role definitions are constructed correspond closely to the nature of the professional dilemma which all lawyers face in cases of divorce. In regard to the client the problem may be broadly stated as whether or not attorneys should openly confront the various psychological and interpersonal issues which threaten the working alliance. With regard to the opposing attorney the dilemma is whether or not to incorporate into one's professional identity the strong, but officially unsanctioned pressures to work cooperatively with the official "adversary." The counselor and advocate stances provide answers, albeit very different answers, to each of these questions. Moreover, each of these answers is readily defensible in terms of important aspects of the work and of legal tradition. The counselor solution attempts to resolve the problems of the role through a more open recognition of the extent to which professional realities depart from official doctrine; the advocate solution opts for a stricter adherence to what has been taught and codified. Whatever other consequences may be involved, the adoption of either stance provides lawyers with a buffer against the contradictions of their job and a rationale for managing the client and the opposing attorney.[8] We turn now to the consequences of that choice for the course and outcome of the settlement negotiations.

8

Counselors, Advocates, and the Quality of Legal Services in Divorce

The Advantages of the Counselor Stance

What is the practical significance of the typology of divorce lawyers? All things being equal, is the divorce client better off retaining a lawyer who is a counselor or one who is an advocate? This is a deceptively easy question, behind which lurk real complexities. It may be useful, however, to begin with a simple answer before proceeding to the necessary qualifications.

The simple answer is that, all things being equal, in the handling of divorce cases counselors are to be preferred to advocates. This, of course, is a probability statement, not an argument that counselors have no defects and advocates no virtues. The impulse to cooperate, in the absence of a realistic appraisal of the client's circumstances and the other party's motivation, can result in victimization; advocacy, on the other hand, may produce superior results for all concerned if advocacy is defined as firm adherence to one's ultimate objectives but flexibility with regard to means. The most notable proponent of this viewpoint among students of bargaining and negotiation is Pruitt (1981). He provides evidence in a number of experimental studies, that "cooperation" in the guise of a too ready willingness to compromise can prevent a truly superior settlement, whereas "competitive" tactics, in the form of a stubborn adherence to relatively high aspirations combined with flexibility regarding means, can work to everybody's advantage. In the Williams (1983) study of Phoenix attorneys, neither cooperative nor competitive lawyers had a monopoly on success; both were included among the ranks of effective negotiators and both types had many traits in common (such as perceptiveness, poise, and analytic ability).[1] The weight of the evidence, however, clearly favors counselors. The advantages of the counselor stance occur on both of the axes from which our typology of lawyers is constructed.

With regard to interpersonal sensitivity, there is much evidence that it facilitates effective professional assistance. Research on the physician-patient and psychotherapist-patient relationships, for example, corroborates the notion that interpersonal skills on the part of the professional are crucial to the establishment and maintenance of rapport, without which technical competence alone is insufficient. Thus, physicians who elicit the greatest cooperation and compliance from their patients are those who are warm, friendly, and interested in the patient (Stone 1979). Patients are also more likely to comply with their doctor's orders when they believe that they are valued and accepted by the physician rather than when there is an atmosphere of rejection or antagonism (Korsch, Gozzi, and Francis 1968) or when the patient's symptoms are viewed in isolation from the whole person (Mentzer and Snyder 1982).

Ironically, it is in the area of psychotherapy, where the value of interpersonal sensitivity was first touted so highly (Rogers 1957), that the most empirical evidence has been generated, demonstrating that interpersonal sensitivity is not as potent in its ability to produce change in patients as was once thought (Parloff, Waskow, and Wolfe 1978). Nonetheless, there is still ample reason to believe that while genuineness, empathy, and positive regard are not sufficient to produce therapeutic progress, they go a long way toward making it possible. (See also Grunebaum's [1983] report that warmth and caring are the characteristics most sought by experienced psychotherapists in choosing their own therapist.)

Certainly the interpersonal and psychological sensibilities of the counselor appear better suited to the conditions of divorce work than the more technical and legal preoccupations of the dedicated advocate. This is so because the client is likely to be emotionally hurting, and therefore more in need of a supportive touch. Also, in the typical case, the legal and technical issues are subordinate to the psychological tensions that interfere with constructive problem solving between the parties and create obstacles to a collaborative lawyer-client relationship. As I have suggested in the preceding chapter, these tensions do not exist solely because of the client's emotional and economic misery. They also reflect the inhospitable circumstances created by the legal system and abetted by legal training.

There is no unequivocal proof that counselors do a better job than advocates in overcoming these obstacles to establish a sense of cohesion and fellow feeling with their clients, but the evidence is suggestive. O'Gorman (1963) found that "people-oriented" lawyers, 80 percent of whom were counselors, were much more likely to say that they enjoyed divorce work than "problem-oriented" or "money-oriented" attorneys, who were predominantly advocates. Presumably, greater liking for the work both reflects and produces greater closeness between lawyers and clients. In our own studies, lawyer antipathy toward the client was more often expressed by advocates than counselors. Although there is no certain way of knowing the degree to which these feelings are communicated to clients, Hochberg (1984), in the only direct evidence on the impact of lawyer stance on client attitudes, reports that clients who rated their attorneys more like counselors than like advocates were also significantly more likely to be satisfied with the legal fees which they paid, with the settlement agreement, and with their postdivorce lives generally.

On the cooperative vs. competitive axis the advantage belongs even more clearly to the counselors. In chapter 2 I have reviewed the extensive evidence which indicates that cooperatively motivated parties experience more pleasurable and rewarding interactions than those who are competitively motivated. In the overwhelming majority of studies which document this effect, cooperative or competitive intent has been created by experimental manipulation (e.g., by telling the research subjects either to be concerned with the other's welfare or to attempt to "beat" the other) rather than reflecting the participants' pre-existing inclinations. However, there are a number of investigations in which the predisposition to behave cooperatively has been shown to have the same advantages over a competitive disposition as are found when cooperation and competition are artificially created (Benton et al. 1969; Cohen 1982; Kelley and Stahleski 1970a, 1970b; McNeel 1973).[2]

The limited evidence from the legal sphere is consistent with the research from the experimental laboratory. In our sample of New Jersey attorneys, peer ratings of the highest competence (taken from the *Martindale-Hubbell Law Directory*) were received only by counselors. (However, ratings were available on only one-third of the sample and the finding was not statistically significant.)

Williams (1983) reports much more extensive evidence on the matter in his study of 350 Phoenix attorneys. Although, as I have just noted, Williams found that both cooperative and competitive attorneys were among those judged highly competent by their peers, 58 percent of the cooperatively-oriented lawyers were rated effective, compared to only 25 percent of the competitive types; only 3 percent of the cooperatives were rated as ineffective compared to a whopping 33 percent of the competitively-oriented attorneys (Williams 1983, 19).

The disadvantages of a competitive stance are also suggested by data on impasses in negotiations. Among attorneys judged as effective negotiators, effective cooperators obtained a settlement in 84 percent of their cases and went to trial with the remaining 16 percent. In contrast, effective competitives settled only 67 percent of their cases and experienced a negotiation breakdown and trial in 33 percent. Williams observes that going to trial is not necessarily bad for the client's case, but notes the high costs involved and the possibility that clients whose cases go to trial may be subsidizing clients whose cases are settled (Williams 1983, 51). Since this was a study of general legal practice it may well underestimate the relative superiority of a cooperative style in divorce negotiations. In divorce, judicial intervention is usually viewed as far less desirable than a negotiated agreement because of the severe emotional and financial costs associated with a trial and the ravaged co-parenting relationship which is often its most enduring memento.

The Modest Role of Lawyer Stance in Determining the Client's Fate

Having made the case for the importance of lawyer role conception, it is important to consider its limitations as an explanatory construct. There are a variety of reasons for so doing.

In the first place, the direct evidence from legal practice on the influence of lawyers is still quite modest, and none of it is based on direct observation of the transactions between lawyers and clients. It is impossible to say, therefore, what transmutations occur in lawyer role orientation in the hurly burly of the settlement process. Lawyer "type" may change radically in the presence of others—clients who are more or less tolerant of a particular stance; judges who penalize (or benefit) attorneys who take one stance rather than the other; and even other attorneys who project acceptance/rejection depending on the stance taken. As I have noted earlier, in spite of the significant legal and methodological problems involved, it is crucially important that we begin to observe the behavior of lawyers at work in order to form some estimate of the relationship between legal attitudes and legal practice.[3]

The importance of lawyer stance is also a function of the degree to which lawyers are involved in the settlement process. The conventional wisdom (along with legal vanity, perhaps) has it that the vast majority of divorce agreements are negotiated by the two attorneys, while the distraught and bewildered clients wait passively in the wings, wringing their hands (and their pocketbooks). Indeed, this was the image my colleagues and I held when we began our research. However, evidence is beginning to appear which suggests that the conventional wisdom may be seriously in error. The results from several recent studies indicate that perhaps as many as half or more of all divorcing couples do most of the settlement negotiations themselves, with only minimal assistance from lawyers.

The strongest conclusion on this point comes from the Cavanagh and Rhode (1976) study of 330 Connecticut divorce filings drawn at random from court records in Bridgeport and New Haven. In more than 50 percent of those filings one of the spouses was unrepresented by a lawyer. This figure changed only marginally in cases in which there was presumptive evidence that important settlement negotiations had occurred. (Thus, in the nearly two hundred settlements involving a financial award of property, alimony, or child support, fully 44 percent of the defendants were unrepresented by counsel.) Somewhat lower, but still sizeable estimates of unrepresented persons, on the order of 20 to 30 percent, have also been reported.[4]

The accounts which the parties in the Cavanagh and Rhode study gave of the legal help which they received corroborates the picture of only a modest lawyer negotiating role. Nearly half the clients (46.7 percent) reported no more than three personal and telephone contacts with their lawyer, a figure which did not change much among clients with children or with decrees containing property or support awards (40 percent in each category). Even in cases in which significant lawyer assistance was reported, almost a quarter of the clients reported the same modest level of contact with their attorney. Although these figures imply that lawyer and client do not typically constitute a close-knit negotiating team, it might be argued that the lawyer's greatest importance is in carrying the negotiating ball in deliberations with the opposing counsel. However, 60 percent of those interviewed indicated that they and their spouse had independently worked things out on *all* issues without resorting to the advice of attorneys! Only 29 percent described situations in which disagreement between them appeared to have been resolved with the help of lawyers. The overall thrust of the study is that in a great many divorces the lawyer is little more than a highly compensated clerk, paid to process a handful of forms and wait around for a couple of hours for the case to be called.

Hochberg's study of New Jersey divorces, which, by design, included only cases involving minor children and the use of attorneys by both spouses, indicates a similar pattern. Less than one-fifth of the sample felt that their lawyers had played the major role in settlement negotiations. Moreover, few of the respondents reported that their attorney had given them very much guidance in handling the relationship with their spouse during the settlement process. Indeed, few seemed to feel a great need for such assistance; less than one-tenth of the sample considered the financial matters to be negotiated particularly complex and only 7 percent reported high levels of disagreement over substantive issues (Hochberg 1984).[5]

There is no unequivocal way of interpreting data such as these. Perhaps they reflect the strained economic circumstances of divorcing persons, even those with property to divide, and the corresponding wish to save money on legal fees. Perhaps they are additional confirmation of the tensions endemic to the lawyer-client relationship and are best regarded as an index of alienation between lawyers and clients.

Perhaps they simply reflect ambivalent public attitudes about lawyers. National survey data suggest that nearly half of the population believes that lawyers should be consulted only after every other possible way of handling a problem has been exhausted (Curran 1977).

Whatever the explanation, the practical implication is that in an undetermined, but sizeable proportion of cases, the lawyer's particular vision of his or her role—be it that of counselor or advocate—has only limited capability to affect the settlement process because the clients do most of the negotiating themselves. Hochberg's data suggest that, by and large, they may be wise to do so. Statistically controlling for a variety of factors such as income, emotional climate, mutuality of the divorce decision, and so on, client, rather than attorney, control of the negotiations was one of the most significant predictors of good postdivorce outcomes. These included compliance with the terms of settlement, reduced prospects of a future court fight, and general good will.

But what is the impact of lawyer stance when the clients do permit their attorneys to play an active negotiating role? There is very little evidence on this crucial matter but what does exist is consistent with the picture that lawyers exercise only a modest impact on the settlement process. Spanier and Anderson (1979) found no relationship between client reports of the degree to which their lawyers encouraged competitive behavior toward the spouse and three separate measures of client postdivorce adjustment. Overall, client satisfaction with the legal process made only a trivial contribution to postdivorce adjustment and one which was less important than factors such as health, economic stress, and postdivorce dating behavior.

Hochberg reports a more significant effect of lawyer involvement. A counselor orientation and cooperative tactical advice from the attorney were significantly associated with better postdivorce outcomes, while competitive tactical advice from the lawyer was associated with worse outcomes. However, the overall contribution of these lawyer related variables was modest (on the order of 2 percent to 3 percent of the total variance). Other factors made equal or greater contributions. These included the economic circumstances of the parties, the degree to which they did their own negotiating, and the manner in which they attempted to influence each other. The thrust of Hochberg's results is that a cooperatively oriented attorney is of help to a divorcing couple. It is even more helpful, however, to have a relationship with *each other* that is cooperative, to keep control of negotiations, and to have enough money.

The nature of the divorcing couple's relationship with each other and its effects on the negotiating process shall be our central concern in the following chapter, but Hochberg's findings illustrate the final point I wish to make regarding the weight which should be given to lawyer style as a determinant of the settlement process. The point is a simple one: *a focus on the characteristics of any single actor in the settlement process is bound to be too narrow.* In chapter 2 I have outlined the argument for this perspective by describing nine major factors which complicate the negotiators' task in the divorce settlement process. These include the destructive or incompetent manner in which the parties may try to influence each other, the imbalances in power and interpersonal sensitivity which may characterize their relationship, a shortage of material resources and high levels of stress. All of these —and perhaps others not yet documented—must be taken into account, along with the contributions of lawyers, by any truly adequate description of the settlement process.

Additional evidence for the futility of explaining divorce settlement outcomes exclusively in terms of the lawyers' behavior and attitudes may be found in the twenty-five-year history of research on the determinants of success in psychotherapy. In a detailed, incisive review of this literature, Parloff, Waskow, and Wolfe (1978) conclude that focusing exclusively on therapist characteristics has produced very little—in part because such studies have ignored other potent variables, such as the type of patient treated, concurrent life events, the respective goals of therapist and patient, and so on. From the area of laboratory research, Bixenstine, Lowenfeld, and Englehart (1981) report that subjects' predisposition for behaving cooperatively or competitively account for no more than a modest 5 percent of the variance in negotiating behavior in an experimental gaming study. Coincidentally or not, the 5 percent figure is nearly identical to the amount of variance in postdivorce settlement outcomes which Hochberg (1984) reports for lawyer type.

Since the tendency to either scapegoat attorneys or mythologize them is so strong I would like to close the discussion of the lawyer's role with a hypothetical, but entirely plausible, illustration of the complex workings of the negotiating system in divorce.

This system is made up of four individuals—the two spouses and their respective lawyers. These actors are influenced and constrained not only by their own characteristics—the husband may be a wealthy alcoholic, his lawyer may be a confirmed advocate, and so on—but by the properties and characteristics of the other actors in the system. For instance, the alcoholic husband may be attempting to extricate himself from a homely woman with only a high school education who is extremely frightened but belligerent. The husband, stimulated in part by his wife's behavior, may be, by turns, guilt ridden, angry, and dictatorial about settlement terms. Considered as a subsystem within the larger structure, their relationship may be described as psychologically enmeshed (see chapter 11). Needless to say, attorneys are affected by the relationship dynamics of this enmeshed subsystem as mediated by their relationship with their respective clients.

Although as yet we have no comparable terms to describe the interpersonal dynamics of the lawyer-client relationship, it too has its unique properties. Among the most important of these may be the degree to which lawyer and client agree on the appropriate stance to assume in the settlement negotiations (e.g., cooperative or competitive); the level of mutual trust between them; the manner in which they interact, especially the tactics by which each tries to influence the other; and their respective desires to please each other. Thus, the husband's lawyer may be eager to satisfy his client, who is an anticipated source of future business as well as a desired high status social contact, and they may treat each other with the utmost tact and mutual regard. The wife's relationship with her attorney may have none of these leavening qualities.

Then there is the relationship between the two attorneys. For example, while the husband's lawyer is an advocate, the wife, quite by accident, may have found herself a counselor. Despite their considerable differences in outlook, however, the two lawyers may have faced each other innumerable times and have developed a grudging respect for each other's skills. Moreover, they may also anticipate a continuing professional relationship once this case is settled.

Surrounding this system of bubbling mutual interest, seething antipathies, and catalytic ambivalence is the surrounding environment, legal and otherwise; e.g., the real estate market may be a shambles making it difficult for the couple to liquidate important holdings, and the wife's contribution as homemaker may have no legal status in the allocation of marital property.

Finally, each set of relationships—husband-wife, client-lawyer, and lawyer-lawyer—may influence the process and outcomes in each of the others. Thus, if the wife is highly distrustful of her lawyer and insists on closely monitoring his behavior, the effect on the lawyer, in spite of his counselor leanings and his affinities with opposing counsel, may be an increase in his efforts to produce a financial "victory" for his client, which will satisfy her and recompense him. The effect of this on the relationship with opposite counsel will be predictably harmful, especially since the husband's lawyer is already predisposed to the adversarial mode. The worsening climate between the two attorneys may well improve the working relationship in each lawyer-client team, while simultaneously aggravating the relationship between the two spouses. When this new level of spousal animosity is fed back into the respective lawyer-client relationships the level of legal warfare between the two attorneys can be expected to increase. Out of such an interplay of forces legal and psychological mayhem is produced.

The point of this illustration is not to devalue the importance of differences in lawyer role orientation. On the contrary, since lawyers are directly involved in three of the four central relationships in the negotiating system, lawyer stance may well be an important intervening variable in predicting settlement outcomes. Nor is it to suggest that settlement negotiations are too complex to be understood. There are emerging models of the negotiating process that appear very well suited to the study of divorce negotiations (see, for example, Adams [1976], whose work on boundary roles in negotiations between competing organizational units has many notable parallels to the case of divorce). However, any attempt to understand the relationship of lawyer type to the course and outcome of settlement negotiations must take into account the characteristics of the entire system in which those negotiations occur. At a minimum this would involve some consideration of the couple's characteristics and dynamics, especially their habitual manner of dealing with conflict and the effect of this on the relationship which develops within each attorney-client pair and between the two attorneys. We shall turn our attention to the psychological dynamics of the divorcing couple in chapter 11.

One final note on the divorce lawyer: Although the role of the attorney in divorce may be exaggerated in the popular imagination, there are hundreds of thousands of cases each year in which the involvement of lawyers is anything but trivial. The time is ripe for systematic elucidation of precisely what a lawyer's impact is in such instances. For students of bargaining and negotiation, who have expended so much of their energy on laboratory studies involving transient, artificial interactions among strangers (Rubin and Brown 1975), divorce negotiations represent an arena of study rich with possibilities. The current void of information on the lawyer-client relationship and its effect on those negotiations is analogous to the veil of ignorance which surrounded the psychotherapeutic relationship prior to the beginning of systematic empirical scrutiny in the 1950s. The data on lawyer typology presented here is but the tip of the iceberg.

The absence of well-documented research on lawyers notwithstanding, public and professional disenchantment with the legal process has led to increasing cries for reform, and the use of divorce mediation has become popular. In the following chapters we shall examine in detail this rapidly expanding innovation.

9

Divorce Mediation: A Critical Overview

The field of divorce mediation is no more than ten years old, and only within the last five years has it gained any real degree of public and professional visibility. We are still far too early in the record to make any definitive assessment of its potential. My aims are modest. Earlier chapters focused on the role of the therapist and the lawyer in negotiating the marital breakup. In this chapter and the next I will define the mediation process in general terms, examine some of the reasons for its growing popularity, and summarize the small but accumulating research findings on its strengths and limitations. Then, in chapters 11 and 12, I shall descend from these somewhat rarefied heights to examine the mediation process at close range as observed by my colleagues and myself in a small but intensive number of case studies, one of which shall be the exclusive focus in chapter 12.

While I am an enthusiastic student of the mediation process, my understanding of mediation in other domains of conflict (Kressel 1972, 1981; Kressel and Pruitt, in press) has convinced me that mediation is a vehicle of social influence which is not inherently superior to any other method of conflict resolution. Like the others, it has its own decided liabilities as well as assets. The polemical claims of its proponents and critics notwithstanding, my study of divorce mediation has done nothing to dissuade me from this view. Indeed, my reading of the record is that divorce mediation, for all its promise, is a complex and stressful social role with difficulties that are remarkably similar to, and, in certain respects, perhaps even worse than, those I have described earlier in considering the headaches of the divorce attorney. In sum, I have attempted to describe divorce mediation with an open but critical eye and to delineate the unique problems which it poses for professional intervention.

I shall begin with a brief description of the mediation process and the practical context in which it occurs, and then proceed to a more analytic look at the claims which have been made on its behalf.

The Professional Context of Divorce Mediation

THE ROLE OF THE MEDIATOR

Within the divorce mediation community there are important differences of opinion regarding the precise nature of the mediator's role. Some of these differences reflect the very different settings in which divorce mediation occurs, others reflect philosophic or conceptual differences of a more profound nature. (We shall examine some of these matters shortly.) In spite of the disagreements and differences, however, it is possible to give an overall characterization which is shared by nearly all schools of divorce mediation.

Divorce mediation refers to a process in which divorcing spouses negotiate some or all of the terms of their settlement agreement with the aid of a neutral and trained third party. Some of the negotiating sessions may involve separate meetings between the mediator and each of the parties, but the emphasis tends to be on face-to-face sessions in which the parties deal with each other directly. The mediator's overarching objective is the establishment and maintenance of a cooperative, problem-solving orientation between the spouses (as opposed to the competitive "I win-you lose" orientation said to surround the adversary use of lawyers). Within this broad objective the mediator's attention is directed to two principal areas: establishing a productive negotiating climate and addressing the substantive issues.

With regard to the negotiating climate, the mediator's principal functions include facilitating accurate and honest communication; seeing to it that anger and hostility are kept within manageable bounds; promoting in each party a feeling of confidence in the process and in their respective abilities to use it to attain their most significant objectives; reminding the parties of the needs and perspective of their children; and inculcating in each side at least the rudiments of a constructive negotiating style—principally in the form of a recognition of the need for compromises and tradeoffs and the value of attention to the other's needs as well as to one's own.

On the substantive side, the mediator's activities include the development of an orderly agenda; the fostering of open and productive sharing of relevant information; providing legal, economic, or psychological information; helping each side identify objectives of greater and lesser importance; making suggestions for settlement; pressing recalcitrant or unrealistic parties to move toward agreement; and translating the agreements reached into a written document.

Typically, lawyers are not directly involved in the negotiating sessions but serve the parties as consultants. This may occur in the form of a single advisory attorney who serves both spouses and the mediator as a source of neutral legal expertise, or each party may be encouraged to retain outside legal counsel, particularly for final advice regarding the settlement document drawn up by the mediator.

THE SETTING

Divorce mediation is either arranged for privately by the parties or is provided to them by a public agency, usually one with direct ties to the court. Pearson, Ring, and Milne (1983) have conducted a useful national survey of mediation service providers in both these areas. Their results suggest that there are important differences between the two sectors. The data that follow are drawn from their report.

Private sector mediation is much more likely than public sector mediation to involve the negotiation of all the issues, including economic ones such as child support, spousal maintenance, and division of marital property, all of which have traditionally been the domain of attorneys. This form of mediation is sometimes referred to as *comprehensive* divorce mediation. For the most part, public sector mediators restrict themselves (or are restricted by the terms of their court sponsorship) to the resolution of custody and visitation disputes. This narrower focus reflects both the court's formal role as ultimate guardian of the children's interests and the much greater willingness of bench and bar to acknowledge the limits of their expertise in matters affecting children.

Private sector mediation is also likely to last longer and to be more expensive than mediation in the public sector. Thus, the average private sector mediation takes almost nine hours and costs about $440 (exclusive of any legal fees which the parties may incur). Public sector mediation averages slightly more than six hours with an average cost of $156.

Private sector mediation is also much more likely to be a voluntary process—one is almost tempted to say a "word of mouth" process. Thus, private mediators report that more than half (56 percent) of their clients are self-referred, with less than a third entering mediation at the suggestion of another professional such as an attorney or a therapist. Fewer than 10 percent of all private mediations involve a referral from the court. In the public sector the situation is reversed, with 82 percent of all referrals coming directly from the court and only 16 percent by self-referral.

The two sectors also orient themselves somewhat differently regarding the involvement of attorneys in the mediation process. Although very few mediation services of either type by-pass the attorneys completely, this is slightly more likely to occur in the private sector than in the public one. Eleven percent of private mediators have no contact with lawyers during mediation compared to 5 percent in the public sector. On the other hand, with specific regard to the draft settlement agreement, which is the usual product in all but a very small percentage of cases in both sectors, it is the public sector mediators who are more likely to eschew any role for the attorney in looking things over (39 to 26 percent).

The overwhelming majority of mediators in the private sector are mental health professionals, principally social workers (42 percent) and psychologists (22 percent). Approximately 15 percent of private sector mediators are lawyers. By contrast, in public sector mediation social workers constitute nearly 75 percent of all practitioners and lawyers do hardly any public sector work (1 percent). Few practitioners in either sector make mediation their exclusive area of practice. Private practice mediators spend about a third of their professional time doing mediation; public sector mediators about half of their time.

One final difference of note: by virtue of their built-in referral base from the courts, public sector mediators are more likely to be experienced at mediation than their counterparts in the private sector. Thus, nearly all (93 percent) of the private sector mediation services polled by Pearson and her colleagues reported handling fewer than fifty cases a year in 1981, and about one half conducted fewer than ten. In the public sector, by contrast, 54 percent of the services conducted more than one hundred mediations per year, a figure matched by only 2 percent of the private sector services.

To date there are no uniform standards for the training of divorce mediators. It is generally felt that mediators should be well versed in both the psychological, economic, tax, and legal aspects of divorce. The precise knowledge required and the relative weight of knowledge desirable in each of these areas are matters of uncertainity and disagreement. According to Pearson, Ring, and Milne (1983), nearly half the mediators in both sectors have been trained by Jim Coogler, the man whom many consider the "father" of divorce mediation. This fact is of more than passing interest for us because it is Coogler's philosophy and approach to mediation that we shall examine close up in chapters 11 and 12.

THE RAPID PACE OF PROFESSIONALIZATION

In spite of its rapid development over the last few years it can hardly be said that at the present moment divorce mediation is a threat to supplant the traditional use of lawyers in the negotiation of divorce settlements. At a rough approximation not more than 3 percent of all such settlements have involved a divorce mediator in any capacity.[1] We may also note that as of 1982, there were probably no more than 400 or so providers of mediation services in the country (Vanderkooi and Pearson 1983)—a fraction of the hundreds of thousands of attorneys standing ready to provide the same result in the traditional manner.

However, there are numerous signs that divorce mediation has begun to establish itself as a legitimate and independent discipline. Given its very recent origins, many of these signs are impressive. We may note the following:

A RAPID RATE OF GROWTH. In 1980 approximately 28,000 divorce mediations were conducted; in 1981 the estimate was well above 34,000 (Pearson, Ring, and Milne 1983)—a growth rate of nearly 25 percent in one year. Nearly half of all private divorce mediators began their practice as recently as 1981 (Pearson, Ring, and Milne 1983).

ACCEPTANCE BY THE COURTS. At the current writing thirteen states now provide divorce mediation through their courts or court-connected social service agencies (Appleford and Pearson 1984). Other states (e.g., New Jersey) are conducting experimental evaluations of mediation with an eye to providing them on a regular basis, usually in cases involving custody/visitation disputes. At least one state (California) has mandated mediation in all such instances.

PROFESSIONAL RECOGNITION. A variety of professional organizations have begun taking a formal interest in divorce mediation. These signs of interest include the offering of workshops in the practice of mediation and the establishment of committees to consider issues and promulgate positions concerning mediation practice and training. Among the organizations that have taken such steps are the American Association of Marriage and Family Therapists, The American Orthopsychiatric Association, and the Association of Family Conciliation Courts. Mediation fever has even spread to the bastion of the legal community: The American Academy of Matrimonial Lawyers has held meetings and workshops on divorce mediation and the Family Law Section of the American Bar Association has formed a standing committee on mediation and arbitration (Milne 1983). Indeed, in 1984 the Family Law Section published a preliminary report entitled, "Standards of Practice for Family Mediators." Although scepticism about mediation is often apparent in these legal discussions, they also represent a clear acknowledgment that mediation has established itself as a force to be reckoned with.

A BURGEONING LITERATURE. Books and articles on divorce mediation, almost unheard of five years ago, are beginning to appear with increasing frequency. By informal count there are now at least six books devoted entirely to that subject (Bienenfeld 1983; Coogler 1978; Haynes 1981; Irving 1980; Saposnek 1983; Shapiro and Caplan 1983). All of them are essentially enthusiastic "how to" manuals addressed to the prospective or novice divorce mediator. In 1983 the first professional journal devoted entirely to mediation, and with a principal focus on divorce mediation, *The Mediation Quarterly,* was established.

A DEVELOPING INSTITUTIONAL STRUCTURE. At the present writing there are two formal national organizations devoted exclusively to divorce mediation—The Family Mediation Association and the Academy of Family Mediators. Both were established within the last several years and each trains increasing numbers of mediators each year. In addition, many states now have private, non-profit divorce mediation organizations which compete with the national organizations in the training of mediators and promote the use of divorce mediation in their states. Although there are as yet no universally agreed upon standards of training or practice for divorce mediators, there are increasing calls that these be developed (e.g., Family Law Section 1984; Milne 1983; Moore 1983).

In short, all the signs point to a field which, in a period of no more than seven or eight years, has attained a relatively high degree of professional visibility, is attracting increasing numbers of adherents, and is well on its way to becoming an established interdisciplinary field. There appear to be two principal factors that account for this rapid emergence and professionalization: widespread disaffection with the traditional use of lawyers and the courts, and a belief, at times verging on the feverish, that mediation is an inherently more humane, rational, and effective vehicle of conflict resolution.[2]

The criticisms of the traditional legal approach to divorce negotiations are founded on what is widely believed to be its overall poor record of performance. The critics, many of whom come from within the legal community, point to the increasingly long and vexing backlogs of cases awaiting adjudication because the parties and their lawyers have been unable to resolve matters. The quality and durability of the settlement agreements have also been found wanting in the aggregate, with noncompliance common, especially in regard to child support and visitation, and with the parties frequently remaining at each others throats emotionally, if not legally, long after the "final" settlement is reached. These matters were reviewed in detail in chapter 1.

Although there are numerous possible explanations for why things work out so badly, the belief persists that the principal cause is an undue reliance on all too defective legal mechanisms. The majority of mediation service providers surveyed by Pearson, Ring, and Milne (1983) invoked disaffection with the traditional legal approach as the principal motive for their existence. This view was taken by 60 percent of the public sector mediation providers and 90 percent of those in the private sector. The presumed flaws in the legal approach have also been reviewed earlier. They include: the competitive "win-lose" orientation fostered by legal norms and training; the strong, if implicit tensions and conflicts of interest between lawyers and their clients; the lawyers' lack of training in matters psychological; the one-sided perspective forced on the lawyer by legal ethics; and the lack of consensus within the legal community on standards for settlement, combined with the unfortunate tendency to construe the professional encounter as one between naive and passive client and controlling legal "expert." It has also been said that the law often fails to get at the underlying issues because of its preoccupation with procedural rules, substituting the concerns of lawyers and judges for those of the divorcing parties (Pearson 1983; Sander 1983).

In contrast to this plaintive list stand the numerous virtues attributed to mediation—virtues thought to flow more or less inevitably from the cooperative ethos on which all models of mediation are built; from the mediator's training and sophistication in matters practical and psychological; and from the structural arrangement which allows the mediator simultaneous access to both parties. Thus, mediation is said to result in a more open and complete sharing of information; a more positive negotiating climate; more flexible and creative agreements; enhanced ability to clarify the priorities of each side; the ventilating of emotions which might otherwise block constructive problem solving; the preservation of a working relationship between the parties, including the development of much needed communication and problem-solving skills; the avoidance of blame; the more rapid recovery from the emotional trauma of divorce; the fostering of a greater feeling of mutual power and psychological ownership of the agreements reached, and hence the production of more durable agreements; and a savings in time and money as the result of a more efficient, less destructive negotiating process. This list of mediation's putative virtues is not necessarily exhaustive. A more complete catalogue may be compiled by consulting any of the leading expositions of the process (Coogler 1978; Haynes 1981). The basic thrust is that the legal system is built on coercion and mediation is built on consent.

The polemical, not to say adversarial quality reflected in these anti-lawyer, pro-mediation arguments is understandable—perhaps even inevitable. To make their way against entrenched ways of doing things and to develop the necessary internal cohesion and espirit de corps, the proponents of new modes of social activity often state their case in an extreme, one-sided fashion (Coser 1956). It is merely an ironic note that this well-established social phenomenon is so easily discernible in the divorce mediation movement, whose fundamental premise is the ultimate destructiveness of the adversarial mode.

On the other hand, it is important to distinguish reality from polemics. Research on the effects of divorce mediation is in its infancy. The results to date are promising, but far from conclusive. Moreover, on analytic grounds there are good reasons to suspect that the complexities and headaches of the mediator's role are no less severe, and in certain ways very similar to those of the divorce attorney. I shall treat each of these matters in turn.

Does Divorce Mediation Work? A Survey of the Research

THE STUDIES

The number of investigations of divorce mediation's effectiveness can be counted on the fingers of one hand. In summarizing what is known I have drawn upon the following reports:

1. Margolin's (1973) investigation of custody or visitation disputes among 150 previously divorced couples, one half of whom were randomly assigned to either an experimental, one session, counseling session (mediation) or to a no treatment control group.
2. Doyle and Caron's (1979) ex-*post facto* analysis of nearly 700 cases of disputed custody/visitation in Hennepin County (Minneapolis), Minnesota, from June, 1975 to June, 1978 comparing clients who, after an initial screening by the court, had been assigned either to custody resolution counseling (mediation) or a traditional custody study.

3. Irving, Bohm, MacDonald, and Benjamin's (1979) comparison of 228 court clients, quasi-randomly assigned to either a conciliation counseling service designed to help resolve outstanding issues related to the divorce ($N=106$) or to the traditional intake service ($N=122$).
4. The Denver Custody Mediation Project (DCMP) (Pearson and Thoennes 1982a, 1984a; Vanderkooi and Pearson 1983). This project involved the random assignment of couples disputing custody/visitation to either an experimental mediation condition or a control group which proceeded with the customary use of lawyers and the courts. Data is reported for over 200 individuals who received mediation and nearly 100 persons in the control condition. An additional group of more than 100 respondents who rejected the offer to mediate were also studied.
5. The Custody Mediation Research Project (CMRP) (Pearson and Thoennes, 1982b; 1984b). This investigation studied a total of more than 500 individuals using court-connected mediation services in Los Angeles, Minneapolis, and throughout the state of Connecticut. Interviews were also conducted with a randomly selected group who had used either mediation or litigation at the Minneapolis site five years earlier and with a contemporary sample of contesting and non-contesting persons in Colorado who did not have access to publicly supported mediation programs.[3]

The evidence available in these studies is germane to two related, but distinct issues: divorce mediation's general level of effectiveness and acceptability and its effectiveness compared to what is usually referred to as the "adversary" or "adjudicatory" system—the traditional use of lawyers and the courts. Given the polemical atmosphere which surrounds the question of divorce mediation's efficacy it is easy to blur the distinction between these two matters. For this reason I have thought it best to discuss separately the findings on mediation's general and comparative effectiveness.

MEDIATION'S GENERAL EFFECTIVENESS

Divorce mediation appears to be generally satisfying to the majority of persons who have tried it, perhaps more satisfying then their experiences with the court process. Thus, in the DCMP approximately 76 percent of all those who tried mediation were satisfied with the process. Only 42 percent of these respondents felt similarly about their court experiences. These findings are generally confirmed in the CMRP. Of those who reached a settlement in mediation, 90 percent expressed satisfaction with the process, but so too did 70 percent of those who could not reach a mediated settlement. In contrast, between 50 to 70 percent of the mediated respondents expressed dissatisfaction with their exposure to the legal system. Whether or not they were able to reach a settlement in mediation, the majority of the respondents in the CMRP also said they were glad they had tried mediation; would recommend it to a friend; and believed that it should be mandatory for couples with custody disputes.

These levels of user satisfaction are comparable, and perhaps even higher, than those reported for public satisfaction with other types of professional services. Thus, in a national probability sample of persons who sought help for a personal problem (Veroff, Kulka, and Douvan 1981), 75 percent of the respondents said the assistance which they received was helpful. Satisfaction rates ranged from between 80 percent for those who consulted either a physician or a clergyman, to 49 percent for those who sought the help of a marriage counselor. Studies devoted exclusively to patient evaluation of medical services (of which, incidentally, there are many more than of client evaluations of lawyers) have yielded satisfaction rates of between 35 to 89 percent, with most clustered in the 45 to 70 percent range (DiMatteo and Friedman 1979).

Even more to the point, user satisfaction with divorce mediation does not suffer in comparison to client assessments of divorce therapists and divorce attorneys. Satisfaction with general divorce counseling services appears to lie in the 60 to 85 percent range for the few studies which have been reported (Sprenkle and Storm 1983). As for satisfaction with the divorce attorney, the data is even more scanty and no strict comparison with mediation is possible. However, Cavanagh, and Rhode (1976) report that nearly one third of their random sample of Connecticut divorces could be classified as dissatisfied with the legal assistance received, and this figure was appreciably higher (64 percent) for those who had relied heavily on the lawyer's help. Curran (1977), in a national probability sample of public attitudes toward lawyers, reports generally positive ratings for "matrimonial" legal services. However, relative to other legal services the divorce attorney did not fair so well. The competency ratings given to divorce services were exceeded by the competency ratings given by persons using lawyers for several other types of legal work and were only higher than the ratings given their lawyers by persons with employment problems, auto accidents, and criminal cases.

In addition to the promising findings on user satisfaction, the settlement rates achieved in mediation are reasonably good, especially given the high levels of conflict typically associated with custody and visitation disputes. The range of reported settlements is between 22 and 97 percent across studies, with most results falling in the 40 to 70 percent range. With one exception (Margolin 1973), no investigators report results comparable to the oft-quoted 90 percent settlement rate achieved by lawyers. It is important to remember, however, that the mediation studies deal precisely with those cases in which the negotiations between the parties and their lawyers have broken down or have seriously threatened to do so.

The settlement rates achieved in divorce mediation compare favorably with the settlement rates reported for the highly regarded and long institutionalized process of labor mediation, where settlement rates of 28 to 57 percent have been reported, and are roughly comparable to the settlement rates reported in studies of mediation in small claims court and across a range of civil disputes.[4] Furthermore, the settlements reached in divorce mediation appear to be generally complied with and have not resulted in a rash of relitigation (Margolin 1973; Pearson and Thoennes 1984a).

MEDIATION VS. THE "ADVERSARY" SYSTEM

The available evidence may also be interpreted as showing that mediation is superior to the traditional use of lawyers and the courts in a number of significant ways. The comparisons most favorable to mediation occur on measures of user satisfaction, compliance, levels of compromise, and financial costs. Many of these findings come from the DCMP, but they are generally corroborated by other evidence.

Thus, whereas three-quarters of those in the mediated group in the DCMP were satisfied with mediation, only 37 percent in the control group expressed satisfaction with their experiences with the legal system. Similarly, 68 percent in the mediation group, compared to 53 percent in the control group, were satisfied with the final decree. Approximately nine months after the promulgation of final orders, 81 percent of those who had been able to settle in mediation, compared to 62 percent of the controls, reported the spouse to be in full compliance with all terms. Moreover, "serious disagreements" were reported by only 9 percent of the successful mediation cases but 35 percent of the control group.

The degree of compromise which occurred during negotiations was estimated by the percentage of respondents choosing joint over sole custody and the proportion of the father's income reflected in child support orders. On both these indices the results suggested that more compromise had occurred in mediation than in the traditional use of lawyers and the courts. Thus, at intake, 22 percent of the couples in the mediation condition were already in agreement on joint custody prior to treatment, compared to 14 percent of the control group. However, in the final settlement, 70 percent of all mediation couples but only 22 percent of the controls had a joint custody agreement—presumably as a result of their respective experiences between initial assessment and final agreement, 48 percent of the mediation couples compared to only 6 percent of the control sample had worked their way toward joint custody. With regard to the proportion of the father's income paid in child support, Pearson and Thoennes (1984a) report that when support was stipulated in the final agreement (and in many instances of joint custody there is no such provision), 34 percent of the fathers in the mediation group agreed to pay at least one quarter of their net monthly income, compared to 22 percent of the control fathers who so stipulated.

Modest but distinctive savings in legal costs were also associated with the use of mediation, especially for those able to reach settlement. The successful mediation respondents reported an average legal fee of $1,630 compared to $2,360 for the comparison group. Based on the experiences of the mediated and nonmediated samples in the DCMP it is possible to estimate that on a national basis the use of mediation in highly conflictual custody and visitation disputes could save a minimum of between $79.5 million to $159 million annually.[5] Pearson and Thoennes (1982a) have also estimated from their data that the public saves between $5,610 and $27,510 per 100 cases sent to mediation. These are very modest savings on a per capita basis, but in the aggregate the savings can be impressive. McIssac (1981) claims that the Los Angeles experiment with mandatory custody mediation saved Los Angeles courts $175,000 in 1978. Partly on this basis the program was enacted into law by the state legislature (Pearson 1983).

Corroboration of the DCMP findings on the relative superiority of mediation compared to adjudicatory modes of dispute resultion may be found in various other studies, both within and outside of the area of divorce conflict. The relatively higher rates of user satisfaction are confirmed by the results on the five-year retrospective sample in the CMRP (Pearson and Thoennes 1984b) and in a range of other dispute settings, including small claims, felony, community disputes (Pearson, 1983), and labor management conflicts (Brett and Goldberg 1983). In an exception to the generally high levels of user satisfaction with the mediation process, Vidmar (in press) reports that satisfaction was *not* related to whether mediation or adjudication was the mode of dispute resolution.

With regard to compliance and compromise rates, corroboration of the DCMP findings comes from the CMRP and the study of small claims mediation by McEwen and Maiman (1981). Thus, in the CMRP, 85 percent of those who five years earlier had been able to reach an initial settlement in mediation reported that the ex-spouse was "generally" in compliance in the current period. The comparable figure was roughly 60 percent for respondents who had experienced only the traditional custody evaluation study or for those who had been unable to reach a settlement in mediation. Joint custody was more likely to be chosen than sole custody by the contemporary mediation respondents at both the Los Angeles and Minneapolis (but not the Connecticut) sites (Pearson and Thoennes 1984b). In the small claims investigation, payment in full occurred in 71 percent of the mediated cases compared to only 34 percent of those which had been adjudicated, and lopsided awards going entirely to the plaintiff occurred in nearly 50 percent of the adjudicatory group, but only 17 percent of the mediated cases. (However, see Vidmar [in press] for methodological problems which call some of these data into question.)

THE EFFECTIVENESS OF DIVORCE MEDIATION: CRITIQUE AND SUMMARY

The evidence just reviewed may be interpreted as demonstrating that divorce mediation is not only generally satisfying and workable but that it is also more effective than the traditional use of lawyers and the courts. In this latter regard the evidence for mediation has been called "impressive" (Sprenkle and Storm 1983) and, based on their analysis of the data from the DCMP, Pearson and Thoennes have concluded that "mediation is the preferable way to resolve contested child custody disputes" (Pearson and Thoennes 1982a).

My own conclusions are less sanguine. There are numerous substantive and methodological grounds for a more cautious interpretation of the evidence. The problems are particularly acute in regard to assessing mediation's merits relative to the traditional approach. On this matter the standards of acceptable proof are considerably more stringent and difficult to establish than they are for establishing mediation's general workability. On balance, I do not think that the case has yet been made. Indeed, after considering the problems with the available evidence, I suspect that the difficulty of making it may have been seriously underestimated.

Before elaborating, I wish to note that, my critical stance notwithstanding, there is much to be admired in the research done thus far. Compared to research on legal services in divorce or the effects of divorce therapy, assessments of divorce mediation are not only more numerous, but, for the most part, they are better realized. (See especially Sprenkle and Storm [1983] on the quality of research done on divorce mediation compared with that on divorce counseling.) This is so despite the fact that divorcing persons spend vastly more time and money on divorce lawyers and therapists than they do on divorce mediators. The work of Pearson and her colleagues is an apt example of the virtues I have in mind. In a number of ways the DCMP and the CMRP are important achievements. The strengths of these investigations include the large numbers of persons whose experience with mediation has been studied; the attempt (in the

DCMP) to randomly assign couples to comparative modes of assistance; the longitudinal designs, providing perspectives on the consequences of mediation over as much as a five-year period; the variety of mediation services investigated, including both quasi-private (DCMP) and a variety of public ones (CMRP); and the wide array of measures on which the effects of intervention have been measured. To my knowledge there is no empirical investigation on the work of lawyers or the courts in the negotiation of divorce settlements which comes close to this catalogue. It is against this generally approving background, and with the hope of making a constructive contribution to what is still very much a fledgling enterprise, that I have undertaken the critical review that follows.

The principal difficulties with the available research on the effectiveness of divorce mediation are these:

THE NUMBER OF STUDIES IS SMALL AND RESTRICTED ENTIRELY TO THE MEDIATION OF CUSTODY/VISITATION DISPUTES. The assessment of mediation's effectiveness rests on a handful of studies. In addition, all of the investigations focus on the mediation of custody and visitation disputes in which the negotiations between the parties and their attorneys have broken down or threatened to do so. Moreover, most examine relatively brief (one to three session) interventions. Mediation's value as a more comprehensive and extended instrument for reaching settlement on all issues, including money and property, remains untested. The majority of divorce mediators in the private sector offer just this type of assistance, and it is this form of mediation which has most raised the hackles of many within the legal community.

IT IS NOT YET POSSIBLE TO SEPARATE THE SPECIFIC EFFECTS OF MEDIATION FROM THE EFFECTS OF NONSPECIFIC FACTORS, SUCH AS THE GENERALIZED EXPECTANCY OF BEING HELPED. None of the existing studies controls for an array of nonspecific factors which might explain the observed differences between the mediated and unmediated groups. At its worst this means that we are unable to estimate the degree to which the putative effects of mediation are more properly attributed not to mediation's unique virtues, but to the positive effects on people of being exposed to a novel, intriguing, and enthusiastically administered form of treatment. The problem is compounded in some studies (such as the DCMP) by providing mediation gratis, while the traditional approach employing lawyers is expensive. The placebo effect is especially likely to contaminate attitudinal measures, such as general satisfaction, which are precisely the ones which have yielded some of the most impressive evidence in mediation's favor.

We are also on uncertain ground in estimating the degree to which the favorable evidence regarding mediation is attributable to factors with which mediation is associated but which are by no means unique to it. These include such important psychological and interpersonal states as increases in cooperativeness, relevant knowledge, and a feeling of being in control of one's fate. To be sure, such qualities are part of the rationale behind mediation, but they may be inculcated in many other ways; ways which may be less costly, simpler, and unattended by the theoretical trappings and aura which surround mediation. One such alternative approach is private or court sponsored lectures and discussion groups on the legal, economic, and psychological factors involved in negotiating a settlement agreement. To my knowledge such a "treatment" has not been systematically implemented and evaluated, but, at least in theory, it could have many of the same positive consequences for the negotiating enterprise as formal mediation.

MEDIATION'S EFFECTIVENESS IS EQUIVOCAL ON A NUMBER OF OUTCOME MEASURES, PARTICULARLY THOSE RELATED TO POSTSETTLEMENT ADJUSTMENT AND RELATIONSHIPS AMONG MEMBERS OF THE POSTDIVORCE FAMILY. An important argument which has been made by proponents of divorce mediation is that its cooperative and psychologically sophisticated approach makes it a better vehicle for improving and sustaining positive relationships among family members than does the competitive, adversarial orientation fostered by laws and legal training. However, the available evidence on this matter is mixed.

It is true that in the DCMP, mediation respondents, relative to persons with no exposure to mediation, were much more likely to say that the assistance they received improved communication, cooperation, understanding, and the ability to handle anger towards the ex-spouse. Very few of those exposed only to lawyers and the courts had comparably favorable things to say about *their* experience. However, judged against the general claims that have been made on mediation's behalf, the results are less impressive. No more than half of mediation respondents felt that the impact of mediation was positive on any of these variables. Although the precise figure is not given, one can calculate that about 40 percent or so simply felt that mediation had no impact whatever on the relationship with the ex-spouse, with another 10 percent feeling that mediation had actually made things worse.[6]

At long-term follow-up, nine months after the issuance of final orders, continued improvement in communication, cooperation, understanding, and the handling of anger were noted by fewer respondents in all conditions, and the advantage for the mediation group relative to those with no exposure to mediation was slight. From data in Pearson and Thoennes (1984a), it is possible to calculate a combined average for all mediation respondents (successful and unsuccessful) with which to compare the figures for the total group exposed only to the adjudicatory process (controls and those who rejected mediation). The comparisons are shown in table 9.1. If one considers the methodological problems (noted later), especially the problems with pretreatment differences between mediation and nonmediation respondents, these differences, while favorable to mediation, are relatively small and may well be without real significance.

The results from the CMRP provide an equally restrained assessment of mediation's impact on the relationship between the parties. Across the three sites whose mediation programs were studied, three-quarters of those who could not reach settlement felt that the mediation experience had no effect on their relationship with their ex-spouse, but so too did between one-half and two-thirds of those who could reach a mediated agreement (Pearson and Thoennes 1982b). As in the DCMP, a minority of persons, between 10 and 20 percent across the three research sites, actually felt that the mediation experience worsened the relationship between them and their ex-spouse. At the Minneapolis site, for example, this was the opinion of 20 percent of the respondents who could not come to an agreement in mediation and 15 percent who could (Pearson and Thoennes 1982b).[7]

The CMRP results also suggest that although the majority of mediation users may be well satisfied with the process, a significant minority are not, at least in the large-scale public mediation services which were studied. A relatively large number of respondents at each site had distinctly negative things to report about the mediation experience. Thus, 25 percent said that "mediation was confusing," and 36 percent that "the mediator did not seem to understand the real issues and problems." On the other hand, only 25 percent felt that the mediation had helped them understand their ex-

Table 9.1

Summary of Long-term Outcomes

Item	*Groups Mediated (N=217)*	*Groups Adjudicated (N=202)*
Improvements Over the Last Three Months in:		
Communication	34.5%	25.2%
Anger	29.9%	28.7%
Cooperation	33.1%	23.7%
Understanding	23.0%	16.8%

SOURCE: From "Mediating and Litigating Custody Disputes: A Longitudinal Evaluation," by J. Pearson and N. Thoennes, *Family Law Quarterly* 17(1984):497–524, table 2.

spouse's point of view, and 25 to 32 percent wanted and expected more legal advice (Pearson and Thoennes 1982b).

The relationship between parents and children is another area in which rather conspicuous claims have been made on mediation's behalf. The evidence, however, is again equivocal. Margolin (1973) reports the most positive findings. At four-month follow-up, compared to the control group, mediation respondents reported that the children were more satisfied with visitation, that both parents and children enjoyed the visits more, and that the children behaved better both during and after the visit. The DCMP provides no information on the quality of the parent-child relationship, but those who were able to reach settlement in mediation reported significantly more days of visitation at both short- and long-term follow-up (eight to nine days per month) than did respondents who either could not reach a mediated settlement or who used only traditional legal services (five to seven days of visitation per month (Pearson and Thoennes 1984a).

These results were not confirmed in the CMRP. In that study there were no statistically significant differences between the mediated respondents and the non-mediated at any of the sites. Moreover, unsuccessful mediation respondents (in Minneapolis and Connecticut) reported even more visitation than their successful mediation counterparts. One year after the settlement significant proportions of respondents across all conditions reported problems with visitation (40 percent were dissatisfied with visitation and approximately one-third reported irregular or infrequent visitation). Mediation respondents fared no better than the nonmediated.

Finally, there were no statistically significant differences between mediated and nonmediated groups on a measure of the emotional adjustment of children although there was a non-significant trend for children in both successful and unsuccessful mediation groups to be less aggressive and depressed (Pearson and Thoennes 1984b). The researchers note that the failure to find significant positive effects for mediation may have several causes, including the possible insensitivity of their measure of child adjustment (which was based on parental reports), the possibility that mediation may only be helpful to parents, and the pressure of so many overwhelming stresses acting on children that the beneficial effects of mediation may have simply been swamped.

Postsettlement litigation is another important outcome measure on which the effects of mediation relative to the traditional process must still be considered equivocal. Findings favorable to mediation have been reported by Margolin and by Pearson and Thoennes (for the DCMP sample). Thus, on a four-month postsettlement follow-up, Margolin (1973) found that only 12 percent of the mediated group, compared to 79 percent of the control group were back in court. In the DCMP, nine months after the issuance of final orders only 4 percent of the successful mediation cases (those who settled in mediation) but 15 percent of the control group, had filed a request with the court for modification of the decree (Pearson and Thoennes 1984a).

Negative results, however, come from the five-year retrospective sample in the CMRP. In that investigation about 15 percent to 20 percent of respondents in all categories had returned to court, with clients who had been exposed to mediation faring no better than anybody else (Pearson and Thoennes 1984b). Pearson and Thoennes (1984a) cite a number of other studies, both in and outside the area of divorce conflict, in which mediation has not done better at reducing levels of postsettlement litigation than traditional adversarial approaches. Mediation has also been reported to be financially more costly than the adjudicatory process alone in cases in which the parties try mediation to resolve a custody/visitation dispute which has arisen after the divorce (Pearson and Thoennes 1982a).

MANY OF THE BENEFITS ATTRIBUTED TO MEDIATION ACCRUE ONLY TO THOSE WHO ARE ABLE TO REACH A MEDIATED SETTLEMENT. Forty to 60 percent of those whose experience with divorce mediation has been studied have not been able to reach a mediated agreement. As Pearson and Thoennes point out, the results from the DCMP suggest that the impact of mediation on these individuals is not particularly good; no better, in fact, than the impact of lawyers and the courts on individuals with no exposure to mediation. The point can be seen vividly in table 9.2 which I have reproduced from Pearson and Thoennes (1984a). The table summarizes the long-term follow-up results on the DCMP's most significant outcome measures for the four groups on which statistical tests were performed. Although the overall tests are significant it is apparent that this is due exclusively to the superior outcomes experienced by those who were able to settle in mediation (the "successful" group). Those who could not reach a mediated resolution of the issues (the "unsuccessful" group) actually do no better on most measures, and worse on some, than the control group or those who refused the mediation offer and proceeded in the traditional manner.

PRETREATMENT DIFFERENCES BETWEEN THE MEDIATED AND NONMEDIATED COMPARISON GROUPS CONFOUND THE INTERPRETATION OF THE DATA. In most of the studies I have reviewed there are serious questions regarding the pretreatment comparability of mediated and nonmediated groups. Typically, the nature of the pretreatment differences is that the less conflicted, more cooperatively oriented, and less disturbed couples end up in the mediation group, while the worst cases go into the "control" or comparison groups. Some-

Table 9.2

Summary of Long-term Outcome Measures

	Mediation: Successful	Mediation: Unsuccessful	Rejecting	Control
Agreement Making				
Those interested in modifying who anticipate reaching decision on their own or in mediation[a,c]	68% (71)	32% (23)	28% (23)	32% (23)
Satisfaction and Compliance				
"Very" or "somewhat" satisfied with mediation process[c]	91% (113)	59% (51)	N.A.	N.A.
"Very" or "somewhat" satisfied with court process[a,c]	52% (60)	34% (31)	34% (38)	39% (36)
"Very" or "somewhat" satisfied with decree[a,c]	68% (85)	48% (43)	54% (61)	53% (47)
Have filed motion to modify custody or visitation	4% (6)	11% (18)	14% (28)	15% (16)
Report serious disagreements have arisen over settlement[c]	9% (11)	30% (27)	21% (24)	35% (31)
Report spouse to be in general or "complete" compliance[a,c]	81% (101)	52% (46)	63% (71)	62% (55)
Relationship with Former Spouse				
Relationship is "friendly" or "strained"[a,b,c]	84% (105)	46% (41)	46% (51)	41% (46)
During last 3 months have been improvements in:				
Communication[a,c]	43% (54)	23% (21)	24% (27)	26% (24)
Anger[a,c]	41% (52)	14% (13)	29% (33)	27% (25)
Cooperation[a,c]	42% (53)	21% (19)	18% (20)	26% (24)
Understanding[a,c]	29% (37)	14% (13)	15% (17)	19% (17)
Relationship with Children				
Average number of days per month noncustodian sees the children[c]	8.8 (118)	7.6 (81)	5.6 (94)	5.2 (70)
TOTAL SAMPLE SIZE	(126)	(91)	(113)	(89)

NOTE: From "Mediating and Litigating Custody Disputes: A Longitudinal Evaluation," by J. Pearson and N. Thoennes, *Family Law Quarterly* 17(1984):519. Reprinted by permission.
[a]Chi square significant at .05 or better.
[b]Lambda indicates improved prediction of dependent variable by 10 percent or more.
[c]F statistics based on mean scores of ordinal or interval level variables significant at .05 or better.

times the differences are the result of pretreatment screening by the courts in which an intentional effort is made to assign only "suitable" cases to mediation. This is true for two of the three sites of the CMRP (Minneapolis and Connecticut) and for the Doyle and Caron project. The DCMP and the investigations by Margolin and by Irving et al. did employ random or quasi-random assignment of cases to the mediation and control conditions. While random assignment is not the exclusive means of obtaining useful information about mediation's workability, it is widely recognized as the single most important methodological condition to be met when the issue is the comparative value of alternative interventions.

Unfortunately, all of the three studies that attempted some random procedure suffer from other interpretive headaches. Thus, in the Margolin investigation only one mediator was used, making it impossible to separate the effects of mediation from the unique effects of the mediator. In Irving et al. the mediators were better trained, had more flexible work schedules, and had smaller case loads than the counselors implementing the traditional intake service with which mediation was compared.

Because it is the most ambitious and, in many ways, the best of the divorce mediation outcome studies, the DCMP has been examined in detail throughout this chapter. Despite its numerous virtues, however, in regard to the issue of pretreatment differences among groups, it has some significant problems. They illustrate the troublesome methodological and analytic difficulties that confront researchers in this area, difficulties for which there appear to be no easy solutions.

The most obvious problem is that fully 50 percent of the couples randomly assigned to the mediation group rejected the invitation, usually because one spouse refused. This high refusal rate appears to be common among all types of voluntary mediation programs (see Roehl and Cook, in press), but it effectively vitiates the intent of random assignment to create comparable groups prior to intervention.

The nature of the bias introduced by the high refusal rate is especially problematic because there is evidence that those who accepted the offer to mediate were less conflictual, better able to communicate, more willing to work together, more affluent, and better educated than those who refused (Pearson, Thoennes, and Vanderkooi 1982). With the exception of level of education, all of these factors have also been correlated with favorable outcomes should mediation be tried (Doyle and Caron 1979), or are suspected of being so by divorce mediators (Pearson, Ring, and Milne 1983). Thus, it is difficult to say whether the more positive results for the mediation group in the DCMP are properly understood as being the result of mediation per se or of the group's more favorable pretreatment characteristics. Pearson and Thoennes (1984a) have begun to explore this possibility via statistical manipulation of their data. The results thus far indicate that the benefits associated with mediation remain on most outcome measures when pretreatment levels of hostility and ability to cooperate, as well as type of custody agreement reached (sole vs. joint) are statistically controlled for. These statistical explorations are encouraging but they can never completely resolve the uncertainty surrounding the cause of the observed differences in outcome between mediated and nonmediated respondents because such large scale deviations from random assignment may well be associated with unsuspected and unmeasured pretreatment differences between groups.

Another problem is raised by the decision to perform the statistical comparisons of outcome on one homogeneous group—those who settle in mediation—against three heterogeneous groups—mediation nonsettlers, controls, and those who rejected the offer to mediate. As Levy (1984) points out, this mode of analysis confounds the mode of intervention with the mode of reaching settlement—a negotiated agreement for all the successful mediation respondents, but a negotiated *or imposed* settlement in all the other groups. It is thus possible to conclude that the results indicate not that mediation is a superior vehicle of conflict resolution but simply that it is better for parties to reach their own accord than to have one dictated by the court.

Pearson and Thoennes argue (1984a) that it is desirable to analyze the successful mediation cases separately (since certain of the claims made on mediation's behalf logically apply only to those who settle) and also to evaluate the possibility that the benefits attributed to mediation may accrue even to those who cannot reach a mediated settlement. But both these objectives might have been accomplished by dividing the mediated and control groups in a parallel fashion. At a minimum this would require separating, for purposes of analysis, control group cases in which a negotiated settlement was reached with the assistance of lawyers only, from those requiring some additional assistance from the court. This latter group could be further subdivided into cases requiring only a custody evaluation before settlement was reached and those which went all the way to trial. Not only do each of these conditions constitute different "treatments," but they are treatments which are probably closely correlated with the preintervention prognosis for conflict resolution.

The comparability of the mediation and comparison groups is also clouded by problems related to the handling of respondent attrition. Over time the project lost 20 percent of the mediated respondents and 25 percent of the control group. In ruling out the possibility that systematic bias has crept into the data these figures are reassuring, as far as they go. However, there are unsolved problems. First, the investigators provide no information about the *reasons* for attrition in the two groups. It is always conceivable that comparable rates of attrition nonetheless mask systematically different motives in the drop-outs in each group. For example, what if the lost cases in the mediation group came primarily from among those respondents whose high initial hopes were most seriously dashed by the actual mediation encounter, whereas attrition in the control group was random with regard to important sources of systematic bias?

Second, no separate attrition rates or reasons are provided for the successful and unsuccessful mediation groups, although here too it is possible that many fewer respondents have been lost from the successful group than for any other group in the study and that those who were lost in this group were the most disenchanted "successes"—e.g., those who may have felt coerced into settlement.

Finally, the attrition rate for the reject mediation group is a disproportionately high 40 percent. The reasons for this high drop-out rate apparently lie in the researchers' decision not to pursue this class of respondents with as much zeal as those in the other groups since the reject group was primarily of interest as a source of information about what types of people are turned off by the idea of mediation. This is a legitimate use of the reject group. The problem arises in the inclusion of the group in the statistical analysis aimed at evaluating the comparative effectiveness of mediation. The statistical tests are predicated on the assumption that respondents in all the groups being compared are from the same underlying population. When this assumption is not met, the statistical robustness of the comparisons is called into question (Cook and Campell 1979).

I do not believe that the methodological and statistical choices that were made in the DCMP are indefensible or difficult to comprehend. For the most part they are understandable reflections of the very early stages of research in this area and the attendant ignorance of the problems that will be encountered. Nor is it obvious that any of the difficulties actually biased the data in such a way as to invalidate the usefulness of the study. All that may properly be said is that the grounds the study provides for concluding that mediation is superior to the traditional use of lawyers and the courts is a good deal less firm than one would wish.

Overall, then, what may be concluded about divorce mediation's effectiveness? First, I am inclined to believe the evidence regarding mediation's general workability, at least with regard to the mediation of custody/visitation disputes. Although the *degree* of effectiveness is probably inflated in the existing studies due to the failure to take into account nonspecific factors and the overrepresentation among the ranks of the mediated of the more cooperatively oriented couples, the positive findings have been replicated across a range of settings, on a variety of outcome measures, on a large number of users, and are generally corroborated by similar findings in at least one mandatory divorce mediation program (the Los Angeles site of the CRMP). The positive findings are also generally consistent with those reported in a variety of nondivorce related mediation programs (Pearson 1983; Roehl and Cook, in press). All of this strengthens the belief that divorce mediation is *not* the threat to the public welfare it has been accused of being by its fiercest critics and that it is a helpful and satisfying procedure for many persons.

On the other hand, the more ambitious claims of its most ardent proponents are also far from having been demonstrated. Mediation is obviously unable to produce settlement in a sizeable proportion of cases, has not been notably effective in altering dysfunctional patterns of family relating, and is still of uncertain value as a tool for helping children. Moreover, many couples who are given the choice do not avail themselves of the opportunity to mediate their differences. Indeed, mediation's usefulness in custody/visitation disputes may be restricted to a rather specific and perhaps narrow brand of divorcing parents: those who are able to negotiate fairly, respect each other as parents, and have similar ideas about child rearing, among other things (Saposnek 1983; Sprenkle and Storm 1983).

If mediation is generally workable, does this mean that it is also *more* workable than something called the "adversary" (or adjudicatory) system? I believe that the available evidence is too weak to reach any firm conclusions. Although the findings of several studies point in that direction (again, only for custody/visitation cases), by the time one takes into account the absence of controls for non-specific factors, the systematically more benign prognosis of the mediation cases prior to intervention, the variety of measures on which mediation has not produced more positive outcomes, and an assortment of other methodological problems, there is little left, in my opinion, on which to judge mediation's virtues compared to the traditional way of doing things. The most that can be said is that, given the very early stages of the research, the results thus far suggest that mediation is certainly no worse and *may,* particularly for the appropriate couples, have decided advantages over exclusive reliance on lawyers and formal court procedures.

These modest conclusions are, in most respects, broadly consistent with those reached by others, both in divorce mediation (Pearson and Thoennes 1984a) and in the mediation of a wide array of civil and criminal legal disputes (Roehl and Cook, in press). However, the practical threat which mediation represents to many attorneys and the opportunity it promises to many mental health professionals, along with the widespread disenchantment with purely legal ways of resolving disputes, can easily cause confusion and misunderstanding in the conduct and interpretation of divorce mediation research. If care is not taken, the promising start that has been made in evaluating mediation's potential may bog down in a polemical swamp. In spite of such signs, students of mediation and dispute resolution in and out of the divorce arena seem agreed on several broad principals which are worth summarizing briefly.

1. There is an obvious need for truly experimental designs employing random assignment to alternative modes of intervention. The bench and bar will need to be vigorously supportive of the need for such studies if the purpose of random assignment is not to be defeated by the paradox that many couples, including precisely those whose experience with the process is most in need of being evaluated, will reject the opportunity to mediate.
2. With regard both to traditional modes of resolving disputes (e.g., lawyer to lawyer negotiating, court evaluations, preliminary hearings, judicial "mediation" and decision making) and to formally labeled mediation there is a need for systematic descriptions of what actually transpires between and among the actors. For one thing, the adjudicatory system is a multifaceted array of interventions and possible interventions, not a homogeneous monolith built exclusively on competitive advocacy. The most informative research designs will recognize that lawyers and the courts employ an array of techniques and strategies to resolve disputes and that these may differ as much from each other as any one of them differs from "mediation" (Levy 1984). Secondly, modes of intervention with very different public reputations may well be more similar than they appear. Thus, I have argued in earlier chapters that lawyers may often attempt to dampen (mediate?) conflict rather than inflame matters and there is reason to suspect that mediators, in divorce and elsewhere may act more coercively than is generally realized (Vanderkooi and Pearson 1983; Vidmar, in press).

   Direct observation will also allow us to determine the specific interventions —whether employed by mediators, lawyers, or the parties themselves— which are most and least productive under specified conditions and at specified stages of conflict. The design and conduct of such research is no simple matter, but it is in this direction that the most adequate understanding of conflict management in divorce is likely to be found.
3. There are many determinants of a successful outcome besides the methods by which a settlement was arrived at. These include the characteristics of the parties and the nature of their dispute as well as the surrounding social and institutional environment. I have attempted to spell out the more important of these in chapter 2. We are beginning to have reports of the role which such factors play on the outcomes of legal representation and mediation. While the evidence is very preliminary, there are hints that the factors that help produce constructive agreements are the same whether lawyers or mediators are or-

> chestrating matters. These include the ability of the parties to cooperate, relatively modest levels of hostility at the time intervention begins, and a cooperative orientation on the part of the professional intervenors. (See the roughly parallel findings of Hochberg and Kressel [1983] for lawyer supervised negotiations, and those of Thoennes and Pearson [in press] for mediated negotiations.) A very good case can be made that studies of this kind are preferable to those which merely pit one "type" of intervention against another without regard to the tremendous internal variations within modes of intervention and the widely disparate circumstances which prevail among disputing parties. The point has been made more than once that the appropriate question is not whether "mediation" is "better" than "advocacy," but for what types of disputes and for which kinds of outcomes what mode of intervention is most suitable (Fisher 1983; Kressel et al. 1979; Saposnek 1983; Wall 1981). This approach has the further advantage of de-polemicizing the study of dispute resolution in divorce since it assumes that the major forms of assistance are all of potential value to *some* important segment of the divorcing population and that the problematic outcomes experienced by so many divorcing families can be laid at no single door.

Assessments of mediation will also be on a more realistic footing if the complexities and stresses of the mediation role are taken into account. The early proponents of mediation have, perhaps understandably, glossed over this issue. Given divorce mediation's recent emergence, a comprehensive analysis of meditation's inherent role tensions is not possible. However, a discussion of the more obvious headaches that mediators confront may make it more understandable why one should not expect mediation to be a panacea. These matters are discussed in the following chapter.

10

The Stresses of the Divorce Mediator's Role

Success as a mediator entails considerably more than the skillful management of conflict. It also requires some adroit wrestling with the often unrecognized but significant internal stresses and demands of the role itself. A combined reading of this section and the earlier chapter treating the stresses of the legal role in divorce will also underscore my belief that, in spite of their well-advertised antagonisms, lawyers and mediators have more to commiserate than to argue about.

The headaches of the mediation role derive from three principal and interrelated sources: the lofty and at times contradictory and ambiguous demands of the role itself; the mediator's intermediate position between the disputants; and the objectively difficult circumstances in which the negotiations typically take place.

There is no precise catalogue of the behaviors and attitudes that are expected of a mediator but there are certain themes which regularly reoccur in the reflections of practitioners and students of the art. I have summarized these for the mediation of international disputes between nations (Kressel 1981). Interestingly enough, the description is apt for the role of divorce mediator as well.

> With regard to the parties, the mediator is expected: to establish and maintain trust and confidence; to demonstrate empathy and understanding for the positions of each side; to be highly expert on substantive and procedural issues, but

> to use that expertise to guide and counsel, not to impose personal views or take sides. With regard to the process, the mediator is expected to foster a procedure of dispute resolution: in which neither party gets all that it is asking, although neither ends by feeling humiliated or defeated; that engages all parties in an active process of give and take, albeit one that is sufficiently controlled so that the risks of conflict escalation are kept to a minimum; and that is based on an objective and realistic assessment of the forces and interests at play. With regard to the settlement, the mediator is expected to promote agreements: that both sides can defend publicly; that each can view as reasonably fair; and that lay the groundwork for improved interaction.

The first thing to note about this description is that fulfilling all of its requirements is a task of no mean achievement, even without regard to any of the situational and strategic complications we shall shortly consider. With due respect to the noble aims of the bar, the demands made on the lawyer are a good deal more straightforward. Lawyers are not bound to strike an even-handed pose between the disputants (indeed, they are forbidden to do so) and they need not trouble themselves with the delicacies of what constitutes a good and fair agreement.

The problems of successful role enactment for the divorce mediator are significantly compounded by the arduous psychological, interpersonal, and economic circumstances in which the parties typically find themselves. The pioneers of divorce mediation have emphasized the mediator's advantages over the lawyer in handling these obstacles (Coogler 1978; Haynes 1981). Much of what they argue is plausible, but there is another side of the coin. In conjunction with the mediator's intermediate position between the parties and the high aspirations encouraged by the role prescription, the difficult characteristics of the dispute may create extremely inhospitable conditions for successful role enactment.

Let me illustrate this theme in terms of the obstacles to a constructive negotiating process outlined in chapter 2. I have illustrated in chapter 2 how discrepancies in the parties' power and interpersonal sensitivity, their inexperience as negotiators, and their ambivalence about the divorce, may create strategic problems for the divorce mediator, just as they do for the divorce lawyer. The difficulties do not end there, however. The remaining obstacles to a constructive settlement process outlined in chapter 2 may also make divorce mediators wish they had gotten into another line of work.

INTRA-PARTY CONFLICT (AMBIVALENCE)

If one or both of the parties to mediated negotiations are ambivalent about ending the marriage or about the desirability of dealing openly and fairly with the spouse, it is logical to assume that the mediator will have a difficult job orchestrating a negotiated agreement. I will elaborate on this point in the chapter which follows. Here let us focus on the ambivalence which the parties may have not about the marriage and each other, but about the mediation process.

Client ambivalence about mediation may derive from conscious or unconscious wishes to wound and attack, rather than to negotiate; from fears of becoming vulnerable because of the other's greater negotiating skills or resources; and from ignorance of the goals and methods of the mediator. There is little precise evidence on how frequently these or other factors temper the parties' stances in mediation, but there are grounds for believing that client confusion, apprehension, or hostility regarding the mediation process is not uncommon. As we have already noted, when given a choice many people are not interested in mediating their differences. Divorce mediators in private practice cite public ignorance and misunderstanding about mediation (along with the opposition or indifference of lawyers) as prime reasons for their difficulties in attracting clients, and mediators in both the private and public sectors believe that the public has only vague and often inaccurate ideas of what divorce mediators do (Pearson, Ring, and Milne 1983).

Public divorce mediation services have little trouble developing case loads because of their direct pipeline to the court system, but in terms of client ambivalence, the problem is probably worse than that facing private practitioners who may presume that those who seek their services voluntarily have at least the rudiments of the appropriate motivation. Interviews with clients at the three court sites studied by the CMRP revealed serious misconceptions of the goals of mediation; e.g., that mediation was intended to save the marriage or that the mediator had the authority to make a final custody decision. Between 20 to 30 percent of the clients at each site felt that "mediation was confusing" (Pearson and Thoennes 1984b). One public sector mediator remarked: "I do not think people have any idea why they are coming here. I think it would be immensely helpful if they did" (Pearson, Ring, and Milne 1983).

One can also infer from the factors associated with the refusal to voluntarily mediate, that if and when divorce mediation becomes mandatory for large numbers of people many of them will be inhospitable candidates. For example, in the DCMP the rejection of mediation was associated with extremely high levels of conflict between the parties, fear and distrust of husbands on the part of wives, and the wish of the husband to reconcile (Pearson, Thoennes, and Vanderkooi 1982). In short, in many cases mediator and clients may, at least in the initial encounters, be working at cross-purposes.

Client ambivalence is obviously a problem for any helping professional in which even a modicum of client cooperation is required. For the divorce mediator client cooperation is not merely desirable; it is crucial. Moreover, the mediator must reckon with not one, but two potentially reluctant or unsuitable players. There is also the hazard that, even if only one of the parties is initially ambivalent, the ambivalence will spread quickly to the other, particularly given the face-to-face format encouraged by the mediation role.

There are ways of handling the problems of client ambivalence about the mediation process, of course. The most obvious is a thorough orientation, in which misunderstandings about the nature and purpose of mediation can be clarified and the disputants socialized into the appropriate norms. However, such efforts, while important, are not always easily realized in the heated climate surrounding many disputes. In addition, there may be both explicit and implicit pressures on the mediator to pay insufficient attention to client misconceptions and misgivings. In the public sector the motivation to ignore client ambivalence may come from the need to process large numbers of cases. Whatever the reason, there is evidence that much less time is devoted to orientation efforts in the public sector than in the private (Pearson, Ring, and Milne 1983). In the CMRP between one-quarter and one-third of all clients reported that the mediation process was too rushed (Pearson and Thoennes 1984b). On average, private practitioners appear to do a more thorough orientation, but even here there is the possibility that with so little demand for their services, combined with such a high level of belief in what they are doing (not to mention the desire to make a living), private sector mediators may be disinclined to inquire too closely into the parties' motivation and suitability for mediation (see chapter 12).

The spread and intensification of ambivalence from one party to the other may also be managed by separating the parties at the early stages until trust in the mediator and in the process has been strengthened. Note, however, that this tactical move may have negative consequences in other directions—e.g., the fostering of distrust in each party of what may be going on between the mediator and the other in private caucuses; the undermining of the parties' confidence that they can deal with each other directly; and the loss to the mediator of important information about patterns of dysfunctional interaction which may be blocking agreement.

In sum, by virtue of having to deal with two, rather than one person, and because the mediation format places the mediator physically and psychologically between the parties, the mediator's task in handling client ambivalence regarding the professional encounter is inherently more complicated than the lawyer's. To be sure, access to both parties is also rich with opportunities denied to the lawyer, but these opportunities have to be seized and the seizing entails risks of its own. This basic theme reoccurs with all of the principal obstacles with which the mediator must wrestle.

WELL-ESTABLISHED, RIGID PATTERNS OF DESTRUCTIVE INTERACTION

In the emerging empirical study of mediation, both in divorce and elsewhere, there is one finding which stands out: the worse the state of the parties' relationship with one another and the more intense their conflict, the dimmer the prospects for effective mediation. Thus, divorce mediation has been found less effective for couples who have a history of prior litigation and postdissolution battles; who describe their ability to cooperate as "just about impossible"; in which severe pathology such as substance abuse or physical violence has occurred; or who have many contested issues (Doyle and Caron 1979; Pearson and Thoennes 1984b). Divorce mediators themselves are most likely to list the ability of the parties to cooperate with one another as the primary predictor of a successful outcome (Pearson, Ring, and Milne 1983). Studies of labor mediation corroborate the findings in divorce mediation. Poor outcomes are more likely under more intense conflict (Carnevale and Pegnetter, in press; Kochan and Jick 1978; Landsberger 1955); greater hostility between the parties (Carnevale and Pegnetter, in press); and an increase in the number of issues in dispute (Carnevale and Pegnetter, in press; Kochan and Jick 1978).

The correlation between high levels of deeply entrenched conflict and poor mediation outcomes is partly a reflection of the greater difficulty in promoting compromise and constructive problem solving between people to whom compromise and cooperation are alien. The findings also support the view that under conditions of intense and long-standing conflict the mediator's role and structural position mid-way between the combatants becomes as much of a handicap as an advantage. This perspective rests on the assumption, well validated by students of various types of mediation, that the sine qua non of effective intervention is the trust and confidence of the parties (Kolb, in press; Kressel 1972, 1981). Maintaining rapport becomes increasingly difficult as the intensity of the conflict increases, since the mediator's acts of consideration or support toward one of the disputants are apt to be perceived as signs of favoritism or bias by the other. The mediator's dilemma is made more acute because it is precisely under conditions of intense conflict that the obligations of the role impel the mediator to intervene actively and forcefully, thereby risking still further the alienation of one or both sides.

As with the management of ambivalence, the mediator has an array of strategic moves for maintaining acceptability while simultaneously intervening to reduce hostilities and effectuate a more promising interpersonal climate. A partial listing of these includes separating the parties, invoking norms of cooperation and fair play, interrupting dysfunctional or hostile exchanges, educating the parties about their mutual role in negative transactions, invoking their mutual interests in the welfare of their children, and so on.

However, as with the handling of ambivalence, any intervention which occurs in the midst of a highly alienated couple must inevitably have about it something of a wing and a prayer quality. The more recent clinical writings of experienced divorce mediators make this abundantly clear.

> [The mediator] will often be disliked by at least one, if not both, of the spouses, and at one point or another may be viewed as uncompassionate, naive, incompetent, unhelpful, destructive, or just plain mean. Whichever spouses loses the leverage typically will try to cast the mediator in the role of troublemaker or incompetent. Often, one spouse will express this negative feeling to some other significant person, such as a lawyer or new spouse: "My mediator doesn't really understand my side, or he wouldn't have been taken in by those lies from my ex-spouse." (Saposnek 1983, 26)

COMPLEX ISSUES THAT THREATEN LOSS OF FACE OR SELF-ESTEEM

There are findings which suggest that divorce mediators are less successful when the scope of the conflict has expanded to include a variety of third parties, including new spouses or lovers, grandparents, and stepchildren (Caron and Doyle 1979; Sprenkle and Storm 1983); when the parties' lawyers are unethusiastic about mediation (Irving et al. 1979, 1981; Pearson and Thoennes 1982a); and when there are a wide range of highly disputed issues, especially concerning the children (Doyle and Caron 1979; Pearson and Thoennes 1982a; Saposnek 1983).

Under all of these circumstances the parties' negotiating flexibility is likely to be minimal, partly because they wish to appear upright, competent, and successful in the eyes of others. The parties' concerns with "face" can create problems for attorneys, but it would appear to represent a more onerous burden for mediators on a number of counts. First, the parties are much less apt to be willing to compromise with one another, since they may fear that compromise will be interpreted as weakness by others. The ability of their clients to compromise is of value to attorneys, but it is crucial to mediators.

Second, the mediator role places a premium on face-to-face problem solving. By definition such encounters are likely to heighten even further the parties' concerns with looking good. For this reason the mediator may eschew conjoint sessions, at least for a while, but such a tactic may be experienced by all parties, including the mediator, as a departure from the normative prescriptions of the role. Finally, their peace-making function encourages mediators to tackle head on any and all obstacles to conflict resolution. If the parties' resistance is based on fears of how others outside mediation will judge them, the mediator, far more than the attorney, is likely to feel an obligation to improve the negotiating climate by such things as telephone calls to the parties' indifferent or antagonistic lawyers, or by invitations to concerned grandparents or new spouses to attend mediation sessions. Such tactical maneuvers can be productive, but they may also place enormous strains on the mediator's patience, diagnostic acumen, and powers of persuasion. The burden may become especially onerous if the mediator feels obliged to deal not only with one, but two disruptive sets of outside influences.

DISRUPTIVE LEVELS OF STRESS AND TENSION

It is often implied in manuals on divorce mediation that an important function of the mediator is to provide an oasis of calm and rationality in which the highly stressed parties may be helped to collect their wits. This is a worthwhile objective. But what of mediators' struggles to collect their own wits because of the stresses to which *they* are exposed? As divorce mediators become more secure in their professional standing we shall doubtless hear more about the trials and tribulations of their work. For the moment, we may simply enumerate some of the clinical pressures and demands that working with highly ambivalent, conflicted, and unhappy couples is likely to involve. The quotations with which I shall flesh out this list are all drawn from Saposnek (1983), whose book on child custody mediation is the first extended treatment of divorce mediation by a seasoned practitioner in which the many problematic aspects of the role are seriously considered. Saposnek's delineation of the stresses of the divorce mediator's role may apply more to the mediation of custody disputes, which are the subject of his book, than to other forms of divorce mediation. His own view is that the differences are more of degree than of kind. In any case, it is with the more conflicted couples that many divorce mediators will find themselves working.

1. *The need for constant vigilance and activity.*

Because the stakes are so high, the tactical struggles between spouses will be numerous. The mediator must be alert if he or she is to stave off the destructive effects of these struggles. There is no time for passive observation, since the couple's interactions rarely calm down. Moreover, at some point during the process, their interactions almost always reach a point of tension that threatens to terminate the mediation process abruptly and prematurely. (Saposnek 1983, 25)

2. *The paucity of information about the couple, combined with the limited time frame in which mediation occurs.*

Because the mediator receives very little information ahead of time and must work within a time limitation, the task can feel quite difficult at the outset. The issues are obscured and the spouses typically very well defended. This situation can be characterized as the mediator stepping lightly across a mine field. If he accidentally steps in the wrong place, the entire process can blow up in his face. (Saposnek 1983, 27)

3. *The discrepancy between the couple's overt behavior and their underlying dynamics.*

Seasoned mediators learn to be cautious with apparently cooperative couples. If the spouses were really all that cooperative with each other, they would not need to seek mediation . . . a mediator working with such a couple should be prepared for the hostility that often erupts during the actual discussion of custody, or it may come as a disheartening shock. The mediator must be prepared to remain skeptical throughout the session and even to expect the worst while working toward the best outcome. This attitude is a necessary survival tool if the mediator is to cope with unpredictability within a session. (Saposnek 1983, 28)

4. *The enormous range of skills demanded of the mediator.*

An effective mediator's style might best be characterized as active, assertive, goal-oriented, and businesslike. He or she must utilize the skills of brief behaviorally oriented family therapy, crisis intervention, negotiation, organizational development, and child development counseling, coupled with a sensitivity to the emotional and psychological aspects of the mediation process. The mediator must deal with the emotional aspects of the process without allowing them to disrupt the problem solving. Too tight control restricts the complexity of the emotional issues that need to be assessed, while too loose control allows the emotional charge to overwhelm the rational structure needed to reach resolution. There is a thin line between these extremes that the skilled mediator must learn to walk.

Mediators who cannot tolerate open and intense conflict will burn out quickly and, moreover, may cause irreparable damage to the couple's potential for future negotiation. (Saposnek 1983, 322–33)

5. *The frequent exposure to emotionally provocative material.*

> The ability to remain nonjudgmental also requires that the mediator be aware of, and reasonably resolved about, his or her own familial issues and personal values, which might be aroused in the course of mediation. . . . it may be difficult for the mediator to deal fairly with spouses who have authoritarian child-rearing practices, religious beliefs that seem extreme or destructive to healthy child development, or vengeful motives for spending time with their child. These issues can elicit what psychoanalytic theory refers to as countertransference reactions and lead a mediator away from the task of fair management of the dispute. Keeping such reactions in check is especially important in mediation work because, unlike psychotherapy, there is little or no time to digest or even dissipate such reactions. (Saposnek 1983, 34–35)

DEFECTS IN THE NORMS AND SOCIAL MECHANISMS OF CONFLICT MANAGEMENT

In chapter 2 I outlined the problems that may be created for constructive divorce negotiations by legal training, norms, and relationships. Since mediation occurs within a legal context, the procedures and norms of the law may also pose a serious threat to the work of the divorce mediator. The most direct agent of the mediator's miseries is likely to be the lawyer. Inadvertently or intentionally, the parties' attorneys may detonate the mediation process. Saposnek gives two such examples. He cites one instance in which a mediation had been going smoothly until the husband received a subpoena from his wife's attorney for a custody hearing. This notice had been sent inadvertently by the lawyer's secretary. Although apologies to the husband were made, his trust in his wife's motives had been damaged beyond repair and he refused to continue the mediation. According to Saposnek, such occurrences are not uncommon in custody mediation (Saposnek 1983, 31).

In another instance, agreement in mediation was forestalled by the wife's rigid insistence on having three-quarters of a day more per week with the children than her husband. On investigation, her motive hinged on her attorney's advice that she negotiate more than 50 percent of the time with the children because this might strengthen her chance of gaining physical custody in the event that she ever moved out of state (she could then argue that the children had become more attached to her). This competitive legal advice was destructive to the mediation efforts and was particularly ironic, since the wife had no intention of relocating and had been perfectly willing to share the time with the children equally until her lawyer intervened (Saposnek 1983, 152).

Problems of this sort are exacerbated because, although collaboration between attorneys and mediators certainly occurs, the majority of practitioners in both groups appear to have relatively little to do with one another. For example, 30 percent of mediators in the private sector and 43 percent in the public sector report that attorneys are not involved in any way in the drafting or review of the mediated agreement. Far fewer than half of the mediators in either sector obtain the attorneys' consent at the beginning of mediation or talk with the attorneys before, between, or after mediation sessions. As a group, lawyers may be contributing significantly to the lack of communication. More than half of the eighty-one New Jersey Family Law Section members whom we interviewed were unenthusiastic about mediation and a minority were decidedly hostile. Very few referrals to mediation come from attorneys (Pearson, Ring, and Milne 1983).

Many mediators are apparently aware of the low esteem in which they are held by the legal community. In the survey by Pearson and her colleagues, only 32 percent of private mediators felt the bench was favorably disposed to mediation; only 20 percent that the bar was so inclined. Significant of the distance between lawyers and mediators, even larger percentages simply didn't know how they were viewed by either bench (41 percent) or bar (39 percent). Moreover, a good number of divorce mediators appear to be concerned that their legal colleagues may be inclined to sue them for the unauthorized practice of law. (Only 3 percent of divorce mediators have actually been taken to court on this issue, but 53 percent in the private sector and 45 percent in the public one are worried about the possibility [Pearson, Ring, and Milne 1983].)

The institutional roots of the mediator's difficulties do not lie exclusively in legal soil, however. Several notable problems arise from within the normative and institutional structure of mediation itself. Among these are the nonjudgmental stance which mediators are obliged to adopt; the liabilities they may incur as a consequence of their official standing as agents of the court; and the lack of consensus within the profession on strategies and tactics of intervention.

THE PHILOSOPHY THAT NEITHER PARTY IS "RIGHT" OR "WRONG."

> It is not uncommon for the mediator to receive calls from a therapist (or even a lawyer) who is aghast at hearing (from the mother) that the mediator is even considering helping a "bad" father continue contact with the "victimized" child. . . . The mediator must deal understandingly with those persons and their concerns but must not be swayed. It is only by adhering to the systems point of view, in which there is typically neither individual truth nor objective reality, but only degrees of descriptive accuracy about the system itself, that the mediator can succeed in resolving the dispute. (Saposnek 1983, 26)

Although not every divorce mediator would necessarily agree with this prescription, it expresses a view which is commonly held. In several respects it is a useful prescription. It conforms to the reality that in most disputes between divorcing spouses there *is* no right or wrong, but simply differences of taste, opinion, and subjective judgment; it reflects well-documented clinical experience regarding how families operate (see chapters 3 and 4); and it offers the mediator valuable protection against the serious blunder (and temptation) of taking sides.

However, there are less functional consequences of the "nobody is right or wrong" philosophy. The mediator's commitment to the notion of indeterminacy can be wearing, especially since divorce mediation occurs in an arena in which the parties' own turmoil may make them very inadequate judges of what is fair or reasonable. There are undoubtedly times, especially in regard to children, when the mediator's judgment is better than that of the parties. In such circumstances the mediator faces some uneasy choices, particularly when the less tractable or rational party also exerts the stronger influence in the deliberations. If the mediator chooses to remain silent an agreement can be reached which does violence to the mediator's obligation to foster lasting and high quality settlements as opposed to merely expeditious ones. If the mediator intervenes vigorously to attempt to persuade the parties to reach an agreement on terms which the mediator thinks advisable, he or she runs the risk of losing acceptability and of thereby ceasing to be an influence altogether, or of arm-twisting the disputants into an agreement that will very quickly be abandoned once they are beyond the mediator's clutches. There is evidence from international and industrial mediation that mediators attempt to steer a delicate path between these various extremes, partly by blinding themselves to the very real, but covert and manipulative quality of their interventions (Kressel 1972, 1981).

PROBLEMS EMANATING FROM THE MEDIATOR'S INSTITUTIONAL AFFILIATIONS. In chapter 7 I discussed the covert conflicts of interest that may adversely affect the relationship between lawyer and client. Divorce mediators are not immune to such problems. For example, public sector divorce mediators work in an institutional context and are thus exposed to the wishes and views of co-workers and superiors. These individuals represent the mediator's own "constituents," and their perspective on the performance of mediation may not be easily ignored. I have considered the problems posed by the mediator's constituents in the international and industrial spheres (Kressel 1972, 1981; see also Wall 1981). The major threat appears to be to maintaining the trust and confidence of the parties because of their suspicion that the mediator's interests are at variance with their own. There is no direct evidence of similar problems in divorce mediation. However, a significant minority of persons who have experienced public sector divorce mediation are displeased with the process and complain of coercive mediator tactics (Pearson and Thoennes 1984b). Vidmar (in press) reports a similar phenomenon in small claims mediation. The use of such tactics may partially be attributed to the pressures on the public sector mediator to produce large numbers of "agreements"—agreements that their superiors need in order to justify to continued use of public funds. I have also noted that, compared to private sector mediators, those in the public sector spend significantly shorter amounts of time orienting clients to the mediation process. This, too, may reflect institutional pressures on the public sector mediator to process large numbers of cases in order to impress the cost conscious and sceptical legal community which controls the purse.

Divorce mediators may also be imbued with considerable power, either in fact or in the imagination of the disputing spouses. Once again, this is particularly likely to apply to the public sector mediator, who functions directly under the aegis of the court. Power and authority can be great assets to a mediator but they are also potential liabilities, even when not explicitly mobilized, since they tend to foster undo receptivity to the mediator's preferences, whereas the mediator's role is to foster the parties' self-determination. Moreover, in particularly intense disputes, or with especially difficult or ambivalent clients, mediators may be sorely tempted to *use* the power at their command. In so doing they are responding to the mandates of their role that they resolve disputes, and, perhaps, to the implicit pressure to appear successful and competent to themselves as well as to those to whom they may be accountable. However, the arm-twisting approach risks alienating the parties and/or producing settlements which are very short lived. Public sector divorce mediators have not yet written on these matters but, as I have just noted, there is evidence that mediator "aggressiveness" is not uncommon in public mediation and that it is resented by a sizeable minority of clients (Pearson and Thoennes 1984b; Vidmar, in press).

THE LACK OF CONSENSUS WITHIN THE FIELD ON MAJOR STRATEGIC ISSUES. Because divorce mediation is in the very early stages of professional development, the individual practitioner may not yet rely on a high degree of professional agreement in confronting many of the everyday problems of professional practice. Instead, mediators must struggle to develop their own private solutions, secure in the knowledge that somebody else who speaks with authority thinks things should be done differently. The questions on which opinion is diametrically opposed are: Should there be formal rules of mediation which the parties sign in advance or should there be no such rules? Should mediation have joint sessions exclusively or should mediation proceed primarily via individual meetings? Should mediators handle only custody/visitation disputes or should they handle all issues, including those over money and property? Does the mediator have an obligation to help promote a "fair" agreement, especially where the welfare of children is concerned, or is the mediator to scrupulously refrain from pushing his or her concept of a good settlement on the parties?

In addition to these questions there are a host of others on which the range of answers put forward for the edification and guidance of the practicing mediator cannot be so simply summarized. These include: What, if anything, should be the formal role of attorneys in the mediation process? Which couples are most appropriate for mediation; which, if any, are inappropriate? Can a couple's therapist continue in the role of mediator, and, if so, with what understandings for later therapeutic involvement? Should divorce mediators deal with "emotional" issues, or stay "task-oriented"? If emotional issues are dealt with, in what ways and for how long should this be done? What should be the structure of mediation sessions (e.g., how long should each session last? How far apart should sessions be scheduled?). Should the parties be permitted/encouraged to speak with each other and their friends, advisors, and attorneys, or should they be asked to take a vow of silence between sessions? What legal risks do divorce mediators expose themselves to? (E.g., is divorce mediation by mental health professionals the unauthorized practice of law? Can attorneys engage in mediation without risking serious violation of legal norms and ethics?)[1]

The effect of all this uncertainty on a mediator's peace of mind is impossible to judge with any degree of accuracy. In some regards it might make life a bit easier, providing mediators with a wider array of acceptable role options than would be the case if role performance were more strictly prescribed. On the other hand, judging from the number of calls for the resolution and clarification of these and other matters of professional practice, the level of concern about how the mediation role should be enacted appears to be high.

The lack of professional consensus about the enactment of the role is not merely a function of divorce mediation's early stage of professional development. There is an inherent ambiguity and indeterminacy about competent performance in the mediation role which no amount of professional consensus seeking can ever completely eliminate. Mediating a dispute is a fundamentally different kind of human activity than fixing a carburetor or removing a gall bladder; there are no precise guidelines for proceeding and the result of intervention is by no means self evident. It is this elusive and vexing aspect of their work to which experienced labor mediators refer when they describe their job as far more "art" than science. Kolb (in press) has given one of the best recent sketches of the issue in her description of the struggles of experienced labor mediators to establish and maintain credibility with the disputants and the ironic headaches they may create for themselves in attempting to do so.

Kolb sketches a number of factors which promote insecurity in mediators. All of them represent certain inherent ambiguities of the peacemaker function, including the fact that the knowledge and skills of the mediator are of a behavioral sort available to many; that it is difficult, both for mediators and disputants, to evaluate competent and incompetent mediator performance; that it is frequently difficult to know when progress is occurring during a case; and that it is often unclear what, if anything, the mediator has contributed to the outcome. The theme of Kolb's paper is to delineate the various strategies that mediators employ to bolster their provisional standing with the parties and themselves. At least some of these strategies have the paradoxical effect of threatening to make the mediator's dilemma worse, rather than better (e.g., name-dropping to establish their "expertise"; inventing "facts" to convey their "knowledge" of the industry; fabricating to one side the efforts they have made in private caucuses with the other to push its position). Such interventions may be effective in establishing the mediator's authority but they may also lead to characterizations of the mediator as a flimflam artist if brought to light. The precise manner in which divorce mediators struggle to establish the basis for *their* authority—and the price which they and the parties may pay for the solutions which they arrive at—have not yet begun to be documented.

Summary

As we have seen, the divorce mediator's role is fraught with difficulty. Some of this is ascribable to the unfortunate psychological and material circumstances of the divorcing couple. However, an important contributor to the difficulties that mediators experience are the lofty, contradictory, and ambiguous nature of the role itself. Mediators may wish and strive to be impartial, even handed, impeccably trustworthy, empathetic, and clear sighted. These objectives will soon be found to conflict with the need to establish their authority and influence, overcome resistance, promote compromise, represent and cope with the needs and wishes of their own constituents, and promote settlements that cause nobody undue pain.

Does this mean that divorce mediation is an inherently "impossible profession" and therefore an unlikely source of help for the miseries which arise during divorce negotiations? I do not think so. Does the analysis imply that the claims of mediation's most eager and impassioned champions ought to be regarded skeptically? Without question.

As we gain more experience with the divorce mediation process and as researchers and practitioners begin to document the more and less adaptive ways in which mediators cope with the challenges of the role, the conditions under which divorce mediation is likely to be most useful, and the varieties of intervention that are required to manage or circumvent the role's inherent problems, will become increasingly clear. In the following two chapters I shall assay a modest contribution to that undertaking by scrutinizing the pioneering efforts of Coogler, one of the most profound influences on the first generation of divorce mediators.

11

Mediation and the Psychological Dynamics of the Divorcing Couple

Thus far the focus has been on the perspective and concerns of the therapist, lawyer, or mediator. I turn now to the perspective and concerns of the divorcing couple themselves. When my colleagues and I became interested in extending our research on the settlement process to the mediation experience, it soon became clear that direct exposure to the views of divorcing persons would be crucial. At this juncture of our research we were extremely fortunate to learn of the work of O. J. Coogler, the man who may rightly be considered the "father" of the divorce mediation movement, and who, until his death, trained approximately half of all practicing divorce mediators (Pearson, Ring, and Milne 1983). When we first contacted him, Coogler was in the process of finalizing the details of the procedure which he referred to as Structured Mediation. At the time, in the spring of 1976, it was the most well-developed approach to divorce mediation in existence. Coogler and his co-workers, Judi Wood and Will Neville, had by then assisted approximately one hundred couples negotiate their divorce settlements. Even more exciting, in terms of our research interests, was that nearly all of those mediations had been fully tape-recorded. What we learned from the intensive study of a small number of those cases is the subject of this and the following chapter.

In presenting this material I would like to express my gratitude to Coogler. His willingness to tolerate, indeed, to welcome critical analysis of his work, particularly at a time when the undertaking was lonely and the criticisms from his legal colleagues many, is testimony not only to his faith in himself and the mediation process, but to his candid recognition that there was much to be learned. It is in that spirit and with great admiration for his accomplishments that I have written what follows.

It was true when my colleagues and I began our study of divorce mediation, and is still largely true today, that accounts of the divorcing process have stressed intrapsychic and individual factors, rather than what goes on *between* the divorcing spouses. Moreover, the accent has been on marital dissolution as an ordered series of "stages," more or less comparable from case to case. This one-dimensional perspective is very much at variance with what we learned from the couples whose experiences I shall be describing. I have tried to do justice to their experiences—and the requirements of effective intervention—by painting a more complex picture of the divorcing process.

I am well aware, of course, that an investigation of a small number of cases, however intensive, is not a vehicle for demonstrating cause and effect relationships or the reliability of descriptive categories. I present these findings not because they are definitive, but because they address in a concrete, detailed fashion two important and related, but largely unexplored issues: the types of couples for whom some form of divorce mediation may be most suitable, and the multidimensional nature of the divorce experience itself.

In this chapter I shall primarily be concerned with describing the typology of divorce decision making which is at the core of our findings and its broad correlation with the ease or difficulty with which the mediators were able to perform their task. I shall also briefly consider the implications of the typology for the ease of adjustment among members of the postdivorce family. In the following chapter I shall focus in on one of the more difficult cases and examine in detail the hazardous psychological currents in which the divorce mediator may, on perhaps many occasions, be obliged to navigate.

Method

THE RESPONDENTS

Two groups were selected for study: nine *mediated* couples who had used the Coogler procedure of Structured Mediation in negotiating their settlement agreements, and five *nonmediated* couples who had used the traditional legal-adversarial system. At the time of the research, the Family Mediation Association (FMA), which Coogler founded and which implements the mediation program, had been in existence for nearly two years in a large Southern city.

The process of Structured Divorce Mediation (Coogler 1978) involves divorcing spouses in direct negotiations over all the terms of the divorce settlement, including financial and property issues as well as those involving the children (e.g., custody, visitation). The couple is assisted by an impartial mediator trained in psychology. An advisory attorney serves as a neutral legal consultant for both spouses. During negotiations the couple is enjoined from seeking outside legal advice. Detailed written guidelines are provided in an initial orientation. The ground rules emphasize the importance of full disclosure, fairness, and mutual respect, and set forth the administrative details of the negotiations. The role of the mediator is complex, but includes assistance with framing an agenda, problem solving, increasing the flow of accurate and nonbelligerent communication, and insuring that both parties participate actively in the negotiating process. Overall it may be characterized as largely task-oriented. Couples are referred elsewhere for help in dealing with emotional problems related to the divorce. Settlements are generally reached within three to eight two-hour sessions.

Since our goal was to get as comprehensive a picture of mediation as possible, we selected for investigation couples who had at least one minor child and who, in the judgment of the FMA staff, were involved in negotiations of some complexity. In addition, at least two cases from each of the FMA's three principal mediators were included.

The nonmediated couples constituted a smaller sample than we had wished, but obtaining nonmediated respondents turned out to be a far more complicated task than anticipated. The initial plan was to sample randomly from court records the divorce settlements filed within the same period as the settlements of the mediated group, and from among these randomly selected divorces, interview those former spouses whose marriages had been most comparable to the mediated group on certain descriptive-demographic characteristics. This plan foundered on the incompleteness of the court records with regard to the present whereabouts of the spouses, and the unwillingness of one or both spouses to speak with us. Ultimately only two couples were successfully located from the court records. The remaining three couples were obtained from inquiries among local church and community groups. (Three additional interviews, two mediated and one nonmediated, were conducted with respondents whose ex-spouses refused to talk with us. The data from these respondents will be used in a supplementary fashion.)

Descriptively, the mediated spouses were slightly younger (35.7 years vs. 40.2 years for the husbands; 33.3 years vs. 36.6 years for the wives) and married more recently (9 years vs. 13 years) than the nonmediated couples. There was an average of two children per family for both groups. The mediated husbands had received somewhat more education and had somewhat higher incomes than their nonmediated counterparts. (Although all husbands in both groups were in professional or managerial positions, one of the mediated men was a physician and another a dentist. Neither of these high status, high income professions were represented in the nonmediated group.) A similar pattern was characteristic of the wives. The tendency for receptivity to divorce mediation to be higher among more affluent, better educated segments of the population has also been reported by Pearson, Thoennes and Vanderkooi (1982). On religious affiliation and importance of religion the mediated and nonmediated couples were comparable, the majority being Protestant. There was one Jewish couple in both groups. All the couples were white. At the time of the interview the mediated respondents had been divorced for a shorter period (median=6 months, range=2 to 18 months) than had the nonmediated respondents (median=14 months, range=6 to 42 months).

For most of the couples the divorce process was relatively long (median =26 months from the earliest point at which either spouse first seriously considered the possibility of divorce to the date of the final divorce decree). The entire process may be subdivided into an extended *decision stage* (median=14 months), during which the couple struggled about the fate of the marriage, and a much shorter *negotiation stage,* typically beginning within a month to three months after the divorce decision, and concluding within a month or two in agreement over terms for a final divorce settlement. The chronological pattern was similar for both mediated and nonmediated groups.

SOURCES OF DATA

The project involved two primary sources of data: the complete audiotapes of each of the nine mediated couples' negotiations (these were recorded by the FMA for research and training purposes with the knowledge and permission of the couples), and extended two-and-one-half- to four-hour postdivorce interviews, designed and conducted by us, with each of the former spouses. Respondents were assured that all material would be kept strictly confidential and that none of their views would in any way be communicated to the former spouse. The interview schedule was a mixture of open-ended questions and bipolar ratings scales covering the entire divorce experience.

The Path to the Bargaining Table: Nonmutuality and Level of Conflict

I will focus my primary attention on the patterned differences among our couples with regard to the dynamics of the divorcing process. I begin, however, with some general observations concerning the nature of the spouses' motivation to divorce, the level of conflict between them, and the parties' overall evaluation of the mediation experi ıce.

NONMUTUALITY OF THE DIVORCE DECISION AND READINESS TO NEGOTIATE

Why did these marriages end? This is at once the most natural question to ask and the most difficult to answer. We had no illusion that in a single interview we would be able to answer it fully.

For the most part, questions about the causes of the divorce elicited stereotypic responses: "problems in communicating," "absence of love," "personality differences," or simply "growing apart." Sexual problems and financial difficulties were mentioned by two or three respondents. In two cases the desire to marry somebody else was the precipitating factor, although in both instances there are clear signs that things had gone wrong in the marriage long before the new love appeared. The only pattern of note was that in half the fourteen cases there was an indication that the wives wanted a more intimate, emotionally closer relationship than their husbands were willing or able to supply.

We can speak more confidently, however, of the motivational pattern with regard to the wish to divorce. Nonmutuality was the prevailing style. Only three of these fourteen divorces were mutually desired at the time of the first serious divorce discussion. Of the nonmutual divorces, seven were initiated by the husband, four initiated by the wife. Even after an agreement to divorce had been reached and negotiations over settlement terms had begun, in only five cases did both spouses characterize themselves as equally ready to end the marriage. These findings are entirely consistent with the empirical literature (see chapter 2). In the termination of intimate relationships there is typically a "leaver" and a "left."

Vastly different temporal perspectives were correlated with these two roles. In general, the noninitiators had far less time with which to prepare for the emotional and substantive issues in the divorce. At the time negotiations began, for example, the initiators had been grappling with the prospects of divorce for an average of ten to eleven months, the noninitiators for only one or two.

More than a simple lack of emotional and cognitive preparedness was involved, however. There are clear indications that strong elements of defensive denial were at work on the part of the noninitiator. Thus, in eight of the fourteen couples the noninitiators report not consciously considering divorce for periods ranging from two to fifteen months after either what they themselves regarded as the first serious mutual discussion of divorce with their spouse (who often put this discussion at a much earlier period), or after the even more concrete sign of rupture—the physical separation. In four of these eight cases the noninitiators did not consider divorce seriously until after both these events had occurred.

As might be expected, the effect of nonmutuality on the negotiating process was unfavorable. In the orientation, when the rules and procedures of Structured Mediation were being explained, both spouses had some difficulty in comprehending fully and asking questions. The difficulties, however, were typically greater for noninitiators. A mutually informed commitment to the mediation process was thus not easily obtained.

Once negotiations began noninitiators tended to adopt extreme and inflexible positions—often couched in terms of protecting the interests of their children—as a means of simultaneously expressing their anger, saving face, and preventing the reaching of a settlement and the ultimate dissolution of the marriage. Initiators typically responded by at first acquiescing to their spouse's demands, and then with anger and inflexibility.

In the large-scale samples studied by Pearson and her colleagues, nonacceptance of the divorce has not been found predictive of a poorly mediated outcome (Pearson and Thoennes 1984b), although it is widely believed to be a crucial complication by mediators themselves (Sprenkle and

Storm 1983), and there is at least one investigation where its negative impact has been verified (Irving et al. 1979). In the FMA couples whose experiences we are considering, the ultimate impact of nonacceptance was a function of the wider pattern of divorce in which it was embedded and which shall be described shortly.

LEVEL OF CONFLICT AND THE DECISION TO MEDIATE

Under what conditions will divorcing spouses prefer the use of lawyers in the traditional adversary process as opposed to negotiating a settlement directly with the help of a mediator? We may shed some light on this important question by a comparison of our mediated and nonmediated couples. Because of the wide publicity the FMA had received in the local community at least one spouse in five of the six nonmediated couples (we are including here one case in which only the husband agreed to be interviewed) knew of the FMA in advance of seeing a lawyer. Why was mediation not used?

In one instance, the parties opted for lawyers as the most familiar and straightforward means to achieve a swift and uncontested divorce in a situation in which the wife was eager to remarry. In all the other cases high levels of conflict appear implicated in the decision not to mediate. Relative to the mediated group, the four remaining nonmediated cases exhibited higher degrees of nonmutuality with regard to the divorce decision; a more negative emotional climate; and less satisfactory experiences with joint counselling prior to the divorce decision. The picture is consistent with Pearson, Thoennes, and Vanderkooi (1982), who found that severe impairments in parental communication and motivation to cooperate were associated with the rejection of free custody mediation.

An additional component in the mediation decision was the attitude of wives. Compared to their nonmediated counterparts, the mediated wives were far more positive in their ratings of the marital climate and the chances for settlement. Indeed, they were the most optimistic group among the respondents generally. We also note that two of the mediated wives were thoroughly familiar with mediation as a result of some training experience with the FMA. On the other hand, mediation was explicitly rejected by one wife because she felt incapable of holding up her side of negotiations without independent counsel. Overall, the findings suggest that mediation is an unattractive alternative for couples who perceive the level of conflict between them as being either quite high—and their own resources for effective self-representation as inadequate—or quite low. Mediation appears to be more appealing to couples experiencing moderate levels of conflict and in whom there is some confidence, particularly on the wife's part, that self-representation can be effectively managed. (I hasten to add that a couple's preference for one or another mode of arriving at a settlement is not necessarily the best indicator of what method would actually serve them best.)[1]

SATISFACTION WITH THE MEDIATION EXPERIENCE

In the postdivorce interviews, five of the nine couples were generally enthusiastic about mediation. They felt, among other things, that the mediator had made useful suggestions for compromise, kept them issue-oriented when anger threatened to become disruptive, reassured them by remaining calm in the face of their own or the spouse's provocation, and left them with a sense of having achieved a settlement that was truly their own.

In two couples the spouses disagreed about the value of mediation, and in two others both spouses regarded the experience as unsatisfactory. The principal complaints were lack of adequate guidance on substantive matters, suspicions of mediator bias, and the belief that the settlement now appeared unfair.

The outcomes experienced by the mediated couples compared favorably to the outcomes experienced by couples who relied exclusively on lawyers. Mediated couples tended to spend slightly less, on average, than did the nonmediated (by about $200 per couple); and described a more positive process. Thus, on the seven-point rating scales, in which the low end of the scale indicated the favorable response, mediated wives rated the settlement process as more constructive, friendlier, less upsetting, and more satisfying. The pattern was similar but less striking for the husbands. There were no major differences between the two groups with regard to satisfaction with most of the terms of settlement except that there were no mediated couples involved in a postdivorce custody dispute, but this had occurred in two nonmediated cases. It must be noted, however, that the mediated couples described the climate *prior* to negotiations in generally more favorable terms than did the nonmediated respondents. Thus, the mediated couples were more likely to report thinking it would be easier to reach agreement; felt more mutual about the divorce; and reported lower levels of initial disagreement.

Because of the small and highly self-selected samples involved, I shall make no pretense that these findings cast any light on mediation's efficacy. The complexities of that issue and the growing evidence on the subject from more large-scale studies have been considered in detail in chapter 9.

Two things are worth noting, however: First, on our rating scale measures, the *subjective* evaluations of the mediation experience were, on average, highly positive. Thus, on the seven-point scales, husbands and wives were highly satisfied with mediation and gave the mediator very high marks for impartiality, supportiveness, competence, and psychological sophistication. On the other hand, when respondents were given a more extended opportunity to expand on their views and when we considered how matters stood six months or more after the settlement, a less positive and more complex picture of mediation's impact was apparent. I note this not to disparage what was accomplished but to suggest that we need to evaluate the mediation process (and the legal one, too) with a variety of tools and should not be unduly impressed with the most easily obtained types of data. Generally, people who have invested time, energy, and money in a process tend to say nice things about it. When they are given an opportunity to elaborate or when other perspectives are brought to bear, matters may look more complicated.

Patterns of Divorce: A Typology and Its Correlates

While nonmutuality and level of conflict played their roles in influencing the approach to negotiations, it was the systematic and patterned differences among our couples in the divorce decision period, rather than any one or two characteristics of this period considered in isolation, that were most highly correlated with the nature and outcome of the settlement process. Research on divorce, like that on acquaintanceship and courtship, has focused on the stages through which the relationship passes, with little attention to the patterned differences among individuals or couples. There is a striking absence of research on the multidimensional nature with which human relationships unfold (Huston and Levinger 1978). In contrast, the complex and differentiated picture of the divorce decision period which our respondents provided suggests very strongly that the process of marital separation is neither uniform nor idiosyncratic. It was possible, in fact, to discern four distinctive patterns by which our couples reached the divorce decision. We have labeled these the *enmeshed, autistic, direct,* and *disengaged* patterns of divorce decision making. The classification is based primarily on three complex and highly intercorrelated dimensions: *degree of ambivalence* toward the fate of the relationship, *frequency and openness of communication* about the possibility of divorce, and the *level and overtness of the conflict* with which the decision was reached.

Because data collection centered on the settlement process, we can say little about the antecedent factors which may have produced these patterns. We can be much more explicit, however, about what appear to be their more notable consequences. First, the negotiating process tended to recapitulate, in a more concentrated fashion and within a more restricted time frame, the major dynamics of the divorce decision period; e.g., degree of ambivalence, openness and frequency of communication, and level and quality of conflict maintained the contours which they had previously assumed. Second, the challenge to effective intervention varied accordingly. Generally speaking, the enmeshed and autistic patterns appeared the most difficult for mediators to deal with. Finally, the patterns were correlated with different levels of postdivorce adjustment. Among the mediated couples the worst adjustments occurred in the enmeshed and autistic patterns, somewhat more favorable ones in the direct conflict group, and the best overall adjustment in couples of the disengaged type. We have organized the descriptions of the four patterns and their consequences in this ascending order of postdivorce adaptation.

THE ENMESHED PATTERN

Seven couples—four mediated and three nonmediated—fit the enmeshed pattern. The hallmarks of this pattern were extremely high levels of conflict and ambivalence about the divorce decision. The parties debated the pros and cons of divorce, often bitterly; agreed to divorce and then changed their minds; and once a "final" decision was made proved unable to implement it. They maintained a common residence after the decision and may have continued sleeping in the same bed and having sexual relations. Marital counseling was tried but proved ineffectual in producing a clear impetus to psychic divorce. In spite of explicit avowals of a wish to divorce the impression was of parties psychically unprepared to let go.

The negotiation period reflected the ambivalent and highly reactive nature of the divorce decision process. On the eve of negotiations the emotional climate was extremely poor—worse, indeed, than in any of the other patterns. One, and sometimes both spouses, approached mediation with grave reservations and gave themselves to the process grudgingly at best. For the nonmediated couples contact with lawyers had a similar flavor—attorneys were retained then dropped, or there were no efforts to retain counsel at all on the part of the noninitiator. Negotiations were long, acrimonious, and frustrating, even when substantive issues did not objectively present major obstacles to settlement. The prolonged squabbling over minutiae seemed to derive from an unconscious resistance to finalizing a settlement. Because it was in opposition to these powerful currents of attachment, the mediator's role was extremely difficult.

The outcomes were as poor as the negotiations which produced them. The parties were bitter towards each other and dissatisfied with the terms of settlement. Blame of the other was the prevailing explanation both for the divorce and the difficulties since. In every instance there were significant adjustment problems with children. The more extreme forms of post-divorce turmoil—initiation of law suits, and (in one case) acts of physical violence necessitating police intervention—occurred only in this pattern, and appear to reflect the same generalized inability to let go that characterized the divorce decision and negotation periods.

The cases of the Whites is representative of the enmeshed pattern:

> Both spouses agreed that Mr. White first brought up the idea of divorce and wanted it more. They tried discussing their problems with no success. Mrs. White said they argued over everything. If he said "black" she said "white." They went to a counsellor, jointly and alone, over a period of two years. Although both expressed satisfaction with this experience, neither seemed to have any real insight as to why they didn't get along. Finally they decided to divorce.
>
> Soon after, the thirty-five-year-old wife became pregnant for the second time (the couple had one child), and the divorce decision was reversed. After three months of pregnancy, Mrs. White had a miscarriage. According to the husband, there was no longer any reason to defer the divorce. Mrs. White, however, continued to strongly oppose the idea, claiming that she still loved her husband. He, in spite of pushing for divorce, continued to live at home.
>
> The Whites first went to the FMA for an orientation session at the suggestion of their therapist, but Mrs. White refused to agree to mediation at that time; she still wanted the marriage. They decided to proceed with the process a month later. Nevertheless, Mrs. White's commitment to it was at first minimal and she occasionally threatened to walk out. Although Mr. White claimed to be determined to divorce he was still sleeping in the same bedroom with his wife and was very unresponsive to the mediator's suggestion that he separate from her. His doubts about mediation, which he had pushed for, can be inferred from his secretly retaining a lawyer, although this is forbidden by the mediation rules and was explicitly discouraged by the mediator.
>
> Although the Whites' mediation was long and acrimonious, they had few substantive issues to resolve. At the second session they agreed that everything should be split equally. Neither spouse seemed really to accept this, however. Mrs. White felt that she deserved more than half because she didn't want the divorce and also because she had worked part-time during the marriage. Mr. White seemed to feel that all marital property was really his, since he had paid for it. Small items such as towels and sheets became matters requiring extensive negotiation.
>
> The mediator's major focus was to attempt to break the cycle of conflict over minor items, at first by trying to help the parties arrive at mutually acceptable methods of division, and, when that failed, to suggest in various ways that they

> were both being unreasonable. Ultimately, the mediator became as frustrated as the parties.
>
> During the postdivorce interview both partners expressed bitterness at their former spouse. Although Mr. White was paying child support regularly, Mrs. White had reported him to the IRS for his failure to give her half of their tax refund from the previous year and they were still fighting with each other over that. Within a few months of the divorce Mrs. White had remarried a man eight years her junior. She was holding down two jobs since her new spouse was unemployed. Mr. White was still stewing over the division of property. Their son was very disturbed by the divorce. The child had begun throwing temper tantrums, couldn't sleep, at first wouldn't eat and then had started overeating. Finally, Mrs. White sent him to a psychologist.

More extreme examples of the nature and consequences of enmeshment are represented in the sample. In one case mediation began but never ended. The couple had an extremely stormy series of sessions and went through two mediators in the process, neither of whom was able to contain the conflict or win the husband's confidence. In this instance it appears that mediation was the vehicle utilized to continue the relationship rather than end it. This motivation could be quite explicit. One nonmediated husband, whose wife initiated their divorce, remarked that if she had agreed with his suggestion that they go to the FMA, he had intended to try to use the process to keep the marriage from ending.

An even more intense pattern of enmeshment is illustrated by the Stewarts:

> From the account of the husband (whose ex-wife would not consent to be interviewed), the marriage appears to have been based on the husband's destructive need to fight with and demean his wife. By his own admission the husband had sought the "meanest bastard" for a lawyer that he could find to help him wage a bitter custody fight which occurred prior to mediation. After $12,000 in legal fees, he finally lost this battle because, during the court fight, he had continued to live at home and sleep with his wife.
>
> At the time of the postdivorce interview he expressed no regrets at any of this. Indeed, both the court fight and the equally tempestuous mediation (his wife is currently suing him for psychiatric and other bills) he viewed with great satisfaction; lawyers, judges, mediators—all, he felt, were highly competent and fair. The impression of an intense and continuing gratification at the heat of marital battle is inescapable.

THE AUTISTIC PATTERN

One mediated and one nonmediated couple fit the autistic pattern. In several respects this pattern is the antithesis of the enmeshed type of divorce decision making. For the autistic couples communication and overt conflict about the possibility of divorce were almost entirely absent. Throughout the decision stage the spouses avoided each other physically and emotionally. Ambivalence about the divorce, although high in at least one partner, did not galvanize interaction during the divorce decision period as it did with the enmeshed couples. Rather, the effects of ambivalence were assimilated to the prevailing pattern of conflict avoidance, and the currents of doubt and uncertainty about the fate of the marriage went completely unarticulated. The two couples exhibiting the autistic pattern during the divorce decision period proceeded very differently.

The more problematic case was that of the Browns who used mediation. Their experience shall be discussed at great length in the following chapter. We may simply note its major contours here.

> Mr. Brown, the initiator of the divorce, said nothing to his wife about his plans to leave her for nearly a year. Finally, he took a separate apartment, ostensibly to be nearer work. For several months during the separation they did not say a word to each other about divorce. Finally, at the prodding of a therapist she had begun seeing, Mrs. Brown raised the issue and with little discussion they agreed to end the marriage. The divorce mediation was short but not sweet as we shall see in the next chapter. Its major characteristic was the absence of any genuine negotiating give and take. Most of the time Mrs. Brown dictated the terms to a guilty, occasionally sullen, but mostly acquiescent husband. Near the very end of the mediation he exploded in a totally unanticipated outburst over child support and she tearfully assented to his demands. Nonetheless, although the deeply buried emotional issues were left unexplored and although the mediator did not draw the parties' attention to the absence of any true negotiating, through his good offices, the Browns were guided into a reasonably equitable settlement.
>
> The emotional context in which negotiations were conducted has, however, cast a long shadow. Visitation, child support, and division of property are all issues of continuing dissatisfaction. The Browns returned to the FMA for one session because of Mrs. Brown's continuing complaints about her ex-husband's refusal to see the children and his counter charges that she harasses him at work and annoys his new wife with phone calls. Although the terms which he agreed to do not seem unreasonable, one year after the divorce Mr. Brown feels bitter and "ripped off." He has consulted a lawyer to see if he has any legal recourse.
>
> The Browns' relationship with each other is strained, but, as during the marriage, a cool distance prevails. She had hoped that they would be able to have the children in common but they don't. When asked if she wished anything between them were different, Mrs. Brown said, "Not any more. From my standpoint it doesn't bother me at all."

In the other instance of an autistic pattern the same hallmarks of noncommunication throughout the decision stage were present, but in the negotiation stage matters were emotionally more straightforward. The wife had fallen in love with somebody else, but the couple was able to divorce with a minimum of conflict and a reasonable amount of good will. The more placid course which the autistic pattern took in this case seems attributable to a variety of factors, including the financial self-sufficiency of the wife, the near independence of all the children, the youngest of whom was seventeen at the time of the divorce, and the genuine respect for each other which both partners had.

THE DIRECT CONFLICT PATTERN

Four of the mediated couples and two of the nonmediated couples had a direct conflict style of divorce decision making. The major characteristics of this pattern were relatively high levels of overt conflict (though not as intense as for the enmeshed couples) and frequent and open communication between the parties about the possibility of divorce. The most distinguishing component was an initially high, but gradually and distinctively moderating degree of ambivalence about ending the marriage in an extended period of "working through" of a year or more duration, during which the possibility of divorce was explicitly discussed both between the spouses and with outside parties, most notably marriage counselors.

Although all but three couples in our sample obtained some joint counseling during the divorce process, only the mediated, direct conflict couples seem to have had a successful therapeutic experience. For these couples therapy fostered the process of psychic divorce by weakening the negative emotional bonds of guilt, sense of failure, and fear of separation that were keeping the parties in a relationship which, in retrospect, they felt had already died. (The nonmediated direct conflict couples either rejected therapy or found the experience unsatisfying.)

In three of these couples there was also a critical premediation conflict over the terms of separation which appears to have had a cathartic effect and led to an increased desire to reach a mutually acceptable settlement. These cases, all husband-initiated divorces, present a nearly identical pattern in which the couple's own efforts at negotiation exploded when the husband's faith that settlement would be easy because of his generous intentions ran aground on his wife's anger or mistrust and the reality of scarce divisible resources.

The negotiation process in the direct conflict pattern recapitulated in a more muted key the major themes of the divorce decision period: an initial superficial period of calm and apparent cooperation, followed by outbreaks of open conflict, and resolution in mutual, although not necessarily amiable, problem solving. Although more profound psychic factors were operative, the conflicts derived primarily from the parties' realistic fears and the relatively uninformed and inferior position of the wives with regard to financial matters.

The role of the mediator (all of whom were evaluated favorably, although less so by husbands) reflected the underlying character of the conflict. The task was not easy, but the largest obstacle was maintaining the good will of the husband in the face of strong pressures to shore up the weaker bargaining stance of the wife, rather than attempting to produce settlement in the face of the couple's fundamental ambivalence about ending the relationship. For the nonmediated couples legal counsel was secured in a direct fashion. Although there were postdivorce complaints about high legal fees and a general air of dissatisfaction with the lawyer's role, the lawyer-client relationship remained intact until settlement was reached.

In discussing postdivorce adjustment it is necessary to distinguish between the mediated and nonmediated couples. For the four mediated couples the postdivorce period produced some dissatisfaction with the terms of settlement, particularly the financial aspects, and lingering, sometimes notable tensions in the parties' relationship with one another. However, in no case did the conflicts approach the intensity of those in the enmeshed pattern. The individual adjustment of the spouses was reasonably good, particularly that of the wives, who were enjoying a gratifying sense of psychological and financial autonomy. Perhaps most notably, the co-parenting relationship was being handled cooperatively, and both parties felt that the children had adjusted well to the divorce.

For the two nonmediated couples the postdivorce period was more conflictual. There was considerable unhappiness with the terms of settlement at the time of the divorce and that dissatisfaction had increased. In both couples the children had become foci of conflict, in one case with regard to visitation, in the other about custody. Personal adjustment was slow, and in both cases the parties complained of difficulty in forming new relationships.

The Kendalls are illustrative of the direct conflict pattern in the mediated group:

> Mr. Kendall wanted the divorce more initially, but they spent a year thrashing out the pros and cons. Their discussions to save the marriage were numerous but

fruitless. They saw a therapist jointly for five or six sessions to help them resolve their impasse. The effect was catalytic and highly satisfying to both. The husband was pleased that the counselor did not blame him and he began to feel less guilty about his wish to divorce. The impact of therapy was greater for the wife (she continued seeing the therapist alone after the decision to divorce was made), freeing her from a sense of failure and a rigid adherence to the dead marriage. The wife also reached out to two women friends, one of whom had had a divorce a year earlier and was able to give her advice, support, and a model of successful coping.

This help notwithstanding, there was still much bitterness when the decision to divorce was made. They could not agree on temporary child support and alimony and ended up in a court fight which was expensive and left them both badly shaken. He "won" in the technical sense, but felt emotionally drained and regretful at how upsetting the experience had been for them both. She felt humiliated by the entire episode.

Mrs. Kendall initiated the contact with the FMA. She heard one of the mediators speak about Structured Mediation and compared to her bitter court experience it sounded like a highly desirable alternative. Mr. Kendall agreed.

The mediation began calmly enough as both spouses appeared eager to avoid a repetition of their previous court battle. In sessions one and two, custody and visitation agreements were quickly reached. In session three, a superficial calm hid growing tensions around money. Mr. Kendall had been asked by the mediator to produce certain financial documents and had not complied. His general posture was passive and noncommital, reflecting perhaps a generalized anxiety about money and a reluctance to face the financial consequences of a divorce.

Mrs. Kendall's bargaining stance was in many ways reminiscent of Mrs. Brown's, but without the same degree of rigidity. She was able to focus on the material issues more objectively, even though she appealed in a highly dependent manner to the mediator to assume much of the responsibility for questioning her husband and articulating her perspective to him.

In sessions five and six, the tensions erupted in mutual recriminations. Finally, an agreement was reached to call in the husband's business consultant to clarify the financial picture. The move proved highly successful. The consultant made several creative suggestions for settlement which both parties were able to accept. With a reduction in anxiety over finances the way was paved for final settlement.

The Kendalls' postdivorce adjustment was the stormiest in the mediated direct conflict group. At the time settlement was reached both partners had been satisfied with the terms. Since then there have been some problems. Mr. Kendall's checks have frequently been late and sometimes they bounce. Mrs. Kendall has "bitched and moaned" to him about this and threatened to see a lawyer. Although lately he has been better about the checks she now feels the settlement is no longer equitable because she feels his income has increased significantly. There have also been some minor squabbles about furniture.

On the other hand, they have been able to work well over visitation. He suggested some increased time with the children to which she readily assented.

She feels his relationship with the children is better than it was during the marriage since now he wants to be with them when he has them. Both support each other as parents and both are optimistic about the future and appear in control of their own lives. This is particularly true of Mrs. Kendall who is enjoying the prospects of a new career.

THE DISENGAGED CONFLICT PATTERN

The disengaged conflict pattern of divorce decision making was typified by two of the mediated couples.

This pattern is distinguished by the notably low level of ambivalence about ending the marriage that characterized the entire period of divorce decision making. Of all our couples these were the ones in which the flame of intimacy had come to burn least brightly—and so too had the heat of conflict diminished. Communication and conflict were nearly as low as in the autistic pattern, but from lack of interest rather than anxiety. There was a relatively long period during which one or both partners seriously considered divorce but relatively few direct efforts at reconciliation. Therapy was explored, but there was no real commitment to it. The overall impression was of two people who were no longer interested enough in each other to work in saving their marriage.

The negotiations for this group were the swiftest of the entire sample. Although the parties described their relationship as tense and there were occasional sharp differences, the overall climate was cooperative. A notable aspect of the parties' orientation was a strong wish on the part of both to avoid intensifying their conflict through the use of lawyers. They engaged in no serious unassisted negotiations prior to mediation because of an explicit fear that their differences would get out of hand. Unlike the direct conflict group, their contact with the FMA was not the result of a personal referral, but of one of the partners reading a newspaper article on Structured Mediation, i.e., the impression was of people looking for a means of handling their differences with a minimum of competitive conflict. Although both spouses were optimistic that mediation would be useful, the husbands were even more favorable to the idea than their wives. Accordingly, the mediator's role was relatively uncomplicated and consisted primarily in providing a framework for negotiations, with occasional reminders about details (e.g., to decide about how to divide an anticipated tax refund). The parties' evaluation of mediation was correspondingly positive. The disengaged pattern was correlated with the most successful postdivorce adjustment in the sample.

Mr. and Mrs. Cook provide a good illustration of the disengaged pattern of divorce decision making.

There is some question about whether Mr. or Mrs. Cook first brought up the possibility of divorce. The husband claims that he brought it up and wanted it more. The wife felt that the decision was entirely mutual. They separated briefly a year before the divorce decision. When they reunited they had only a few discussions about saving the marriage. The husband's view is that they no longer had much in common. The wife felt that her husband was very unemotional; she couldn't draw him out and got tired of trying. According to the husband, they saw a therapist jointly for three sessions. He was displeased with these meetings, feeling that the therapist was "biased" and didn't understand their situation. The wife did not even mention the therapy episode. Both describe the emotional climate at the time of the divorce decision as tense and unsatisfying, but it is clear that both had lost interest in the struggle to keep the relationship going.

Mr. Cook read about the FMA in a newspaper article. Neither spouse looked forward to a court fight, which they considered destructive and unnecessary, so Mrs. Cook went along with her husband's suggestion that they try mediation. Both parties described the emotional climate at this time as poor.

Their negotiations were efficient and brief. There was some ambivalence expressed about the divorce, particularly by Mrs. Cook, but it had none of the intensity and disruptive force on negotiations that was characteristic of the enmeshed couples. Each of the partners remained basically fair and oriented not only to self-interest but to the interests of the other and their child. There were some sharp exchanges over how to liquidate their common business venture, with the wife pushing for independence via liquidation of the assets and the husband arguing for continued joint ownership. There were also conflicts over child support and spousal maintenance. However, neither party made any wildly unrealistic demands and they remained responsive to the communications they got from each other. The mediator was able to refocus them on problem solving whenever emotions threatened to get out of hand.

Both Mr. and Mrs. Cook were extremely satisfied with the divorce settlement and with the mediation experience. Their postdivorce relationship was tinged with the same tensions that marked their mediation: Mr. Cook continues to try to help his former wife with business matters and she experiences this as meddling and an attempt to prevent her from gaining full independence, but the overall picture was favorable. Both parties felt that their son had made a very good adjustment to the divorce. He is encouraged by both of them to openly express his feelings on the subject. Neither of the Cooks seems to have had any serious problems with their postdivorce social relationships, although Mrs. Cook claimed that it was very hard to find "sharp, bright men who are available—or even unavailable."

The one discordant note in the disengaged pattern was the danger that constructive problem solving could become the victim of excessive cordiality. This would seem to have been the case with the Lees. Although relative to the rest of the sample their individual adjustment is quite good, during negotiations neither party stopped to consider the effects the wife's proposed one hundred-mile relocation would have on their co-parenting relationship. The consequence has been that Mrs. Lee now complains of her husband's infrequent visitation and failure to give the agreed upon two weeks notice. Also, the child support checks have begun to arrive late. Both Lees noted that their older daughter has had difficulties accepting the divorce. According to Mrs. Lee, she never saw them fight while they were married and therefore cannot understand why they don't stay together.

Implications of a Typological Approach to Divorce

Because of the small size and unique nature of the sample, the preceding typology of divorce has primarily suggestive value. Certainly I do not claim that it exhausts the ways by which divorcing couples may be meaningfully classified, nor even that our own respondents could only be categorized in that particular fashion. Indeed, had the focus been only on degree of nonacceptance of the divorce or on the level of overt conflict, the sample could have been divided differently and with relevance to the processes of conflict management which concern us. On the other hand, for our particular respondents the typology captures an underlying coherence on a variety of dimensions. The patterns are sensible and of potential usefulness, particularly with regard to the prognosis for settlement negotiations.[2] Certain implications of a typological approach to divorce, and of this typology in particular, are worth additional comment.

IMPLICATIONS FOR RESEARCH ON POSTDIVORCE ADJUSTMENT

A good deal of interest in the divorce literature centers around questions of postdivorce adjustment: How does the mental health of the divorced compare to that of other groups in the population? What is the impact of divorce on the adjustment of children? Do men adjust to divorce better than women? Our results suggest that a good deal of needed precision can be brought to answering questions such as these if some effort is made to distinguish among subtypes in the divorced population based on the interactional pattern between the parties.

That family, and particularly spousal interactive patterns, may be an illuminating way of understanding individual problems in adjustment is a fundamental tenet in much of the family therapy literature. The power of that approach is exemplified in the work of Minuchin and his colleagues (Minuchin 1974; Minuchin, Rosman, and Baker 1979) with which, indeed, our typology of divorce has some affinities. (The terms "enmeshment" and "disengagement" have been used extensively by Minuchin to describe a continuum of dysfunctional relating in intact families.) A common theme among family clinicians is the dysfunctional consequences of conflict avoidance, particularly between husband and wife. Although there is little systematic empirical evidence for this proposition (see Rausch et al. [1974] for some evidence to the contrary), the poor postdivorce adjustment in the enmeshed and autistic patterns lends support to the idea. Although on the surface they appear quite different, both patterns may be viewed as sharing the same underlying inability of the spouses to engage each other in constructive patterns of conflict identification and resolution.

One may also speculate that the quality as well as the direction of postdivorce adjustment—either in adults or their children—may be a function of the type of divorce in question. For instance, although both patterns may well have negative consequences for children, the covert nature of the conflict between the spouses in the autistic divorce presents children with a very different context of separation than does the flamboyant parental hostility of the enmeshed type. The consequences for the kind of coping responses the child develops may be correspondingly different.

As I have noted, I can say little about the factors that may have produced the divorcing patterns my colleagues and I have identified. One approach to this issue might be to search for antecedents in the personality structure and characteristics of the individual spouses. Perhaps a more fruitful approach might be to delineate the relationship between patterns of divorce and the pre-existing patterns in the marriage. For example, in the autistic divorce of the Browns, patterns of interaction which were characteristic of an earlier stage of the relationship seem to have exerted a powerful influence over what developed subsequently.

IMPLICATIONS FOR MEDIATION AS AN ALTERNATIVE TO THE ADVERSARY PROCESS IN DIVORCE

As I have suggested earlier, in evaluating divorce mediation it is important to ask not whether mediation is preferable to the adversary system, but rather, what types of interventions are most likely to be useful for what kinds of couples. The typology of divorce decision making indicates why this is the appropriate type of inquiry and suggests some tentative answers.

The style of mediation exemplified in these cases was of the task-oriented variety. The tapes indicate that mediators largely avoided commenting on matters of the couple's interactional style and the latent conflict between the parties, and worked instead to keep the spouses focused on concrete issues. This was in keeping with the explicit policy of the FMA that couples be referred elsewhere for help with "emotional" problems.

This task orientation worked well with couples of the direct and disengaged types. With these couples there was an overall congruence between the mediator's goals and those of the couple—to arrive at an equitable settlement in an efficient and even-handed manner. The problems faced by the mediator in that kind of situation were not always easy to solve, but they were of a functional or problem-solving kind that fit the common framework shared by all the parties. The better postdivorce adjustment of the mediated direct conflict couples compared to that of their nonmediated counterparts suggests that this is the kind of situation in which divorce mediation may well be superior to the adversary process.

On the other hand, the task orientation seems to have been less successful with couples of the enmeshed and autistic types. In these patterns there appears to have been a fundamental, albeit unarticulated divergence among the participants. In the enmeshed pattern the mediator's goals of achieving settlement were at odds with the strong forces of psychic attachment at work in the parties. In the autistic pattern the parties' phobic attitude toward open communication, particularly around themes of conflict and disagreement was counter to the mediator's emphasis on informed problem solving.

What to do, then, with enmeshed or autistic couples, or, if one prefers to suspend judgment about the specific typology, with any couples in which strongly dysfunctional patterns of communication and conflict resolution predominate? A definitive answer must await systematic study, but several approaches suggest themselves.

One answer is to begin every mediation with a thorough diagnostic assessment. Such an assessment should certainly survey the parties' respective levels of ambivalence about ending the marriage and, especially, the patterns of communication and conflict which characterized their "negotiations" in arriving at the divorce decision. In effect, those negotiations are probably an excellent prognostic sign of how the formal settlement negotiations will proceed and the kinds of problematic interactions with which the mediator will have to deal. The more detailed the mediator's picture of how the parties function as a decision-making unit, the better.

If the prognosis is poor there are two tactical possibilities. The couple can be encouraged to consider a period of exploratory divorce therapy of the kind described in chapter 4. I have argued in that chapter that exploratory divorce therapy may actually be the treatment of choice for such couples. If it is successful in modifying destructive patterns of interaction and giving the parties insight into their respective contributions to the interactional dynamics, the handling of the formal settlement process may well proceed smoothly whether lawyers or mediators are the vehicle by which the negotiations are conducted.

The other tactical approach is to focus on the operations of the marital system during the mediation process itself. I shall elaborate on this notion in chapter 12. I believe there is much to be said for it, at least on theoretical grounds. We know from research in individual and marital therapy that the elimination of dysfunctional responses to the environment—including that which family members provide for each other—is often facilitated when there is a concrete task or problem around which therapeutic interventions can be structured. Strangely enough, this perspective has thus far rarely been mentioned in the debate within the mediation community on the distinctions between therapy and mediation. A popular view appears to be that confusing mediation with therapy is among the most serious of tactical blunders (Kelly 1983; Saposnek 1983). However, "therapy" is usually defined in these discussions as either a historical trek into the marital past to address unresolved attachment issues or the encouragement of emotional catharsis. Therapy defined as attention to and education about palpable interactions occurring before everybody's eyes in the course of mediation is rarely alluded to (see Barsky [1983] for a notable exception).

Conclusion

I have suggested that there are intercouple variations in the divorce experience; that these variations can be grouped into a limited number of distinctive subtypes; and that these subtypes make a difference, both in terms of the tenor and quality of settlement negotiations and the postdivorce adjustment of the parties. I have also suggested that divorce mediation must take these patterned differences into consideration through diagnostic screening or modification of its largely task-oriented focus. Let us pursue these and related strategic issues in the detailed examination of one couple's mediation experience.

12

Can Mediation Be Therapy? The Case of the Browns

We have been introduced to the Browns and their autistic interpersonal style in the previous chapter. In this chapter I would like to trace their mediation experience and its aftermath in more detail. The case is of interest on a number of counts. The Browns' mediator was Coogler, the "father" of divorce mediation. Although this was an early case, it captures much of the flavor and many of the formal elements of his system of structured mediation, an approach that is still widely taught and practiced. While Coogler was at the early stages of his development as a mediator in this case, most divorce mediators are no more experienced, and many a lot less so, than he was here.

My principal reason for choosing this case for extended treatment is because it raises in a particularly focused way an important strategic question: to what extent is it the mediator's task to function "therapeutically"—that is, to educate the parties about their dysfunctional style of dealing with each other and to make direct efforts to modify that style? I shall advance the view that a therapeutic focus of this type is not only appropriate, but, in cases such as this one, an absolute necessity. Specifically, I shall argue that the formal rules of mediation and the mediator's stringently task-oriented focus unwittingly amplified the Browns' highly dysfunctional approach to problem solving and conflict management. In examining the Browns' postdivorce adjustment, I shall suggest that the failure to address interactional issues during mediation abetted the autistic elements in their relationship with unfortunate consequences for the durability of the agreement and the parties' feelings about the mediation experience.

In holding the mediator responsible for not having vigorously addressed the couple's dysfunctional interpersonal style I have employed a criterion with which many expert mediators, both within and outside the area of divorce, would strongly disagree. For example, it is a deeply help belief among most experienced labor mediators, that the mediator's *only* responsibility is a negotiated agreement. Attempting to change the underlying quality of the relationship between the parties is not viewed as part of the mediator's mandate (Kressel 1972). Similarly, in the area of community dispute resolution (e.g., disputes between neighbors and relatives) the focus on mediation is typically on the immediate substantive issues; rarely on the underlying dynamics that may be fueling the dispute (Roehl and Cook, in press). Although the literature on divorce mediation is still in its formative stages it is already clear that a major and influential segment of practitioners is ready to write off "therapeutic" interventions as inappropriate and unrealistic, given the constraints of time and purpose under which divorce mediation occurs (Kelly 1983; Saposnek 1983).

Coogler's own position on this matter is unclear. On the one hand, he appears to have favored the view that mediation ought not to be confused with therapy. Parties with clearly unresolved emotional issues were referred to therapists on this ground. On the other hand, he encouraged the idea that the mediator must be equipped to address dysfunctional patterns of communication (Coogler 1978, esp. pp. 75–76, 83). My own belief as a clinician is that divorce mediation without an avowed focus on the patterns of communication, conflict management, and problem solving is a much less exciting vehicle for resolving conflicts, and probably not much different from the use of skillful and cooperative lawyers. It is to sharpen debate around this issue that I have chosen this case.

Several cautionary words are in order before proceeding, however. First, an evaluation of mediation's effects in a single case is inevitably open to alternative interpretations. The outcomes, whether good or bad, may reflect forces or events occurring outside of mediation; forces over which the mediator has no control. Second, weighing the pros and cons of the mediation experience is inevitably a subjective exercise. While I have made every effort to be realistic and even-handed, others looking at the same set of materials might reasonably arrive at different conclusions.

Lastly, in order to sharpen the strategic issues between mediation and "therapy" I have necessarily adopted a critical stance toward the participants in this mediation. However, I would very much like to express my admiration of both the couple and the mediator. The Browns are to be admired for their courage in experimenting with the mediation procedure, for sticking with it when the going got rough, and for their willingness to share their experiences with us. Although I shall have some sharp things to say about their problematic style of relating, I imply no malice of forethought on either of their parts. Both of them did their best under trying psychological and economic circumstances.

Much the same can be said of the mediator. This was one of Coogler's earliest cases, and it was not an easy one. In spite of this, the overall result, while flawed, was not unreasonable, considering the underlying marital dynamics. His performance here may also be unrepresentative of how he would have handled things later in his career. Moreover, my analysis has had the benefit of the "retrospectoscope"—a marvelous device unavailable to the mediator.

The analysis draws upon the fully recorded mediation sessions and a separate, intensive, postdivorce interview with each of the principals approximately one year after the conclusion of mediation. I have altered names and biographical details to protect the anonymity of the couple. The presentation is divided into four major sections: the premediation background, the mediation experience, the postdivorce aftermath, and an analytic reprise.

The Premediation Background

THE MARITAL BACKGROUND

The Browns had been married for twelve years. Mr. Brown, age forty, was a school teacher and part-time musician with an annual gross income of $16,000 when the mediation occurred. At the time we spoke with him, five months after the end of mediation, he was remarried. He had become involved with his present wife while still married to the first Mrs. Brown.

Mrs. Brown was thirty-eight years old at the time of the mediation. She is a freelance technical writer. She worked at intervals during the marriage with variable earnings. At the time of the postdivorce interview she was earning $18,000 a year, although at the time of the mediation she had just resumed active part-time work.

The signs of a conflict-avoidant, noncommunicative interpersonal style in the marriage are well documented in the circumstances leading up to the decision to divorce. The Browns physically separated when Mr. Brown decided to take an apartment away from his family, ostensibly to be closer to his job and the music studio where he practiced with his band two nights a week. There is no indication that this departure was the occasion for any significant discussion between the Browns of the state of their marriage or its future. In Mrs. Brown's view her husband had already decided to end the marriage when he left home, but the issue had never been discussed between them. By his own account, Mr. Brown had indeed begun seriously considering a divorce at that time.

The Browns' first serious discussion with each other about the possibility of divorce occurred some six months later. Technically both agree that she was the one to raise the issue but they also agree that he was the one who really wanted the marriage to end. According to Mrs. Brown, her husband was unwilling to mention the word "divorce" but indicated his disenchantment with her and the marriage in every other way. She, on the other hand, had begun psychotherapy and her therapist had begun prodding her to consider if *her* needs were being met in the marriage—with the obvious implication that they were not. This was the recognition that prompted Mrs. Brown to ask her husband for a divorce.

Once she raised the issue with him, they came almost immediately to an agreement to dissolve the marriage, with little discussion of the pros and cons and no real attempt to understand what had gone wrong. They never went for joint counseling although Mrs. Brown suggested it. According to her, "he was afraid of what he would learn about himself."

Mrs. Brown's own therapy lasted only five or six sessions. As noted, it catalyzed the divorce decision and she also applauded the therapy for helping her gain some "emotional control" at a time of great anxiety. She claims also to have gained a general understanding of herself. However, the brevity of the therapy and her unhappy postdivorce adjustment suggest a flight from handling internal conflicts parallel to the avoidance of conflict endemic to the marital relationship.

In the postdivorce interviews Mrs. Brown was better able than her husband to articulate a meaningful psychological account of why the marriage foundered. Her explanation is an apt description of the autistic marriage. She attributed the divorce to "years of noncommunication. We reached a point where we didn't know each other." She blamed herself for her inability "to speak with somebody I'm emotionally involved with. He would get mad if I cried. I also don't fight well." In his characteristically terse style Mr. Brown said simply that they divorced because of "a lack of love."

Both the Browns admitted that they had trouble talking about whether or not to divorce. Mr. Brown's explanation for the difficulty in joint decision making conveys his contribution to the couple's avoidant style: "Emotional problems—knowing you want something but not knowing all the reasons why and being *forced* to verbalize them anyway" (emphasis added). Mrs. Brown's explanation: "Because I always cried and he would get mad. I couldn't keep it 'business-like' enough for him." The "business-like" was spoken with irony, but she herself was ashamed of her crying and felt that strong "emotional" displays of this or any other type were signs of weakness. This inhibited perspective was undoubtedly an obstacle to communication during the marriage. During the mediation it seriously interfered with the mediator's efforts to encourage joint problem solving.

THE STEPS LEADING TO MEDIATION

For about one month after their decision to divorce, the Browns made some unaided efforts at reaching agreements on settlement issues. No real negotiations appear to have occurred during this time, however. They relied principally on the *de facto* arrangement which had been in effect since his departure nine months earlier (and had never been the subject of any informed discussion), whereby he continued to pay for the home and the children. According to Mrs. Brown, they had some preliminary discussions regarding a more permanent arrangement that went very smoothly. "He wanted to give me everything. That had to do with his guilt complex." Neither child support nor visitation were discussed in any meaningful way, but based on this early experience she felt it would be fairly easy to arrive at a settlement agreement. From the very different perception of Mr. Brown, it is clear that the characteristic pattern of noncommunication was well entrenched in this negotiating preamble. He remembers feeling that they were very far apart on a number of items, especially visitation, division of property, and child support. Overall, he thought it would be "very difficult" to reach agreement.

Although Mrs. Brown at first tried to hide the news of her impending divorce from family and friends she began to find them a source of support and reassurance "because I felt lower than low; I felt I was being duped." This sense of victimization was an integral component of her stance throughout the negotiating period. Mr. Brown, on the other hand, spoke with nobody. In retrospect he feels that perhaps he should have tried counseling but doubts that it would have done much good.

The initiative to use mediation came from Mrs. Brown, and both parties agreed that she wanted to use the process much more than he. She had learned of the mediation center from her therapist who had strongly recommended it, especially in light of Mrs. Brown's tendency to "give in" too easily and not look out for herself. In addition, Mrs. Brown wanted a settlement that would be fair. "I didn't want bitterness. They [the mediation center] knew what would be good for us." She thought mediation would be extremely useful "because they were expert; they were supposed to know it all."

Mrs. Brown felt that her husband was less enthusiastic than she about mediation and that he agreed for two reasons: because she threatened him ("We either do it this way or we both get lawyers and fight it out"), and because "He wanted to do it the cheapest way." In fact, Mr. Brown was less certain about how useful mediation would be, but had mildly positive expectations: "It sounded like a good way to do it and seemed less expensive as well."

Mrs. Brown had consulted a lawyer very briefly during her husband's nine-month absence to find out what her legal rights might be in case of a divorce, but neither of the Browns had retained a lawyer for serious representation prior to the first mediation meeting. As far as could be ascertained, neither consulted a lawyer during mediation.

The Mediation Experience

The Browns' mediation lasted three sessions, including the orientation meeting in which the rules of Structured Mediation were explained and questions about the process answered. Each session was one to one-and-a-half hours in length. All issues save child support were resolved in the two working sessions. The mediation was completed in approximately one month. The final agreement on child support came the day after the last meeting when Mrs. Brown decided to accept the final offer that Mr. Brown had tendered at the end of session three. Both parties and the mediator were present at all sessions. The joint format was used throughout. A female trainee was present at sessions two and three. The final mediation agreement was incorporated into the final decree of divorce which was granted about six weeks after the end of mediation.

I have described the mediation with enough detail to convey the major themes of each session, highlighted by verbatim accounts of key incidents or highly illustrative exchanges. There is no perfectly satisfactory way in which to integrate analytic comments with this material. I have chosen to provide a running analytic commentary rather than reserving all of my critical reflections to a separate section following the account of mediation. This approach has the disadvantage of breaking the narrative flow and precludes the reader from making wholly independent judgments about what is occurring during mediation. The advantage is that the relevance of the analytic observations can be more readily judged, not only in terms of the immediate event to which they refer, but to subsequent ones as well.

THE ORIENTATION SESSION

The session begins with the distribution of the mediation rules, one copy to each party. The rules are detailed and lengthy, covering approximately seven or eight legal-size pages. The Browns examine these silently for approximately five minutes. Responding to several sceptical sounding questions from Mr. Brown, the mediator comments on the virtues of mediation as opposed to the traditional use of lawyers. Mr. Brown questions the purpose of the arbitration clauses, by which the parties agree that in the event of an impasse they will submit the disputed issue(s) to an arbitrator selected under the rules of the American Arbitration Association. The mediator explains the difference between mediation and arbitration: under mediation the final decisions are theirs; in arbitration a third party, after listening to both sides, makes a binding recommendation. The purpose of the arbitration clause is to give them a more flexible, quicker, and cheaper alternative to the court room in the event mediated negotiations break down.

The discussion turns to the matter of fees. Mr. Brown asks: "What is the quickest anybody has completed mediation?" This straightforward sounding question is a harbinger of things to come. Throughout the mediation, Mr. Brown's preference will be for doing things quickly, not well. He also wants to know how much mediation costs relative to the use of two attorneys. The mediator's response emphasizes the greater savings that can normally occur in mediation and the tremendous expenses that can occur when lawyers become involved.

Although the opening ten minutes suggest that Mr. Brown has doubts about mediation, all the parties act on the assumption that the decision to proceed has been made. That assumption is never checked. The mediator's failure to carefully question the parties' commitment to mediation and the manner in which they have arrived at the decision to mediate is noteworthy on several counts.

In the first place, it cost the mediator the parties' wholehearted loyalty and enthusiasm. When we interviewed the Browns one year later both felt that they had committed themselves to something they did not really understand. For example, although he rated the mediator's presentation of the procedure as clear and competent, Mr. Brown felt that "he didn't get answers in terms he would have liked," either because "I didn't ask the right questions or didn't understand what was happening." Similarly, Mrs. Brown admitted that a good part of the orientation passed over her head completely. "I was in such an emotional state I don't know what he (the mediator) said. I was tense. There were papers to read and sign. I *knew* this is what I wanted to do so maybe I didn't listen. . . . It was clear enough that I knew I wanted to go through with it."

Second, as these last remarks from Mrs. Brown hint, and as the unfolding events of the mediation eloquently testify, the lack of deliberation regarding the decision to mediate parallels the Browns' own tendency to arrive at hasty, ill-conceived decisions in the midst of emotional turmoil. In that sense the mediator unwittingly abetted a dysfunctional process rather than starting to shape a superior one. The Browns' experience was not atypical. A great many respondents from the larger sample remarked unfavorably on the haste with which mediation began and the wish that they had had more time to think things over.

By carefully exploring the manner by which a couple has arrived at the decision to seek mediation, the mediator may also develop an idea of what he or she will be in for once the negotiations begin. Explorations of this kind, in the form of neutral questioning regarding the details of each party's contribution to the mediation decision and the way in which each handled their doubts also may serve to begin the parties' education about their decision-making style. Such an education is the cornerstone on which later efforts at modifying problematic patterns of decision making may be built.

In any case, the mediator chose not to pursue these potentially valuable, but murky, diagnostic waters. He kept instead to the narrow task-oriented tack to which he bore more or less unswervingly throughout, taking down factual information (e.g., the dates of the marriage and physical separation, names and ages of children, etc.) before turning to the present state of affairs. In response to his inquiry, Mrs. Brown indicates that she has custody of the children. Mr. Brown volunteers that he is agreeable to her having permanent custody.

MEDIATOR: What about visitation?

MR. BROWN: I'd like to see them whenever I want.

MRS. BROWN: That's fine, but I want some time specified. Maybe two weekends a month and one week during the summer. My point is that I want some time for myself. Otherwise I'm agreeable.

The mediator asks about marital property. They have two cars, some stocks amounting to a few thousand dollars—which he is willing for her to do with as she likes. They also have a savings account and a house. The mediator suggests that an inventory of household things be made as an aid to distribution. Mr. Brown resists this idea. He is going to keep the house. She can take whatever she likes of its contents. Mrs. Brown does not contest this. Apparently there has been some prior understanding between them on the house. She will bring to the next session a list of household goods that she wants. The mediator says that this is a good idea which will eliminate any misunderstandings. Once again, he shows no curiosity about the Browns' decision-making style.

To this point in the session both Browns are calm, businesslike, and even friendly in manner. There are no discernible traces of anger or rudeness, only Mr. Brown's mild suspicion about mediation. He is also solicitous of Mrs. Brown concerning the house and asks, "Who will help you move out?"

The mediator distributes budget forms and explains that they will be used in the next session to help the Browns arrive at an agreement on child support. He explains that it is as important for Mr. Brown to complete a budget as for his wife. They will probably find that the total of both their budgets will exceed their joint income. That will have to be dealt with in their negotiations, but the goal is to develop budgets that provide for some of life's pleasures as well as the needs of the children.

The mediator asks the Browns if they are both aware of the other's assets and liabilities. Mrs. Brown says "pretty much" but she is unsure of "certain things." In response, the mediator explains the importance of full disclosure on both sides to insure a fair agreement. He encourages each of them to bring their salary stubs to the next meeting. Mrs. Brown indicates that she does not receive a salary stub. Mr. Brown reassures her that he needs no proof of her earnings. He goes on to indicate that he wants the house appraised and would like to give her one-half of the equity, he would like all stock put in the children's names, and he wants the savings account to go to his wife. The tone here is of a man bending over backward to be fair—even generous.

The mediator asks if they have a temporary support agreement in effect. They do. Mr. Brown is giving his wife $700 a month, but he does not feel he can keep it up much longer. The mediator suggests they try to reach an agreement now on temporary child support. The Browns quickly agree on $600 per month, with the mediator playing an active role in helping them with the practical details. By a prior agreement there will be no temporary alimony. Again, the mediator does not explore how this decision was reached and whether or not the process of agreement is at all characteristic of their general problem-solving style.

The mediator then asks who is making the mortgage payments. The wife is, in the amount of $270 per month. He inquires when she plans to move out. She is not sure. It depends on when she finds an apartment for herself and the children. At this juncture the only real conflict in the session suddenly erupts. It is the only clue during the meeting that the Browns have deep, unresolved animosities, but the tension disappears as quickly and unexpectedly as it arose. The incident is triggered by the mediator's question to Mr. Brown: will he pick up the mortgage payments once he takes possession of the house?

MR. BROWN: "Not if I have to pay her $600 per month."

MRS. BROWN: (Angrily) "Yes you will. You just get some roommates. Its a big house. I'm not going to live in an efficiency with two kids."

Mr. Brown backs down immediately, agreeing to pick up the mortgage payments when they arrive at a final settlement. Mrs. Brown closes the exchange, reiterating that he can always get a roommate. The session ends with the mediator having completed the temporary agreement, explaining to them that it should help avoid tensions from developing during the negotiation process.

SESSION TWO

This was a crucial session in which the Browns' difficulties in negotiating with one another are amply illustrated. The fundamental dynamic was that of an angry, bitter wife dictating terms to a docile, guilt-ridden husband. The pattern was given shape by Mrs. Brown's waving of the banner of parental obligation before the contrite Mr. Brown, while simultaneously trumpeting that she wanted nothing for herself. The mediator occasionally challenged her and tried to breathe some life into the listless Mr. Brown. Both of these efforts foundered, however, on the treacherous currents created by the couple's well-entrenched style of conflict avoidance.

The mediator opens the session by asking if the Browns have had any further discussions with each other since the last meeting. There have been none. The mediator directs them to a discussion of the budget forms they have completed between sessions.

Mrs. Brown begins. She answers that she has taken into account only the needs of the children. She expects nothing for herself. Her total budget for the children comes to $665 per month but she will accept $600. (This represents about two-thirds of Mr. Brown's monthly take-home.) Mr.

Brown says he cannot afford this much. Mrs. Brown responds in an angry, lecturing tone: She is not interested in what he can or cannot afford. She expects him to do part-time work to augment his earnings if necessary; she expects him to support his children, period.

In a calm tone of voice the mediator asks her to read her budget figures aloud, item by item. She complies, reiterating at the end that her husband can do free-lance work and make an additional $50 per day. She will not accept the idea of settling for $200 per month (an exaggeratedly low figure). Her tone continues to be angry and insistent. Mr. Brown is quiet, saying only that he wants to pay as much as he can in child support.

They discuss his budget. The total is $550 per month. Mrs. Brown repeats her idea that he take in roommates. At the request of the mediator Mr. Brown gives his wife an item by item breakdown. She does not find his budget unreasonable. She simply repeats that she needs what she needs:

> The point I'm trying to make to you Joseph is that I have custody of the children twenty-four hours a day. I take care of them and you support them. You couldn't hire anybody to take care of them cheaper than I do.

The discussion turns to the marital home. Mrs. Brown suggests that her husband sell the house as a way to meet his parental responsibilities. She does not want it for herself since she cannot afford it on what she makes. The mediator endorses this as realistic and, a bit incredulously, asks Mr. Brown how he can afford the house, given that he can barely afford the $100 a month apartment in which he now resides. Mrs. Brown jumps in saying that she sees no problem with him maintaining the house if that is what he wants, adding:

> The reason I came here [to mediation] is because I thought you would tell us what we needed—what I need to protect the children in the future; things I have no idea about. We don't know these things and we can't make decisions.

In response, the mediator begins an examination of the equity tied up in the house. This amounts to roughly $8,800. Mrs. Brown wants her share *now,* not when her husband sells it, which may be in five to six years.

The female observer interjects and asks Mrs. Brown why she is forego-ing alimony. The question appears to be stimulated by Mrs. Brown's "nothing for myself" negotiating posture. Mrs. Brown says she was under the impression she was not entitled to alimony since she works. The mediator clarifies, indicating that the law offers few guidelines in divorce settlement negotiations. In an apparent effort to alter Mrs. Brown's aggressive passivity, he notes that settlement negotiations are inherently ambiguous. No court will be able to tell them what is "right" and even the mediator can only make suggestions. It is *they* who have to do the negotiating and make the agreements.

To the mediator's inquiry if she is satisfied with her husband's representation about his income, Mrs. Brown replies that she is but thinks he could be making more. Mr. Brown disagrees. The mediator notes that they can agree on a re-negotiation clause for later years, noting that one function of mediation is to help them make creative and flexible provisions for upward and downward revisions of the financial settlement.

Mrs. Brown says that she distrusts her husband and inquires sceptically how she can keep him honest in the future. The mediator responds, indicating that, for example, they can stipulate her right to examine future tax returns. Mrs. Brown is dubious—what if he barters his services? How will she be able to keep track of that? The mediator says it *is* possible to track things down; hiding income is hard. She dismisses this proposition; she has no time for tracking things down. The mediator (somewhat testily): "You're asking me, 'what if.' I'm telling you." He hopes that such audits would not be necessary.

Apparently sensing that Mrs. Brown has parried his efforts to dislodge her from her unproductive stance, the mediator mounts a direct assault on her inflexibility. He stresses that their income *right now* is insufficient to meet their mutual needs. The task they must both confront is to clearly specify and agree on the needs. This is the only real "guideline" they can hope for. He adds that it is impossible to get payments exactly right. The chances are good that Mr. Brown will be paying either too little or too much. The best they can do is to agree on some reasonable method for arriving at agreements and for revising them should the need arise in the future. Pointedly turning to Mrs. Brown he ends his exhortation:

> It is important that your *own* needs be taken into account. You haven't said anything about this except that you don't want anything. Remember though, it won't be a sound solution unless your personal needs are met in some way.

For these sensible and much needed words of advice, Mrs. Brown has little use.

> MRS. BROWN: I can always make enough to meet my needs for food. That's all I need.

Although torpedoed by Mrs. Brown, the mediator's intervention has temporarily emboldened Mr. Brown, who now chips in that it does not seem fair that his wife is asking him to live on about $300 per month while she would be living on the $600 she is asking for in addition to her own earnings of about $500. However, while his words are assertive, Mr. Brown's tone is docile. Mrs. Brown quickly dispenses with him: while she is taking care of the kids on weekends and evenings he can be out working and making the equivalent of whatever income she has! The mediator sternly intervenes: "Are you aware that you are *telling* him how much he can be making? How about asking him?"

Mrs. Brown complies, with angry questions to her husband on the possibility for part-time work, establishing in the exchange that in previous years he has not reported all of his income on his tax returns. Mr. Brown sticks to his belief that the prospects for augmenting his income are poor.

MEDIATOR (to Mrs. Brown): Do you believe him?

MRS. BROWN: Partly, but people who want to can find work. His *primary* responsibility is to his children, even if he has to eat hot dogs.

She is willing, however, to bring down her demands by $50 per month, "since you're hurting so bad" (said sarcastically).

The mediator defends Mr. Brown's right to have his personal needs met. Once again emboldened by this support, Mr. Brown begins to defend himself, albeit rather lamely, "If I don't have the money I can't pay." Mrs. Brown repeats firmly that he can *get* the money, adding with the tone of a person making a concession, that she won't throw him in jail if he should lose his job through no fault of his own but that she has confidence that he can make a good living if he really wants to. The mediator interjects that jailing somebody for nonsupport is easier said than done, but the wind has already gone out of Mr. Brown's sails. He starts talking about leasing the house and continuing to live in an apartment. The lease might just cover his mortgage payments. On this basis he agrees to his wife's demand for $550 a month in support although his biweekly take-home pay is only $450. The mediator questions him sharply: wouldn't he have the feeling that he is being "ripped off"? The mediator's choice of language is an unflattering slap at Mrs. Brown and is probably ill-advised, but it doubtless reflects his frustration at the lack of any informed negotiating give and take between the parties. Mr. Brown responds quickly: "He would not feel ripped off in the least; that's what the kids need to live on." In a subdued tone the mediator reminds him that he has accepted his wife's version of the children's needs without any question.

At Mrs. Brown's initiation they proceed to a discussion of how Mr.

Brown will pay her the additional $50 per month that she says the children need but which he cannot presently afford to give her. Mr. Brown offers that on his very first raise he will give the first $50 to his wife. She pushes to sharpen and clarify this concession, pushing for him to agree that *every* raise he gets up to $50 per month he will give to her in increments of $25. Mr. Brown agrees and they begin going over his pay stubs to see how it can be determined what any anticipated raise amounts to. It is interesting how quickly they have arrived at this point, apparently in the unspoken assumption that he must assume total support of the children. Her salary and future earning power have received no consideration except in so far as she is asking for no alimony.

The mediator again asks Mr. Brown if he is satisfied with his wife's version of the children's needs. This time Mr. Brown responds with a suggestion for an annual re-examination of the children's circumstances, but closes by asking the mediator what *he* would advise. The mediator suggests re-examination at two years, with a return to mediation if they cannot agree at that time by themselves.

They then proceed in a very business-like way to divide up savings, a mutual fund account, automobiles and so on. This is all done on the basis of a 50–50 division. The mediator's role is mainly that of asking, "What's next?" and advising on some practical details. Occasionally he tries to prod Mr. Brown into a more active negotiating stance but the results are always the same:

MEDIATOR TO MR. BROWN (with implied scepticism): Are you obligating yourself to pay for all the children's medical and dental bills?

MR. BROWN (laughing ruefully): I guess I am.

The session ends with a discussion of visitation. It is a brief, characteristic, and, in light of postsettlement developments, ominously revealing exchange.

The mediator opens the topic with the notion that the mediation center prefers to think of visitation as "shared custody" and that their view is that terms should be made specific so that the children have some assurance that they will get to see their father and so that Mrs. Brown can have a predictable social life. Mr. Brown announces that such a procedure is impossible because of his unpredictable work schedule.

The mediator immediately indicates that he can put in a clause that visitation be left completely open. This is a puzzling response, since it essentially duplicates the couple's own tendency to reach agreements without any exploration of underlying realities. Some inquiry into the nature of Mr. Brown's work-connected travel and the degree to which he has control over such plans might have been informative. It would also have shown the Browns the kind of problem-solving behavior which is crucial to an informed negotiation. The response may be partly understood as the mediator's wish to encourage autonomy and to respect the parties' right to make their own agreements. It also illustrates the role ambiguity inherent in mediation: is the mediator's primary allegiance to settlement or to a thorough process of negotiations? If the latter, how hard is the mediator entitled to push the parties off the path which comes most naturally to them?

In any event, left to their own devices the Browns' familiar pattern repeats itself. Mrs. Brown accepts without scrutiny the "impossibility" of detailing visitation, coupling this with a lecture to her husband on the responsibilities of being a parent and a demand that he agree to visitation on the first weekend of every month.

MRS. BROWN (to Mr. Brown): Do you *want* them a weekend a month?
MR. BROWN: Sure.
MRS. BROWN: You want to get up with the bottles, the diapers, and the trash?
MR. BROWN: No, but that's part of it.
MRS. BROWN (with great anger): Sure as hell is.
MEDIATOR (abruptly): O.K. So what are you agreeing to?

Mrs. Brown is firm and lectures Mr. Brown about how he has to be *responsible* for the children, no "personal business" or work should come first. Mr. Brown is silent. She wants him to take the children the first weekend of every month. He agrees without argument or discussion.

Sticking to his narrow task-orientation, the mediator presses the Browns to at least be detailed about a holiday visitation schedule. The pent-up anger that the dysfunctional interaction has generated in Mr. Brown vents itself at last—on the mediator: "You hear us, we don't want to specify!" The episode is a perfect example, in miniature, of the displacement of aggression that results when the principals to a conflict are unable to deal constructively with each other.

The final exchange of the session symbolizes the entire meeting. Mrs. Brown wants Mr. Brown to deposit $250 into the savings account of each child. This was money her parents gave her to cover certain home repairs, with instructions to put it into savings when the repairs were paid off. She also wants his name off the children's accounts so that he can nave no access to them. He agrees to both stipulations.

MEDIATOR: Anything else?
MRS. BROWN: Not on my list.

MEDIATOR (to Mr. Brown): Anything on your list?
MR. BROWN: I didn't have a list.

SESSION THREE

This session began in the same spirit as the preceding one with a haughty, demanding wife and a passive, acquiescent husband. One-third into the meeting things went into reverse. Mr. Brown became the adamant party and Mrs. Brown turned helpless. The change was more superficial than real, however, since the dynamics of the previous session continued to operate. Whether adamant or meek, Mrs. Brown enacted the role of overwrought victim and, for all his momentary outspokenness, Mr. Brown remained vulnerable to the sight of her distress, to his guilty conscience, and to his fear of conflict.

The session opens with a discussion of the house. The Browns have obtained an appraisal and agree that they have about $8,800 in equity, half of which will go to Mrs. Brown. Mrs. Brown's main concern is getting her money out as quickly as possible. In one-and-one-half years she wants half of her equity, and wants the remainder within three years. Mr. Brown says he will make every effort to get her what she wants. The mediator's role is largely that of expert and neutral advice giver, trying to assist them in accomplishing the mutual goal of getting Mrs. Brown paid off as quickly as possible. The tone is entirely characteristic of the first two meetings. A sample dialogue:

MRS. BROWN: I don't care how you do it, but by next year I want half.
MR. BROWN: O.K.
MEDIATOR (to Mr. Brown): That's agreeable to you?
MR. BROWN: Yeah.

Mrs. Brown continues on in her insistent mood: even if she gets half her money in one-and-one-half years she still has no money to get a new car, which she will need because she can't get credit—"You get all the credit out of the marriage and I get nothing." Mr. Brown asks the mediator what his wife's chances are of getting a loan. The mediator feels that things are getting easier for divorced women. Mrs. Brown takes issue with this. A department store wants to *give* him a card on the phone but she can't get one. The mediator acknowledges the truth of what she says—immediately after a divorce women do have trouble getting credit. The observer notes that one bank in town has been easier about giving credit to divorced women.

Mrs. Brown asks the mediator for advice about whether to change her name. Is it better to keep her married name so that she and the children will have the same last name? The mediator notes that most women did keep their married name, but that things are changing. He gives her information on the technical details of a name change.

Now the crucial reversal in the dynamics of the session begins. The mediator starts to recapitulate the terms of settlement so that he can draft the final agreement. Mr. Brown interrupts. He has serious doubts about the child support stipulation. He cannot afford the $600 he agreed to last time. "I just think that was too high." He can afford only $450 per month. Even that is too high, and he will simply not go any higher. All of this is said in a low, depressed voice, but very firmly. Mrs. Brown says nothing.

The mediator suggests that perhaps they need a more detailed accounting of the children's actual needs. This is a useful sally since one of the symptoms of the Browns' autistic style is that they throw numbers at each other with no attention to facts. The intervention is also aimed at tactfully challenging Mrs. Brown's imperious posture, but Mr. Brown does not pick up on it in any constructive way. Instead he expresses unhappiness that some of the money he pays in child support will actually go for his wife's needs. The mediator says there is no way this can be avoided. She lives in the same house with the children and eats the same food. Still Mrs. Brown is silent. The mediator returns to a recital of the items on which they are in agreement. Mr. Brown interrupts to say that he wants a review of the child support provision at the end of one year, rather than in two years as they had earlier agreed (or within three months of the request of either party).

This leads to an explanation by the mediator of what would happen at the end of one year if they disagree on child support. If they could not resolve the issue in mediation they would go to arbitration. Mr. Brown asks if the agreement to return to mediation or to arbitrate is legally binding. The mediator explains that the highest state court has ruled that people cannot *legally* commit themselves to mediate or arbitrate a dispute that they have not yet had; therefore, the answer to Mr. Brown's question is "no." The mediator adds, however, that the mediation center hopes that couples will honor the arbitration clause, noting that in certain professions there is an arbitration provision which is also legally unenforcable but which most parties honor in order to avoid the costs, time, and energy of going to court. Mr. Brown agrees to the arbitration clause.

Mrs. Brown finally speaks. She is willing to drop her child support request to $500 per month with the provision that it is increased to $600 as his salary increases. Mr. Brown responds instantaneously: "We're at an impasse. We might as well call it a day, 'cause I'm not going to give her any more." He challenges Mrs. Brown to take him to court if she's not happy with his offer.

Mr. Brown's response is surprising only in that the adamant sentiments are now being expressed by him rather than by his wife. Otherwise the pattern is familiar: when one of the Browns makes a move toward a negotiating posture—which is the import of Mrs. Brown's offer to lower her request for child support by $100—the other withdraws or sabotages the effort. The exchange also marks a crucial moment in the Browns' mediation. In responding to it the mediator redirected his efforts to get the Browns to stop hurling demands at each other and to begin to grapple with the issues that divide them in a realistic manner.

The mediator's first tack is to seize upon the arbitration provision as a lever to force the Browns to deal with one another or face the prospect of having the matter taken out of their hands entirely. There is doubtless something to be said for this strategy, but in the case of the Browns it amplified rather than challenged their noncommunication pact.

Mrs. Brown side-steps the mediator's query about whether she wishes to go to arbitration. She responds instead that she has a detailed list of her children's needs and that her request for child support is reasonable and fair. The following dialogue then ensues:

MR. BROWN (to his wife): You also don't realize that what you've been living on the past couple of years is a lot better than what you're going to have to get used to.

MRS. BROWN (playing on his guilt): Joseph, you've got to support your children according to the standard they're living under when you divorce me. You don't transfer them into the slums.

MEDIATOR (trying to counter the guilt-inducing message): You don't transfer them into the slums but it's also realistic that both sides are not going to have as much money as they had before.

MRS. BROWN (sending another message to Mr. Brown's conscience): I don't care about me, but my kids are not going to be hurt by this. (She begins to cry and starts to leave the room.) There's no way I can talk now so we may as well call it quits.

MEDIATOR (in a calm, reassuring voice): I'd rather you wouldn't do that. You need a little time to get yourself together. I want to explain to both of you what your rights are.

The mediator then explains (over the continuous sobbing of Mrs. Brown) that he will draw up the entire agreement, including the statement that Mrs. Brown wants the original amount of child support ($550) but that Mr. Brown is offering only $450; in a week they will come back to sign the settlement agreement and the disputed child support issue will go to the American Arbitration Association. They will need a $100 deposit for the AAA at that time, as stipulated in the rules of the mediation center.

Mr. Brown now suggests that they should set up one more mediation session for next week. In the interim he will talk to his wife. The mediator indicates that he would prefer that Mr. Brown not talk with his wife outside mediation.

MEDIATOR: I think this is the place to make your settlement.
MR. BROWN: Well, she's not able to talk now.
MEDIATOR: I am aware that she's upset right now, but I think you need to work on that here.

This sequence represents the mediator at his best. His calm but firm insistence that Mrs. Brown collect herself and stay in the room and his opposition to Mr. Brown's equally strong impulse to flee were remembered by Mrs. Brown as the highlight of the mediation. ("Because if I had walked out then, thinking 'I can't handle it,' it would have been harder to handle the next time.") The intervention positions the mediator to begin to help the Browns jointly confront their inability to handle conflict constructively. The injunction that "this is the place to make your settlement" is also an implicit reminder that one of mediation's theoretical advantages over the use of lawyers is the opportunity to observe and modify dysfunctional transactions. Alas, the mediator does not pursue this course, but continues in the same concrete manner. Since he adds no new element to the interpersonal geometry, the old pattern of conflict avoidance reasserts itself.

Mr. Brown, in a tone that is much softer than his adamant position of a few minutes earlier, repeats that he is not ready for arbitration right now. The mediator takes up the gauntlet again and tries to return the Browns to negotiations.

MEDIATOR (to Mrs. Brown): He's saying he wants to negotiate some more. You have the option to say you want to negotiate or go to arbitration.
MRS. BROWN (tearfully): I don't know what to do. I figured out what they [the children] needed; I asked for less and then he knocked me down again, and now I'm willing to go down *again*. . . .
MEDIATOR: I want you to do what you think is right for you.
MRS. BROWN (angrily, with tears): . . . and through all this crap I'm thinking of the $100 which he is going to have to put out [for arbitration]. I don't know why I am so stupid. [This is not stupidity, but her characteristic and unconscious embrace of the martyred victim role.]
MEDIATOR: I realize it's money and we're talking about a whole lot more than $100; we're talking about child support.

MRS. BROWN: O.K. Let's go to arbitration.

MEDIATOR (intentionally misperceiving): I want to be clear. Are you offering to renegotiate with him?

MRS. BROWN (explaining): Well, that means he's going to have to pay more and just a second ago he said he's not going to.

The mediator, now side-stepping the arbitration possibility, tries to get the Browns to begin an appraisal of their respective views on the children's needs, on the grounds that the child support issue can only be realistically resolved if they both have a clear idea of how much the children need and for what. Until now the couple's dynamics have effectively short-circuited any such discussion. The mediator tries to get a dialogue going in a variety of ways, but the autistic pattern reasserts itself at each step.

The mediator first tries to coax Mrs. Brown into asking Mr. Brown what it is about her budget for the children that he would like more information on. The Browns start to argue unproductively. The mediator suggests they stop fighting and they get clear what kinds of information and facts about the children Mr. Brown wants from Mrs. Brown so that in the next session they can begin to negotiate instead of hurting each other by name-calling.

MR. BROWN: I don't *know* what information I need. I need to get satisfied in my own mind first.

MEDIATOR: How are you going to do that?

MR. BROWN: I don't know.

MEDIATOR: She has a right to know from you what you want [by way of documentation]; otherwise, it's not fair to object to what she's asking for.

This is the same concrete approach the mediator has been trying all along. As before, it leads nowhere. Pressed to ask "fact" questions, Mr. Brown can only respond that his wife's monthly requests for the children's schooling is about $20 too high; for rent about $50 too much. The mediator invites him to explain his objections, but Mr. Brown ignores this request and simply goes down her budget indicating several items that he feels are excessive. Mrs. Brown repeats that they should go to arbitration. The mediator makes one last effort to get a dialogue started: is there anything that Mrs. Brown can provide information about that would clarify things for Mr. Brown? No, says Mr. Brown, he just thinks that $600 a month is too much money.

Here, as elsewhere, the mediator does not direct the parties' attention to the patterns by which they avoid constructive grappling with conflict. In this case the problem is Mr. Brown's inability to ask his wife useful questions, indeed, any questions whatever. The consequences of this inhibition for informed decision making and at least a rudimentary understanding of the sources of Mr. Brown's difficulty (guilt? fear of upsetting Mrs. Brown?) would appear matters very much in need of explication.

Mrs. Brown introduces a new issue: what happens when her kids get older if she only has a fixed amount of child support?

> MR. BROWN: For Christ's sake, I hope that when they're fourteen I'll be making more money than I am now. [Note that although he is angry there is a persistent assumption that the total responsibility for child support is his, in spite of the fact that his wife has reasonable earning power of her own—one year after the divorce she was making nearly as much as he.]

The mediator reminds them that they have agreed to re-mediate and that in two years or so they may well have a *better* idea of what their needs are. He indicates that there is no way of knowing what an arbitrator would find, but that there is no sense negotiating any more unless they get down to concrete discussions. Mr. Brown agrees to up his offer to $500 a month, but with no escalation clause. Mrs. Brown tearfully says she will refigure everything and consider his $500 offer. They all agree that she will call him up to say whether she will accept the $500. If not, they will go to arbitration.

The mediator indicates that he will help facilitate the administrative contacts with the American Arbitration Association and that, since this is the first use of arbitration by the mediation center, the Association will probably not charge. Mr. Brown indicates that he does not want the mediator to serve as arbitrator. The mediator assures him that he will not. He asks Mrs. Brown if she could get her decision to him by tomorrow since he has to leave town and would like to draft their agreement before he does. The next day she called to accept her husband's final offer.

The final settlement document was prepared by the mediator and signed by both parties one week after the last mediation session. Mrs. Brown took this document to an attorney who filed it with the court. Approximately one month after signing the mediated settlement agreement, the Browns were legally divorced. Mr. Brown was not represented by counsel. There is no evidence that Mrs. Brown used her attorney in anything but a *pro forma* manner.

The Postdivorce Aftermath

The Browns' mediation, while not a model of constructive conflict resolution, produced some favorable results. However, the positive achievements had more to do with the objective dimensions of the settlement. In terms of the parties feelings about each other and the mediation experience and especially in the badly crippled co-parenting relationship, the signs were not so good.

THE POSITIVE OUTCOMES

The major accomplishments of the mediation appear to be these: The negotiations were swift and inexpensive. The total cost of mediation and the legal fees connected with it was $385 (all of which was paid by Mr. Brown).

Considering the difficult psychological and financial circumstances, the terms of settlement were reasonable. Mr. Brown agreed to child support payments representing approximately 38 percent of his annual income. This figure is within published court guidelines for a family with two minor children in the state in which the Browns resided (see Coogler, 1978). One year after the divorce Mr. Brown was in full compliance with the child support stipulation, a notable achievement given the national epidemic of noncompliance.

A serious defect which Mr. Brown did not complain about, was the failure of the parties to take into account the present and future earning power of Mrs. Brown, except in the sense that they both agreed that no alimony would be paid. Mr. Brown assumed the entire responsibility for the children's medical and dental expenses and the entire eventual cost of sending them to college. Given the likelihood of Mr. Brown's starting a new family and the significant alienation which already existed between him and his children, this lopsided victory for Mrs. Brown may turn out to be pyrrhic. In this connection it is also of note that at the time of the postdivorce interview Mrs. Brown's salary was already two-thirds of that of her ex-husband.

On the other hand, Mr. Brown did retain sole ownership of the marital home, a significant economic prize and something that he very much wanted, undoubtedly because of his plans to remarry. With very minor exceptions, all other property was split 50–50. Ancillary, but important matters such as health and life insurance provisions, along with an agreement to resolve any future disputes via mediation or arbitration, were also part of the final agreement. All things considered, and in comparison with available data on the quality and thoroughness of typical settlement agreements negotiated in the traditional manner, these results are nothing to be ashamed of.

Although Mrs. Brown had criticisms of mediation and the mediator, on the whole she was relatively satisfied at having used the process. She commented favorably on the mediator's efforts at helping create an orderly agenda and at bringing up issues that needed to be discussed. She was also pleased that the mediator "didn't tell us what to do." Although she had expected that he would "put his two cents in more," she liked the fact that he made her feel that the settlement was more her own. She would recommend the process to a friend.

She also appeared to have made strides towards economic self-reliance and savvy. She felt that the divorce had had a markedly favorable impact on her ability to handle business and financial matters. Since the divorce she had bought a house, established credit, and gotten a loan. These positive developments may be at least partly attributable to the mediator's assistance in helping her remain in negotiations when her own instinct was to run from this responsibility, as evidenced by her teary collapse toward the end of the last session.

Finally, although it does not seem to have accomplished much, the Browns voluntarily sought one postdivorce mediation session on the topic of visitation. This suggests at least a minimal level of confidence in the process.

THE NEGATIVE OUTCOMES

The negative side of the ledger is more extensive. Mr. Brown was bitterly dissatisfied with the financial provisions of the final settlement, especially the terms of child support. He still could not see how "all that money could be going to the children." He was sufficiently disturbed about this to consult an attorney. The lawyer advised him that under the laws of the state he would have to wait two years before requesting a modification and if he does so his chances of winning relief are slim since his salary will be higher. This advice dissuaded him from pursuing the postdivorce litigation which he had been contemplating. He was extremely angry with himself for making the child support agreement. He felt "stupid" about the settlement and has learned the unhappy lesson that he is incapable of making sound decisions when he is in a state of emotional turmoil.

Mr. Brown was also unhappy with the mediator and the mediation process. In comparison to his wife, who felt that negotiations had gone rather satisfactorily, Mr. Brown rated them as destructive, hostile, and upsetting. Along with child support, he also rated visitation and division of property as issues on which there had been considerable disagreement during the sessions. Since the recordings of the mediation meetings indicate that visitation and division of property were arranged with very little debate, his ratings reveal more about his inner turmoil and his inability to find expression for that turmoil in constructive engagement with his wife than they do about what transpired during mediation.

He would recommend mediation only to couples who had little by way of property or other assets, or for couples who had had a previous divorce and were therefore more experienced about the issues to be negotiated. He would especially not recommend mediation to divorcing friends with children. He held the mediator largely responsible for what he regarded as an undesirable financial settlement. He felt that the mediator's calmness and professional demeanor lulled him into a false sense of security. He also believed that the mediator favored his ex-wife. He acknowledged that this might be an "emotional reaction" but he felt strongly that the mediator had "missed something" on child support and division of property. If he had it to do over again he would skip mediation altogether and get himself a lawyer.

Although Mrs. Brown was more satisfied with mediation than her husband, she too had complaints. She felt that the mediator had not succeeded in gaining full disclosure from her ex-husband and had been so preoccupied with remaining impartial that he had failed to provide them with necessary information.

> I felt very much at a disadvantage. I thought we were going to get more professional advice—on the economics; what the children are going to need; what's fair, stuff like that. He didn't tell us and we weren't allowed [by the rules of Structured Mediation] to get outside help. I felt all the burden was on me and what did I know? That's why I was there, but because they were trying to remain so neutral they didn't give us the help.

She also complained of the mediator's failure to see her side of things.

> I would get mad at the direction things were going so I'd say something and the mediator would say, "Now you must listen to him; you have to hear what he has to say." But I felt I knew what he was saying more than the mediator. I just felt he [the mediator] was not seeing my point.

The visitation agreement was a shambles. This was probably the most pathognomic development in the postmediation period and the clearest example of how the Browns' inability to face their differences constructively came back to haunt them.

At the time of settlement Mrs. Brown remembered feeling very satisfied with the visitation agreement; Mr. Brown indicated that he had been satisfied, but less so. She liked the fact that she would have one weekend a month to herself and that he could see the children "whenever he wanted." He liked the idea that he would see his children once a month but he was dissatisfied with "all the arguing" they had in getting to the agreement.

After the divorce, matters deteriorated. They had serious conflicts and returned for one mediation session entirely devoted to visitation. Her version was that "he wouldn't take the children at all." With an unhappy sigh she added that in the year since the divorce he has had them for maybe two weekends and a couple of single days. His version was that he hasn't been able to take them as much as he agreed to because he was traveling a lot in connection with his job and was working long overtime. His distorted memory of the visitation agreement is that he agreed to take the children one weekend a month *when in town.* In fact, the agreement as written, obligated him to *at least* one weekend of visitation a month.

The postdivorce mediation session occurred because Mrs. Brown began calling her ex-husband at home, wanting to know why he wasn't coming to take the children. This riled Mr. Brown because his new wife didn't like answering such calls. In the postdivorce session the former Mrs. Brown agreed to call him only at work if he would agree to take the children for a whole weekend each month. She felt she needed some time for herself away from them. In the interview Mrs. Brown noted that to make things easier for him she agreed on any weekend a month he chose to accommodate his work schedule.

Mediation after the divorce does not seem to have been notably more successful for the Browns than it was the first time around, except that there was a reversal of unhappiness. Mrs. Brown was now quite dissatisfied with the current state of affairs, and Mr. Brown was reasonably satisfied. The upshot appears to be that he still was not seeing the children. According to the distressed and saddened Mrs. Brown, "he can't be bothered." Mr. Brown claims that he does see the children "every three to four months" and would like to see them more, but his work schedule prevents this. He does try to take his older son out to dinner once a week (although Mrs. Brown made no mention of this). He is happy that at least his ex-wife is no longer bothering him about the children.

Perhaps the worst aspect of the visitation debacle is that neither party evidenced the slightest understanding of why things were not working out and of their own possible contributions to the problems. If the mediation tapes are at all indicative it is not too difficult to imagine what the nature of those mutual contributions are; i.e., that Mrs. Brown manages to convey her continuing disappointment with her ex-husband and the heavy burdens which she alone must carry, and that he reacts to all her signs of distress with guilt and phobic avoidance. The postdivorce interviews provide support for this thesis. Thus, Mrs. Brown had hoped that after the divorce they would be able to talk and "be friends," but they can't. She felt things between them might have been different if he hadn't remarried immediately. Now she believes "he would just as soon the marriage had never existed." When asked if she wished anything between them were different she replied, "Not any more. I thought we'd be able to have the kids in common, but it hasn't worked out that way. From my standpoint, it doesn't bother me at all."

Mr. Brown's comments on the co-parenting relationship were simply that it had gotten less "emotional" and more "business-like"—trends which he prefers. His brevity is an eloquent summary of his continuing difficulty with the interpersonal demands of close relationships.

Analytic Reprise: Mediation as a Therapeutic Encounter

At the outset of this chapter I indicated that my primary purpose in choosing the case of an autistic divorce for analysis was to pursue the issue of whether divorce mediation can legitimately aspire to accomplish broadly therapeutic purposes through avowedly therapeutic stratagems. I have hinted at what those stratagems might be in my annotated account of the Browns' mediation sessions. Here I would like to make the notion of the therapeutic functions of the divorce mediator more explicit and consider several implications of a therapeutic approach for the development of the profession. Before doing so several general comments are in order.

First, I should like to reiterate that the degree to which Coogler may be criticized for his handling of this case is debatable. Aside from the obvious fact that hindsight is sharper than foresight, the outcomes of the Browns' mediation were not all bad. Second, the immediate presence of a new wife, combined with the couple's limited economic resources, were external complications which may have contributed significantly to the postdivorce difficulties. There may have been other complications of which we remain ignorant. Finally, the couple's deeply entrenched problems with handling conflict might not have yielded to even the most adroit and prescient handling.

I am also wary that my critical reflections may be taken as revealing an implicit bias that the Browns would have done better with lawyers. Obviously, there is no certain way of knowing whether the traditional legal approach would have produced a better result, but I think it would not have. The strongest thing that may be said on behalf of the legal approach is that it may have alleviated the manifest discontent of Mr. Brown, especially his feelings of having been taken to the cleaners financially. He himself was of the view that a good lawyer would have prevented such an outcome. Mrs. Brown did not complain of unfair terms, but she too was unhappy that the mediator did not provide her with more concrete information and support of the kind that a competent attorney might have been expected to provide. Finally, both sides felt that the mediator was somehow partial to the other. This is an inherent risk of the mediation role to which the advocate attorney is much less susceptible.

On balance, however, I do not find the arguments in favor of lawyers compelling. In the first place, the final terms were not badly skewed, Mr. Brown's opinion notwithstanding. The settlement was not strikingly creative, but given the parties' economic and psychological circumstances, and bearing in mind the not too high quality of the typical settlement produced by attorneys (Cavanaugh and Rhode 1976), it passes muster reasonably well. Moreover, Mr. Brown's perception that the mediator allowed his pockets to be picked is not supported by the tapes of the mediation. On the contrary, the mediator made numerous efforts to alert Mr. Brown to his passive negotiating style (albeit with little examination of its sources or consequences) but got little thanks for his efforts. As for Mrs. Brown, I believe that her yearnings for more substantive guidance from the mediator touch upon a central point, but tell us less about how she would have done under legal tutelage and more about her psychological need to play the helpless victim. In any case, she herself was of two minds about the mediator's restrained role. It is probably her better side which was in evidence when she spoke approvingly of the mediator's refusal to serve as her knight in shining armor.

The argument for lawyers falls flatest when it comes to the Browns' autistic negotiating style. That style was the product of elements to which each party contributed heavily and those contributions were made in simple but exquisite synchronization: Mrs. Brown's anger and messages of victimization cued Mr. Brown's passivity and acquiescence; at a certain point passivity and acquiescence turned to inflexibility and rebelliousness, which cued Mrs. Brown's helplessness and returned Mr. Brown to his earlier psychological posture (in spite of the fact that he clung tenaciously to his position on child support). Restricted to the one-sided perspective provided by their respective clients, lawyers would have had neither access to this dysfunctional system nor, in all likelihood, the training or motivation to do anything about it.

Indeed, a plausible case can be made that the Browns are precisely the sort of couple whose conflicts could well have escalated under adversarial representation. From the evidence on the tapes, the tendency of the marital system was to return perpetually to a state of chronic, but repressed, conflict. Dealing through lawyers, and thus freed from their restraining gyroscopic effect on one another, all hell might have broken loose. In the sense that it permitted access to the marital system and thus raised the possibility of altering its trajectory, mediation may be viewed as having had decided strategic advantages over the use of lawyers. That the mediator may not have seized upon these advantages in the most effective way is another matter.

This is not to say that Coogler was unaware of the interpersonal dynamics standing in his way. However, he chose to address the interpersonal issues within the confines of a rather narrowly construed task orientation. Thus, he countered Mrs. Brown's posture of self-abnegation with explicit admonishments that it was appropriate and necessary for her to think of her own needs. He repeatedly attempted to strengthen Mr. Brown's negotiating resolve by urging him to defend his own position and look out for his own interests and he pressed both parties to deal in facts and figures rather than insult and injury. He advocated norms of full disclosure, countered fantasies that there are perfect solutions to complex problems, and tried to inject flexibility and energy into the negotiations. With few exceptions these frontal assaults on the Browns' autistic interpersonal style fell flat.

THE THERAPEUTIC ROLE OF THE MEDIATOR

If there was a significant shortcoming in Coogler's grappling with this case it may be summarized as an underemphasis on mediation's therapeutic possibilities. *I define as therapeutic all efforts on the mediator's part to explore, understand, and alter patterns of spousal communication, problem-solving, and conflict management which are manifestly interfering with a constructive negotiating process.* A more precise designation for this approach might be *process-therapeutic,* since it is the process by which the couple interacts (rather than their individual or marital histories) which provides the grist for the therapeutic mill.

What are the specific kinds of strategies and tactics by which a mediator may enact a process-therapeutic role? In my running analytic commentary of the Brown's mediation I have suggested many of them. A mediator enacts a therapeutic function when he or she: expresses curiosity about how the couple has arrived at decisions directly related to the mediation effort, implicitly models more constructive patterns of problem solving, and attempts to educate the parties about and directly modify dysfunctional interaction patterns.

The first two of these strategies are by no means incompatible with a more task-oriented style of mediation (although neither was employed to a very high degree by Coogler in his work with the Browns). However both strategies tend to serve more extended purposes in a process-therapeutic approach. The direct attempt to modify dysfunctional patterns by description and education is the strategy of therapeutic mediation as I have defined it.

THE MEDIATOR EXPRESSES CURIOSITY ABOUT HOW THE COUPLE HAS ARRIVED AT DECISIONS DIRECTLY RELATED TO THE MEDIATION EFFORT. A therapeutically focused mediator will be extremely active with regard to exploring their decision-making style with the mediating couple. The Browns' case is representative of the numerous relevant opportunities to do so. The foremost of these is the decision to agree to mediate in the first place. Others include the decisions, made outside mediation, that the house would remain the husband's, that there would be no spousal maintenance, and that a detailed visitation provision was impossible because of the husband's work schedule. Note that it is *not* necessary to ask general questions concerning the long-buried (and forgotten) marital past for clues to what the relationship patterns have been. There is more than enough material of this type which is directly relevant to the settlement negotiations to make such historical excursions unnecessary.

There are several purposes to such explorations. First, they educate the mediator to the kinds of interactive dynamics that are likely to interfere with the mediation process. This is an important diagnostic activity since there is very good reason to believe that interactive patterns which characterized the couple during the preliminaries to mediation will almost certainly make themselves felt during it. Second, by inquiring closely, in a non-judgmental way, about how decisions have been arrived at, the mediator implicitly models the importance and value of understanding the marital dynamics as a tool in the negotiations. In the case of the Browns, inquiries into the process of joint decision making would almost certainly have revealed Mrs. Brown's unconscious (but skillful) management of Mr. Brown's guilt and his passively acquiescent, but covertly resistant style of reacting to her.

THE MEDIATOR IMPLICITLY MODELS MORE CONSTRUCTIVE PATTERNS OF PROBLEM SOLVING. In approaching the negotiations the mediator should act to establish certain problem-solving norms. Foremost among these are the value of deliberation rather than haste and the need for a careful search for all relevant facts—psychological as well as practical.

The first opportunity for setting a good example and countering dysfunctional norms of decision making comes with the introduction to mediation and the committment to use mediation as the forum for negotiations. I believe that it is incumbent on the mediator to foster as deliberate and thorough a process in this regard as possible. The mediator should prepare an adequate written description of the mediation process which can be mailed to prospective clients prior to the orientation and which can assist the parties to ask informed questions at the orientation meeting. In the orientation itself the mediator should convey throughout that the purpose is to make a decision regarding mediation in a deliberate and mutual way. The potential virtues of mediation may be set forth enthusiastically, but care should be taken that the mediator's belief in the approach not become an implicit coercion to forego other means of reaching settlement. Doubts about the process should be examined in detail. As noted earlier, the contours of the couple's prior discussions regarding the decision to try mediation should be examined closely and an attempt made to clarify the motives and decision-making style which characterized those discussions.

It is also advisable to allow some time between the orientation and the beginning of mediation, during which the couple ought to be encouraged to think over what they have learned in the initial contact, discuss it with each other, consult with others whose opinion they value, and recontact the mediator with further questions. There is no doubt that this course of action entails the risk that highly ambivalent couples, who might nonetheless be excellent candidates for mediation, will choose not to avail themselves of the mediator's services. It is a risk that has the associated virtue of not only modeling a functional approach to joint decision making, but of inculcating a desirably high level of psychological commitment to the mediation enterprise. (These strictures regarding gaining a commitment to mediation obviously apply more to private sector mediation, whose prospective clients are free agents, than to public sector mediation in which couples are ordered to mediate by the court.)

Another central component of modeling constructive patterns of problem solving is the generous provision by the mediator of substantive guidance. In the Browns' mediation Coogler tended to eschew an active role in this regard. He typically deflected questions about substantive matters (such as requests for guidelines on child support), arguing that it was far more important that the couple search for solutions which fitted their unique circumstances and made sense to *them.* There is some truth to this, but on the whole I believe it is crucial that the mediator play a more active role on substantive matters.

There are several reasons for embracing the role of substantive expert more avidly. In the first place, the typical divorcing couple has a legitimate need for such information. The issues to be resolved are often complex, anxieties are likely to be high, and the couple's ignorance is often extensive. When one adds to this list entrenched patterns of defective communication and problem solving, the need for substantive guidance from the mediator is likely to be genuine.

The generous provision by the mediator of substantive advice and information also may serve a useful diagnostic function. If the couple's wish for such help is due to simple ignorance and the more or less normal anxieties associated with divorce, the provision of the wanted assistance should produce a reduction in tensions and movement in the negotiations. If, on the other hand, the mediator's guidance and advice lead nowhere it is a good bet that attention needs to be paid to faulty patterns of interaction or unresolved emotional issues.

Finally, to successfully enact the more robust therapeutic functions of changing dysfunctional patterns it will be crucial that the mediator have the trust and confidence of the parties to the highest possible degree. Without such rapport, efforts to interest the couple in modifying the necessary aspects of their interactive style are likely to fall very flat indeed. It is no secret that enacting the role of expert in substantive areas is one of the surest means by which mediators may establish themselves in the hearts and minds of the disputants. A few minutes with any experienced labor mediator will make this abundantly clear (Kolb, in press; Kressel 1972).

Two caveats about enacting the role of substantive expert: First, much depends on how the task is carried out. Obviously I am not talking about efforts to manipulate the parties in to doing the "right" or "normal" thing by providing information in a biased or heavy-handed way. Second, care must be taken that the information provided not be assimilated by a highly dysfunctional marital style—as by passive acceptance of everything the mediator has to offer with little or no evidence that the parties are considering it in the light of their particular circumstances or values. If the mediator's substantive interventions are reacted to in a dysfunctional way the parties need to be made aware of it.

THE MEDIATOR ATTEMPTS TO EDUCATE THE PARTIES ABOUT, AND MAKES DIRECT EFFORTS TO MODIFY, DYSFUNCTIONAL PATTERNS OF INTERACTION. This is the core meaning of a therapeutic orientation to the role of the divorce mediator. When negotiations bog down because of a problematic style of interaction, the mediator with a therapeutic style attempts to serve as an "observing ego"—educating the parties to those aspects of their interaction which are hindering negotiations and, by his or her powers of persuasion, attempting to modify those patterns just enough to facilitate more productive exchanges.

Although it is not given the title "therapeutic," something closely akin to this approach to mediation is commonly advocated. All of the major expositions of divorce mediation with which I am familiar make the point that it is the mediator's task to take cognizance of well-established dysfunctional patterns of interaction. The emphasis, however, is typically on circumscribing and containing the problematic forms of exchange, rather than on attempting to help the parties gain command of them through insight into their nature, cause, and consequences. Haynes, for example, writes that "certain patterns of behavior that exist between the parties will, of course, be part of the relationship during the negotiations. Where those patterns interfere with open and equal negotiations, the mediator must intervene to *circumvent* the normal behavior and permit negotiations to continue" (emphasis added) (Haynes 1981, 112).

It is clear from the descriptions of strategies and tactics of intervention given by others that the notion of dealing with destructive patterns of conflict through circumvention, rather than by education and direct modification, is widely shared. Most commonly it is advocated that the mediator deal with destructive or dysfunctional patterns by explicitly forbidding certain types of interaction ("Telling Jane she is stupid is not helpful"); keeping the parties task-oriented; allowing for cooling off periods; invoking the interests of children to induce cooperation; bringing weight to bear on the parties through their attorneys; and altering "power imbalances" by building self-esteem in the weaker party (see Haynes [1981], Kelly [1983], and Saposnek [1983]).

It is apparent that Coogler himself was under the influence of this conflict containment view of the mediator's role in his work with the Browns. Coogler, like many divorce mediators, emphasized to the couple the value of mediation as a means of "avoiding tensions." This is sensible for couples whose primary presenting style is of the enmeshed variety—openly and destructively conflictual. With a couple like the Browns it appears to have unwittingly reinforced unrealistic fears about the dangers of "fighting" and displays of emotion. One year later Mrs. Brown was still feeling "embarrassed" about her emotional tendencies rather than being aware of how her displays of emotion served to control Mr. Brown (because of his own anxieties about emotional fireworks) or how they effectively undermined the co-parenting relationship which it was her conscious wish to foster.

The therapeutic approach to divorce mediation and the more narrowly circumscribed conflict containment approach are not mutually exclusive.

The therapeutic focus ought to be called into play only when the underlying patterns do not yield to more directly task-oriented means of channeling destructive modes of conflict. However, when the conflict containment approach fails, I believe the mediator has little choice but to make the observed dysfunctional patterns the active grist for the mediation mill.

Therapeutic interventions may be made at the level of the individual or the couple. It is clear, for example, that Mr. Brown's inability to adopt a negotiating posture or deal in an active way with his wife's anger and hurt were a serious obstacle to an informed negotiation. This inhibited style needed addressing. There are many ways to do this sort of thing, but the major approaches include pointing out the style and its consequences; inquiring, in a sympathetic way, into its sources; challenging any unwarranted or misleading assumptions on which the dysfunctional style is built (e.g., that a more assertive posture on his part will only make his wife angrier or more helpless); and suggesting more adaptive ways of responding. Similar strategies might have been employed in dealing with Mrs. Brown's unproductive use of guilt inducement and helplessness to coerce her husband to grant all her demands.

Efforts to help the parties see and modify their unproductive individual contributions to negotiations can be made during joint sessions, with the advantage that the other partner gains some insight into the motives and characteristic anxieties of the other. The disadvantage is that defensiveness is likely to be high when the other is present, making it difficult for the mediator to say what has to be said without serious risk of alienating the target of his or her instruction. For this reason individual sessions are often the most productive setting in which to teach many of the lessons that need to be learned.

Interventions aimed at the level of the couple are more profitably made in the context of joint settings. For example, it is apparent, as I have noted earlier, that the Browns played out their respective roles in direct response to one another. The most sophisticated, and potentially the most useful type of intervention a mediator can make along therapeutic lines, is to point this out as it is happening, making explicit each side's contribution and the consequences for the negotiating enterprise.

The wife's teary collapse at the husband's first serious signs of gumption in the last session and his miserable but rigid insistence on his position in the face of her emotional "collapse" is a good case in point. Coogler rightly and skillfully blocked Mrs. Brown's impulse to leave the mediation session. On the other hand, he did not help either of the parties see what this significant exchange was all about or what its consequences were for the future of any agreements they might reach. By this time in the mediation a description of the conflict avoidant style could have been forcefully made, with numerous illustrations from earlier exchanges. An emphasis on each side's contribution would have made this more palatable although it would not have completely eliminated the risks to rapport that are part of any effort to impart insight.

One cannot force couples to be interested in material of this kind, but one can make supportive, but firm efforts to convince them that they should be. "Do you think we should try to understand why you both continue to run from real negotiations?" is the kind of intervention I have in mind here. Let us suppose that Mr. Brown's response to such a query is something along the lines of: "We can't negotiate because she refuses to be sensible and realistic." This permits the mediator to ask Mr. Brown if he has noticed *his* part in the flight from constructive bargaining—by acquiescing to all of her demands, running scared when she cries or gets angry, failing to question her budget figures in a fair but serious way, and so on. Mr. Brown may not care for this perspective at first hearing and he may retort that *his* style is only the product of his wife's behavior. A mediator should welcome a dialogue along these lines because it provides the opportunity to suggest to Mr. Brown first, that he may well be underestimating his role in producing the very behavior in his wife that he complains of, and second, that it will be more productive if both he and his wife focus on understanding and modifying their own contributions to the faulty negotiating process rather than on insisting that all the changes in behavior need to be made by the other. These points, too, are debatable, but it is precisely because they need to *be* debated that a dialogue with Mr. Brown, in earshot of Mrs. Brown, is worth provoking.

For her part, Mrs. Brown needed to be helped to articulate why serious negotiating overtures were so difficult for her to respond to. Quite possibly her intransigent style was masking despondency about the divorce. There may have been deeper psychological issues with roots in her family of origin, such as a traumatic history with a dominating, hypercritical father, who left her bereft of any confidence in her own powers of persuasion and problem solving in an intimate setting.

How deeply is a mediator obliged to pursue material of this kind? Only far enough to either move the couple into a productive negotiating pattern or to determine that the obstacles are too deep or the parties too resistant to make mediation a viable modality. If more than two or three sessions addressing dysfunctional patterns are needed this is a likely sign that the couple is unsuited for mediation. They should be presented with this diagnosis and invited to ask questions about it. The spirit of this discussion should be accepting of the parties' right to be as they are, but firm on the prerequisites for effective mediation. The mediator should also convey the belief that being unwilling or unsuited to mediate is nothing to feel ashamed or despondent about. The mediation experience has well served its purposes if it is now clearer than it was at the outset that a brief period of individual therapy or exploratory joint therapy is needed before substantive negotiations are likely to be productive or that more traditional legal approaches are better suited to the couple's preferred style of resolving differences.

REFLECTIONS AND CAUTIONS REGARDING A THERAPEUTIC APPROACH TO DIVORCE MEDIATION

Several additional observations and caveats about my delineation of the process-therapeutic approach to divorce mediation are in order.

First, my use of the word "therapeutic" differs from the usual employment of that term in most prior discussions of divorce mediation with which I am familiar. Most commonly, the therapeutic approach to divorce mediation is taken to mean interventions aimed at helping the parties resolve ambivalence about the divorce through an examination of the marital history and the process of divorce decision making. Emotional catharsis is often included as a necessary component of such a therapeutic stratagem. Proponents of this approach argue that unless unresolved feelings of psychological attachment are put to rest no constructive negotiations are possible. Consequently the mediation process is geared to resolving such feelings prior to embarking upon a direct engagement of the substantive issues. (Milne [1978] has given perhaps the most thorough exposition of this approach.)

By and large, this conception of the mediator's role has not been well received. When the warning is given not to confuse divorce mediation with therapy it is this generic sense of the word therapeutic that is typically being invoked. The detractors of the "mediation as therapy" philosophy feel that it is simply unrealistic and unworkable given the time constraints under which mediators typically work and the necessity of coming quickly to important practical agreements (Kelly 1983; Saposnek 1983). Pearson et al. (1983) quote one such divorce mediator: "It is tempting for us to try to do counseling with newly divorced people. You see so clearly how attached they are to each other and they need to learn how to detach. I have learned that I cannot help them with that" (p. 23). Saposnek argues that more often than not delving into the causes of the divorce as part of the mediation process leads nowhere because one spouse is likely to assert, "I don't want to dwell on the divorce, I just want to settle the custody problem—so let's get on with it" (Saposnek 1983, 169).

These anti-mediation-as-therapy views strike me as sensible. Unresolved attachment feelings are better handled in a short course of exploratory divorce therapy (see chapter 4) prior to the commencement of mediation. However, there is room for more than a single meaning of the word "therapeutic" as it applies to divorce mediation. Attempting to modify patterns of flawed communication, problem solving, and conflict resolution which directly interfere with the negotiation experience is a "therapeutic" effort that is entirely consistent with the mediator's mandate to resolve substantive issues.

Even with as obviously problematic a couple as the Browns, however, a case can be made against trying to do so. The argument might run as follows: interventions aimed at changing interpersonal dynamics are still too much like therapy; therapy is not what the couple expects and they are likely to balk at paying for it. The therapeutic style is also unlikely to be effective because long-standing patterns of relating cannot be changed in a short-term intervention like mediation. If mediation is extended to achieve therapeutic purposes, costs will escalate, thereby undermining one of the principle arguments for mediation over the use of lawyers.

I do not find these assertions compelling. Given the high levels of public ignorance about the mediation process (see chapter 10) there is no reason to assume that a couple's readiness to accept and pay for therapeutically-oriented divorce mediation is better or worse at the outset than their enthusiasm for any other kind. No matter what the mediator's approach a good deal of education as to the nature of mediation will usually be necessary. Making it clear to the parties that one of the mediator's tasks is to help them see and overcome at least some of their problematic ways of communicating and resolving differences does not seem a more arcane piece of enlightenment than explaining the pros and cons of, say, arbitration or the role of the advisory attorney.

As to effectiveness, experience with short-term marital and family therapy suggests that salutary changes in problematic styles of relating can occur without long courses of treatment. Such changes may even be facilitated by having a concrete focus which can give added meaning to therapeutic interventions.

The argument that a process orientation will prolong mediation and thereby escalate costs hinges on the definition of "costs." If costs refers to the short-term expense of paying to get a settlement agreement, then therapeutically-oriented mediation may prove more costly than the strictly task-oriented approach. Even here, however, the additional expense should run no more than a few additional sessions, for as I have indicated, the need for *extensive* attention to problematic interactional patterns suggests strongly that mediation is premature or unwise. If we are talking about long-term costs, however, a process orientation during mediation may well save the couple thousands of postdivorce legal dollars by promoting a more durable agreement, to say nothing of a more propitious climate in which to raise their children.

There is, however, a less luminous side to the process-therapeutic approach to divorce mediation. In the first place, it is not the model of choice for everybody. At the most benign and cooperative levels a therapeutic approach may be superfluous, whereas, at the highest levels of dysfunction it may be necessary to stick with a highly directive task orientation lest the roof fall in. At the present writing it is not yet clear how this type of diagnostic assessment is to be made with any degree of confidence. There are also more subtle distinctions among styles of mediation than the stark contrast between the task and process-therapeutic forms which I have been discussing. A truly adequate contingency model of mediation would be capable of identifying alternative permutations and combinations of mediator behavior which might be appropriate for differing types of couples. We are not remotely close to this level of sophistication.

The process-therapeutic approach also adds certain complications to the professional life of the divorce mediator. For one thing, it suggests that mediators either must know the limits of their competence to handle a therapeutic role or must do something to increase their competence where it may be lacking. The notion of incompetence in divorce mediation—practicing beyond the scope of one's training—is usually mentioned by lawyers who criticize mediators for inexperience in legal and financial matters. But a similar point can be made with regard to the handling of interpersonal issues. When a couple requires such assistance, a mediator should have the requisite training in individual and marital dynamics, or be assisted by somebody who does. This is one reason why the idea of lawyer-therapist mediation teams has an appeal to many observers. In any case, more training or more team work involves additional expense and effort on the part of mediators.

Invocations of a process-therapeutic style of mediation also provides another opportunity to comment on the stressful and complex nature of the mediation role set forth at greater length in chapter 10. Coogler's task orientation was consistent with a time-honored interpretation of the mediator's role: to keep a modest profile, to encourage the parties' autonomy, and to avoid, even by suggestion, the adoption of standards of settlement foreign to them. This approach may not have worked wonders for the Browns but, from the mediator's perspective, it had the virtues of clarity, simplicity, and tradition.

The assumption of a therapeutic orientation seems to me to expose the mediator to greater hazards. Most notable among these are the heavy demands made on the mediator's diagnostic skill and powers of persuasion, and the attendant risk of losing ambivalent clients or of sufficiently alienating them so that no useful result occurs. For example:

- The therapeutically-oriented mediator's allegiance to modeling a deliberate and thorough approach to joint problem solving entails the risk of losing clients who are unable or unwilling to maintain such a high standard. Thus, the mediator may lose ambivalent clients at the outset by encouraging a careful approach to the decision to mediate.
- Although other approaches to mediation often involve highly directive interventions that may alienate the parties, interpreting dysfunctional behaviors and inquiring, however sympathetically, into their source, is a delicate diplomatic task. Even if done with great skill it may still bruise tender egos to the point of no return—especially since the joint format may increase personal sensitivities.
- The interpretive mode also requires an active shuttling between individual and joint sessions with various associated problems. These include: the diagnostic quandary of when to switch from individual to joint sessions and back again; the possibility of unintentionally revealing "secrets" which have been divulged in individual sessions; the possible loss of trust in the mediator due to each party's fear of what is going on with the other in the individual sessions. Coogler's preference for exclusively joint sessions is partly to be understood as a way to avoid such potential pitfalls.
- The mediator is asked not only to diagnose dysfunctional patterns, no simple task in its own right, but to constantly monitor the mediation process for signs that the mediator's own interventions are being assimilated to the couple's dysfunctional style. This can be wearing. With the autistic couple I have stressed the need to actively provide substantive support. However, doing so may play into the dysfunctional pattern. That is, the parties may passively accept the information or advice, and in so doing continue to avoid any true grappling with their differences. Similarly, the invocation by the mediator of arbitration or any other form of "leverage" to move parties who are stuck may simply amplify an already defective relationship style. This happened with the Browns. The pressure which Coogler exerted by announcing his readiness to move them into arbitration precipitated a full-fledged attack of negotiating rigor mortis in a system already strongly inclined toward the morgue.

In sum, although I have advocated a process-therapeutic style as a necessary component of the divorce mediator's kit bag, I am well aware that this is a prescription that is easier to give than to take. It implies a level of diagnostic acumen we do not yet possess (except perhaps in hindsight); it adds a degree of complexity and stress to a role which is already difficult; and it raises complex issues regarding the appropriate training and professional background of mediators.

Another way of saying all of this is to restate a basic theme which has emerged in our exploration of all forms of professional assistance in divorce: there are many obstacles to a constructive settlement process—and many of them have as much to do with the difficulties and ambiguities of the professional role as with the unhappy circumstances of the parties.

13

Conclusions and Implications

The focus of this book has been the process of divorce settlement negotiations—the informal negotiations by which the divorcing couple arrives at the decision to terminate their marriage and the formal negotiations over money, property, and children. In particular we have been concerned with understanding the role of lawyers, therapists, and mediators in attempting to assist the parties in these two negotiating arenas. It would be premature to claim that we have now arrived at a definitive statement on these matters. On the contrary, one of our major themes has been the remarkable lack of research on divorce "negotiations" in light of the incredible frequency with which these occur and the vast sums spent in the endeavor. I shall attempt to summarize the major gaps in our knowledge and specify particular research issues at the end of this chapter. My primary concern, however, is a modest summary of what we now know and the implications of this knowledge for divorcing couples and those who assist them. There is some good news here but by and large my concluding notes are written in a somber key.

I shall first present the practical import of our work in terms of some general themes regarding the divorce process. I shall then address the implications for seeking and using the services of therapists, lawyers, and mediators.

Some Practical Themes Regarding the Divorce Settlement Process

When we began our research my colleagues and I set as our goal an understanding of the manner in which the formal terms of settlement were negotiated. We were particularly interested in the nature of the conflict which developed during those negotiations and the manner by which professionals attempted to channel that conflict along more productive lines. Our research focus was based on the premise that the forces set in motion by the settlement negotiations could profoundly influence, for better or worse, not only crucial practical arrangements, but the psychological environment which came to prevail among the members of the post-divorce family. In other words, our practical hope was ameliorative: that we might learn something of value for those who struggle to make divorce as positive an experience as one can reasonably expect.

CONFLICT, EVEN DESTRUCTIVE CONFLICT, HAS ITS USES

It is evident from clinical experience that divorce proceeds in stages and that, particularly in the earlier stages, destructive forms of conflict are to be expected. The practical circumstances—the shortage of cold hard cash and its various equivalents—doom any easy generosity, and the psychological task of giving up deep emotional ties seems to require some degree of emotional fireworks for most people. Even later in the process, angry outbursts are not necessarily to be shunned or viewed with dismay. Anger helps us to see more clearly what is wanted or where the real needs are. Indeed, one of the most serious pathologies of destructive conflict in divorce is the absence of conflict where one expects it to be. The principle is nowhere better embodied than in the concept of the "autistic" divorce and its unhappy aftermath.

THE KEY TO THE CONSTRUCTIVE MANAGEMENT OF CONFLICT IS A COOPERATIVE NEGOTIATING ORIENTATION

Enlightened professional opinion generally holds that the most effective approach to the settlement process is a cooperative orientation to conflict management. While each party should actively strive to protect and advance their own interests this should be done with a view to seeking arrangements that will benefit the other party as well. The notion of striving cooperatively rather than with the competitive motivation to score a "victory" over the other is consistent both with the reality of the continuing ties which bind divorcing parents and with three decades of research on the social psychology of conflict.

The importance of inducing a cooperative orientation to divorce conflict is the key conceptual notion underlying the premiere strategy of the divorce therapist, what we have called "orchestrating the motivation to divorce." Therapists proceed on the notion that unless each side is in an approximately equal state of acceptance of the divorce no constructive approach to conflict management is likely, because the will to seek a mutually beneficial end to the marriage does not exist. Among attorneys, opinion regarding the value of cooperatively oriented conflict is more divided, but even here, at the bastion of adversarial conflict, we find that a very sizeable number of professionals—those whom we have labeled "counselors"—share the view that cooperation is vastly preferable to competition in the negotiating process. It is among the proponents of divorce mediation that the cooperative ethos has reached its zenith. Although it is an oversimplification, divorce mediation's key strategic goal is to engender a cooperative pursuit of settlement terms.

There are two additional points about the value of a cooperative negotiating ethos that are worth discussing. First, as just noted, one should not expect cooperation to be the hallmark of a constructive negotiating process from beginning to end. The early stages of divorce may actually require what appear on the surface to be destructive outbursts. Premature cooperation may indicate a pathological intolerance of conflict in one or both parties. Second, it is beneficial for the parties, as well as their therapists, lawyers, and mediators, to bear in mind that it is unlikely that there will be any single villain or cause for the difficulties which arise at the bargaining table. I have reviewed in chapter 2 the numerous obstacles that stand in the way of a constructive divorce settlement process. Both the parties and their agents are struggling with many sources of inflexibility, tension, and ill will that none of them have intentionally created and that none of them control. In divorce settlement negotiations a little sympathy is due everybody.

EXPLORATORY DIVORCE THERAPY IS A POTENTIALLY VALUABLE AND FREQUENTLY OVERLOOKED AID TO SETTLEMENT NEGOTIATIONS

In chapter 4 I have touted the virtues of divorce therapy for increasing the prospects of a constructive process of settlement negotiations because such therapy may help encourage mutuality of the divorce decision, strengthen battered self-esteem, and increase interpersonal sensitivity. Our typology of divorcing couples suggests, however, that the greatest value of exploratory divorce therapy may be in modifying dysfunctional patterns of problem solving, communication, and conflict. A strong case can be made that, in the early stages of divorce, particularly during and immediately after the decision to end the marriage, a course of exploratory divorce therapy may well be the treatment of choice. There are several aspects of the divorce process that argue in this direction:

1. The decision to end a marriage is of such profound importance and entails such serious dislocations in personal and family functioning that it should only be taken after the most strenuous marital and self-examination.
2. The probability for a flawed divorce decision process is quite high. Although many people give lip service to the idea that both spouses contribute to a bad marriage, in actuality most divorcing persons find it difficult to conceptualize their own contribution to the marital difficulties in any but the most perfunctory ways—e.g., "I never should have married the bastard." This lack of understanding only contributes further to the difficulties and almost guarantees continued suffering, whether or not divorce ensues.
3. The divorce decision-making process is likely to embody all of the dysfunctional elements of the marital relationship itself. There is a very real possibility that the modification of these patterns might enable the marriage to survive in a positive fashion. Even if the marriage is unsavable, the modification of dysfunctional styles of relating is likely to be a boon to the ensuing settlement negotiations.

In sum, probably the best advice anybody can give a divorcing couple is the admonishment, "Don't just do something; stand there." Divorce therapy is a potentially constructive means of "standing still."

THE LAWYERS ROLE IN SETTLEMENT NEGOTIATIONS MAY BE LESS EXTENSIVE AND LESS DESTRUCTIVE THAN THE POPULAR STEREOTYPE

The popular stereotype has it that the central professional actor on the stage of divorce is the attorney. In this version attorneys are the prime advisors, negotiators, and handholders of the anguished and confused divorce client. In somewhat opposite fashion, attorneys are also widely reputed to be the chief professional bounders in the divorce process. Even among their own colleagues, the "matrimonial" specialist is said to rank little higher than the proverbial ambulance chaser. Divorce lawyers have been referred to with such unflattering encomiums as "the proctologists of the legal profession."

Since empirical evidence on the actual role and performance of the divorce attorney is woefully lacking, a definitive counter to these stereotypes is not possible. Undoubtedly, like many stereotypes, they are based on a kernel—perhaps more than a kernel—of truth. Yet, among the more unexpected and striking findings of our research is that the role of the attorney in divorce is probably both less important and more positive than is generally suspected.

In the first place, as far as can be established in any objective way, the vast majority of divorcing persons do *not* appear to make very extensive use of lawyers. When asked, two-thirds or more of recently divorced people, including those with property and children, say that they did most of the settlement negotiating directly with their spouse and with scarcely any lawyer input whatever. Even more striking, apparently between 20 to 50 percent of all divorces involve not the proverbial duo of attorneys—but a single lawyer. The assumption is that the attorney in these cases has served as little more than a clerk—a highly paid one, to be sure—but a clerk nonetheless.

It is possible, of course, that the conclusion that lawyers play a limited role in the settlement process is in error. It is, after all, a conclusion based on only a handful of studies and the data admit of differing interpretations. Perhaps the samples are not truly representative, or perhaps the version of the respondents is inaccurate. The client's sentiment that the lawyer did little of the work may reflect skillful, rather than absent, legal management (since it is preferable that the clients *believe* that the agreement is their own), together with the client's own vanity. Maybe, but I doubt it. There is little evidence in our extensive interview data that even the highly "psychologically" minded legal counselor is sophisticated and subtle in the arts of impression management. As for vanity, it would appear at least as robust in the attorney as the client. Also, low levels of legal utilization are consistent with a variety of other factors surrounding divorce negotiations. These include the strained financial resources of the typical divorcing couple, which may produce a strong desire to keep legal costs to a minimum; the widespread public distrust of attorneys; and lawyers' own lack of enthusiasm for the kinds of personal attention and careful interpersonal management which negotiations between divorcing or divorced spouses require.

It is also striking that a relatively small percentage of attorneys—no more than perhaps 10 to 15 percent—appear to embody the snarling portrait of the competitive, conflict escalating "son-of-a-bitch" about whom we had heard so much. On the contrary, both by their own accounts and by those of the few clients whose views on the subject have been solicited in any systematic way, the preponderance of lawyers appear motivated to dampen spousal hostilities and to profer counsel of moderation. Thus, somewhere between a third to two-thirds of attorneys fit more neatly under the *counselor* rubric than under that of *advocate*—and even the majority of the advocates appear a rather tame lot.

The popular stereotype of the belligerent attorney may owe more to certain aspects of legal life in divorce than to the realities of how lawyers actually behave. The portrait of the lawyer as a competitive zealot out to screw things up for the sake of a "victory" and a fat fee is consistent with the common human desire to find a simple scapegoat for unhappy, but complex events; with the lawyer's unfortunate role as the bearer of unpleasant economic and legal tidings; and with the high visibility and good "copy" of the legal *gladiators,* combined with their often pivotal harmful effect on the other settlement negotiators.

The limited use which the divorcing public appears to make of attorneys and the reasonably benign posture of most lawyers towards the settlement negotiations, leads to the surprising and sobering conclusion that legal help may be underutilized rather than overutilized in divorce. In other words, the generally miserable aftermath of the settlement process in terms of such things as noncompliance and postdivorce litigation may partly reflect the failure of divorcing persons to actively seek and properly make use of competent legal assistance. I realize that this possibility is very much at variance with doctrinaire anti-lawyer views. Moreover, the proposition can scarcely be said to rest on an impeccable base of evidence. The case can nonetheless be made that the divorce attorney has been given a bum rap (albeit a well-compensated one).

I am not asserting, mind you, that more active legal involvement is *the* answer. That would be going too far in the opposite direction. As I have already suggested, the power of legal assistance to make things better—like that of the power of therapists and mediators—is strongly circumscribed by the numerous obstacles over which nobody has very much control. Moreover, as I shall reiterate shortly, *all* of the professional roles in divorce are beset by internal problems which add a degree of difficulty to the uncoupling process. I am asserting that the service of a good divorce attorney is a healthy and reasonable objective to strive for.

DIVORCE MEDIATION IS A PROMISING ADJUNCT TO THE EXCLUSIVE USE OF ATTORNEYS, AT LEAST FOR CERTAIN TYPES OF COUPLES

I have cast a jaundiced eye on the extravagant claims that have been made by the early proponents of divorce mediation. The miserable circumstances likely to prevail at the divorce bargaining table preclude, in my view, any simple solutions. Moreover, for all its appeal, mediation is not an easy solution at all, but a highly complex and stressful mode of intervention under many circumstances. Even the rudimentary and defective empirical evidence on divorce mediation's success rate bears out its distinct limitations. I have reviewed all these matters in detail in chapters 9 and 10. The main difficulty suggested by the empirical evidence is that mediation appears to work only for those who are able to reach a mediated agreement, rather than for all those who try. This latter group may represent 40 to 60 percent of the total. Moreover, even for the successful cases, mediation appears to have only limited benefits for altering dysfunctional relationships among divorced parents and their children, an area where some of the more extravagant claims have been made. There is no reliable evidence that mediation is *superior* to the use of attorneys.

However, a critical perspective is not intended to disparage mediation's value, and it would be ironic if the critical words I have written on the subject were turned to that use by mediation's opponents. The empirical record on mediation, while not supportive of the more extreme claims which have been advanced, is far from bleak. The preponderance of couples who have used mediation give it relatively high marks, marks at least as high as those received by other forms of professional assistance, including that provided by therapists and lawyers. For those most vexing and difficult of all divorce disputes—those over custody and visitation—the mediation alternative appears a desirable adjunct to the use of attorneys and, for the most part, the legal community has been willing to grant this.

There are certain couples who may be particularly well suited to mediation; for whom, indeed, it may be the approach of choice. Again, the early evidence is still too fragmentary for definitive conclusions, but combined with clinical experience, the target population for comprehensive divorce mediation (that is, mediation of *all* the issues, including money and property, as well as child-related matters) appears to be divorcing couples in which both spouses have accepted the need to end the marriage; in which both have a modicum of trust in the other; in which the mutual ability and willingness to cooperate remains sufficiently intact to permit joint problem solving; in which there is no more than a moderate imbalance in financial and psychological resources (power); and in which there has either been a history of some success in joint decision making (especially in regard to children) or else a period of therapy preceding the mediation in which such skill has been developed.

The percentage of the divorcing population which fits this description is unknown. The figure probably ranges from somewhere between 10 percent to 30 percent of the whole. There is also undoubtedly a percentage of couples outside this optimal type who can derive considerable benefits from mediation, particularly a mediation which is geared to addressing their dysfunctional patterns of relating, which has the active support of their attorneys, and at which, for whatever reasons, the parties are willing to work. Among this group, I suspect, are those who have burnt themselves out, emotionally and financially, in legal warfare, and thus arrive at the mediator's doorstep prepared to make constructive use of the mediator's services. (Incidentally, this is a particularly interesting category of disputants. It is from their ranks that some of the more enthusiastic testimonials regarding mediation have come. Note, however, that as mediation becomes more widespread we shall doubtless begin to see testimonials of a contrasting hue; from couples who have exhausted themselves in mediation and are then prepared to embrace legal representation as the solution to their miseries. Neither lawyers nor mediators should place too much faith in such cases as evidence of the virtues of their respective approaches until it has been ascertained to what degree the happy resolution of the conflict is due to the prior history and its motivating effects.)

Even in its very early stage of growth perhaps the most valuable contribution of the mediation movement has been its openess to empirical scrutiny. Much of the little we now know about how divorcing spouses conduct themselves during the settlement process has come from the study of divorce mediation. If legal interests are going to use that research to disqualify the mediation alternative it will behoove them to do so on the basis of an equally intense scrutiny of what transpires between lawyers and their clients.

THE STRESSES AND COMPLEXITIES OF THE PROFESSIONAL ROLES IN DIVORCE MAY CONTRIBUTE TO THE DIFFICULTIES OF ORCHESTRATING A CONSTRUCTIVE DIVORCE PROCESS

When my co-workers and I began our study of the divorcing process I was optimistic about the prospects that we could contribute much to the improvement of what most people agreed was a dreary situation. I felt that knowledge of the social psychology of conflict combined with a thorough survey of expert professional views could be blended into much more workable approaches to dispute resolution in divorce. That perspective was based partly on naivety, partly on the enthusiasm which accompanies the start of any new line of investigation. I have not completely abandoned my hopes but I am more somber now about the possibilities.

Any approaches to attenuating destructive conflict in divorce and converting it into something constructive will have to reckon with two imposing obstacles: the profoundly unhappy and difficult practical and psychological circumstances in which divorced persons find themselves *and* the inherent stresses and tensions likely to be involved in rendering professional assistance during divorce. The former theme I have explored in detail in chapter 2 and at various other points throughout the book. I believe that the poor psychological and practical circumstances surrounding the typical divorce place restrictive, if as yet indeterminate, limits on what can be accomplished, even by highly trained professionals. The second theme regarding the discomfitures of the professional role is the most unanticipated and perhaps the most significant of our findings.

We have seen that therapists, lawyers, and mediators each face considerable difficulty in enacting their roles. In some important measure the problems arise not simply because the circumstances of the parties are bad, but because of certain problematic aspects of each of the professional roles themselves.

This notion is illustrated in its mildest form in the chapters on the divorce therapist. There we described the difficulties of maintaining rapport in the midst of the couples' own intense antagonisms and the well-known difficulties inherent in all family work, which may be conveniently, if oversimplifiedly, summarized under the heading of countertransference problems. It is in the depiction of the circumstances of the lawyer and the mediator that we have described in greatest detail the stresses and strains inherent in the professional role.

Thus, the lawyer emerges in our research as the unhappy victim of some difficult, and often unacknowledged professional problems. These include the notable, if hidden conflicts in the lawyer-client relationship; the cross-pressures on the attorney to play the role of competitive zealot and cooperative problem solver in the absence of clear guidelines on when to follow which path; the inability of the attorney to predict with any confidence how the marital dynamics will affect the settlement proceedings over which he or she is nominally in charge; and, ironically enough, the not inconsiderable probability that the lawyer will be matched with an opposing attorney whose approach to the form and substance of settlement negotiations are very much at variance from his or her own.

Divorce mediation has been widely touted as the solution to the problems of the legal role. However, the position of the divorce mediator is probably no better and may, in certain circumstances, be a good deal worse, than that of the attorney. The mediators' problems derive principally from the extremely lofty, and at times contradictory and ambiguous things prescribed by the mediator role; the extremely high degree of professional uncertainty about important aspects of the work; and the headaches imposed by the mediator's structural position midway between the parties.

In the following section I shall consider some of the implications of the problematic professional roles for those seeking professional help in divorce. For those who offer it I would advise modest aspirations and a keen appreciation for the obstacles arrayed against you. This is particularly needed advice, I suspect, for the emerging cadre of divorce mediators, whose enthusiasm and inexperience may combine to produce wholly unrealistic expectations for success. I believe the danger in this regard is greatest in the public sector mediation of child custody disputes. Empirical evidence is still highly fragmentary, but, as I have outlined in chapter 10, this form of mediation, despite its superiority to strictly legal approaches, may offer the most inhospitable terrain of all for effective intervention at the same time that it is most likely to be accepted by the legal community. The conjunction may not be accidental.

Since all types of divorce practitioners share highly similar difficulties in the enactment of their roles, there is also much to be said for a truce on rival claims of superiority. Rather, there is a need for sharing experiences and mutually exploring alternative ways of handling role difficulties. Lawyers and mediators are especially good candidates for professional cross-fertilization. Although the adversarial climate which has surrounded the emergence of mediation may be something of a barrier here, there are encouraging signs that lawyers and mediators are beginning to recognize their kindred problems.

Some Suggestions for Seeking and Utilizing Professional Help in Divorce

Sensible advice on the selection and use of professional help in divorce is available in a number of popular books on the divorce process (Ware 1984; Wheeler 1980; Women in Transition 1975). I shall not attempt to duplicate it here. However, our research, as well as my own clinical experience as a therapist and mediator, suggest a number of practical ideas to bear in mind during the help-seeking process. I offer them as general guidelines, not as rigid prescriptions. There is too much individual variation from divorcing couple to divorcing couple, and the process of intervention in all the professional arenas, including that of the law, are still more art than science to permit the application of rules of thumb for the help-seeking encounter. I am also aware that advice of this type is generally easier to give than to take. What follows is offered in this modest spirit.

GENERAL THEMES IN HELP SEEKING

To begin with, there are certain general themes in the utilization of professional help in divorce that apply with equal cogency to finding and using either a therapist, mediator, or lawyer. The key themes may be summarized in three words: Care, Initiative, and Cooperation.

CARE IN THE SELECTION OF THE HELPER. Seek professional help in a careful, deliberate manner. The success of your experience with a professional in a delicate and emotional area such as divorce hinges to a great degree on a feeling of trust and confidence in the person retained and a significant measure of rapport in the professional-client relationship. Not everybody who is competent and qualified to offer their services to you is also somebody who is suitable to your particular needs, circumstances, or personal style—and you may not be suitable to theirs. Consequently, take your time in selecting help.

In practical terms careful selection means asking for an initial consultation. Although some professionals will provide an hour or so of their time gratis for a get acquainted meeting, many will not. You should be willing to pay for an hour's consultation and consider it money well spent. The major purpose of a consultation is to see if you are comfortable with the therapist, mediator, or lawyer. Do you find him or her easy to talk to, patient, and empathic? Do you appear to share at least some common ideas about reasonable ways to proceed?

Although you may feel sufficiently comfortable after the first meeting it is usually a good idea to take some time to think things over before making a formal commitment to proceed. Given the opportunity to consider the initial meeting in relative tranquility, you may find yourself with more questions or doubts about the initial encounter than you realized you had at the time. If you do have doubts or are uneasy on any grounds, another consultation, either with the same individual or another, is certainly in order. Consulting with at least two prospective candidates is not a bad idea in any case.

There are at least two warning signs that should alert you to the possibility that you are in the wrong office: extravagant claims of benefit and any qualms or reluctance on the part of the professional to let you think things over before deciding whether or not to plunk down your money.

One word of caution: if, after consultations with two or three different professionals, you are still unable to decide whom to retain, the problem may lie with your own psychological unreadiness to accept the divorce or some other psychological conflict which needs to be understood. The appropriate arena for such work is psychotherapy. Fight your ambivalence and find a therapist who can help clarify what's bothering you.

INITIATIVE IN UTILIZING PROFESSIONAL ASSISTANCE. An active stance in the use of professional assistance in divorce is crucial. There are two reasons, at least, for this rule. First, it is your life and your family. Nobody can know as much or be as much concerned as you about the consequences of professional assistance. Furthermore, divorce is largely an area of values and subjective choices. There are few clear "correct" decisions, even over material disbursements, and these often need to be subordinated to more important values or personal considerations. Second, as we have seen, the professional-client relationship has many hidden tensions and the professional role has many pressures that can work to the clients' disadvantage. This is not a reason to avoid professional help, but it is a reason to help the professional by staking out a clear and active involvement in every phase of the deliberations.

In practical terms this means expecting to keep the professional as fully informed as possible about your needs, values, uncertainties, and wishes. It means questioning professional advice and opinion until their basis is clear to you. It means expecting to be kept informed about the professional's view of the case, especially when you are uncertain how things are going or whether the two of you are on the same wave length. It means the willingness to change helpers after sincere efforts to iron out differences or feel more comfortable have not succeeded.

The principal of cooperative, but skeptical and vigorous questioning and attention to professional ministrations is as important with your therapist and mediator as with your lawyer. The client who takes nothing for granted in the professional encounter—allowing always the willingness to be guided—does better justice to the hidden currents in the professional-client relationship and increases the likelihood of satisfactory service.

Again, a caution: repeated dissatisfaction with professional help is most probably a sign of your own unresolved conflicts about yourself or the divorce. Therapy should be seriously considered to identify the underlying problem.

A COOPERATIVE STANCE VIS À VIS YOUR SPOUSE AND THE HELPING PROFESSIONAL. As I have indicated throughout this book, a cooperative orientation is the key to a constructive divorce process. Adopting such an orientation toward your spouse helps improve the chances for a successful experience with your professional helpers as well, since it makes the professional's task a more realistic one and establishes a better climate for informed problem solving. This is especially useful advice in approaching your lawyer, since there are strong professional pressures on your attorney to adopt a destructively competitive relationship in the external negotiations with your spouse and your spouse's lawyer.

Maintaining a cooperative orientation also applies to the direct relationship with your lawyer, therapist, or mediator. In discussing the need for client initiative earlier, I have stressed the need for self-assertion and questioning of professional opinion. There is a necessary balance which needs to be struck, however. Persistent mistrust or doubt, unwillingness to be guided, and resistance to taking an open, receptive stance to professional input is just as deleterious to a constructive management of the divorce as passive acceptance. Ask yourself this about the relationship with therapist, lawyer, or mediator: Do I tend to react skeptically or with little enthusiasm to nearly everything I am told or asked? Am I keeping important concerns hidden from the professional out of fear or mistrust? Am I late for or do I cancel appointments on a regular basis? Am I reluctant about paying bills or taking my financial obligations in the relationship seriously?

If the answer to any of these questions is "yes," the requisite degree of cooperation and trust in the professional-client relationship is lacking. The source of the difficulty may lie with the professional, with you, or with both of you. If this is the first divorce professional with whom you have worked, I would not lose too much sleep over trying to apportion the blame. If a candid discussion or two cannot ease your fears about the relationship, find somebody else to work with. On the other hand, if this is the second or third professional with whom things have not worked out, serious self-scrutiny is in order. The best advice here is to suspend relationships with lawyers or mediators and work through the problem. In most instances this is best done in therapy.

USING A THERAPIST

Though in the traditional view they take second place to lawyers, in many ways therapists are the key professional consultants in divorce. The therapeutic role is central because many of the crucial obstacles to a constructive divorce process are psychological and emotional (even though they may have some of their roots in stressful practical realities). Unfortunately, therapeutic wisdom in the area of divorce counseling has not yet crystalized and there are widely divergent approaches to the therapeutic task. It is possible, however, to give some general guidelines for seeking and using a divorce therapist.

SEEK A THERAPIST EARLY. Many a marriage which is *theoretically* salvageable and good is *practically* beyond the pale of even the most skillful therapeutic help because the marital climate has been polluted for too long. Therapeutic help has the best chance of working if it is sought when marital problems are first looming and before a process of destructive relating has taken firm hold. Certainly therapeutic assistance is best sought before lawyers or mediators have become involved. Effective use of these latter sources of assistance is predicated on the resolution of intense emotional attachment and healthier modes of problem-solving and conflict management, both of which are the province of therapy.

Note also: the absence of fighting and even talk of a "friendly" divorce are by no means signs that therapeutic help is unnecessary. In the early stages of the divorce process, guilt, along with ignorance of the hard realities to be negotiated may create a false climate of apparent good will. The "peace" may also rest on a pathological inability to handle differences and manage conflict. Talk of divorce should mean talk of a therapeutic consultation.

SEEK THERAPY JOINTLY. The initial consultation should be sought jointly. The joint approach makes the most sense because the first task of therapy is to get a clear reading on two principal diagnostic questions: Is the source of difficulty in the marital system or in a reactive psychological crisis which has its locus in only one of the partners? Regardless of the source of the difficulty, have matters passed the psychological point of no return, beyond which there is no practical means of saving the marriage? Both these queries are more efficiently addressed by direct exposure to both spouses.

In the majority of cases the diagnostic assessment will reveal that both partners are making significant contributions to the marital difficulties. In this case, continuing in joint counseling is the treatment of choice. In the case of a reactive divorce, individual therapy for one partner may be indicated, at least for a time. The signs of a reactive divorce include: (1) A clear psychological stressor or other psychologically signal event in the life of the divorce initiator. Such events may be external (e.g., the death of a parent or close friend; a major career disappointment) or internal and symbolic (e.g., reaching the age at which a parent died). (2) Denial by the initiator that anybody in the family, including spouse and children, will be greatly affected by the divorce. (3) An unwillingness or inability to talk about the motivations to divorce in a convincing or realistic way. (4) Complaints about the marriage that appear exaggerated or have the quality of flight.

The immediate need in a reactive divorce is to slow the headlong rush to flee the marriage and to begin, via individual sessions, to uncover and come to terms with the underlying intrapsychic conflict. Individual therapy may also be the treatment of choice when one partner's self-esteem or general functioning is so abysmal that no effective joint work is immediately possible. In all these cases, however, the eventual use of joint sessions is highly probable.

FOCUS ON YOURSELF. Regardless of the therapeutic format attempt to use therapy as a vehicle for self-understanding and the modification of your own contributions to the dysfunctional patterns of relating with your partner. Seeking therapy for the purpose of vindicating yourself and gaining a verdict of "guilty" from the therapist for the other's "wrongdoings" is counterproductive.

A corollary of this injunction is to proceed with individual therapy when your spouse refuses to see a counselor jointly. There is no justification for the belief that the *only* effective way to treat a troubled marriage or set in motion a more constructive divorce is if both parties are in treatment. In the first place, your spouse may soon be willing to join you in therapy as a result of seeing your commitment or by changes in your behavior or attitude brought about by therapy. Second, positive changes in an interpersonal relationship can often be produced by changes initiated by only one of the parties.

STAY IN THERAPY AFTER A DECISION TO DIVORCE HAS BEEN REACHED. A great many people who seek therapy abandon it if a decision to divorce is reached during the therapeutic process. This is often a mistake. Our depiction of the enmeshed and autistic divorces suggests why: frequently the divorce process will be a highly destructive one because dysfunctional patterns of communicating and conflict management remain very much intact after the decision to divorce has been reached. However, while the expert practitioners whose views are recounted in chapters 3 and 4 appear to favor continued joint therapy after the divorce decision has been reached, in practice, it is difficult to sell this idea to most couples. Individual therapy for both partners is perhaps a more realistic way to proceed. In my experience, destructive patterns of interacting are often as effectively addressed in individual therapy and without the attendant risks of fostering the fantasies of reunion which are often associated with the joint format.

BE PATIENT. The problems for which people seek help from a marital or divorce therapist did not develop overnight and they will not be solved overnight. Divorce therapy should not drag on for years, but it must be given a fair chance. Ten to 12 sessions is an arbitrary, but reasonable length of time to commit to the process before deciding whether or not it can be helpful. It often takes that long for sufficient trust to develop and for the therapist to become familiar with the underlying issues which need to be addressed.

BE FLEXIBLE BUT INQUISITIVE. Although there appear to be many common themes in the practice of divorce therapy, there are also wide variations in the structure and focus of treatment. Therapists of equal competence may have very different styles. Be willing to be guided by your therapist's inclinations, with the provison that the rationales behind them are explained and make sense to you. When you are unsure of the wisdom of a therapeutic approach (say the value of examining your relationship with a parent or of dropping the joint format for a while in favor of individual meetings) say so and ask the therapist to explain further.

USING A LAWYER

I have argued earlier that lawyers may often attempt to play a more constructive role in settlement negotiations than is generally realized. This does not mean, however, that enabling them to play that role is an easy matter to arrange. In chapters 7 and 8 I have described the numerous difficulties which beset the legal role in divorce, including the very notable, if unarticulated tensions in the lawyer-client relationship. The responsibility for making the most of the lawyer-client relationship rests as much with the client as with the attorney.

THE BEST TIME TO SEEK AND RETAIN A LAWYER IS WHEN THE GROUNDS FOR SERIOUS NEGOTIATIONS HAVE BEEN WELL LAID. In particular, this means when the decision to divorce has been arrived at in a thorough and considered manner, preferably after a course of exploratory divorce therapy, and certainly after the most intense emotional and practical upheavals have had a chance to subside. In my experience most divorcing persons who become actively engaged with lawyers do so prematurely and with the mistaken assumption that the major solutions to their worries are legal.

AN ATTORNEY OF THE COUNSELOR VARIETY IS PREFERABLE TO AN ADVOCATE; HOWEVER, IT IS PROBABLY MORE CRUCIAL THAT THE ATTORNEY CHOSEN BE ONE WITH WHOM THE SPOUSE'S ATTORNEY IS COMFORTABLE. From everything our legal respondents have told us a key ingredient in a constructive settlement process is mutual respect and a similar outlook on the part of the two lawyers (assuming, obviously, that the attorneys' views and style are also acceptable to the clients). When lawyers have worked together harmoniously in the past, the theoretical advantages of legal representation—increased rationality, moderation, and experience in the handling of settlement negotiations—are more likely to be realized. When lawyers have not worked together before, or when they are actively antagonistic or uncomfortable with one another, the chances for constructive negotiations are probably nil unless the two clients are extremely cooperative, share well-defined objectives, and are able and willing to give their lawyers firm directives.

IT IS VITAL THAT THE CLIENT PLAY AN ACTIVE ROLE IN THE LAWYER-CLIENT DIALOGUE. I have already emphasized this theme, but it is worth repeating because nowhere is client passivity more commonplace than in the legal arena and nowhere is it more likely to cause serious problems. The passivity stems, I suspect, from the air of mystery inculcated by legal terminology and legal procedures, and the lack of first hand experience that most people have with legal matters. Throw in the confusion and demoralization which is characteristic of the typical divorce client and you are likely to have a very passive client indeed. As noted, client passivity is especially unfortunate in utilizing legal assistance because the lawyer is exposed to pressures emanating from the opposite counsel and from legal training and procedures which may well be at variance with the client's best interests. If the client does not provide a counterweight, so to speak, even the well-intentioned attorney may provide less than optimal service.

Client initiative means, among other things, that the client must be informed about the law and the issues to be negotiated. Information on these matters is widely available. It also means that the client has an obligation to probe closely all prospective legal counsel as to experience, fees, negotiating philosophy, attitudes towards custody arrangements, alimony, etc. The selection of a lawyer is not a time to be shy. If you are shy, take a friend to the initial consultation. Prepare questions in advance and make a vow to retain nobody on the spot. Take a day or two to make the decision about whether or not the lawyer suits you. A lawyer who cannot see the need for such deliberation is almost certainly not the lawyer to use. Once a lawyer has been retained it is essential for the client to challenge, in a constructive and appropriate way, all of the lawyers suggestions for the conduct of the negotiations until the attorney's rationale is clear and acceptable. If you don't understand or don't agree, say so. If the lawyer can't or won't explain, get another.

THE MOST APPROPRIATE EXPECTATIONS FOR WHAT LEGAL SERVICE CAN ACHIEVE ARE MODEST ONES. The difficult circumstances under which settlements are negotiated place very distinct limits on what any lawyer can do. Divorce, for most couples, is an unhappy emotional and economic event and no lawyer, however skillful, can change that fact. In addition, "victories" which are inspiring on paper are likely to prove short-lived in reality. A lawyer who promises "victory" is not, in most instances, a useful ally.

Communicating modest expectations to the attorney makes the task of legal representation easier; insisting on "winning" makes the lawyer's task more difficult.

There are divorces in which a victory of sorts is indicated. These are the cases in which the client has been in a truly abusive marriage. Here, zealous legal assistance abets a healthy personal step and is not only necessary, but desirable. Alas, the belief that one has been in a one-sidedly abusive relationship appears to be far more common than the reality. Here, too, a course of exploratory divorce therapy can serve the valuable function of either validating or correcting assumptions regarding who is to "blame" for the marital woes.

USING A MEDIATOR

The general advice that I have given for the effective use of a divorce therapist or a divorce lawyer—Care, Initiative, and Cooperation—applies to finding and effectively using a divorce mediator also. However, since divorce mediation is a far more recent area of professional specialization, it is difficult to be precise regarding the kinds of couples most likely to benefit from it and exactly what ought to be expected by way of professional competence. I shall restrict the necessarily general guidance which follows to private sector mediation, rather than the public variety provided by the courts, since it is in the private sector where my own research and clinical experience has been concentrated.

MEDIATION IS APPROPRIATE ONLY FOR COUPLES FOR WHOM A MODICUM OF COOPERATION ALREADY EXISTS OR WHERE THE PROSPECTS FOR DEVELOPING IT QUICKLY ARE RELATIVELY GOOD. Although research on the kinds of couples most and least likely to benefit from mediation is still in its early stages, there is an emerging consensus that mediation is unsuitable for couples in which extreme conflict is the prevailing mode of relating. Serious impairment in the ability to think and plan in a rational and systematic way are also contraindications, since mediation places the weight of negotiating squarely on the parties' shoulders. Therefore, mediation seems an inappropriate vehicle if either you or your spouse have a drinking or drug problem, if there is an ongoing history of physical violence in the family, or if serious mental disorder, such as clinical depression or diagnosed psychotic behavior are present. On the other hand, high levels of anger and emotional distress, are not in themselves contraindications for mediation. Indeed, a degree of destructive conflict is the expectable norm in divorce, particularly in the early stages of the process, and it is precisely for such cases that mediation may be most helpful.

During the mediation process itself a cooperative spirit is crucial to success. In practical terms this means approaching the decision to mediate as a joint problem-solving venture. Nothing will sink the prospects for mediation faster than an attempt to impose the process on a reluctant spouse. The decision to mediate should make sense to both sides. Once the mediation process begins it will be the mediator's task to help develop and maintain the requisite level of cooperation. You can greatly facilitate the work by seeking agreements which are mutual beneficial, which means keeping an eye on achieving your partner's objectives as well as your own, and fostering awareness of your common interests, such as the welfare of the children.

THE FIRST PHASE OF MEDIATION SHOULD BE DIAGNOSTIC CONSULTATION. Because it is such a new and unfamiliar process and because many couples may not be suited to it, an initial diagnostic consultation at which both you and your spouse are present is a prerequisite in mediation. Finding a mediator with whom to have such a meeting is likely to be more difficult than finding a competent attorney or therapist. In appendix 3 I have listed several national organizations from whom an appropriate referral may be secured.

The initial consultation has several purposes. First, it should answer your own questions about the mediation process. Come prepared to ask questions on cost, duration, the mediator's conception of his or her role, and the mediation rules and procedures. Second, the consultation should deal with your suitability for the mediation process. The prospective mediator should make some assessment of your interpersonal style with one another, especially regarding the way in which immediate decisions have been made (including the decision to divorce and to seek mediation). On the basis of this reconnoitering and a general history of your individual and joint wishes and fears related to the divorce and to the mediation process, the mediator should be able to give a diagnostic opinion as to whether or not mediation will be of help. Finally, the consultation should help you decide whether you are likely to feel comfortable with this particular mediator.

Do *not* make an immediate commitment to mediation during the initial consultation. Give yourselves a week or so after the first meeting to decide if mediation is for you. Seek advice and talk things over with each other, as well as with trusted friends or advisors. Get back to the mediator if you have unanswered questions. The mediator should actually foster this kind of deliberation in word and deed. Optimally, the consultation process should be spread out over two or more sessions and include individual as well as joint meetings. If this kind of thoroughness and deliberation is absent you may be in the wrong office.

MEDIATION SHOULD BE USED IN CONJUNCTION WITH THERAPY AND LAWYERS. Although some divorce mediators prohibit the parties from retaining outside legal counsel, this view is no longer popular. It is generally recognized that competent legal counsel is a valuable part of the mediation process. Lawyers are not usually present at mediation sessions, but the parties are generally encouraged to consult with their attorneys during mediation and to have their attorneys thoroughly review the draft memorandum of agreement that is the final product of the mediation. While it is the mediator's job to keep negotiations on track and to insure constructive communications between you, the mediator is by definition impartial. Consequently, your lawyer's job is to advise you on your legal rights and responsibilities and to be a committed spokesperson for your interests *as the attorney understands them*—a role difficult for the impartial mediator to play. Your job, and it may not be an easy one, is to balance the advice and perspective of lawyer and mediator, and not to follow the direction of either one slavishly.

You will help yourself enormously in this task if you select an attorney who is well disposed to the mediation alternative and has at least a general familiarity with the goals and procedures of mediation; if you require that lawyer and mediator communicate with each other to clarify their respective roles; and if you insist that no legal actions (e.g., subpoenas) be taken while mediation is in progress. If guarantees of this kind cannot be made, then either you, your partner, and/or one or both of the lawyers are too ambivalent about mediation to give it a fair chance.

While consultation with a lawyer should generally be maintained during the mediation process, therapeutic consultation is best obtained prior to starting mediation, as I have noted earlier. The problems most likely to sink mediation, and which mediation is least well equipped to handle, are precisely those that fall squarely within the therapeutic realm. These include seriously flawed patterns of problem solving and conflict management and a faulty process of divorce decision making which has left in its wake abysmally low levels of self-esteem in one partner, extremely high levels of guilt in the other, and ambivalent yearnings for the dead marriage in both. Mediation is not a way to hang on to a marriage; if you are hoping that you can use it to move a reluctant spouse in that direction, forget it. Likewise, mediation will not work if you are feeling totally miserable about yourself as a person. Under these and similarly inhospitable conditions, therapy is the treatment of choice—preceding in usefulness any form of formal settlement negotiations, whether orchestrated by mediators or lawyers.

Should a therapist who has worked with a couple in divorce counseling continue to serve them in the role of mediator? Opinions differ on this matter, but I believe that if the therapist possesses the requisite skills the advantages to the couple of having the therapist continue in the role of mediator can be considerable. The obvious advantage is that trust and confidence have been established and the therapist cum mediator will be intimately familiar with the interpersonal issues and patterns that may threaten the negotiation process. Therefore, if a divorce decision has been made during therapy, it would be wise to inquire if the therapist is able and willing to continue as mediator over settlement terms. At the present writing few therapists are equipped to mediate, but more and more are learning to do so.

IF NEGOTIATIONS GET BOGGED DOWN, MEDIATION SHOULD ADDRESS "THERAPEUTIC" MATTERS AS WELL AS PRACTICAL AND FINANCIAL ONES. Although faulty patterns of relating are best dealt with in therapy, this theoretically sound advice is not always practicable. I have recorded in chapter 12 my firm conviction that, when necessary, the mediator should be ready and willing to educate you and your partner about problematic aspects of your interaction with one another. This may mean doing more than simply channeling or prohibiting dysfunctional behavior. It may involve trying to understand the cause and consequences of the pattern and efforts to better equip you both to modify it.

Divorce Negotiations as an Arena for Research

When my colleagues and I began the work reported here we had only a few general ideas to guide us. I will not pretend that our research program developed systematically and according to some strict internal logic. It is possible to imagine us pursuing some other collection of investigations, given the basic themes which interested us at the start. Now, however, it is possible to sketch the kinds of studies that would put empirical flesh on what at times has been more educated speculation than anything else. For expository purposes these can be conveniently, if somewhat artificially divided, into those touching more strongly on either practical or conceptual issues.

PRACTICAL RESEARCH ON THE PROCESS AND OUTCOMES OF DIVORCE NEGOTIATIONS

Perhaps our most striking finding is the degree to which divorce negotiations—particularly the formal negotiations required by our legal procedures—have been neglected as a subject of systematic inquiry. The relatively few studies suffer from the expectable weaknesses which are likely to beset any fledgling research enterprise: small and unrepresentative samples; too much self-report and too little direct observation; measures which are more convenient than robust; research designs which are inadequate to bear the conclusions which rest upon them. All in all it would be difficult to imagine a more ubiquitous form of interpersonal conflict where so little is known of what actually occurs between the parties and those with whom they consult. Some of the issues on which it would be useful to have knowledge are described in the following paragraphs.

WHAT ARE THE MOST IMPORTANT DETERMINANTS OF A CONSTRUCTIVE NEGOTIATING OUTCOME IN DIVORCE? ARE THESE FACTORS EQUALLY IMPORTANT WHETHER LAWYERS OR MEDIATORS ARE AT THE HELM? I have identified nine major obstacles to a successful negotiating process but these reflect clinical experience and educated hunches more than anything else. Have important factors been omitted or are certain factors which I have included less important than they seem from our limited vantage point? For example, our expert divorce therapists felt very strongly that nonmutuality of the decision to divorce is a serious impediment to a constructive divorce negotiation. I have endorsed that view. However, Pearson's research on mediation (Pearson and Thoennes 1984b) and Hochberg's (1984) on the use of lawyers do not corroborate the idea. I believe that this is because it is difficult to get clinically accurate measures of the actual state of the parties' feelings about a divorce, but this is assertion, not proof. There is even less evidence for such variables as discrepancies in interpersonal sensitivity (probably the most speculative of my nine factors) and the inexperience of the parties in the art of negotiating.

IS EXPLORATORY DIVORCE THERAPY AS GERMANE TO A CONSTRUCTIVE PROCESS OF FORMAL NEGOTIATIONS AS I HAVE CLAIMED? MAY IT BE EQUALLY OR MORE HELPFUL IN THIS RESPECT THAN DIVORCE MEDIATION? These questions are at least as easy to test as the comparative merits of mediation vs. lawyers. In my view they are as relevant to test, as I have argued in chapter 4.

WHAT IS THE NATURE OF THE LAWYER-CLIENT RELATIONSHIP? There are a host of questions here. I believe that the *counselor-advocate* distinction conforms to an underlying reality, but its precise impact on the settlement process is uncertain. Regardless of how they respond to a questionnaire on legal practice in divorce and attitudes towards the client, do counselors and advocates *behave* in systematically different ways regardless of circumstances or are these two orientations heavily influenced by the characteristics of the client, the client's orientation towards the attorney, the behavior and attitudes of the other attorney, and so on? If the lawyer's stance is modifiable in the course of the settlement process are there still convincing reasons to prefer one legal type over the other? Are there other relevant types of lawyers besides counselors and advocates?

Are there different types of legal *clients* and is it possible to classify the lawyer-client relationship in a manner analogous to our typology of spousal relationships? If the lawyer-client relationship can be described according to subtypes, on what dimensions can this be done and what, if anything, is the relevance of these types to the course and outcome of settlement negotiations and satisfaction with legal services?

What role do judges play when they are given (or seize) the direct opportunity to influence the deliberations between the parties and their lawyers? In particular, what interpersonal stratagems do judges employ to bring about a negotiated agreement? Can judges, like lawyers, be classified according to their distinctive preferences for intervening? What judicial interventions are most and least effective under which circumstances. The research of Wall and his colleagues (Wall, Schiller, and Ebert 1983; Wall and Rude, in press) has made a useful start in this general direction but the focus has not been specifically on divorce.

How do the various components of the negotiating sytem in divorce—lawyer-client, lawyer-lawyer, client-client, judge-lawyer (if it comes to that)—interact to influence the course and outcomes of settlement negotiations? How do each of these components affect what occurs in the others and which of the components are most crucial to the eventual outcome?

FOR WHAT TYPES OF COUPLES IS WHAT FORM OF PROFESSIONAL ASSISTANCE MOST LIKELY TO BE HELPFUL? Here again, many issues present themselves. I would not claim, for example, that our typology of divorcing couples represents the final word on that complex subject, nor that the implications of a typological approach for effective intervention can be clearly seen from our present vantage point. Much more research, on far larger and more representative samples is needed before we can even be confident that we have put our finger on the most meaningful dimensions from which to construct a typology, or having done so, that reliable and meaningful categories of couples can be isolated.

I have also argued that a quasi-therapeutic approach to divorce mediation, in which efforts are made to understand and alter dysfunctional patterns of interaction, is necessary for certain kinds of problematic couples. I believe this is a worthwhile observation, but as a practical matter it leaves important questions unanswered. Can we specify, for example, the levels of marital disruption under which this approach will and will not be effective? At the highest levels of marital mayhem *no* form of mediation may be workable; at slightly diminished levels of chaos mediation may work, but only if it is of the aggressive and practical kind and eschews any therapeutic objectives. For couples at the most functional end of the spectrum therapeutic approaches to mediation may be superfluous. Only for moderately disturbed couples may a therapeutic orientation on the part of the mediator prove workable. Research on leadership—and the mediator is a type of leader—has made fruitful use of approaching the understanding of interpersonal influence in terms of identifying the conditions under which contrasting interpersonal styles have their most effective impact (Fiedler 1978).

An even more fundamental question involves the comparative virtues of entire systems of conflict resolution. The debate in this regard has crystalized around mediation vs. the adversary system. I have suggested that this is a misleading way of approaching the issue and is likely to produce more heat than light. Neither mediation nor the traditional use of lawyers represent monolithic, homogeneous approaches. Even on the early evidence it is clear that mediation means different things to different practitioners. No clear consensus on the enactment of the role is evident. The range of interventions which characterize the adversary system are at least as diverse, and probably more so. Some couples make very limited use of attorneys, others extensive use; some attorneys play a highly competitive role, others are far more cooperatively oriented; many couples never experience a court evaluation or have direct exposure to a judge, others do. Meaningful comparative evaluations will need to be based on a more sophisticated accounting of the "treatments" to which divorcing couples are exposed.

The debate on mediation vs. lawyers may also have obscured the very real possibility that many other equally useful approaches to conflict management are being overlooked. Many of the virtues attributed to mediation, for example, may be capable of inculcation without the time and expense which mediation may involve. Thus, experiments with court run "courses" on divorce negotiations, at which lawyers, judges, and mental health experts might lecture could encourage the realism and cooperation which lawyers and mediators may strive to encourage at a much higher price.

A final word about conducting research in an area which touches so directly on legal concerns and institutions: it is imperative that social scientists be able to work collaboratively with lawyers, judges, and court personnel. Our own research efforts have benefited greatly from the willingness of members of the legal community to speak with us. However, the more difficult and sensitive collaborative tasks lie ahead. This is particularly so with regard to the need to observe in some direct manner what transpires between key actors in the legal system. The lawyer-client relationship is the most crucial relationship where such data is needed. To forge a working alliance with the legal community, social scientists will have to do at least two important things: take seriously and be willing to work assiduously to resolve the very real legal and ethical problems which such research entails, and make the relevance of the enterprise to legal practice clear in unmistakable terms and free of the jargon and abstraction for which we, no less than lawyers, have become so infamous.

DIVORCE NEGOTIATIONS ARE AN ARENA FOR THEORETICAL RESEARCH

In my own mind it is very difficult to make a sharp distinction between "pure" and "applied" research. I am very much taken with Kurt Lewin's axiom that there is nothing so practical as a good theory. It is true, however, that certain of the issues raised by our research on the divorce settlement process have a more conceptual and theoretical cast than those which I have just outlined. In particular, I believe that the divorce settlement process is a hospitable site for several important subjects of general theoretical interest within my home discipline of social psychology.

THE SOCIAL PSYCHOLOGY OF CONFLICT RESOLUTION. To the degree that our research began with strong conceptual and theoretical concerns, they obviously lay in this area. I shall not rehash here the debate within the discipline between the experimentalists and the field investigators. It is clear to many of us that both forms of research are valuable and complementary. It does appear, however, that social psychologists have continued to be more wedded to the experimental laboratory in the study of negotiation and conflict than to real world settings. This was true at the start of our research (Rubin and Brown 1975) and remains largely true now (Pruitt 1981). There is an obvious need to verify and extend our laboratory findings and insights by exposure to settings in which the participants care deeply about the issues at stake and about each other and are embedded in a social and institutional context where the full panoply of factors influencing conflict resolution is at play. Divorce negotiations are a particularly attractive setting in which to accomplish such a purpose. By contrast, arms control conferences or international disputes are far more rare, exotic, and less accessible settings in which to study the management of conflict. In chapter 2 I have also made a preliminary essay at showing how research on divorce negotiations is relevant to a comparative study of other forms of conflict and vice versa. The comparative study of conflict is another way in which the search for theoretical understanding advances.

GENDER DIFFERENCES. In chapter 2 I made some suggestions about the manner in which psychological differences between the sexes might adversely affect the settlement process in divorce. As with the study of interpersonal conflict, much of the research on the subject of gender differences has occurred in the artificial confines of the laboratory or been conducted with strangers or with children. Divorce negotiations represent a cross-sex situation of considerable power and importance which is anything but artificial.

THE MANAGEMENT OF PROFESSIONAL ROLE STRAIN. Mediators and lawyers appear to face extremely stressful professional roles. In the chapters on lawyers I have suggested that the development of the counselor or advocate stance is, at least partially, to be understood as a mechanism of coping with that strain. The notion is obviously in need of further testing and elaboration, but it illustrates the potentially close relationship between professional circumstances and the adaptation of individual practitioners. The thought is not a new one, by any means, but previous studies of occupational role strain have tended to focus more on the measurement of role strain and its "productivity" effects than on individual mechanisms of adaptation. The adaptive responses of mediators to the strains of their role is much less clear because the field itself is so new. The recent emergence and still unformed state of the field provide fertile ground for research on how institutional responses may shape and be shaped by the coping responses of individual practitioners.

Appendix 1

The Lawyer Role Questionnaire (LRQ)

This questionnaire is an important supplement to the interview which was conducted with you. It will help us get as complete a picture of your views as possible and will allow us to cover some specific issues that may not have been dealt with during the interview. It should take no more than twenty minutes to complete.
Thank you again for your cooperation.

NAME ____

I. The Goals of Settlement

Below is a list of possible goals which a lawyer might have in divorce cases. Indicate how important each of the goals is to you by assigning each goal a number from 1 to 100 according to the following scale:

1 = A goal I do *not* usually strive for

100 = A goal I usually *do* strive for

Since we are interested in the *relative* importance to you of each goal, no two items should receive exactly the same rating.

NOTE: A goal may be desirable or worthwhile without necessarily being an objective which you personally strive to achieve (e.g., some goals you may view as impractical for a lawyer or not within the scope of the lawyer's role).

1. Getting my client the best possible financial settlement. ______
2. Getting a settlement my client is satisfied with, regardless of how anybody else feels about it. ______
3. Reaching a settlement which I consider equitable to both parties. ______
4. Getting a settlement which both parties feel they can live with. ______
5. Creating a cooperative postdivorce climate between the ex-spouses. ______
6. Protecting the welfare of the children. ______
7. Achieving emotional health and adjustment for the client. ______

II. The Obstacles to Settlement

What are the major obstacles to reaching a settlement in divorce cases? Below are possible obstacles to settlement. Indicate the degree to which you have generally found them to be obstacles to settlement by using the following scale:

1	2	3	4	5	6	7
usually not a major obstacle						usually a major obstacle

1. The inherently neurotic personality of most divorce clients. ______
2. The temporary emotional instability of divorce clients deriving from the stresses of divorce. ______
3. Differences of goals and/or philosophy between the opposing attorneys. ______
4. Differences of settlement goals between the divorcing spouses. ______

5. Differences of settlement goals between attorney and client. _______

6. The highly charged emotional atmosphere between spouses. _______

7. The inadequacy of current New Jersey divorce laws. _______

8. Lawyers' lack of training in psychology and family dynamics. _______

9. The emotional strain on the lawyer of becoming involved in somebody else's personal problems. _______

10. The lack of clear criteria for arriving at a settlement. _______

11. The ambivalence of the clients about whether or not they really want a divorce. _______

12. Unrealistic client expectations about what is legally or materially feasible. _______

13. The amount of property or assets available for division. _______

14. The attitudes and/or training of certain judges. _______

Other (please specify):

____ _______

____ _______

III. The Major Sources of Satisfaction in Divorce Work

What are your major sources of satisfaction in doing divorce work? Below are possible sources of satisfaction. Indicate the degree to which each is a source of satisfaction to you by using the following scale:

1	2	3	4	5	6	7
not a major source of satisfaction						a major source of satisfaction

1. The technical legal challenge of producing a good case. _______

2. Financial rewards. _______

3. Producing equitable settlements. _______

4. Winning for my clients. _______

5. Gaining professional recognition. ______
6. The challenge of legal combat against another attorney. ______
7. Helping a person in a time of need. ______
8. Gaining insight into the reasons for divorce. ______
9. Learning something about human psychology. ______
10. Protecting the welfare of children. ______

Other (please specify):

______________________________ ______

______________________________ ______

IV. The Role of Mental Health Professionals

In what ways, if any, do you feel that mental health professionals can be useful in assisting the divorce lawyer or the divorce client? Below are possible ways in which a mental health professional might be useful. Indicate the degree to which mental health professionals can be useful in serving each function.

1	2	3	4	5	6	7
not at all useful						very useful

1. Relieving the lawyer of the burden of listening to the client's emotional problems. ______
2. Buttressing a case. ______
3. Reducing the tension between the spouses. ______
4. Protecting the overall welfare of the family during and after the divorce. ______
5. Helping the client achieve social reintegration. ______
6. Giving the lawyer insight into the client's emotional state. ______
7. Protecting the welfare of the children. ______
8. Helping make sound custody decisions. ______

9. Helping the parties resolve their differences on substantive issues. ______

Other (please specify):

______________________________ ______

______________________________ ______

V.

The items below concern your attitudes toward divorce, divorce clients, and legal work in divorce. How strongly do you agree or disagree with each item? Indicate your feelings by using the following scale:

1	2	3	4	5	6	7
strongly disagree						strongly agree

1. To the extent that divorce clients exhibit irrational behavior, it is a temporary reflection of the stress of their marital difficulties. ______
2. Personal selfishness is a major cause of divorce. ______
3. Staying together for the sake of the children is no reason for staying in a bad marriage. ______
4. People who get divorced are generally the least mature, emotionally most unstable people in society. ______
5. Given sound legal and practical guidance from the lawyer, divorce clients are as capable as anybody else of making sound decisions. ______
6. Effective legal representation in divorce requires as much an understanding of the client's psychological makeup as of the practical and legal issues. ______
7. It is not the lawyer's job to provide emotional support. ______
8. The lawyer's job is primarily to carry out the wishes of the client, not to intrude his own views of what's fair and equitable. ______
9. In terms of the settlement negotiations, it is often part of my job to tell my clients when they are being unfair to their spouse. ______

10. In terms of the settlement negotiations, it is often part of my job to tell my clients when they are being unfair to their children. ______

11. Based on my experience, mental health professionals can be very useful in divorce cases. ______

12. A strong adversarial relationship with the opposing attorney is usually necessary for effective legal representation in divorce. ______

13. There is rarely such a thing as a good outcome for the client in divorce cases. ______

14. The present legal system of divorce is not meeting the emotional and psychological needs of divorcing people. ______

15. Particularly where children are involved, it is the duty of the lawyer to give great attention to the possibility of reconciliation. ______

VI.

We are interested in the overall view which you hold of your role in divorce cases. Below are six descriptions of the ways in which lawyers representing divorcing clients might define their own role. Indicate how accurately each description conforms to *your own* view of the lawyer's role in divorce. Use the following scale in responding:

1	2	3	4	5	6	7
very close to how I see my role						very far from how I see my role

Description A

Divorce work is an extremely difficult and emotionally unrewarding task for a lawyer in which really good outcomes are rarely possible. Divorce clients are emotionally unstable people who make very irrational clients. I may occasionally refer them to mental health professionals to relieve me of the necessity of listening to their emotional problems, but I do not have a very high expectation that any real good will come of such referrals. I do divorce work because I make my living by using my legal skills in ways that people need and are willing to pay for. The part of divorce work I enjoy most is using the adversary process to its fullest when this is indicated.

Rating ______

Description B

Good outcomes in divorce generally consist of getting the best financial terms for the client and/or getting clients what they want within the limits of the law. In divorce work, my role is principally that of a legal technician. My clients are adults who are capable of knowing their own minds and I treat them accordingly. The aspect of divorce work I enjoy most is the legal thinking and guidance which it requires.

Rating ______

Description C

My basic task is to get an equitable and fair negotiated settlement, and that means devoting most of my time to establishing a good relationship with the opposing attorney. I try not to get involved in my client's emotional problems, but I will try to appeal to their sense of fairness when I feel their demands are excessive. Referrals to psychiatrists are very often useful as a means of producing a calmer, more reasonable client. A good outcome is one both sides can live with. The aspect of divorce work I enjoy most is serving as a kind of mediator in the negotiating process.

Rating ______

Description D

My major concern is with my client's post-divorce adjustment and overall welfare. I also try to maintain a perspective on the entire family unit: What kind of settlement will be best for all? I welcome the involvement of psychiatrists to help my client deal with the stress of divorce. I don't think divorce is a good solution to most marital problems and will thoroughly explore the possiblity for reconciliation. The part of divorce work I enjoy most is helping people decide what is right for themselves and their families.

Rating ______

Description E

The lawyer can only do his job in divorce correctly if he has a thorough understanding of the client's psychology. In fact, my job isn't all that different from that of a psychiatrist. Divorce is a trying time for all my clients and I try to understand and support them emotionally. The current legal system is not meeting the needs of divorcing people and is causing more problems than anything else. The part of divorce work I like most is ferreting out human motivations and using that understanding for the welfare of my client.

Rating ______

Description F

A good outcome in divorce is one in which the welfare of everybody, but especially the children, is protected. The lawyer in divorce should not hesitate to express his own views of right and wrong to the client, particularly with regard to the welfare of children. Children have no legal representation in divorce and clients are too disturbed during divorce to see the children's interests clearly. To be an effective advocate, the lawyer must become emotionally invested in the case and have a clear sense of right and wrong. The part of divorce work I like most is seeing that justice and fair play occur to the greatest degree possible.

Rating ______

VII. Biographical Information

1. Age: ______ 2. Sex: M ______ F ______
3. Current marital status: ______ single ______ married
   ______ separated ______ divorced
   ______ widowed
4. Have you ever been divorced? Yes ______ No ______
5. From which law school did you graduate? ______________
6. How long have you been practicing law? ______________
7. a) Approximately how many divorce cases did you handle last year? ______

   b) About what percentage of *all* cases you personally handled did this represent? ______

   c) In what percentage of these divorce cases did you represent the husband? ______
8. Do you consider yourself a specialist in matrimonial work?
   Yes ______ No ______

9. What is the approximate average combined annual family income of your divorce clients?

   _______ less than $15,000
   _______ $15,000 to $24,999
   _______ $25,000 to $34,999
   _______ $35,000 to $49,999
   _______ $50,000 to $74,999
   _______ Above $75,000

10. We realize that it is difficult to respond to general questions about legal fees; but based on your experience, what would your *average* fee be in cases in which:

    a) The parties agree on every issue and need your services only for drafting the settlement agreement and filing the necessary papers? _______________

    b) The parties have some serious disagreements which can be settled out of court but which necessitate considerable negotiations between you and the other attorney? _______

11. What was your approximate average fee last year for a divorce case? _______________

Appendix 2

Sampling Procedures and Characteristics of the Respondents

Prospective respondents were initially selected randomly from a statewide membership roster of the Family Law Section provided by the New Jersey State Bar Association. However, practical considerations of geographical proximity between interviewer and attorney resulted in nonrandom additions and deletions from the initial sample.

Descriptive information is available on the respondents (n=46) who returned completed questionnaires. They ranged in age from twenty-five to fifty-six ($\bar{X}=37.5$, $SD=7.4$). Most were married (77 percent), with no previous history of divorce (83 percent). The sample was almost entirely male (90 percent)—a close approximation to the sex-distribution of the Family Law Section, 85 percent of whom are men. Respondents came predominantly from public (55 percent) and Catholic (37 percent), rather than independent, (8 percent) law schools.

Three-quarters of the respondents considered themselves specialists in matrimonial practice. For the average practitioner in the group, divorce constituted almost half of their annual case load. The average number of years in legal practice was 10.5 ($SD=7.9$). Four of the respondents were legal aid attorneys, the remainder were in private practice.

The average fee of the private practitioners was approximately $600 for an uncontested divorce in which little, if any, negotiations were involved, and approximately $1,600, in cases requiring more extensive attorney assistance. Overall, the reported average divorce fee was $1,280. These fees, which appear high in comparison to recent reports of legal costs (Cavanaugh and Rhode 1976; Curran 1977), undoubtedly reflect the middle-class clientele (average family income, $28,000) served by the respondents. (Nine percent of the sample had clients with average incomes above $50,-000. However, 10 percent of the private practitioners and all four of the legal aid attorneys served clients with average annual incomes of less than $15,000.)

Appendix 3

Sources for Finding a Divorce Mediator

Since divorce mediation is still in its early stages, finding a competent mediator may require more looking than locating a competent attorney or therapist. The following sources are good places to begin the search.

ORGANIZATIONS

The following organizations maintain rosters of practitioners who have undergone some degree of professional specialization as mediators. The mediators on these lists are drawn primarily from the fields of psychology, social work, and law. Since a consensus on the appropriate training of mediators has not yet emerged and since there are presently no statutory licensing or certification procedures for divorce mediators, the watchword is caveat emptor. Securing a name or two should therefore be regarded as only the first step in the selection process. As discussed in the text, an initial consultation with two or more prospective mediators is highly recommended.

1. The Academy of Family Mediators
   P.O. Box 4686
   Greenwich, Conn. 06830
   (203) 629-8049
2. The American Arbitration Association
   140 South 51st Street
   New York, N.Y. 10020
   (212) 484-3235

3. The Family Mediation Association
   5530 Wisconsin Avenue, Suite 1250
   Chevy Chase, Md. 20815
   (301) 530-1220

DIRECTORIES

The following sources provide lists of divorce mediation service providers.

The Directory of Mediation Services. Published in May, 1982, by The Divorce Mediation Research Project, 1720 Emerson Street, Denver, Colorado 80218. This volume is the closest thing to a national listing of divorce mediation service providers. Developed as part of a research project on divorce mediation, the *Directory* was funded by a grant from the Children's Bureau at the National Institute for Mental Health.

Sharing Parenthood After Divorce, by Ciji Ware. Published by Bantam Books in 1984 (paperback). While this book contains a more limited roster than the *Directory* listed above, it is especially useful for its advice on selecting and using a divorce mediator.

Notes

Chapter 1

1. It is difficult to reliably estimate the percentage of individuals who receive psychotherapy *during* the divorce process. Most recent reports are based on small and not necessarily representative samples. Wallerstein and Kelly (1980) report that more than half of the women in their widely cited investigation of divorce sought therapy because of marital problems. In the majority of cases this was individual treatment which was used as a springboard out of the marriage. More than one-third of the husbands also entered therapy, but in most cases this was joint treatment, sometimes undertaken to appease a wife who otherwise refused to grant the husband's wish for a divorce. Higher estimates of help seeking for marital distress, on the order of 60 percent, are reported by Hunt and Hunt (1977), in a convenience sample based largely on members of Parents Without Partners; much lower estimates, in the neighborhood of 10 to 20 percent, are reported by Hetherington, Cox, and Cox (1976).

Perhaps the most representative data on help seeking as a function of marital status are to be found in the national survey of help seeking for psychological problems, conducted in the mid-1950s and repeated twenty years later, as reported by Veroff, Kulka, and Douvan (1981). In 1976, 54 percent of the separated or divorced women and 46 percent of the separated or divorced men had received some form of professional help for psychological problems. The figures for both sexes were greater than what they had been twenty years earlier, but the increase was especially notable among the men (up from 23 percent). The figures do not reveal, however, what percentage of the therapy occurred before, during, or after the divorce.

2. The researchers report that in approximately half of the uncontested divorces studied one attorney was used jointly by both spouses.

3. Cavanagh and Rhode, 1976. The researchers timed uncontested divorces in New Haven and Bridgeport, Connecticut in 1975.

4. The Fulton study is probably biased in the direction of high-conflict couples, since the sample included *all* available cases in which there had been either a court contest at the time of divorce or a settlement just prior to going to trial. A 10 percent random sample of all uncontested divorces rounded out the sample, but the preponderance of respondents seem to have come from the more disputatious groups. The Jones's sample appears more representative, although it is much smaller and the respondents were much closer to the time of physical separation and filing. Thus, although the two studies report similar rates of dissatisfaction it is impossible to say whether this is an accurate reflection of prevailing levels of discontent or merely coincidental.

5. The principal studies summarized in the text are those of Eckhardt (1968), Chambers (1979), and Johnson (1978). Supplementary data, highly consistent with these findings, are reported in Goode (1956), Jones (1977), and Fulton (1979).

Not every divorced mother is awarded child support. Estimates of the percentage of divorced mothers to whom child support is to be paid range from as low as 44 percent to as high as 88 percent. Espenshade (1979), citing a survey of American women, gives the figure of 44 percent. Goode (1956) reports that two-thirds of his respondents had a child support award, and Sawhill (1981), citing census data for 1978, reports a 59 percent frequency. Weitzman and Dixon (1979), in their random sample of uncontested California divorces, report a frequency of support awards of 80 to 85 percent over three time periods (1968, 1972, and 1977), and Cavanagh and Rhode's (1976) random sample of Connecticut divorces turned up an 88 percent frequency of child support in divorces involving minors. When child support is not ordered in a divorce involving minor children, it is presumably because of the unemployment, institutionalization, or disappearance of the noncustodial parent.

6. Data on proportions of child support paid are reported in Jones, Gordon, and Sawhill (1976); Espenshade (1979); and Cassetty (1978).

7. On the more positive side, Ahrons reports that about two thirds of her sample described the co-parenting relationship as "supportive." As has been noted previously, however, both the Goldsmith and Ahrons studies probably underrepresent more conflicted and chaotic divorcing couples.

8. The father-child relationship, in spite of its well-documented problems, had a rosy glow about it compared to what was going on between the divorced mother and her children. Relative to divorced mothers, divorced fathers had less antagonistic behavior directed at them, had a stronger impact on modifying the child's behavior, and had their own mood and anxiety less effected by the child. Initially, divorced fathers were especially prone to try to please their children and refrained from criticism or setting limits. By the second year this Santa Claus-like style had begun to disappear in favor of more realistic efforts at parental discipline (Hetherington, Cox, and Cox 1979b).

Chapter 2

1. The need for a gradual approach in negotiations and a shift from a hostile to a more constructive style of interaction is also consistent with Deutsch's (1973) speculation that constructive conflict resolution has many parallels with creative thinking. As Deutsch notes, a pattern of experienced tension, outmoded efforts of resolution, withdrawal, and the gradual emergence of more productive solutions is characteristic of many creative activities.

2. While both clinical and empirical reports suggest that nonmutuality of the decision to divorce is quite common, precise evidence from representative samples is lacking. The studies by Ahrons (1981), Goldsmith (1980), and Zeiss, Zeiss, and Johnson (1980) employed random samples drawn from court records, but in each instance certain restrictive criteria were first applied to identify the "eligible" pool of respondents (e.g., continued residence in the same county, relatively frequent visitations, etc). In addition, in all three investigations a large number of potential respondents either could not be contacted or refused to participate.

It should also be noted that a simple distinction between initiator vs. noninitiator is an undoubted oversimplification. The breakdown of a marriage and the decision to end it are more likely to be the result of mutual contributions and subtle (and not so subtle) processes of mutual influence. I have stressed nonmutuality because nonmutuality captures a partial but important truth: the greater willingness, for whatever reason, of one spouse to push for the end of the marriage and the consequences that this has for the negotiating process.

3. The evidence summarized by Gottman is corroborated by other recent observational studies of marital interaction (Billings 1979; Jacobsen, Waldron, and Moore 1980; Margolin and Wampold 1981; Koren, Carlton, and Shaw 1980).

4. The few studies on the effects of stress on international negotiations summarized by Walcott, Hoppman, and King (1977) suggest that when tensions mount in the relations

among nations their dealings with each other over the bargaining table also suffer. This is a somewhat different proposition than the one pursued in the text, in which sources of tension apart from the parties' relationship with each other are viewed as problematic for the negotiating process.

5. Welch and Price-Bonham (1983) present evidence that the decline in the wife's bargaining power with the shift from fault to no-fault statutes may be less precipitous than the studies cited in the text. The researchers analyzed data from Georgia and Washington that corroborate the decline in alimony awards going to the wife and the increased likelihood that she will have to share the legal costs of the divorce. However, the differences were relatively modest. There was no evidence that child support awards had declined with the advent of no fault.

6. Our research on divorce negotiations and related research on the divorce process have led me to highlight gender differences in economic power and to suggest a discrepancy in psychological power between the sexes as well. Other, non-gender related, aspects of psychological power, particularly those tied directly to the dynamics of the divorce process itself, are clearly in need of investigation.

7. Several studies report evidence that on subjective measures of well being, men report more distress than women. In an investigation of premarital breakups among college students (Hill, Rubin, and Peplau 1976) the investigators report a tendency for the men to confess more depression, loneliness, unhappiness, and less freedom one year after the breakup than did the women whom they had been dating. (On the other hand, the women felt more guilt.) Aside from the uncertain relevance of this study to marital dissolution, the group on whom the conclusions regarding adjustment to breaking up were drawn constituted a subset of only 15 of the original 231 couples in the sample. The investigators make it clear that their conclusion is tentative and impressionistic.

Chiriboga, Roberts, and Stein (1978) studied a sample of 126 men and 183 women filing for divorce in San Francisco and Alameda counties in California. On a single question ("In general, how happy are you these days?") separated men reported significantly more unhappiness than did separated women (31 percent of the men vs. 16 percent of the women admitted they were "not too happy"). However, the women were significantly angrier, more depressed, and more uneasy, and were experiencing more tension.

8. Reports of admissions to public outpatient facilities give a less clear-cut picture regarding usage of psychotherapy by divorced men and women. According to a review of this evidence presented by Bloom, White and Asher, (1979), in three out of five possible comparisons between separated and divorced men and women, women were more frequent applicants to such clinics than men. Presumably psychotherapy constitutes a good deal of the service provided by these outpatient facilities, but they are also undoubtedly serving a high percentage of former psychiatric inpatients for whom psychotropic medication may be prescribed more often than psychotherapy. As noted in the text, divorced men are far more likely than divorced women to have had the status of psychiatric inpatient.

9. National data related to marital status and physical health have been reviewed by Ortmeyer (1974), Bloom, White, and Asher (1979), and Verbrugge (1979). The conclusion of all these reports is that while separated and divorced women are more likely to become ill, seek help for their illness, and have illness restrict their activities, separated and divorced men have higher mortality rates. These conclusions hold whether one compares incidence rates of divorced men and women directly or in terms of ratios of the divorced to the married. The mortality ratios of divorced to married are higher for men than for women on all causes of death except cancer of the genital organs. It does appear that separated women are especially vulnerable to illness and disability. In her review of National Health Data for the 1960s and 1970s, Lois Verburgge (1979) has pointed out that the disadvantaged position of women on indices of health and health care is especially striking for the separation period where separated women are more limited by chronic conditions, have much higher rates of short-term disability, especially for respiratory and other acute conditions, and have higher rates of hospitalization and lengths of hospital stay than divorced

women, in spite of similar incidence of illness. There is no such differential between separated and divorced men.

10. In their review of the experimental bargaining research bearing on the effects of interpersonal orientation, Rubin and Brown (1975) make a somewhat different case for the problems created in negotiations by a high degree of interpersonal sensitivity. In their view, social psychological research on bargaining suggests that individuals who are highly interpersonal in orientation tend to attribute variations in another's behavior to enduring aspects of personality rather than to situational pressures. When negotiating conditions are favorable and the other party behaves in a cooperative, trusting manner, the interpersonally sensitive person ascribes the behavior to enduring personal qualities ("He's a nice guy trying to be decent") and reciprocates, thus amplifying the climate of good will. Alas, when negotiating conditions are more difficult, and the other behaves in a competitive or exploitative way, even if only occasionally or because of misunderstandings, the reaction of the interpersonally sensitive party may be unduly personal ("He's sneaky and out to get me")—and defensive and retaliatory behavior of great intensity is likely (Rubin and Brown 1975, 159).

In support of this perspective, Rubin and Brown note that in experimental bargaining research employing the Prisoner's Dilemma, a format which tends to elicit competitive responses because of its restrictions on communication, females tend to play in a "vindictive" manner, choosing competitively and persisting in competitive behavior longer than do males. However, in more cooperatively oriented experimental formats in which communication is permissible females tend to behave more cooperatively than males. Of course, the tendency to overreact to the competitive responses of another by "personalizing" a conflict is also consistent with the insecurities which arise from low power status. In divorce negotiations the wife's economic dependence on her husband, in combination with the already dismal negotiating circumstances, rather than any inherent tendency to personalize, may be the root of the problem.

Chapter 3

1. In seeking to resolve their differences with one another divorcing couples may turn to a variety of sources other than professionals. They may consult informally with friends, relatives, and acquaintances, as well as read books and articles on divorce and the legal and quasilegal aspects of settlement negotiations. Little of a systematic nature is presently known about the frequency with which such resources are tapped or their effects, when utilized, on the relationship between divorcing parties. The absence of information of this type is unfortunate since the important role of informal social support networks in coping with stress and crisis has been well documented in other domains of human experience.

The clergy represent perhaps the single most important source of informal, nonprofessional help in divorce, although programs in pastoral counseling are so widespread that many clergy might be viewed as having professional or quasiprofessional standing. Elsewhere we have reported our study of clergymen who are without formal degrees in psychological counseling but who possess a high level of experience in the special problems of divorcing persons (Weinglass, Kressel, and Deutsch 1977).

2. This study was originally published in *Family Process* 16 (1977):413–43.

3. Quoted material is taken verbatim from the transcripts with only minor syntactical corrections. Quoted comments have generally been chosen as those best summarizing the views of the respondents as a group. The identities of the speakers have been omitted to focus attention on substantive matters and to emphasize our desire to sketch the range of therapeutic views rather than the profiles of individual therapists.

4. In chapter 2, a shortage, rather than an abundance, of resources was noted as one major complication for settlement negotiations. That large assets can also cause problems,

especially when emotional and interpersonal conditions are poor, seems likely. However, since a minority of divorcing couples are wealthy, it is probably a less common source of difficulty.

5. These and other limitations and caveats regarding the research literature on the adjustment of children and adults to divorce are discussed in several useful papers, including Emery (1982), Kitson and Raschke (1981), and Levitin (1979).

Chapter 4

1. An extreme example of a highly structured approach to diagnosis is the use by two of the respondents of the Ravich Train Game Test. The pattern of interaction which results from the couples' play is said to be a diagnostic aid, and in some cases, highly predictive that divorce will occur (Ravich 1972). The game is itself an adaptation of an experimental procedure developed by Deutsch (1973) to explore general hypotheses in the area of conflict resolution. The diagnostic value of the Train Game Test for marital distress, however, has been called into question (Liebowitz and Black 1974). See also the rejoinder by Ravich (1975).

2. Since the focus of this study was on the therapeutic role during the divorcing process, little information was gathered about postdivorce interventions. It is apparent, however, that such help, usually in individual sessions with only one partner to the former marriage, is common. Postdivorce therapy may concern itself with the rebuilding of self-esteem, the working through of unconscious factors in new romantic attachments for purposes of permitting a sound remarriage, and assistance in dealing with postdivorce adjustment in work, child rearing, and social life.

There is also a type of postdivorce therapy in which divorced husband and wife jointly seek therapy for a problem child. The cause of the child's difficulty in these cases was conceptualized as the parents' uncompleted psychic divorce. The child's problem becomes the means by which marital involvement of an intense kind can be continued with neither partner admitting, or aware of, the true motivation for seeking therapy. In such instances one respondent spoke of the necessity of "remarrying the spouses in order to divorce them," i.e., of revivifying the matrimonial fantasies for the purpose of successfully laying them to rest. (For illustrative approaches to postdivorce therapy see Goldman and Coane [1977] and Isaacs [1982].)

Chapter 6

1. An orthogonal factor analysis with varimax rotation was performed on the questionnaire data. Because factor loadings are unstable with a sample this small, refined statistical criteria for deciding on the number of factors and the items to be included in a given factor were not employed. Going beyond four factors explained little additional variance and added nothing to the interpretability of the data. If an item loaded .40 or better on one of the four principal factors it was arbitrarily assigned to that factor. Three items loading .40 or better on two of the factors were assigned to the factor on which they loaded highest.

2. The general aim of cluster analysis is to group objects or individuals, in this case lawyers, into a number of homogeneous groups on the basis of their similarity over a set of n variables, here the items of the LRQ. The cluster analytic program employed (Johnson 1967) uses input distances (or proximities) as a basis for partitioning the subjects into a set of non-overlapping clusters. This hierarchial technique begins by forming one cluster for the data on each lawyer in the analysis. The two closest clusters are combined into one cluster, then the two closest of the new set of clusters are combined into a cluster and so forth. The distance between two clusters is defined to be the maximum Euclidean distance between an

observation in one cluster and an observation in another. The basic statistical goal is to minimize variation on the variables within each cluster. The standardized factor scores for each subject were the input data.

3. Two subclusters were also identifiable: a group of four lawyers breaking off from the advocate group who merit the designation *gladiators,* and a group of ten attorneys within the counselor classification whom we dubbed *journeymen.* I have omitted these two subtypes from the body of the text because of greater confidence in the stability of the two group solution (given the small overall size of our sample), and in order to keep the main theme clearly in focus. At any rate, the gladiator subtype is entirely consistent with that theme, since gladiators are best characterized as a more extreme variant of the advocate type in terms of their enthusiasm for a combatative, adversarial stance, their negative view of the client, and their rejection of psychological objectives and values in their interaction with the client.

The journeymen are the only new type revealed by the four cluster partition of the sample. The label is based primarily on the group's lack of identification with any of the dimensions important to the other types. That is, these were lawyers for whom, relatively speaking, neither a psychological nor an adversarial stance had much appeal; who were not notably interested in issues of child welfare or family readjustment; and who saw the divorcing client's psychological and other characteristics as posing no particular problems for the lawyer. Our speculation, corroborated by indirect evidence, is that these are attorneys who find themselves doing more and more divorce work—not out of any special aptitude, or interest, but because in a highly competitive market for legal services divorce is increasingly where the business lies. The journeyman type may not have emerged in our first study because of the elite nature of that sample. The reader interested in more details on gladiators and journeymen is urged to consult our original report (Kressel, Hochberg, and Meth 1983).

4. The specific average standardized scores of counselors and advocates on each of the four dimensions of the LRQ are as follows:

	Factor			
Lawyer Type	*Psychological*	*Advocacy*	*Social Work*	*Client as Problem*
Counselors	.43	−.62	.28	−.32
Advocates	−.46	.67	−.30	.32

5. The differences between items in table 6.3 reflect the extent to which the items distinguish counselors from advocates. They do not, however, indicate true probabilities since the groups were not derived independently, but were intentionally constructed by producing maximal separation on the standardized factor scores.

6. On the basis of the interviews alone, thirty-five attorneys were classified as counselors, thirty-six as advocates (ten interviews were unclassifiable). This breakdown corresponds closely to the ratio of counselors to advocates obtained in the cluster analysis of the LRQ. We had less success, however, validating the classification of respondents based on the LRQ data with the views they expressed in the interview.

It was possible to compare the interview classification with the cluster analysis classification for twenty-seven respondents. (Of the forty-six individuals who completed both a usable questionnaire and an interview, seventeen returned questionnaires without identification, making it impossible to pair the two sets of data for these respondents. In two additional cases the interview notes were too sketchy to be rated.) Of this group, 63 percent were identically classified by both methods. By type, 58 percent (seven of twelve) of those classified as counselors in the cluster analysis were similarly classified based on the interview data; the comparable figure for the advocates was 67 percent (ten of fifteen). Neither percentage was significantly different from chance. A combination of inexperienced student interviewers and skimpiness of recorded interview material may have been responsible for this unsuccessful "hit" rate. Generally speaking, the interview notes of respondents whose interview classification did not match the classification they had received in the cluster analysis were shorter and less detailed than the interview notes of respondents classified identically by both methods. The judge's confidence in his interview classifications supports this explanation in the case of the counselors. The interviews of the seven counselors whose interview classifications were consistent with their cluster analysis classifications received a mean confidence rating on the interview of 1.9; the five interviews with counselors whose interview classifications were as advocates received a mean confidence rating of only 4.0. The difference is statistically significant ($t=2.37$, $p < .05$). In the case of the advocates, the interviews of the ten respondents classified as advocates by both methods received a mean confidence rating of 4.4; the interviews of the five classified as counselors based on the interviews received a confidence rating of 5.3. This difference, however, was not statistically significant ($t=.71$, ns).

7. A useful elaboration of some of the problems in conducting research in legal settings may be found in Carlson (1976), Danet, Hoffman, and Kermish (1980), Ladinsky (1976), and Rosenthal (1976, 1980).

8. Part of the problem in regard to small sample size was the unexpectedly high rate of attrition among lawyers who consented to be interviewed but who did not subsequently return the LRQ on which our statistical analyses were based. The nearly 50 percent attrition rate may be attributable to the respondents' perception that they had already stated their views during the interview, and/or from an unsatisfactory experience with the (largely law) student interviewers. Whatever the cause, it is clear that our efforts at classifying the respondents are based on a small and perhaps selectively motivated group of attorneys.

9. The interviews, as well as informal discussions with attorneys, suggest that future revisions of the LRQ should include items concerning the strategies and tactics of legal negotiations (both with the client and the opposing counsel), as well as items concerning motivation for doing divorce work. The interviews also point to a need for items on the LRQ regarding the attitudes toward the proper distribution of power and responsibility in the lawyer-client relationship. For example, during the interview, a small but significant number of respondents of both the counselor and advocate persuasions indicated the need for the lawyer to take an authoritarian, controlling approach in influencing the client's decision making. However, a degree of client autonomy has been found significantly related to positive outcomes in personal injury cases (Rosenthal 1974).

10. As with our own research there are several methodological caveats that apply to Williams's investigation. First, of course, is the subjective nature of the data. In this case Williams's respondents were not describing themselves, but another attorney. Such an approach may or may not yield greater accuracy than self-reports but it is still a big step removed from an objective record of lawyer negotiating style. Second, only 35 percent of the one thousand randomly selected members of the Phoenix, Arizona bar responded to the questionnaire, raising the possibility of self-selection bias; e.g., perhaps the more competitively oriented lawyers were inclined not to respond to the researchers' questions—a likelihood which might be expected if our findings on the disdain for psychological concerns of confirmed gladiators is any guide.

11. In theory, the two dimensions which underlie the counselor-advocate typology could yield a four-fold typology of lawyers. In actuality, however, there is probably a strong tendency for a cooperative motivational orientation to be highly correlated with a socio-emotional one. Conversely, a competitive orientation is likely to be associated with a disavowal of socio-emotional interests in favor of a task orientation (Deutsch 1981).

Chapter 7

1. The debate within psychology over whether traits (personality) are more influential than states (motivations produced by circumstances) in predicting behavior has been raging

for over a decade. The argument favoring situational ascendancy over personality was made most strongly by Mischel (1968), and has been countered by Epstein (1980), among others. Pervin (1978) provides an excellent review of the entire debate.

2. Cavanagh and Rhode (1976) and Curran (1977) report client dissatisfaction with fees on the order of 50 to 65 percent, and Hochberg (1984) nearly 40 percent.

3. Low husband income was also significantly associated with active lawyer involvement. Since lawyers have no economic incentive to become involved in cases where the client cannot afford a stiff fee the correlation suggests that the attorneys felt pressured to intervene by the conflicts generated between the spouses by a lack of money.

4. For example, Hochberg (1984) reports that approximately one-quarter of his respondents described a relationship with their spouse on the eve of settlement negotiations which was highly competitive, and 30 percent described themselves as apprehensive about communicating with their spouse. See chapter 1 for an additional discussion of overall levels of conflict among divorcing couples.

5. Goldman gives two very illuminating examples of the impact which the counselor-advocate distinction may have on the client's outcomes and the lawyer's satisfaction (Areen 1978, 348–51).

6. I am aware of only two studies which analyzed the terms of settlement as recorded in the official documents filed with the court (Cavanagh and Rhode 1976, Hochberg 1984). The Cavanagh and Rhode study is widely cited as evidence that vague and inadequately detailed settlements are acceptable to the courts. It has been also taken as demonstrating the poor overall quality of the services which lawyers provide in divorce cases. However, it needs to be remembered that in more than half of the cases in this investigation only one lawyer was involved. Hochberg, whose sample included only cases in which both spouses were represented by counsel, reports much more highly detailed agreements. For example, in the Cavanagh and Rhode study the terms of visitation were detailed in only 8 percent of the agreements; in the Hochberg study this was true 45 percent of the time. The reason for the differences between the two studies is unclear. Presumably, however, Hochberg's respondents had more positive attitudes towards and/or greater needs for legal assistance. The greater detail on settlement terms in the Hochberg study might also be used as an argument that two lawyers are better than one.

7. McKenry, Herman, and Weber (1978) report that a majority (66 percent) of the twenty-two attorneys whom they interviewed indicated that they made efforts to be emotionally supportive to their divorce clients, but 86 percent expressed doubt that lawyers are actually helpful as sources of emotional comfort. Eighty-two percent said they would find training in counseling helpful, but 54 percent saw a distinct conflict in trying to combine the role of legal advisor and emotionally supportive counselor. A sense that professional training is matched poorly with professional responsibilities can also produce a chronic sense of demoralization or defensiveness. I am aware of no direct evidence for this proposition for legal training, but Sell, Brief, and Schuler (1981) cite at least one investigation (of nurses) in which role expectations developed during training which were unmet by actual work experience were associated with role conflict and feelings of role ambiguity.

8. The journeyman classification which emerged in our study of New Jersey lawyers may represent yet a third adaptive mechanism for coping with the strains of the lawyer's role. I have not emphasized it here because the counselor-advocate distinction rests on a more substantial base of evidence. However, the journeymen's stance of "neutrality" toward all the major issues of divorce work on which counselors and advocates had such strong and contrasting feelings is consistent with research which indicates that one consequence of high degrees of role strain may be a degree of emotional blunting and psychological withdrawal from the work and those associated with it (Sell, Brief, and Schuler, 1981). In this vein, Carter (1983) has identified a posture of "professionalism" and distance as one of the more notable ways by which legal aid attorneys cope with the dilemmas of their role.

Chapter 8

1. Williams (1983) also claims that effective negotiators of both the cooperative and competitive stamp are also likely to be rated as trustworthy, honest, ethical, and obedient to the "customs and courtesies" of the bar. My reading of Williams's published data is less sanguine. The cooperators seem to get higher marks on all these attributes. Since Williams provides no statistical analysis in this initial report intended for a lay audience it is difficult to say where the truth lies.

2. In a series of laboratory investigations Thibaut and Walker (1975) reported that adversarial methods are perceived as more fair, produce less bias, and uncover a greater array of relevant information than do non-adversarial methods. Since their original report additional research suggests that matters are more complex (Hayden and Anderson 1980; Sheppard and Vidmar 1980). In any event, the relevance of much of this research to divorce negotiations is questionable since many of the studies have used conflicts of interest which have little or no integrative potential and in which there is no anticipation of future interaction between the disputants. In such delimited circumstances many of the arguments in favor of a non-adversarial, cooperative orientation to conflict disappear (e.g., that it produces greater mutual respect, gives the parties a greater sense of ownership over the agreement, etc.).

3. The available studies have other limitations as well. Both O'Gorman's research and our own were primarily descriptive. Neither was directly concerned with the relationship of lawyer stance to outcomes. Williams's investigation is valuable, but the criteria of negotiating effectiveness was based entirely on a single, ill-defined rating made by a fellow lawyer. Hochberg's study is the most germane but represents only the retrospective judgements of a relatively small group of clients. Moreover, lawyer role type was *not* significantly related to postdivorce compliance with settlement terms or general postdivorce cooperation, areas where it might be presumed to have its greatest advantages.

4. Curran's (1977) national probability sample indicates that only 72 percent of divorcing persons report using a lawyer. Spanier and Anderson (1979), reporting on a non-random sample of 210 persons in Pennsylvania, found that 21 percent of their sample consulted a lawyer jointly. Hochberg (1984) also reports the involvement of only one lawyer in approximately 25 percent of the divorces filed in Middlesex County, New Jersey over a one-year period in 1980–1981.

5. Hochberg's study, like many others on divorce which draw their samples from court records, suffered from a very high rate of non-response from those initially contacted. Only 20 percent of those in the available subject pool participated. It is possible, therefore, that his sample underrepresents couples with significant levels of conflict, complex negotiating issues, and more intense lawyer involvement. Hochberg presents evidence that this may indeed have been the case, at least with regard to level of conflict. However, on a wide range of other indices, including a host of demographic and background factors and complexity and detail of the settlement agreement, responders and nonresponders did not differ significantly.

Chapter 9

1. Pearson, Ring, and Milne (1983) estimate that there were 34,400 divorce mediations conducted in 1981. Assuming that there are roughly one million divorces per year this yields the 3 percent share for mediation's part of the divorce negotiation business. The percentage of mediations per year as a function of the total potential pool of divorce disputes may actually be lower since I have not included postdivorce conflicts in the calculation. To the best of my knowledge there is no accurate national estimate of how many such disputes occur annually.

2. The rise of divorce mediation also appears to be part of a more general search for alternatives to strictly legal methods of dispute resolution. The interest in mediation has occurred in such diverse areas as consumer complaints, disputes between tenants and landlords, minor civil and criminal cases, disputes involving the allocation of public resources (such as money and land), and conflicts between neighbors (Kressel and Pruitt, in press).

3. I have excluded from my review of research on divorce mediation's effectiveness both the investigation by Bahr (1981) and the study of my colleagues and I (Kressel et al. 1980). Both of these projects involved quite small samples and non-random assignment of cases. Thus, their usefulness regarding mediation's virtues compared to those of the adversary system is virtually nil. They are of potential value, however, for descriptive and analytic purposes. This is the use which I have attempted to make of our own study in chapters 11 and 12.

4. The settlement rates reported for divorce mediation are as follows: 20 percent (Irving et al. 1979); 40 percent across the three sites in the CMRP (Pearson and Thoennes 1984b); 51 percent over a four-year period in the Minneapolis court program (Caron and Doyle 1979); 60 percent in the DCMP (Vanderkooi and Pearson 1983); 70 percent (Irving et al. 1981); and 97 percent (Margolin 1973). In addition, the service providers surveyed by Pearson, Ring, and Milne (1983) estimated an average rate of settlement of 61 percent, with somewhat higher percentages of success reported by private as compared to public sector mediators (65 and 56 percent, respectively).

It is an interesting commentary on the lack of a necessary relationship between popularity and proof of efficacy, that labor mediation, which has been firmly rooted in American industrial relations for at least sixty years, has only recently become a subject for empirical evaluation in any serious way. However, there are several studies of recent vintage which report on its ability to produce settlements. Settlement rates ranging from 28 to 57 percent have been reported (Hiltrop, in press; Kochan and Jick 1978; Lewin et al. 1975). Settlement rates for civil mediations in the Neighborhood Justice Programs fall in the 65 to 78 percent range (Pearson 1983) and there are two studies of mediation in small claims court which report settlement rates of 31 percent (Vidmar, in press) and 66 percent (McEwen and Maiman 1982).

I hasten to add that the studies from which these figures have been drawn are a heterogeneous lot with regard to method and purpose and cannot be said to be necessarily representative of the disputes in their respective areas. The comparisons across settings are obviously of only suggestive value.

5. The estimate of annual savings may be calculated as follows from the data given in Pearson and Thoennes (1984a) and Pearson (1983): the smallest per person savings is for the average legal costs of all mediated individuals (those who reached a mediated agreement and those who did not), minus the average costs for all adjudicated respondents (controls plus those who rejected mediation). This figure is approximately $265 in favor of mediation. The calculation applies only to persons with serious conflicts over custody and visitation, since this is the group studied by the DCMP. Assuming one million divorces annually, of which approximately 60 percent involve minor children, and of which 30 to 50 percent involve serious conflicts (see chapter 1), we end up with between 180,000 to 300,000 divorces annually to which our estimated savings apply. This translates into an annual national savings of between $47.7 million to $79.5 million on a per person basis, or between $95.4 million and $159 million on a per couple basis. Folberg (1981) has estimated potential national savings associated with divorce mediation of $181.7 million.

It should be noted, however, that in other forms of mediation there is evidence that mediation programs may actually be more expensive on a per case basis than adjudication (Pearson 1983). This is because such programs lack large volume, often attract cases that would not otherwise get on a court docket, and result in failures to settle that may then require additional court time. Roehl and Cook (in press) suggest that in regard to mediation provided by the Neighborhood Justice Centers, cost-effectiveness relative to adjudication is "notoriously difficult" to calculate and that reliable comparative data on costs are still unavailable.

6. Precise figures for the short-term impact of mediation on the ex-spousal relationship are not given in the most recent report on the DCMP (Pearson and Thoennes 1984a), at least not for the full mediation group (those who settled in mediation as well as those who did not). The investigators report the exact figures only for successful mediation individuals. For the unsuccessful mediation cases, they provide only a blanket 25 percent figure as the proportion citing improvement on each of the relationship variables. Using this blanket figure yields an average improvement rate for all those exposed to mediation of 52 percent for the communication item, 45 percent for anger level, 53 percent for cooperation, and 41 percent for understanding.

7. With regard to the effects of intervention on the parental relationship, the Hochberg (1984) study of uncontested divorce negotiations involving the use of lawyers by both spouses reports figures roughly parallel to those reported in the CMRP for mediation. Thus, about 18 percent of the respondents in both studies said that intervention—whether by lawyers or mediators—improved things in the parental relationship; roughly three-quarters described "no change"; and close to 10 percent said intervention "made things worse." Of course, these are inconclusive findings, since the Hochberg sample was of uncontested cases, whereas the CMRP respondents would appear to represent significantly more intense disputes. In addition, only 18 percent of the persons contacted by Hochberg returned the questionnaire sent them, suggesting that his findings may not be at all representative. Nonetheless, there remains the distinct possibility that, at least with regard to altering long established dysfunctional patterns of relating, neither attorney nor mediator assistance (at least of the relatively brief kind represented by the CMRP cases) can be reasonably expected to have much effect.

Chapter 10

1. Even a cursory reading of the growing literature on divorce mediation will turn up many of the clinical questions and issues enumerated in the text. Among the sources which produced my list are Coogler (1978); Coombs (1984); Family Law Section (1984); Haynes (1981); Markowitz and Engram (1983); Moore (1983); Pearson, Ring, and Milne (1983); and Saposnek (1983).

Chapter 11

1. My suggestions about the appeal of mediation are provisional not only because of the small number of cases, but because the respondents' understanding of "mediation" is unclear. In certain instances, particularly those in which the couple's pattern of divorce was of the type we have labelled "enmeshed," it is apparent that mediation was seen as an attractive alternative to the use of lawyers because it was viewed by at least one of the spouses as a means of holding onto the marriage—a cognitive distortion consistent with the underlying marital dynamics.

2. Elgart (1981) has provided additional evidence that patterns of divorce decision making are prognostic of settlement outcomes. In a questionnaire survey of fifty-eight members of Parents Without Partners she corroborated the existence of distinctive divorce decision-making patterns, two of which were highly similar to the autistic and enmeshed styles and which had a similar negative relationship to postdivorce conflict. Late in the preparation of this book, I learned of a study by Little (1982) which also delineates a typology of divorce conflict in the context of the mediation of child custody decisions. Unfortunately, there was insufficient time to make use of her findings.

Bibliography

Adams, J. S. 1976. The structure and dynamics of behavior in organizational boundary roles. In *Handbook of industrial organizational psychology,* ed. M. E. Dunnette. Chicago: Rand McNally.

Ahrons, C. R. 1981. The continuing co-parental relationship between divorced spouses. *American Journal of Orthopsychiatry* 51:415–28.

Albrecht, S. L. 1979. Correlates of marital happiness among the remarried. *Journal of Marriage and the Family* 41:857–67.

———. 1980. Reactions and adjustments to divorce: Differences in the experiences of males and females. *Family Relations* 29:59–68.

Albrecht, S. L., and Kunz, P. R. 1980. The decision to divorce: A social exchange perspective. *Journal of Divorce* 3:319–37.

American Bar Foundation. 1978. *Final report of the Special Committee to Survey Legal Needs.* Chicago: American Bar Association.

Appleford, R., and Pearson, J. 1984. *An overview of divorce and child custody.* Unpublished paper. Divorce Mediation Research Project, Denver, Colo.

Areen, J. 1978. *Cases and materials on family law.* Mineola, N.Y.: Foundation Press.

Association of Family Conciliation Courts. 1982. *Directory of mediation services.* Denver, Colo.: Divorce Mediation Research Project.

Bach, G. R., and Wyden, P. 1968. *The intimate enemy.* New York: Avon.

Bahr, S. J. 1981. Mediation is the answer. *Family Advocate* 3:32–35.

Bales, R. F. 1950. *Interaction process analysis.* Cambridge, Mass.: Addison-Wesley.

Bane, M. 1976. Marital disruption and the lives of children. *Journal of Social Issues* 32:103–17.

Barry, W. A. 1970. Marriage research and conflict: An integrative review. *Psychological Bulletin* 73:41–54.

Barsky, M. 1983. Emotional needs and dysfunctional communication as blocks to mediation. *Mediation Quarterly* 1(2):55–66.

Bass, H. L., and Rein, M. L. 1976. *Divorce or marriage: A legal guide.* Englewood Cliffs, N.J.: Prentice-Hall.

Beal, E. W. 1980. Separation, divorce, and single-parent families. In *The family life cycle: A framework for family therapy,* ed. E. A. Carter and M. McGoldrick. New York: Gardner Press.

Benton, A. A., and Druckman, D. 1974. Constituent's bargaining orientation and intergroup negotiations. *Journal of Applied Social Psychology* 4:141–50.

Benton, A. A., Gelber, E. R., Kelley, H. H., and Liebling, B. A. 1969. Reactions to various degrees of deceit in a mixed-motive relationship. *Journal of Personality and Social Psychology* 12:170–80.

Berman, W. H., and Turk, D. C. 1981. Adaptation to divorce: Problems and coping strategies. *Journal of Marriage and the Family* 43:179–89.

Bermant, G., Nemeth, C., and Vidmar, N., eds. 1976. *Psychology and the law.* Lexington, Mass.: Lexington Books.

Bienenfeld, F. 1983. *Child custody mediation.* New York: Science and Behavior Books.

Billings, A. 1979. Conflict resolution in distressed and non-distressed married couples. *Journal of Consulting and Clinical Psychology* 47:368–76.

Binion, V. J. 1982. Sex differences in socialization and family dynamics of female and male heroin users. *Journal of Social Issues* 38:43–57.

Bixenstine, V. E., Lowenfeld, B., and Englehart, C. E. 1981. Role enactment versus typology: Another test of the triangle hypothesis. *Journal of Personality and Social Psychology* 41:776–88.

Black, M., and Joffe, W. 1978. A lawyer/therapist team approach to divorce. *Conciliation Courts Review* 16:1–5.

Blake, R. R., and Mouton, J. S. 1964. *The managerial grid.* Houston, Tex.: Gulf.

———. 1979. Intergroup problem-solving in organizations: From theory to practice. In *The social psychology of intergroup relations,* ed. W. G. Austin and S. Worchel. Monterey, Calif.: Brooks/Cole.

Blake, R. R., Shepard, H. A., and Mouton, J. S. 1964. *Managing intergroup conflict in industry.* Houston, Tex.: Gulf.

Blashfield, R. K. 1980. Propositions regarding the use of cluster analysis in clinical research. *Journal of Consulting and Clinical Psychology* 48:456–59.

Bloch, D. 1980. Divorcing: Clinical notes. In *Dimensions of family therapy,* ed. M. Andolfi and I. Zwerling. New York: Guilford Press.

Block, J. H. 1980. *Personality development in males and females: The influence of differential socialization* (Master Lecture Series). Washington, D.C.: American Psychological Association.

Bloom, B. L., White, S. W., and Asher, S. J. 1979. Marital disruption as a stressful event. In *Divorce and separation; Context, causes, and consequences,* ed. G. Levinger and O. Moles. New York: Basic Books.

Blumberg, A. S. 1967. The practice of law as a confidence game: Organizational cooptation of a profession. *Law and Society Review* 1:15–39.

Boss, P. G. 1980. The relationship of psychological father presence, wife's personal qualities and wife/family dysfunction in families of missing fathers. *Journal of Marriage and the Family* 42:541–49.

Brett, J. M., and Goldberg, J. B. 1983. Mediator-advisers: A new third-party role. In *Negotiating in organizations,* ed. M. H. Bazerman and R. J. Lewicki. Beverly Hills, Calif.: Sage.

Brown, P., Felton, B. J., Whiteman, V., and Manela, R. 1980. Attachment and distress following marital separation. *Journal of Divorce* 3:303–17.

Brown, P., and Manela, R. 1977. Client satisfaction with marital and divorce counseling. *The Family Coordinator* 26:294–303.

Cain, M. 1979. The general practice lawyer and the client. *International Journal of the Sociology of Law* 7:331–54.

Campbell, A., Converse, P. E., and Rodgers, W. 1976. *The quality of American Life: Perceptions, evaluations, and satisfactions.* New York: Sage.

Caplan, P. 1979. Beyond the box score: A boundary condition for sex differences in aggression and achievement striving. In *Progress in experimental personality research,* Vol. 9, ed. B. Maher. New York: Academic Press.

Carlin, J. E. 1962. *Lawyers on their own: A study of individual practitioners in Chicago.* New Brunswick, N. J.: Rutgers University Press.

Carlson, R. J. 1976. Measuring the quality of legal services: An idea whose time has not come. *Law and Society Review* 11:287–316.

Carnevale, P. J., and Pegnetter, R. In press. The selection of mediation tactics in public sector disputes: A contingency analysis. *Journal of Social Issues.*

Carnevale, P. J., Pruitt, D. G., and Seilheimer, S. D. 1981. Looking and competing: Accountability and visual access in integrative bargaining. *Journal of Personality and Social Psychology* 40:111–20.

Caron, W., and Doyle, P. 1979. Contested custody intervention: An empirical assessment. In *Child custody: Literature review and alternative approaches,* ed. D. Olson. Minneapolis: University of Minnesota Child Custody Research Project.

Carter, H., and Glick, P. 1976. *Marriage and divorce: A social and economic study* (rev. ed.). Cambridge, Mass.: Harvard University Press.

Carter, R. 1983. *Role strain and the legal service attorney.* Unpublished doctoral dissertation, Columbia University, New York.

Cassetty, J. 1978. *Child support and public policy: Security support from absent fathers.* Lexington, Mass.: Lexington Books.

Cavanagh, R. C., and Rhode, D. L. 1976. The unauthorized practice of law and pro se divorce: An empirical analysis. *Yale Law Journal* 86:103–84.

Chambers, D. L. 1979. *Making fathers pay: The enforcement of child support.* Chicago: University of Chicago Press.

Chiriboga, D. A., and Cutler, L. 1977. Stress responses among divorcing men and women. *Journal of Divorce* 2:95–106.

Chiriboga, D. A., Roberts, J., and Stein, J. A. 1978. Psychological well-being during marital separation. *Journal of Divorce* 2:21–36.

Cline, D. W., and Westman, J. C. 1971. The impact of divorce on the family. *Child Psychiatry and Human Development* 2:78–83.

Clingempeel, W. G., and Reppucci, N. D. 1982. Joint custody after divorce: Major issues and goals for research. *Psychological Bulletin* 91:102–27.

Cohen, J. 1982. Cooperative and competitive styles: The construct and its relevance. *Human Relations* 35:621–33.

Cohen, S. 1980. Aftereffects of stress on human performance and social behavior: A review of research and theory. *Psychological Bulletin* 88:82–108.

Coogler, O. J. 1978. *Structured mediation in divorce settlement.* Lexington, Mass.: Lexington Books.

Cook, T. D., and Campbell, D. T. 1979. *Quasi-experimentation: Design and analysis issues for field settings.* Chicago: Rand McNally.

Coombs, R. M. 1984. Noncourt-connected mediation and counseling in child-custody disputes. *Family Law Quarterly* 17:469–95.

Cooper, H. M. 1979. Statistically combining independent studies: Meta-analysis of sex differences in conformity research. *Journal of Personality and Social Psychology* 37: 131–46.

Coser, L. 1956. *The function of social conflict.* Glencoe, Ill.: Free Press.

Crandall, V. V. 1967. Achievement behavior in young children. In *The young child: Reviews of research,* ed. W. W. Hartup and N. L. Smothergill. Washington, D. C.: National Association for the Education of the Young.

Crossman, S. M., Shea, J. A., and Adams, G. R. 1980. Effects of parental divorce during early childhood on ego development and identity formation of college students. *Journal of Divorce* 3:263–71.

Curran, B. 1977. *The legal needs of the public.* Chicago: American Bar Foundation.

Danet, B., Hoffman, K. B., and Kermish, N. C. 1980. Obstacles to the study of lawyer-client interaction: The biography of a failure. *Law and Society Review* 14:905–22.

Dean, G., and Gurak, D. T. 1978. Marital homogamy the second time around. *Journal of Marriage and the Family* 40:559–70.

Deaux, K. 1976. *The behavior of women and men.* Monterey, Calif.: Brooks/Cole.

Deutsch, M. 1969. Conflicts: Productive and destructive. *Journal of Social Issues* 25:7–41.

———. 1973. *The resolution of conflict.* New Haven, Conn.: Yale University Press.

———. 1981. Interdependence and psychological orientation. In *Living with other people: Theories and research on cooperation and helping behavior,* ed. V. Derlega and J. L. Grzelak. New York: Academic Press.

Dixon, R. B., and Weitzman, L. J. 1980. Evaluating the impact of no-fault divorce in California. *Family Relations* 29:297–307.

———. 1982. When husbands file for divorce. *Journal of Marriage and the Family* 44:103–15.

Douglas, A. 1962. *Industrial peacemaking.* New York: Columbia University Press.

Douvan, E., and Kulka, R. 1979. The American family: A twenty-year view. In *Psychology and women: In transition,* ed. J. E. Gullahorn. Washington, D.C.: V. H. Winston.

Dreyfus, E. A. 1979. Counseling the divorced father. *Journal of Marriage and Family Therapy* 5:79–85.

Eagly, A. H., and Carli, L. L. 1981. Sex of researchers and sex-typed communications as determinants of sex differences in influenceability: A meta-analysis of social influence studies. *Psychological Bulletin* 90:1–20.

Eckhardt, K. W. 1968. Deviance, visibility, and legal action: The duty to support. *Social Problems* 15:470–77.

Eider, V. 1978. Shared custody—an idea whose time has come. *Conciliation Courts Review* 16: 23–35.

Elgart, C. K. 1981. *A typology of divorce decision experiences.* Unpublished master's thesis, Rutgers University.

Emery, R. E. 1982. Interparental conflict and the children of discord and divorce. *Psychological Bulletin* 92:310–30.

Epstein, N. B., and Santa-Barbara, J. 1975. Conflict behavior in clinical couples: Interpersonal perceptions and stable outcomes. *Family Process* 14:51–66.

Epstein, S. 1980. The stability of behavior. II. Implications for psychological research. *American Psychologist* 35:790–806.

Epstein, Y., and Karlin, R. 1975. Effects of acute experimental crowding. *Journal of Applied Social Psychology* 5:34–53.

Espenshade, T. J. 1979. The economic consequences of divorce. *Journal of Marriage and the Family* 41:615–23.

Everitt, B. S. 1974. *Cluster analysis.* London: Halstead Press.

Family Law Section, American Bar Association. 1984. Standards of practice for family mediators. *Family Law Quarterly* 17:455–60.

Federico, J. 1979. The marital termination period of the divorce adjustment process. *Journal of Divorce* 3:93–106.

Fiedler, F. E. 1967. *A theory of leadership effectiveness.* New York: McGraw-Hill.

———. 1978. The contingency model and the dynamics of the leadership process. In *Advances in experimental social psychology,* Vol. 11, ed. L. Berkowitz. New York: Academic Press.

Fisher, M. S., and Fisher, E. O. 1982. Toward understanding working relationships between lawyers and therapists in guiding divorcing spouses. *Journal of Divorce* 6:1–15.

Fisher, R. J. 1983. Third party consultation as a method of intergroup conflict resolution: A review of studies. *Journal of Conflict Resolution* 27:301–34.

Folberg, H. J. 1981. The changing family: Implications for the law. *Conciliation Courts Review* 19:1–6.

Folberg, H. J., and Graham, M. 1979. Joint custody of children following divorce. *University of California at Davis Law Review* 12:523–81.

Fulton, J. A. 1979. Parental reports of children's post-divorce adjustment. *Journal of Social Issues* 35:126–39.

Galanter, M. 1974. Why the "haves" come out ahead: Speculations on the limits of legal change. *Law and Society Review* 9:95–160.

Gersick, K. E. 1979. Fathers by choice: Divorced men who receive custody of their children. In *Divorce and separation,* ed. G. Levinger and O. Moles. New York: Basic Books.

Glenn, N. D. 1975. The contribution of marriage to the psychological well-being of males and females. *Journal of Marriage and the Family* 37:594–600.

Glenn, N. D., and Weaver, C. N. 1977. The marital happiness of remarried divorced persons. *Journal of Marriage and the Family* 39:331–37.

Glick, P. 1979. Children of divorced parents in demographic perspective. *Journal of Social Issues* 35:170–82.

Goldman, E. 1978. Couseling the divorce client. In *Cases and materials on family law,* ed. J. Areen. Mineola, N.Y.: Foundation Press.

Goldman, J., and Coane, J. 1977. Family therapy after the divorce: Developing a strategy. *Family Process* 16:357–62.

Goldsmith, J. 1980. Relationships between former spouses: Descriptive findings. *Journal of Divorce* 4:1–20.

Goode, W. J. 1956. *Women in divorce.* New York: Free Press.

Gottman, J. M. 1979. *Marital interaction: Experimental investigations.* New York: Academic Press.

Grote, D. F., and Weinstein, J. P. 1977. Joint custody: A viable and ideal alternative. *Journal of Divorce* 1:43–53.

Grunebaum, H. 1983. A study of therapists' choice of a therapist. *American Journal of Psychiatry* 140:1336–39.

Gunter, B. G., and Johnson, D. P. 1978. Divorce filing as role behavior: Effect of no-fault law on divorce filing patterns. *Journal of Marriage and the Family* 40:571–74.

Gurin, G., Veroff, J., and Feld, S. 1960. *Americans view their mental health.* New York: Basic Books.

Gurman, A. S., and Kniskern, D. P. 1978. Research on marital and family therapy: Progress, perspective, and prospect. In *Handbook of psychotherapy and behavior change: An empirical analysis,* ed. S. L. Garfield and A. E. Bergin. Toronto: Wiley.

———. 1981. Family therapy outcome research: Knowns and unknowns. In *Handbook of family therapy,* ed. A. S. Gurman and D. P. Kniskern. New York: Brunner/Mazel.

Hall, J. A. 1978. Gender effects in decoding nonverbal cues. *Psychological Bulletin* 85:845–75.

Hancock, E. 1982. Sources of discord between attorneys and therapists in divorce cases. *Journal of Divorce* 6:115–24.

Hayden, R. M., and Anderson, J. K. 1980. On the evaluation of procedural systems in laboratory experiments: A critique of Thibault and Walker. *Law and Human Behavior* 3:21–38.

Haynes, J. M. 1981. *Divorce mediation: A practical guide for therapists and counselors.* New York: Springer.

Hazard, G. C. 1965. Reflections on four studies of the legal profession. *Social Problems* 13 (Summer Supplement):47.

Hermann, M. G., and Kogan, N. 1977. Effects of negotiators' personalities on negotiating behavior. In *Negotiations,* ed. D. Druckman. London: Sage.

Hetherington, E. M., Cox, M., and Cox, R. 1976. Divorced fathers. *Family Coordinator* 25: 417–28.

———. 1979a. The development of children in mother-headed families. In *The American family: Dying or developing,* ed. D. Reiss and H. A. Hoffman. New York: Plenum.

———. 1979b. Play and social interaction in children following divorce. *Journal of Social Issues* 35:26–49.

———. 1979c. Stress and coping in divorce: A focus on women. In *Psychology and women: In transition,* ed. J. E. Gullahorn. Washington, D.C.: V. H. Winston.

Hess, R. D., and Camara, K. A. 1979. Post-divorce family relationships as mediating factors in the consequences of divorce for children. *Journal of Social Issues* 35:79–96.

Hill, C. T., Rubin, Z., and Peplau, L. A. 1976. Breakups before marriage: The end of 103 affairs. *Journal of Social Issues* 32:147–68.

Hiltrop, J. In Press. Mediator behavior and the settlement of collective bargaining disputes in Britain. *Journal of Social Issues.*

Hochberg, A. M. 1984. *Determinants of constructive and destructive divorce settlement outcomes.* Unpublished doctoral dissertation, Rutgers University.

Hochberg, A. M., and Kressel, K. 1983. *Determinants of successful and unsuccessful divorce settlement outcomes.* Paper presented at the meeting of the American Psychological Association, Anaheim, Calif.

Holmes,J.G.,andLamm,H.1979.Boundaryrolesandthereductionofconflict.In *Thesocialpsychologyof intergroup relations,* ed. W. G. Austin and S. Worchel. Monterey, Calif.: Brooks/Cole.

Hunt, M., and Hunt, B. 1977. *The divorce experience.* New York: McGraw-Hill.

Huston, T. L., and Levinger, G. 1978. Interpersonal attraction and relationships. *Annual Review of Psychology* 29:115–56.

Ikle, F. C. 1964. *How nations negotiate.* New York: Harper & Row.

Irving, H. 1980. *Divorce mediation: The rational alternative.* Toronto: Person Library Publishers.

Irving, H., Bohm, P., MacDonald, G., and Benjamin, M. A. 1979. *A comparative analysis of two family court services: An exploratory study of conciliation counseling.* Toronto: Department of National Health and Welfare and the Ontario Ministry of the Attorney General.

Irving, H., Benjamin, M. A., Bohm, P., and MacDonald, G. 1981. *A study of conciliation counseling.* Toronto: Department of National Health and Welfare and the Ontario Ministry of the Attorney General.

Isaacs, M. B. 1982. Helping Mom fail: A case of a stalemated divorcing process. *Family Process* 21:225–31.

Jacobsen, N. S., Waldron, H., and Moore, D. 1980. Toward a behavioral profile of marital distress. *Journal of Consulting and Clinical Psychology* 48:696–703.

Jacobson, D. S. 1978. The impact of marital separation/divorce on children: II. Interparent hostility and child adjustment. *Journal of Divorce* 2:3–19.

Johnson, D. W., Maruyama, G., Johnson, R., Nelson, D., and Skon, L. 1981. Effects of cooperative, competitive, and individualistic goal structures on achievement: A meta-analysis. *Psychological Bulletin* 89:47–62.

Johnson, S. C. 1967. Hierarchial clustering schemes. *Psychometrika* 32:241–54.

Johnson, W. D. 1978. Child support: Preventing default. *Conciliation Courts Review* 16:27–32.

Jones, C. A., Gordon, N. M., and Sawhill, I. V. 1976. *Child support payments in the United States.* Washington, D.C.: Urban Institute.

Jones, F. N. 1977. *The impact of divorce on children.* Unpublished manuscript, Family Court Services, Oregon City, Ore.

Kahn, R. L. 1980. Conflict, ambiguity, and overload: Three elements in job stress. In *The study of organizations,* ed. D. Katz, R. L. Kahn, and J. S. Adams. San Francisco: Jossey-Bass.

Kalmuss, D. S., and Straus, M. A. 1982. Wife's marital dependency and wife abuse. *Journal of Marriage and the Family* 44:277–86.

Kaslow, F. W. 1981. Divorce and divorce therapy. In *Handbook of family therapy,* ed. A. S. Gurman and D. P. Kniskern. New York: Brunner/Mazel.

Kelley, H. H., and Stahelski, A. J. 1970a. Errors in perception of intentions in a mixed-motive game. *Journal of Experimental Social Psychology* 6:379–400.

———. 1970b. Social interaction basis of cooperators' and competitors' beliefs about others. *Journal of Personality and Social Psychology* 16:66–91.

Kelly, J. B. 1983. Mediation and psychotherapy: Distinguishing the differences. *Mediation Quarterly* 1(1):33–44.

Kelly, J. B., and Wallerstein, J. S. 1976. The effects of parental divorce: Experiences of the child in early latency. *American Journal of Orthopsychiatry* 46:20–32.

Kerr, C. 1954. Industrial conflict and its resolution. *American Journal of Sociology* 60:230–45.

Kessler, S. 1978. *Creative conflict resolution: Mediation.* Atlanta, Ga.: National Institute for Professional Training.

Kitson, G. C. 1982. Attachment to the spouse in divorce: A scale and its application. *Journal of Marriage and the Family* 44:379–93.

Kitson, G. C., and Raschke, H. J. 1981. Divorce research: What we know; what we need to know. *Journal of Divorce* 4:1–37.

Kitson, G. C., and Sussman, M. B. 1977. The impact of divorce on adults. *Conciliation Courts Review* 15:20–24.

———. 1982. Marital complaints, demographic characteristics, and symptoms of mental distress in divorce. *Journal of Marriage and the Family* 44:87–101.

Kitson, G. C., Lopata, H. Z., Holmes, W. M., and Meyering, S. M. 1980. Divorcees and widows: Similarities and differences. *American Journal of Orthopsychiatry* 50:291–301.

Kochan, T. A., and Jick, T. 1978. The public sector mediation process: A theory and empirical examination. *Journal of Conflict Resolution* 22:209–40.

Kolb, D. In press. To be a mediator: Expressive tactics in mediation. *Journal of Social Issues.*

Komarovsky, M. 1976. *Dilemmas of masculinity: A study of college youth.* New York: Norton.

Korelitz, A., and Schulder, D. 1982. The lawyer-therapist consultation team. *Journal of Marriage and Family Therapy* 8:113–19.

Koren, P., Carlton, K., and Shaw, D. 1980. Marital conflict: Relations among behaviors, outcomes, and distress. *Journal of Consulting and Clinical Psychology* 48:460–68.

Korsch, B. M., Gozzi, E. K., and Francis, V. 1968. Gaps in doctor-patient communication. I. Doctor-patient interaction and patient satisfaction. *Pediatrics* 42:855–71.

Kressel, K. 1972. *Labor mediation: An exploratory survey.* New York: Association of Labor Mediation Agencies.

———. 1980. Review of *The Family Advocate,* by The American Bar Association. *Journal of Marriage and the Family* 42:1050–51.

———. 1981. Kissinger in the Middle East: An exploratory analysis of role strain in international mediation. In *Dynamics of third party intervention: Kissinger in the Middle East,* ed. J. Z. Rubin. New York: Praeger.

Kressel, K., Hochberg, A., and Meth, T. S. 1983. A provisional typology of lawyer attitudes towards divorce practice: Gladiators, advocates, counselors, and journeymen. *Law and Human Behavior* 7:31–49.

Kressel, K., and Pruitt, D. G., eds. In press. The mediation of social conflict. *Journal of Social Issues.*

Kressel, K., Lopez-Morillas, M., Weinglass, J., and Deutsch, M. 1979. Professional intervention in divorce: The views of lawyers, psychotherapists, and clergy. In *Divorce and separation: Context, causes, and consequences,* ed. G. Levinger and O. Moles. New York: Basic Books.

Kressel, K., Jafee, N., Tuchman, B., Watson, C., and Deutsch, M. 1980. A typology of divorcing couples: Implications for mediation and the divorce process. *Family Process* 19: 101–16.

Ladinsky, J. 1976. The traffic in legal services: Lawyer-seeking behavior and the channeling of clients. *Law and Society Review* 11:207–23.

Landsberger, H. A. 1955. Interaction process analysis of professional behavior: A study of labor mediators in twelve labor-management disputes. *American Sociological Review* 20: 566–75.

Lazarus, A. A. 1981. Divorce counseling or marriage therapy? A therapeutic option. *Journal of Marital and Family Therapy* 7:15–22.

Leik, R. K. 1963. Instrumentality and emotionality in family interaction. *Sociometry* 26:131–45.

Lempert, R. O. 1976. Mobilizing private law: An introductory essay. *Law and Society Review* 11:175–89.

Levinger, G. 1964. Task and social behavior in marriage. *Sociometry* 27:433–48.

Levitin, T. E. 1979. Children of divorce: An introduction. *Journal of Social Issues* 35:1–25.

Levy, R. J. 1984. Comment on the Pearson-Thoennes study and on mediation. *Family Law Quarterly* 17:525–33.

Lewin, D., Feuille, P., and Kochan, T. A. 1977. *Public sector labor relations.* Glen Springs, N. J.: Horton and Daughters.

Liebowitz, B., and Black, M. 1974. The structure of the Ravich interpersonal game test. *Family Process* 13:169–83.

Lind, E. A., Kurtz, S., Musante, L., Walker, L., and Thibact, J. W. 1980. Procedures and outcome effects on reactions to adjudicated resolution of conflicts of interest. *Journal of Personality and Social Psychology* 39:643–53.

Little, M. 1982. *Family breakup: Understanding marital problems and the mediating of child custody decisions.* San Francisco: Jossey-Bass.

Lockheed, M. E. 1976. *The modification of female leadership behavior in the presence of males: Final report.* Princeton, N.J.: Educational Testing Service.

Maccoby, E. E., and Jacklin, C. M. 1974. *The psychology of sex differences.* Palo Alto, Calif.: Stanford University Press.

McEwen, C., and Maiman, R. 1981. Small claims mediating in Maine: An empirical assessment. *Maine Law Review* 33:237–68.

McIssac, H. 1981. Mandatory conciliation custody/visitation matters: California's bold stroke. *Conciliation Courts Review* 19:73–81.

McKenry, P. C., Herman, M. S., and Weber, R. E. 1978. Attitudes of attorneys towards divorce issues. *Conciliation Courts Review* 16:11–17.

McNeel, S. P. 1973. Training cooperation in the prisoner's dilemma. *Journal of Experimental Social Psychology* 9:335–48.

Mallen, R. E. 1978. On guard! How to avoid that malpractice suit. *Family Advocate* 1:10–13.

Margolin, F. M. 1973. *An approach to resolution of litigation disputes post-divorce: Short-term counseling.* Unpublished doctoral dissertation, United States International University.

Margolin, G., and Wampold, B. E. 1981. Sequential analysis of conflict and accord in distressed and non-distressed marital partners. *Journal of Consulting and Clinical Psychology* 49: 554–67.

Markowitz, J. R., and Engram, P. S. 1983. Mediation in labor disputes and divorces: A comparative analysis. *Mediation Quarterly* 1(2):67–78.

Marks, F. 1976. Some research perspectives for looking at legal need and legal services delivery systems: Old forms or new? *Law and Society Review* 11:191–205.

Marks, F. R., Hallaver, R. P., and Clifton, R. 1974. *The Shreveport Plan: An experiment in the delivery of legal services.* Chicago: American Bar Foundation.

Martin, P. A. 1976. *Marital therapy manual.* New York: Brunner/Mazel.

Maru, O. 1972. *Research on the legal profession: A review of work done.* Chicago: American Bar Foundation.

Mentzer, S. J., and Snyder, M. L. 1982. The doctor and the patient: A psychological perspective. In *Social psychology of health and illness,* ed. G. Ganders and J. Suls. Hillsdale, N.J.: Lawrence Erlbaum Associates.

Miles, R. H., and Perreault, W. D. 1976. Organizational role conflict: Its antecedents and consequences. *Organizational Behavior and Human Performance* 17:19–44.

Milne, A. L. 1978. Custody of children in a divorce process: A family self-determination model. *Conciliation Courts Review* 16:1–10.

Milne, A. L. 1983. Divorce mediation: The state of the art. *Mediation Quarterly* 1(1):15–31.

Minter, R. E., and Kimball, C. P. 1980. Life events, personality traits, and illness. In *Handbook on stress and anxiety,* ed. I. L. Kutash and L. B. Schlesinger. San Francisco: Jossey-Bass.

Minuchin, S. 1974. *Families and family therapy.* Cambridge, Mass.: Harvard University Press.

Minuchin, S., Rosman, B. L., and Baker, L. 1979. *Psychosomatic families.* Cambridge, Mass.: Harvard University Press.

Mischel, W. 1968. *Personality and assessment.* New York: Wiley.

Mitchell, T. R. 1979. Organizational behavior. *Annual Review of Psychology* 30:243–81.

Mnookin, R. H., and Kornhauser, L. 1979. Bargaining in the shadow of the law: The case of divorce. *Yale Law Journal* 88:950–97.

Moore, C. W. 1983. Training mediators for family dispute resolution. *Mediation Quarterly* 2:79–89.

Morley, I., and Stephenson, G. 1977. *The social psychology of bargaining.* London: Allen and Unwin.

O'Brien, J. E. 1971. Violence in divorce prone families. *Journal of Marriage and the Family* 33:692–98.

O'Gorman, H. 1963. *Lawyers and matrimonial cases: A study of informal pressures in private professional practice.* New York: Free Press.

Olson, D. H. 1981. Family typologies: Bridging family research and family therapy. In *Assessing marriage: New behavioral approaches,* ed. E. E. Filsinger and R. A. Lewis. Beverly Hills, Calif.: Sage.

Olson, D. H., Russell, C. A., and Sprenkle, D. H. 1980. Marital and family therapy: A decade review. *Journal of Marriage and the Family* 42:973–93.

O'Rourke, J. F. 1963. Field and laboratory: The decision-making behavior of family groups in two experimental conditions. *Sociometry* 26:422–35.

Ortmeyer, C. E. 1974. Variations in mortality, morbidity, and health care by marital status. In *Mortality and morbidity in the United States,* ed. C. L. Erhardt and J. E. Berlin. Cambridge, Mass.: Harvard University Press.

Parloff, M. B., Waskow, I. E., and Wolfe, B. 1978. Research on therapist variables in relation to process and outcome. In *Handbook of psychotherapy and behavior change,* ed. S. L. Garfield and A. E. Bergin. New York: Wiley.

Parsons, T., and Bales, R. F., eds. 1955. *Family, socialization, and interaction process.* Glencoe, Ill.: Free Press.

Pearson, J. 1981. *The Denver Custody Mediation Project: Progress report no. 5.* Denver, Colo.: Center for Policy Research.

———. 1983. *An evaluation of alternatives to court adjudication.* Unpublished paper, Center for Policy Research, Denver, Colo.

Pearson, J., and Thoennes, N. 1982a. Mediation and divorce: The benefits outweigh the costs. *Family Advocate* 4:26–32.

———. 1982b. *A preliminary portrait of client reactions to three court mediation programs.* Unpublished paper, Center for Policy Research, Denver, Colo.

———. 1984a. Mediating and litigating custody disputes: A longitudinal evaluation. *Family Law Quarterly* 17:497–524.

———. 1984b. *Research on divorce mediation: A review of major findings.* Unpublished paper, Center for Policy Research, Denver, Colo.

Pearson, J., Ring, M. L., and Milne, A. 1983. A portrait of divorce mediation services in the public and private sector. *Conciliation Courts Review* 21:1–24.

Pearson, J., Thoennes, N., and Vanderkooi, L. 1982. The decision to mediate: Profiles of individuals who accept and reject the opportunity to mediate contested child custody and visitation issues. *The Journal of Divorce* 6:17–35.

Pedersen, F. A. 1976. Does research on children reared in father-absent families yield information on father influences? *Family Coordinator* 25:459–64.

Perlman, J. L. 1982. Divorce—a psychological and legal process. *Journal of Divorce* 6:99–114.

Pervin, L. A. 1978. *Current controversies and issues in personality.* New York: Wiley.

Pino, C. 1980. Research and clinical application of marital autopsy in divorce counseling. *Journal of Divorce* 4:31–48.

Price-Bonham, S., and Balswick, J. O. 1980. The noninstitutions: Divorce, desertion, and remarriage. *Journal of Marriage and the Family* 42:959–72.

Pruitt, D. G. 1981. *Negotiation behavior.* New York: Academic Press.

Rabkin, J. G., and Struening, E. L. 1976. Life events, stress, and illness. *Science* 194:1013–20.

Radloff, L. 1975. Sex differences in depression: The effects of occupation and marital status. *Sex Roles: A Journal of Research* 1:249–65.

Raush, H. L., Barry, W. A., Hertel, R. K., and Swain, M. A. 1974. *Communication, conflict, and marriage.* San Francisco: Jossey-Bass.

Ravich, R. A. 1972. The marriage/divorce paradox. In *Progress in group and family therapy,* ed. C. J. Sager and H. S. Kaplan. New York: Brunner/Mazel.

———. 1975. The Ravich Interpersonal Game/Test: Comments on Liebowitz and Black's paper. *Family Process* 14:263–67.

Renee, K. S. 1971. Health and marital experience in an urban population. *Journal of Marriage and the Family* 33:338–50.

Rice, R. W. 1978. Construct validity of the Least Preferred Co-worker score. *Psychological Bulletin* 85:1199–1237.

Rindfuss, R. R., and Bumpass, L. L. 1977. Fertility during marital disruption. *Journal of Marriage and the Family* 39:517–28.

Rodin, J., and Janis, I. L. 1979. The social power of health care practitioners as agents of change. *Journal of Social Issues* 35:60–81.

Roehl, J. A., and Cook, R. F. In press. Issues in mediation: Rhetoric and reality revisited. *Journal of Social Issues.*

Rogers, C. R. 1957. The necessary and sufficient conditions of therapeutic personality change. *Journal of Consulting Psychology* 21:95–103.

Roman, M., and Haddad, W. 1978. *The disposable parent.* New York: Holt, Rinehart, and Winston.

Rosenthal, D. E. 1974. *Lawyer and client: Who's in charge?* New York: Russell Sage Foundation.

———. 1976. Evaluating the competence of lawyers. *Law and Society Review* 11:257–85.

———. 1980. Comment on "Obstacles to the study of lawyer-client interaction: The biography of a failure." *Law and Society Review* 14:923–29.

Ross, H. L. 1970. *Settled out of court: The social process of insurance claims adjustments.* Chicago: Aldin.

Rubin, J. Z. 1980. Experimental research on third-party interaction in conflict: Toward some generalizations. *Psychological Bulletin* 87:379–91.

———. 1983. The use of third parties in organizations: A critical response. In *Negotiating in organizations,* ed. M. H. Bazerman and R. J. Lewicki. Beverly Hills, Calif.: Sage.

Rubin, J. Z., and Brown, B. 1975. *The social psychology of bargaining and negotiation.* New York: Academic Press.

Ryckman, R. M., and Sherman, M. F. 1974. Locus of control and attitudes of workers and college students towards members of selected occupations. *Journal of Applied Social Psychology* 4:351–64.

Sabalis, R. F., and Ayers, G. W. 1977. Emotional aspects of divorce and their effects on the legal process. *Family Coordinator* 26:391–94.

Sander, F. E. A. 1983. Family mediation: Problems and prospects. *Mediation Quarterly* 1(2):3–12.

Santa-Barbara, J., and Epstein, N. B. 1974. Conflict behavior in clinical families: Preasymtotic interactions and stable outcomes. *Behavioral Science* 19:100–110.

Saposnek, D. T. 1983. *Mediating child custody disputes.* San Francisco: Jossey-Bass.

Sawhill, I. V. 1981. *Developing normative standards for child support and alimomy payments*. Washington, D. C.: The Urban Institute.

Seal, K. 1979. A decade of no-fault divorce. *Family Advocate* 1:10–15.

Sears, R. 1977. Sources of life satisfaction of the Terman gifted men. *American Psychologist* 32:119–28.

Sell, M. V., Brief, A. P., and Schuler, R. S. 1981. Role conflict and role ambiguity: Integration of the literature and directions for future research. *Human Relations* 34:43–71.

Sellman, J. R. 1979. When your client has crossed the line. *Family Advocate* 1:33–35.

Shapiro, D., Drieghe, R., and Brett, J. In press. Mediator behavior and the outcome of mediation. *Journal of Social Issues.*

Shapiro, J. J., and Caplan, M. S. 1983. *Parting sense: A couples' guide to divorce mediation.* Lutherville, Md.: Greenspring Publications.

Sheppard, B. H. 1983. Managers as inquisitors: Some lessons from the law. In *Negotiating in organizations,* ed. M. H. Bazerman and R. J. Lewicki. Beverly Hills, Calif.: Sage.

Sheppard, B. H., and Vidmar, N. 1980. Adversary pretrial procedures and testimonial evidence: Effects of lawyer's role and Machievellianism. *Journal of Personality and Social Psychology* 39:320–32.

Sherif, M. 1966. *In common predicament: Social-psychology of intergroup conflict and cooperation.* Boston: Houghton Mifflin.

Shinn, M. 1978. Father absence and children's cognitive development. *Psychological Bulletin* 85:295–324.

Shneidman, E. S., and Farberow, N. L. 1961. Statistical comparisons between committed and attempted suicides. In *The cry for help,* ed. N. L. Farberow and E. S. Shneidman. New York: McGraw-Hill.

Sklar, L. S., and Anisman, H. 1981. Stress and cancer. *Psychological Bulletin* 89:369–406.

Snyder, D. K. 1979. Multidimensional assessment of marital satisfaction. *Journal of Marriage and the Family* 41:813–23.

Spanier, G. B., and Anderson, E. A. 1979. The impact of the legal system on adjustment to marital separation. *Journal of Marriage and the Family* 41:605–13.

Spanier, G. B., and Casto, R. F. 1979. Attachment to separation and divorce: A qualitative analysis. In *Divorce and separation: Context, causes, and consequences,* ed. G. Levinger and O. Moles. New York: Basic Books.

Sprenkle, D. H., and Storm, C. 1981. The unit of treatment in divorce therapy. In *Questions and answers in the practice of family therapy,* ed. A. S. Gurman. New York: Brunner/Mazel.

———. 1983. Divorce therapy outcome research: A substantive and methodological review. *Journal of Marital and Family Therapy* 9:239–58.

Stacks, S. 1980. The effects of marital dissolution on suicide. *Journal of Marriage and the Family* 42:83–92.

Stake, J. E., and Stake, M. N. 1979. Performance-self-esteem and dominance behavior in mixed-sex dyads. *Journal of Personality* 47:71–84.

Steinberg, J. L. 1980. Towards an interdisciplinary committment: A divorce lawyer proposes attorney-therapist marriages or, at the least, an affair. *Journal of Marital and Family Therapy* 6:259–68.

Stone, G. C. 1979. Patient compliance and the role of expert. *Journal of Social Issues* 35:34–59.

Straus, M. A. 1980. Wife-beating: How common and why? In *The social causes of husband-wife violence,* ed. M. A. Straus and G. T. Hotaling. Minneapolis: University of Minnesota Press.

Strube, M. J., and Garcia, J. E. 1981. A meta-analytic investigation of Fiedler's contingency model of leadership effectiveness. *Psychological Bulletin* 90:307–21.

Suarez, J. M., Weston, N. L., and Hartstein, N. B. 1978. Mental health interventions in divorce proceedings. *American Journal of Orthopsychiatry* 48:273–83.

Tapp, J. L. 1980. Psychological and policy perspectives on the law: Reflections on a decade. *Journal of Social Issues* 36:165–92.

Thibaut, J., and Walker, L. 1975. *Procedural justice.* Hillsdale, N.J.: Lawrence Erlbaum.

Thoennes, N., and Pearson, J. In press. Predicting outcomes in mediation: The influence of people and process. *Journal of Social Issues.*

Toomin, M. K. 1972. Structured separation with counseling: A therapeutic approach for couples in conflict. *Family Process* 12:299–310.

Tucker, M. B. 1982. Social support and coping: Applications for the study of female drug abuse. *Journal of Social Issues* 38:117–37.

U.S. Department of Commerce, Bureau of the Census. 1979. *Divorce, child custody and child support.* Current Population Reports.

Vanderkooi, L., and Pearson, J. 1983. Mediating divorce disputes: Mediator behaviors, styles, and rules. *Family Relations* 32:557–66.

Verbrugge, L. M. 1979. Marital status and health. *Journal of Marriage and the Family* 41:267–85.

Veroff, J., Kulka, R. A., and Douvan, E. 1981. *Mental health in America.* New York: Basic Books.

Vidmar, N. In press. An assessment of mediation in small claims court. *Journal of Social Issues.*

Walcott, C., Hopman, P. T., and King, T. D. 1977. The role of debate in negotiations. In *Negotiations: Social-psychological perspectives,* ed. D. Druckman. Beverly Hills, Calif.: Sage.

Wall, J. A. 1981. Mediation. *Journal of Conflict Resolution* 25:157–80.

Wall, J. A., and Rude, D. E. In press. Judicial mediation: Techniques, strategies, and situational effects. *Journal of Social Issues.*

Wall, J. A., Schiller, L. F., and Ebert, R. J. 1983. *Should judges grease the slow wheels of justice? A survey of effectiveness of judicial mediary techniques.* Unpublished paper, University of Missouri.

Wallerstein, J. S., and Kelly, J. B. 1980. *Surviving the breakup: How children and parents cope with divorce.* New York: Basic Books.

Walton, R. E. 1969. *Interpersonal peacemaking.* Reading, Mass.: Addison-Wesley.

Walton, R. E., and McKersie, R. B. 1965. *A behavioral theory of labor negotiations.* New York: McGraw-Hill.

Ware, C. 1984. *Sharing parenthood after divorce.* New York: Bantam.

Weinglass, J., Kressel, K., and Deutsch, M. 1977. The role of the clergy in divorce: An exploratory survey. *Journal of Divorce* 2:57–82.

Weiss, R. 1975. *Marital separation.* New York: Basic Books.

Weitzman, L., and Dixon, R. 1979. Child custody: legal standards, and empirical patterns for child custody, support, and victimization after divorce. *University of California at Davis Law Review* 12:473–521.

Welch, C. E., and Price-Bonham, S. 1983. A decade of no-fault divorce revisited: California, Georgia, and Washington. *Journal of Marriage and the Family* 45:411–17.

Wheeler, M. 1980. *Divided children.* New York: Norton.

Whetten, D. A. 1978. Coping with incompatible expectations: An integrated view of role conflict. *Administrating Science Quarterly* 23:256–71.

White, L. K. 1979. Sex differentials in the effect of remarriage on global happiness. *Journal of Marriage and the Family* 41:869–76.

White, K. R., and Stone, R. T. 1976. A study of alimony and child support rulings with some recommendations. *Family Law Quarterly* 10:75–91.

Williams, G. R. 1983. *Legal negotiation and settlement.* St. Paul, Minn.: West.

Williams, G. R., England, J., Farmer, L. C., and Blumenthal, M. 1976. Effectiveness in legal negotiation. In *Psychology and the law,* ed. G. Bermant, C. Nemeth, and N. Vidmar. Lexington, Mass.: Lexington Books.

Wills, T. A., and Langner, T. S. 1980. Socioeconomic status and stress. In *Handbook on stress and anxiety,* ed. I. L. Kutash and L. B. Schlesinger. San Francisco: Jossey-Bass.

Women in Transition, Inc. 1975. *Women in transition: A feminist handbook on separation and divorce.* New York: Scribner.

Woolley, P. 1979. *The custody handbook.* New York: Summit Books.

Wright, G. C., and Stetson, D. M. 1978. The impact of no-fault divorce law reform on divorce in American states. *Journal of Marriage and the Family* 40:575–80.

Zeiss, A. M., Zeiss, R. A., and Johnson, S. M. 1980. Sex differences in initiation and adjustment to divorce. *Journal of Divorce* 4:21–33.

Index